Woodrow Wilson's Right Hand

Woodrow Wilson's Right Hand

THE LIFE OF
COLONEL EDWARD M. HOUSE

Godfrey Hodgson

Yale University Press ∾ *New Haven and London*

Published with assistance from the foundation established in memory of Amasa Stone Mather of the Class of 1907, Yale College.

Printed in the United States of America.

Library of Congress Cataloging-in-Publication Data
Hodgson, Godfrey.
Woodrow Wilson's right hand: the life of Colonel Edward M. House / Godfrey Hodgson.
p. cm.
Includes bibliographical references and index.
ISBN 13: 978-0-300-09269-1 (alk. paper)
ISBN 10: 0-300-09269-5 (alk. paper)
1. House, Edward Mandell, 1858–1938. 2. Wilson, Woodrow, 1856–1924—Friends and associates. 3. Statesmen—United States—Biography. 4. United States—Foreign relations—1913–1921. 5. United States—Politics and government—1913–1921. 6. World War, 1914–1918—Peace. 7. Treaty of Versailles (1919). 8. Political leadership—United States—History—20th century. I. Title.
E748.H77H63 2006
973.91'3092—dc22
[B]   2005044732

A catalogue record for this book is available from the British Library.

The paper in this book meets the guidelines for permanence and durability of the Committee on Production Guidelines for Book Longevity of the Council on Library Resources.

10 9 8 7 6 5 4 3 2 1

Frontispiece: Colonel Edward M. House. Corbis.

For all those who work for peace on earth

Mr. House is my second personality. He is my independent self. His thoughts and mine are one.

—Woodrow Wilson

Contents ᘘ

Preface ☙

THE PAST FEW YEARS have not been a happy time for those who believe, as I have done since I first went to work as a reporter in Washington in 1962, that the peace of the world will be best served by a broad and tolerant understanding between Americans and the friends of democratic government and peace everywhere in the world. It was predictable that the end of the Cold War would persuade some in America that they no longer needed allies and would tempt many in Europe to feel they no longer needed to concern themselves with what Americans felt. What was less predictable was the stab of Islamic terrorism. We now face the danger that the alliance between the United States and its friends, which guaranteed an imperfect peace for almost half a century after the end of World War II, could unravel, leaving the world more dangerous than it has been since the defeat of the dictators in 1945.

These developments have made it more important than ever to study the second decade of the twentieth century and to draw the right conclusions from such a study. That time, as I have written in this book, was the last moment when the world's structures were plastic, clay for the hands of potters like President Woodrow Wilson and Colonel Edward House. It was a time of great hopes betrayed in an age of innovation; of democratic aspirations and cultural ferment; and of global economic change—in short, in many ways, a time much like our own.

In 1914 the hopes of a peaceful and prospering world were abruptly plunged into the abyss of war by an unexpected failure of what seemed, to those at least who did not look too closely, a robust political and diplomatic system. With disconcerting speed, the international system crumbled to pieces. Four great powers—Russia, Austria-Hungary, Ottoman Turkey, and in the end even imperial Germany— cracked under the strains of war. Britain and France, as imperial powers and as societies, were tested almost to destruction. Revolution consumed Russia, China, Mexico, Japan, and India, and the Muslim Middle East was shaken. Only the United States seemed to have emerged strengthened from the storms, and within a decade American society too was sorely tested by the world recession of 1929.

Woodrow Wilson and Edward House saw the danger. They tried to prevent the world war, and as soon as it started, they tried to stop it. They also saw it, however, as an opportunity to impose American ideas on the world. Specifically, they hoped to use the war to convert the world to the American conviction that political power should be founded in the consent of the governed. They also wanted to replace what they saw as a corrupt, elitist system of international relations with a new diplomacy—open, democratic, and respectful of the rights of the weak.

So far, so good. But one of the themes of this book is that President Wilson, in particular, failed because for temperamental reasons he failed to confront the awkward realities of the international situation and indeed certain uncomfortable truths about human nature. To an extent, this book is therefore a rehabilitation of the reputation of Wilson's collaborator, Colonel House, who, I believe, has been unjustly blamed for failures that can be more fairly laid at the door of Wilson's weaknesses.

Another topic illustrated by the narrative of House's work is the emergence of a particular style in American diplomacy that remained characteristic of the American interface with the world at least until the Vietnam War fifty years later. Because so few Americans were interested in the world as it was, as opposed to as they thought it was, and because therefore so few American politicians took what happened in the rest of the world seriously, the case for American involvement in the world, and the shaping of that involvement, became the province of a remarkably narrow cluster of Americans, predominantly members of a quite small, markedly homogeneous elite. Through his patronage of the Inquiry, a group of American scholars working on postwar settlement, Colonel House played an important part in that process.

House's life, though, and in particular the dialogue of his collaboration with Woodrow Wilson in the search for peace, have had more important and more enduring lessons for America's relationship with the world. Ever since the collapse of the Soviet Union and the discrediting of socialism, there has been a revival of the strategy known as "Wilsonian"—that is, the idea that it is the destiny of the United States to use its great power to spread American ideas of democracy and the American version of capitalism to the world. Although many elements go to make up the foreign policy of the George W. Bush administrations, it is unmistakably Wilsonian. So it is easy to forget that the Clinton administration too saw itself as Wilsonian. In its early months, President Bill Clinton himself and three of his leading colleagues—Secretary of State Warren Christopher, national security adviser Anthony Lake, and United Nations ambassador Madeleine Albright (later to succeed Christopher)—all explicitly proclaimed loyalty to a Wilsonian commitment to spreading democracy to as much of the world as possible.

This, therefore, is a moment when it is opportune to reassess the original Wilsonianism and in particular to reexamine the debate at the heart of the Wilson administration's foreign policy between Wilson himself, with his faith in the transforming power of American ideals (as expressed in blazing, biblical rhetoric), and the more patient, realistic political skills of Colonel House. The debate was not essentially, as House's enemies tried to suggest, a difference of policy. It was in part a matter of personality: the contrast between a child of Mary and a child of Martha. But it also represented a division, intensely relevant today, between those, like Wilson, who in exceptionalist terms contrasted American idealism and innocence with the corrupt ways of the Old World and those, like House, who took the trouble to study the world enough to confront it as it actually was and to see what could be done not to redeem but to reform it.

Several writers, including the founder of psychoanalysis himself, have been fascinated by the psychological contrast presented by what journalist George Sylvester Viereck in 1933 called "the strangest friendship in history." I have tried to bring to light the difference underlying that contrast, between two ways of looking at America's relationship with the world, one idealist, the other realist. Just as Colonel House's contribution to the Wilsonian vision has been unjustly underestimated, so it was a tragedy for the world, as well as for him, that his political gifts were wasted when they were most needed. And perhaps the Wilsonian simplicities of contemporary leaders could do with the greater common sense of a latter-day House.

Acknowledgments ❧

THIS BOOK WOULD NOT HAVE BEEN WRITTEN if my name had not been suggested as a possible author by that perceptive admirer of Colonel House, my old friend Philip Bobbitt. Phil Bobbitt has kept before me the historical importance of Edward House, steered me to materials in Austin, and welcomed me as the most generous of hosts. I am equally in debt to Professor Gaddis Smith of Yale University for his initial support and invaluable detailed editorial suggestions and to Professor Lewis L. Gould of the University of Texas at Austin, who read the Texas chapters and not only made excellent suggestions, but also preserved me from error.

I am, as always, more grateful than I can say for the hospitality of Harry and Tricia McPherson in Washington, whose kindnesses over the years are, as the sands of the sea, innumerable; to Doris O'Donnell in New York; to Olivia and the late David Nyhan in Boston; and to many other friends, old and new, who helped and encouraged me over more than four years of work.

I would like to acknowledge the generosity of friends who have lent me books for long periods, especially Professor Richard Crampton of St. Edmund's Hall, Oxford, and David Shapiro.

I owe much to the friendly help and advice of the staff of several great libraries, especially the Department of Manuscripts and Archives at the Sterling Library at Yale University; the Vere Harmsworth Library at the Rothermere American

Institute at the University of Oxford; and the London Library. I am also grateful to the staff of the Library of Congress, the Nicholas Murray Butler Library at Columbia University, the Center for American History at the University of Texas at Austin, and the Austin History Center of the Austin Public Library, as well as the Somerset Archive and Record Service in Taunton, England.

Thank you too to the staff of the Graduate Club at Yale; to Al Davis of Houston, Texas, who provided valuable information on the House family; to my Oxford research assistant, Adrian Hall; to Dr. Catherine Coolidge Lastavica; to Mark Stolle of Manchester by the Book in Manchester, Massachusetts, and to the archivists and librarians who helped me in the search for illustrations.

It has been a privilege to work with Larisa Heimert, Christopher Rogers, Keith Condon, Molly Egland, and the rest of the staff at Yale University Press and with Bojana Ristich, an exacting and meticulous editor. They have set a high standard, and I have tried to meet it.

Several members of my family, in addition to showing tolerance for my grumpiness and preoccupation, made specific timely contributions from their rich bank of skills. My son Pierre drew my attention to a number of French sources; my son Francis lent me his expertise with online photographic libraries; and my daughter Laura helped at a crucial moment with editorial and computer skills. My daughter Jessica was as cheerfully supportive as ever, and my wife Hilary helped in more ways than I can describe, let alone repay.

I can only hope that this book does justice to the expectations of all who have encouraged me and to its subject and his noble aspirations.

1 A Coming Together and a Falling Apart ❧

ON NOVEMBER 24, 1911, a tallish, lantern-jawed man whose fair hair was almost gray visited the Gotham Hotel at Fifth Avenue and 56th Street in New York City. He was shown up to visit, for the first of many times, the apartment of a quiet Texan and his wife.

The visitor was Thomas Woodrow Wilson. Liberal in politics but conservative in everything else, Wilson was a professional historian, a Southerner (born in Staunton, Virginia, and raised in Atlanta), a Presbyterian, and a son and grandson of the manse. His gentlemanly manners and surprisingly juvenile sense of humor concealed inner tensions and fierce ambition. As president of Princeton University, Wilson had proved intensely controversial. Faculty, student body, and especially alumni were bitterly divided over his plans for the university.[1] Wilson quarreled rancorously with those too unenlightened to grasp the rightness of his ambitions for Princeton. Later he despised anyone who did not see the rightness of his vision for the world.

Woodrow Wilson's host that late fall day at the Gotham was Edward Mandell House, a slight, quiet man who, at fifty-three, was two years younger than Wilson. Trim and correct, with a clipped gray mustache and striking eyes, he was gentlemanly and considerate in his manner and carefully ethical in his behavior. He had a southern accent and spoke softly, like a man in a cathedral, as someone said.

Yet in spite of his chronic poor health and mild manner, he was impressive, even formidable.

He was always known as "Colonel" House, though he was not a military man. The title had been bestowed on him, as was the custom in nineteenth-century Texas, by the governor of the state, Jim Hogg, in recognition of House's services in helping to get Hogg elected. House affected to be embarrassed by his colonelcy. He told people that he had given away his colorful colonel's uniform to an African American servant who wore it to meetings of his lodge. House's quiet manner and steadfast refusal to run for office concealed banked fires of ambition. His discretion was legendary. Someone called him "a Sphinx in a soft felt hat."[2] When Congressman Albert S. Burleson of Texas asked blind senator Thomas P. Gore of Oklahoma (Gore Vidal's grandfather) what he thought of House, the senator replied, "Take my word for it. He could walk on dry leaves and make no more noise than a tiger."[3] In Wilson, House had found the man who could be the instrument of his desires.

For more than seven years House labored in Woodrow Wilson's vineyard. He was the most intimate of friends, the most valued of counselors. Then, abruptly, he fell from grace. He was left in the icy distances of outer space as far as Wilson, his second wife, and an envious coterie were concerned.[4]

Less than two years earlier, Wilson had run for governor of New Jersey and, even more surprisingly, had been elected. Once in the governor's mansion in Trenton, he quarreled with Senator Jim Smith, boss of the New Jersey Irish Democratic machine, which had won the election for him.[5] Now, after the briefest experience of politics, he had set his sights on the highest peak of all. He was running for the Democratic nomination for president of the United States. His most influential early supporter was Colonel George Harvey, publisher of *Harper's Weekly* magazine, and no sooner had he won the nomination than Wilson quarreled with him too.[6] Was it true, Harvey asked Wilson politely at the Manhattan Club, that his support, that of a man close to Wall Street, was an embarrassment? There were those, Wilson replied loftily, who thought that it was, especially in the West, and with that he swept out of the club. Wilson knew what he was doing. He had been nominated by a coalition of Southern and Western populists, Northern working men, and middle-class Progressives. If he was to win the election, it would have to be with the help of angry provincials, not as the candidate of Wall Street and the Manhattan Club.

Since the South's surrender at Appomattox forty-seven years earlier, the Democratic presidential nomination had been no great prize. In all that time, only one Democrat, Grover Cleveland, had opened the Republican lock on the White House, though admittedly Cleveland had done it twice. Three times—in 1896, 1900, and 1908—William Jennings Bryan, whose many admirers called him the "Great Commoner" and whose equally numerous detractors called him "the boy orator from the Platte," had gone down to defeat.[7] In 1904, when the Democrats tried a conservative candidate, Judge Alton B. Parker, instead, it made no difference. But now, with Theodore Roosevelt, "as fit as a Bull Moose," leading the Progressive wing of the Republican Party against President William Howard Taft, there was a real chance for the right Democrat.

Wilson thought he was the right man. Four contenders for the Democratic nomination were in the field as the 1912 campaign got under way. Two of them, Congressman Oscar Underwood of Alabama and Governor Judson Harmon of Ohio, were both arch-conservatives. Democratic handicappers who thought neither had a snowball's chance in a year of Progressive incandescence had prevailed upon the Speaker of the House of Representatives, James Beauchamp Clark of Missouri (known as Champ Clark), to get into the race. But Wilson, the scholarly college president, meant to be the champion of the shoeless army who had fought and been beaten under Bryan.

The deep background to the extraordinary circumstances of 1912 was the contrast between the prosperity brought to some Americans by the ebullient growth of the economy and the miserable conditions afflicting millions of others in both cities and country. That contrast had caused a yearning for reform that meant different things to different categories of Americans.

Direst of all was the plight of the farmers, who, with their small-town neighbors, still made up half the population. The two generations since the Civil War had seen many farmers, especially in the South, forced by steadily declining prices into a form of peonage called the crop lien system.[8] (The price of both wheat and cotton had halved between 1860 and 1890.)[9] Year after year, farmers, black and white, raised a crop of cotton without the slightest hope that they could pay off the loans they had contracted to pay for seed, food, and everything else they needed.[10] Sometimes the landowner and the merchant were one and the same person. Some farmers sold their land and worked for the merchant as sharecroppers, most often "on the halves." Many owed their soul to the company store—or rather to the "furnishing merchant." Others sold their farms and "went West." Often they just scrawled on the door of their abandoned family farm, "GTT": Gone to Texas.

The great Wall Street Panic of 1907 was short-lived. But though the country was not in depression in 1912, many pressures for reform were making themselves felt. Rapid industrial concentration since the formation of United States Steel in 1901 fueled concern over "the trusts." There was unease about the new world role the United States had had thrust upon it by victory in the Spanish-American War and the conquest of the Philippines. There was labor unrest, discontent among immigrants, and disquiet among others at the sheer numbers of immigrants. A new, aggressive feminism had appeared. As the historian Richard Hofstadter observed decades ago, "the already forceful stream of agrarian discontent was enlarged and redirected by the growing enthusiasm of middle class people for social and economic reform."[11] That middle-class movement was itself promoted by the rage of those at the bottom of the pile in the North and Midwest—immigrants, industrial workers, and slum dwellers, led by various strands of anarchists, socialists, labor union organizers, and "Wobblies" (International Workers of the World). The human cost of building the American industrial machine was revealed by the anarchist outrages of the 1880s and the violent strikes of the early 1900s. At the same time middle-class people were made aware of the corruption and misery of the cities by the new muckraking journalism. The general theme of this Progressive movement, Hofstadter said, was "the effort to restore a type of economic individualism and political democracy that was widely believed to have existed earlier in America and to have been destroyed by the great corporation and the corrupt political machine."[12]

The anger of those who paid the price for the rampant expansion of the Gilded Age, in Pennsylvania coal mines or on East Texas farms, was now matched by the indignation of the middle classes, shocked by the gross disparity between the sordid poverty of the Lower East Side, on the one hand, and the vulgar splendor of New York's Four Hundred, on the other.

As the two turbulent streams of yearning for political and economic reform, in city and country, flowed together, the 1912 election became momentous. It marked the end of the post–Civil War Gilded Age and the beginning of a dynamic but troubled modern America, nostalgic for the Jeffersonian past but hurtling, coal-powered on steel rails, toward the urban, industrial, and international world of the twentieth century. In the end it marked the final triumph of a "Progressivism" that rejected the populist revolt and accepted the dominance of corporate business as the default repository of political power in America. But would the Progressive forces turn to Theodore Roosevelt and his Republican rebels? Or would they find their home in the Democratic Party? Everything would depend on whether the Democrats would accept the leadership of Woodrow Wilson.

Texas would be crucial. There had been waves of agrarian discontent, translated into waves of political activism, from Minnesota to Georgia. But Texas had been the center of the radical Farmers' Alliance since the 1870s and a hotbed of the People's Party in 1896. And Texas was already big. It had forty votes in the Democratic nominating convention, set for Baltimore in July 1912.

In 1910 Colonel House had been driven north in those pre-air-conditioning days by his inability to tolerate the heat. He divided his time between a big house with a deep porch in Austin, a small apartment in New York, and a rented seaside home on the North Shore outside Boston. (His father had left him tens of thousands of acres of plantation and range land. By shrewd investment and careful management he had a secure annual income of $20,000–25,000—enough to live on very comfortably.) He was bored with his backstage role in Texas politics, and the new men in Texas were not his crowd. He was looking for a candidate to help on the national scene as he had helped four men into the governor's chair in Texas.

Wilson had been persuaded to go and see House by two of the latter's friends: David F. Houston, an economist who was an expert on the tariff—a key issue of the day—and Walter Hines Page, one of the partners in the New York publishing house of Doubleday, Page.[13] A couple of weeks before the fateful meeting with Wilson, House had been visited by the ill-assorted pair who were managing the Wilson campaign. One was William F. McCombs, a Princeton pupil of Wilson's turned New York lawyer, alcoholic and neurotic in the extreme.[14] The other was William Gibbs McAdoo, an Arkansan born who had a successful business career behind him building the tunnels that linked Manhattan to its New Jersey suburbs and a career in Democratic politics ahead of him that stopped only just short of the presidency itself.[15]

On their way to the Gotham, McAdoo, who had never heard of Colonel House, asked who he was.[16] "He has the entire state of Texas in his vest pocket," McCombs answered with characteristic hyperbole. Pressed for detail, he allowed that House was reputed to be "a man of wealth, dignity and honor," that he had never held political office, but that he was nevertheless a man of vast influence in Texas politics.[17]

In the meantime House himself had approached Wilson with a characteristically subtle stroke. In October 1911 he had written to Wilson, saying they had so many mutual friends that he felt he needed no introduction.[18] He reported that he had just received a letter from his friend Senator Charles Culberson, whose campaign manager and gray eminence he had been in Texas. "There is a good deal of talk," House quoted the senator as saying, "about Governor Wilson's attitude to the party in the past, and it is not doing him any good."[19] Culberson said it was being circulated that Wilson had refused to vote for Bryan in 1896, 1900, and 1908 and even voted against Parker in 1904. Wilson wrote back frankly, saying that he had never voted for a Republican in his life but that it was true that in 1896 he had voted against Bryan in a primary because he did not agree with him on the monetary question. So House suggested to Wilson, even before they met, that he was a friendly influence in Texas, a key state for the Democratic nomination.

Historians unfriendly to House have suggested that House had nothing whatever to do with Wilson's support in Texas.[20] That goes too far. It is true that others—for example, Thomas B. Love, Thomas H. Ball, and Cato Sells—had more to do with lining up the Texas delegation.[21] But these men, and indeed Senator Culberson himself, were House's friends, moderate liberals in a Texas sharply divided between populist radicals and conservatives. House did not deliver the Texas delegation to Wilson. Others did that. But he did have influence in Texas. Indeed the network of his friends amounted to a kind of statewide machine.

In any case, on November 24, 1911, Woodrow Wilson duly went to the Gotham, and within an hour, as House put it himself later, "we found ourselves in such a complete sympathy in so many ways, that we soon learned to know what each was thinking without either having expressed himself."[22]

Wilson was, it seemed to House, a godsend. And so, at the time, was House for Wilson. In 1915 House dictated for his diary a conversation he had had with Wilson: "I asked him if he remembered the first day we met, three and a half years ago. He replied, 'Yes, but we had known one another always, and merely came in touch then, for our purposes and thoughts were one.' I told him how much he had been to me; how I had tried all my life to find someone with whom I could work out the things I had so deeply at heart, and I had begun to despair, believing my life should be more or less a failure, when he came into it, giving me the opportunity for which I had been longing."[23]

House's biographer, Charles Seymour, records the answer Woodrow Wilson gave to a politician who asked whether House represented him accurately on a particular matter. "Mr. House," was the president's reply, "is my second personality. He is my independent self. His thoughts and mine are one." It is a remarkable enough statement for any brilliant and dominant man to make about another. It illustrates how close House and Wilson were before the accidents of life split them apart. It is a fact with which those who have sought to portray House as little more than a toady to Wilson must deal. Colonel House addressed his friend in the White House as "Dear Governor," as did other close associates, such as Wilson's son-in-law and treasury secretary, William Gibbs McAdoo. Wilson began his letters to House "Dear Friend"; sometimes "My dear, dear Friend"; and in a time of intense collaboration, between the summer of 1915 and the end of 1916, "Dearest Friend."[24]

House fell ill in January 1912 and remained in Texas for several weeks. During that enforced absence from the national political scene, he distilled his political beliefs into an anonymous tract disguised as a novel, *Philip Dru: Administrator.* (Wilson took it to Bermuda to read on his vacation.)[25] Early in the campaign he began to give Wilson advice on campaign strategy and tactics.[26]

House also played an important part in bringing William Jennings Bryan around to endorse Wilson. Because of Bryan's iconic status in the West, his support was crucial if Wilson were to be nominated. House was not in sympathy with Bryan's belief that the country's ills could be cured if only silver could be freely coined at a ratio to the value of gold of 16:1. But the Houses and the Bryans had known one another well in Austin since the winter of 1898–1899.[27] Bryan's daughter had been ill, and he and his wife wanted to escape the Nebraska cold by moving to Austin for the winter. House helped to find them a home next door to his own, and as the Bryans came every winter, the two families became well acquainted. So in the spring of 1912 House was able, with the help of Mary Beard Bryan, to persuade the Great Commoner to take a favorable view of Wilson, though Bryan did not formally endorse Wilson until the Baltimore convention, perhaps because Bryan still clung to a slender hope of winning the nomination for himself.

House played only a minor part in the pre-convention phase of Wilson's election in 1912. He went to Europe for the summer, as was his habit, leaving on the very day the convention met. He stayed abroad, traveling as far east as Moscow, until August 6. He wrote Wilson from London, however, promising that from the moment the *Laconia* docked in Boston on August 14, "every hour of my time will be devoted to your cause."[28] He returned in time to knock McAdoo's and McCombs's quarreling heads together, a not inconsiderable service to Wilson in itself, and to come down on the side of McAdoo.

It was after Wilson was elected that House's influence really bore fruit. Over the winter of 1912–1913 House and Wilson saw one another and communicated by letter and telephone constantly. Whenever Wilson was in New York, he would dine with the Houses and go with them to see some frothy play such as *Peg o' my Heart* (January 17, 1913) or *Years of Discretion* (February 14, 1913).

Wilson was not the slightest bit interested in patronage. (In New Jersey, to the horror of professional politicians, he consigned the whole grubby business to his political secretary, Joseph Tumulty.) House's influence over the formation of Wilson's administration was extraordinary. As we shall see, he was instrumental in four of his friends joining the cabinet, as well as in other key appointments. House quickly became the man you had to see if you wanted anything at all from the Wilson administration.

From the start, House had a significant influence on the policies as well as the personnel of the Wilson administration. He advised Wilson to try for three main legislative goals in his first term: reform of the banking and currency system, tariff reform, and the building of a larger merchant marine.[29] The first two were indeed major landmarks of the first Wilson administration. It was in foreign policy, however, where Wilson's ignorance was initially almost total, that House's contribution was greatest. He was able to use his personal acquaintance with powerful figures in the Liberal government and in the Foreign Office in London to calm down a potentially ugly row between London and Washington over the Panama Canal. The resolution of this incident was the foundation of his trusting relations with leading British statesmen. On Mexico, then in the throes of civil war, he was heavily involved as an adviser, though he, like the administration as a whole, found the Mexican situation perplexing.

House's role grew until he became a sort of assistant president for foreign affairs. (He turned down the office of secretary of state after Bryan resigned in 1915.) He went to Europe in the spring of 1914 to try to prevent the outbreak of war.[30] In 1915, 1916, and again in 1917 he was back in Europe as a neutral, trying to negotiate an end to the war. In 1917, once America was at war, House represented the United States on the Supreme War Council.

In America's wartime relations with Britain, House was the key figure. He worked closely with the British intelligence agent Sir William Wiseman and dealt as an intimate equal with the British war leaders, Herbert Asquith, Arthur James Balfour, and David Lloyd George. He went everywhere in Britain: he stayed at Cliveden with the Astors, dined with the prime minister in Downing Street, and got on famously with the king. He was shown the Admiralty's secret war room by Admiral Sir John Jellicoe and had an arrangement with the British foreign secretary, Sir Edward Grey, that he could drop around for a chat before dinner every Sunday.[31]

In Paris, House lunched with the president of the republic whenever he was in town. In Berlin he saw Chancellor Theobald von Bethmann-Hollweg when he could not see the kaiser. Arthur Zimmermann, sender of the famous telegram that helped bring America into the war, was one of House's correspondents, and House was also on friendly terms with Admiral Sir Reginald "Blinker" Hall, the head of British naval intelligence whose men intercepted Zimmerman's telegram. House "knew everyone" in the early twentieth century. His diary records meals with Henry James, Edith Wharton, and Rudyard Kipling, as well as with the virtuoso pianist Ignazy Jan Paderewski, who became president of Poland. He mingled with politicians, generals, bankers, academics, journalists, and society hostesses in New York, Paris, and London. He knew J. P. Morgan Jr. well enough to call him "Jack," and he dined with Henry Clay Frick in the house that became his great art museum.

The deep porch of the great house he built for entertaining in Austin, it was said, had seen much of Texas politics for twenty years. The carpets of his successive apartments in New York too—first at the Gotham and then on East 53rd Street—were worn by the steady tramp of genius, ambition, intrigue, and earnest liberal mugwumpery alike.

At the Paris peace conference, House upstaged the secretary of state, Robert Lansing, as completely as Henry Kissinger, as President Richard Nixon's national security adviser, overshadowed Nixon's official secretary of state (William D. Rogers). The cruel joke in Washington went, "How do you spell Lansing?" "H-o-u-s-e."

House was pressed to take cabinet secretaryships, embassies, and political offices of all kinds, but he always steadfastly refused.[32] In part, this refusal was motivated by poor health. In part, it was a function of the very refinement of his ambition: it was more tempting to be the gray eminence than the jack in office. His quite extraordinary influence, arguably greater than any single adviser has ever had over an American president, was earned by steady hard work, wise counsel, and unfailing tact, protected by shrewd manipulation when necessary. It was anchored in extraordinarily intimate friendship until that was eroded by the jealousy of others.

Countless references in the letters exchanged between House and Wilson and in House's diary attest to their closeness. Wilson wrote to the colonel as "my dearest, dearest House." House wrote in 1916 that "from that first meeting and up to today I have been in as close touch with Woodrow Wilson as with any man I have ever known." Again, Wilson told someone, "House is my second personality. He is my independent self. His thoughts and mine are one. . . . If anyone thinks he is reflecting my opinion by whatever action he takes, they are welcome to the conclusion."[33]

"Now this," the most perceptive of Wilson's biographers has written, 'is an exceptional statement for any man, let alone a president of the United States, to make."[34] Yet in some way the friendship was more intimate, more intense, than even that statement would suggest. When House stayed at the White House, Wilson would wander into his bedroom in his robe to say good night. In the summer of 1915, after the death of the first Mrs. Wilson, Woodrow Wilson told House, "I have an intimate personal matter to discuss with you. You are the only person in the world with whom I can discuss everything."[35] The "intimate matter" was whether or not he should marry the second Mrs. Wilson so soon after the death of his first wife. Edith Wilson suspected House, unjustly, of intriguing to prevent the marriage, and she never forgave him.

Early in Wilson's time as president, House came to stay in the White House, as he was to do many, many times over the next five years. (There was even a bedroom there known as Colonel House's room.) On this particular occasion, House picked up a volume of Kipling's poems and asked Wilson to read a favorite poem, "L'Envoi," out loud. Wilson read it "with much feeling," and they "fell to discussing religion for a moment and the imagination of man."[36] The poem begins:

> When Earth's last picture is painted and the tubes are twisted and dried
> When the oldest colors have faded, and the youngest critic has died
> We shall rest, and faith we shall need it—lie down for an aeon or two
> Till the Master of All Good Workmen shall put us to work anew

And this is how it ends:

> And only the Master shall praise us, and only the Master shall blame
> And no one shall work for money, and no one shall work for fame.

At four o'clock they went for a drive. Wilson had something to show his friend: the poignant figure of Grief in the cemetery behind Washington's Soldiers' Home; it had been commissioned from Augustus St. Gaudens by Henry Adams to commemorate his great love for his wife, Clover, who had committed suicide. It affected House "much as some mournful strain of music would." The two friends sat for a long time in front of the marvelous statue, talking about ancient Greek ideas of beauty, and House asked Wilson why "the teeming millions of the twentieth century" could produce so little that was as good.[37] Two inhibited Anglo-Saxon gentlemen, brought up in the Victorian Protestant culture of the Old South, found they could overcome their instinctive constraints together and talk about life, death, and love.

Wilson's first wife, Ellen, died on August 6, 1914. The fourteen months between her death and Wilson's marriage to Edith Bolling Galt—and especially the first few months, before the second Mrs. Wilson had been able to assert her dislike of her future husband's only close friend—saw the zenith of House's influence. Wilson was desperately lonely. He was aware, in spite of self-confidence amounting to arrogance, of how ill-equipped he was to deal with the war in Europe. House had dreamed for years of political influence at the national level. He was, as he admitted himself, highly ambitious. He claimed in his "Memories" that he could have been first governor, then U.S. senator, and would have "tried for the Presidency." But he says he "definitely put behind me all thought of ever accepting office."[38] As his intimacy with Woodrow Wilson, candidate and then president, developed, House was delighted by the meeting of minds. He was also dazzled by the influence his friendship with the president gave him. He reveled in the sense that the friendship gave him of being an initiate admitted to the innermost sanctum of political influence.

Edith immediately sensed that House was the chief impediment to her influence on Woodrow and set herself, timidly at first, then with increasing blatancy, to exclude him from the president's inner circle. "You are going to love House some day," the lovelorn widower wrote to her, "if only because he loves me and would give, I believe, his life for me." "You must forgive me," his inamorata wrote back; "I know he is fine and true, but I don't think him vigorous and strong. Am I wrong?"[39] The thin end of a broad and sharp wedge had been inserted.

Four years later, the David and Jonathan friendship between the president and the colonel was split like a dry pine log, and it was shrewd blows from Edith Wilson's beetle hammer that drove in the wedge. The end of their friendship was disastrous for both men (and for the world). The occasion for the end was not a thoughtless word, such as can damage an ordinary friendship. It came of disagreements that affected the future peace of the world. Behind a clash of temperaments, vast issues of policy were at stake.

From the very beginning of the Wilson administration, House was the indispensable counsellor. As noted, in 1914, with Wilson's approval, he launched a bold attempt to prevent the world war by a kind of shuttle diplomacy among Washington, London, and Berlin. After war started, he tried repeatedly to end it. He persuaded his friend Sir Edward Grey to agree to the House-Grey Memorandum, threatening American intervention if Germany did not agree to negotiate peace.

He set up the Inquiry, harnessing American scholars to plan the postwar settlement. That influenced the whole development of the American foreign policy establishment.

He helped to draft the Wilson speech that spelled out the Fourteen Points, the terms on which the president thought the war should be ended. Wilson's strongest point as a statesman, perhaps, was the eloquence of his great set-piece speeches. Again and again the documents show House either suggesting the theme for a major Wilson speech or emending significantly a draft his friend had sent him.

House helped to draft the covenant of the League of Nations, the master plan with which the two friends hoped to usher in a lasting world peace.

In October 1918, as the war was drawing to an end at last, the president sent the colonel to Europe as his confidential agent in the negotiations to bring about German surrender. House brilliantly played the cards dealt him by Wilson. Their plan was to induce the Germans to surrender on the basis of the Fourteen Points, then finesse the Allies into going along with a peace settlement of Wilson's, not their, design. House was the most influential member, after the president, of the American delegation to the Paris peace conference.

When Wilson returned from Paris to Washington in February 1919, he left House to carry on negotiations with the Allies, and he explicitly gave him carte blanche to do as he thought fit. House, proud of his diplomatic ability, pushed the negotiations forward. He was always careful, though, that the president would have the final decision. When he reported what he had done, Wilson—so his wife and her friends recall, and the incident lost nothing in their telling—was aghast. He suspected his "dearest friend" of betraying his cherished project for a League of Nations by allowing the Allies to separate the peace treaty from the league's covenant so as to carve out an early agreement with the British and the French. The suspicion was unjustified but deadly.

Wilson, physically sick after a series of strokes and suddenly aware that his whole political strategy was threatened by Republican victories in Congress, lost faith in House, who was airbrushed out of the president's intimate circle. House was not even invited to Wilson's funeral.

Disastrously, House forgot that his influence was in the last analysis wholly dependent on his friendship with Woodrow Wilson. He had no other political base. Wilson had only to turn away, as he did, and House was naked to the vengeance of all who had resented his reflected glory.

All politicians' careers end in failure, said Enoch Powell.[40] Woodrow Wilson and Edward House both failed in one obvious sense. They made it their grand objective to replace the ancient power politics of nation-states—the so-called "Westphalian system"—with a league of nations led by the United States. They failed to persuade Congress and public opinion that the league was in America's interest. They sought to replace the "militarism" the nation-states had created with a regime of international law that would lead, so they believed, to lasting peace. Therein was a contradiction. It was not, as they imagined, the moral force of America but precisely its economic predominance over the exhausted powers of Europe that put them in a position to impose their ideals. And there is a further irony. It was not the cynical elites of Europe, as Wilson and House saw them, who frustrated the Wilsonian dream but the ultimately nationalist reluctance of the American people to share its sovereign power of making war with foreign nations.

Wilson, and House, failed to establish a just and lasting system of international relations. They also failed to fulfill Wilson's vision of self-determination. Indeed, they did not seem to comprehend that it was far from obvious which "peoples" should determine their own future as independent nations and which should not. (Kurds, Chechens, Armenians, Kashmiris, Kosovars, and minorities in almost every country on earth confirm that this conundrum has not been definitively resolved more than eighty years later.) Still, they did breathe life into independent nations, some of which (like Poland) have endured, while others (Czechoslovakia, Yugoslavia) have not. They did succeed in persuading the peace conference to accept their solutions for intricate territorial problems. Some of these fixes—the return of Alsace-Lorraine to France, Italy's Alpine frontier—have held. Others— the British mandates in Palestine and Iraq, the settlements in the Balkans and the Caucasus—have left behind some of the world's most envenomed conflicts.

There are those who continue to cherish a Wilsonian dream of using American power to impose American ideals. They have not yet been successful. Wilson's dream of a world made peaceful by American ideals, which House shared and worked with all his skill and patience to bring about, has not yet come true.

How far should House share the blame for Wilson's failure? A powerful school of historians, defending Wilson, has blamed House and accused him of betraying Wilson's ideals. That claim will be examined in this book and largely rejected. But it is true that House and Wilson did not always agree. They were divided by temperament even more than by policy.

Like Wilson, House hated war. (He had grown up on the losing side in the bitter aftermath of the War between the States.) He hoped to prevent, then to end, World War I, and then to make any future war impossible. He shared Woodrow Wilson's distaste for the old diplomacy, with its corrupting secretiveness and cynicism, though he admired some men, like Sir Edward Grey and Lord Robert Cecil, bred in that tradition. He was a passionately patriotic American. (Incidentally, or not, he was a patriotic Texan as well. In his diary he faithfully recorded Texas independence day as it passed.) He had strong ideals. Yet, unlike Wilson, he was willing to work with the imperfect clay of the world as he found it.

The word "realist" has been appropriated by an academic school. Not in that technical sense but in the common meaning of the word, Colonel House was a realist. He understood that a safer world could be built only with the materials of life as it was. He understood—to take as an example the issue between him and Woodrow Wilson that, more than any other, led to the breach between them—that it was no good telling a French nation, which had seen 2 million of its young men die as a result of German invasion, that it should rely for its security on a league of nations that was not yet in existence.

House understood that if Woodrow Wilson wanted to create a new European system, based on the self-determination of nations, he had at least better find out what the existing Europe was actually like, and he should also be realistic about the politics of his own country. House believed to the end that it would be possible to meet the objections of the league's enemies; Wilson never even tried to do so and indeed appears to have thought that to do so would have been dishonorable.

House's apprenticeship in Texas politics had been long, but his active career in world politics was short. He did not appear on the international stage at all until 1913, when he was fifty-five years old, and then only as an adviser. He first flew solo in the spring of 1914, and his career was virtually over within five years. For that short time, though, in that deadly second decade of the twentieth century, in which the nineteenth-century system bled to death and the brutal "short twentieth century" of ruthless ideological struggle began, House was at the very hub.[41] He observed from the seat of a privileged observer the collapse of the Russian, German, Austrian, and Ottoman empires and the eclipse of British and French world power. He watched as a new Europe and a new Middle East were born, and he helped to redraw the map of the world. Dean Acheson, President Harry Truman's great secretary of state, called his memoirs *Present at the Creation*. He was referring to the creation of the Cold War. Edward House was present at the creation of what have survived the end of the Cold War: American world dominance and the intractable problems it still has to confront.

House's trajectory is yet another reminder of how short American history is. He grew up in Houston when it had six or seven thousand inhabitants. As a child, he watched the violent clashes of Reconstruction, and as a young man, he grew up in a rangeland Texas, where a man had better have a revolver in his pocket if he sat down to a game of cards. He saw the United States grow from a raw country, almost ignored by the Great Powers of Europe, to be acknowledged as the greatest power of all. He lived to sit in the Crillon Hotel in Paris, dealing out the cards to the world's principalities and powers.

It fell to Woodrow Wilson and to Colonel House to confront the reality created by the collapse of the European system, the emergence of American economic and military power, and a revolutionary upheaval against the traditional structures of power. The second decade of the twentieth century was one of those rare moments in world history when everything was malleable. Empires were melting in the fires of war. House shared with Woodrow Wilson the vision of a new world converted to American democracy. House's instinct was to focus on restoring peace to a continent devastated by the four horsemen of the modern apocalypse: war, revolution, epidemic pestilence, and famine. The dilemma that divided Wilson's self-righteous idealism from House's realistic accommodation of principle with the way of a naughty world still torments men and women everywhere.

2 *Origins of a Texas Gentleman* ॐ

EDWARD HOUSE WAS ONLY TWO YEARS OLD when the Civil War broke out and not quite seven when Abraham Lincoln was assassinated. One of his earliest memories was of going down to the dock at Galveston to see one of his father's ships, which had been battered almost to pieces by Union gunboats. He remembered driving along the beach at Galveston and seeing the silhouettes of the gunboats five miles out to sea.[1]

His father, Thomas William House, was one of the most prominent of the blockade runners who kept the South's lifelines open and made a fortune in the process. By the end of the War between the States he was a rich man, with $300,000 in gold with Barings Brothers' bank in London and another healthy balance with his cotton brokers in Liverpool.[2] By the end of his life he was said to have a quarter of a million Texas acres, as well as a bank and a store in Houston and many other valuable properties.

The family's main home was a two-story white house in Houston, but its Galveston home, in an orange grove, was a substantial red brick mansion that covered a whole block. If the weather was stormy, House's father would send one of his ships out, and in the morning he would climb up to the cupola to see if any of the gunboats had gone off station. If the Federal ships were all there, he could be pretty sure that his own ship had slipped through the blockade.[3] The steamers would slip out to Havana, where they would transship their cargo of cotton into ocean-going steamers to Liverpool. On the return journey would come weapons of war for the Confederate armies.[4]

T. W. House lost some of his ships. The *Mary* was caught by the gunboats on April 4, 1864, and so was his schooner *Pet* in February 1865. But most of the blockade runners got through. As the Atlantic ports were closed to the Confederacy one by one, Galveston was the only port where the Confederacy could import gunpowder. Galveston was brought under Union control by a squadron led by a Federal navy vessel, the famous gunboat *Harriet Lane*. Three months later a Confederate force led by General John B. Magruder boarded the *Harriet Lane* and killed five of the crew in hand-to-hand fighting. She was sold to T. W. House, who was shrewd enough to pay for her with Confederate scrip. She eventually made it to Havana, where she was ultimately sold for $90,000.

The elder House was a staunch supporter of the Confederate cause. When the Houston Light Guard marched off to join Hood's brigade in the Army of Northern Virginia, it was called the Kid Glove Gentry because T. W. House had presented all its troops with white kid gloves. In a remarkably short time since he had arrived in America as an immigrant, House had become one of the leading citizens of Texas.

The colonel's father was born in 1814 in the English village of Stoke St. Gregory, in deeply rural Somerset, the youngest of seven brothers.[5] The village sits on a low, sandy ridge above the drained marshlands of the Somerset Levels. Until they were drained in the thirteenth century, the levels were an inlet of the sea. This was the site of Avalon, where in legend King Arthur threw the sword Excalibur and a woman's arm rose from the waters to receive it, "clothed in white samite, mystic, wonderful."[6] On the neighboring ridge, Athelney, legend has it that the young King Alfred, disguised as a cook's boy to hide himself from the invading Danes, burned the cakes he was supposed to be watching. A few miles across the marsh, in 1685, the peasants rose against Catholic King James II and were routed at Sedgemoor in the last battle fought on English soil.

The Houses of Stoke St. Gregory are prosperous folk now. But when T. W. House left to seek his fortune in America, West Somerset was a hungry place, with much unrest and little work.[7] Even then, some Houses must have been prosperous, since one of the bells in St. Gregory's church was donated by John House and John Miller only a dozen years before their kinsman emigrated.[8]

Colonel House believed his family originally wrote the name "Huis" and came from Holland.[9] There is a possible explanation for the Dutch spelling. In 1607, a great storm burst the sea wall in Somerset, and the land was flooded twelve feet deep.[10] King Charles I brought in engineers to drain the Levels. The Dutch already had great experience of land reclamation. There is no specific evidence that Dutchmen worked in Somerset, but extensive drainage did take place there, and it is entirely plausible that a Dutchman called Huis might have come to work there and married a local girl.

At any rate, Thomas William House from Stoke St. Gregory emigrated to New York in 1835 at the age of twenty-one and, like the young King Alfred, worked as a pastry cook. The owner of the famous St. Charles Hotel in New Orleans liked his work so well that he offered House a job. In 1836 House moved to Texas and fought in the revolution against Mexico. He was rewarded with a land grant in Coryell County and moved to Houston, where by 1838 he had set up the firm of House and Loveridge, bakers and confectioners. The firm prospered, and soon House ran what became the leading store in the raw little town.[11] (Before the War between the States, Houston had fewer than five thousand inhabitants.) In 1840 he married Mary Elizabeth Shearn, who had also been born in Somerset.[12] She was the daughter of Charles Shearn, later chief justice of Harris County. The pastry cook was on his way to becoming a patrician.

In 1853 House expanded into wholesale trade. He bought out the jobbing business of James H. Stevens and Company, for which he paid $40,000—at that time the largest sum of money ever to change hands in Houston.[13] He went into cotton brokerage and soon found himself advancing crop loans to planters. Cotton factoring led to a bank, one of the biggest in Houston until it fell victim to the Panic of 1907. T. W. House, in fact, was one of the leading citizens of the growing city of Houston. He was elected mayor of Houston in 1862. He helped to create a steamship company plying between Houston and Galveston. After the Civil War he organized the city's first utility, the Houston Gas Company; the first street railway; and the Board of Trade and Cotton Exchange, and he invested in several railroads.

Edward House would spend much of his life in New York and Massachusetts, but (like Woodrow Wilson) he was a Southerner, brought up with the South's sense of loss (even though his father's successful trading sheltered his family from the privations much of the South suffered), and he shared the Southern bitterness at the victorious Union army and its carpetbagger regimes. Thomas W. House was a slave owner, though he disapproved of slavery on principle.

"My first impressions," Colonel House wrote in 1929, "were of human conflict, men battling against men, individually and collectively." The only toys he and his brothers had to play with were guns, and he handled firearms long before adolescence. Riots were frequent. "The market house bell would ring violently. . . . Citizens would seize their rifles, shotguns and six-shooters and scurry away to Market House Square." Carpetbaggers "like jackals were preying upon a broken and impoverished people."[14] A disbanded Texas regiment looted the town, and House's father had to stand at the door of his warehouse with a shotgun. The worst disturbances, though, as House remembered them, were between the prewar white citizens, on the one hand, and armed "Negroes and carpetbaggers," on the other. House's view of Reconstruction, in a word, was unreconstructed. It has long since been exploded by serious historians.

Edward House, in short, grew up in the small antebellum elite of Texas, defeated but not dispossessed by the Civil War. He was the youngest of seven brothers, only four of whom survived to share their father's affluent inheritance. House recalled that an "old darkey nurse" used to tell him of the old superstition that if he had not been the seventh son of a seventh son, he would never have survived.[15] His oldest brother, Thomas W. House Jr., was educated in England for a time and toyed with the idea of becoming a Church of England parson, but his father would hear nothing of it. He accidentally shot off half of his face and hung between life and death for weeks but lived to be "Houston's foremost citizen," a banker and a booster.[16]

The two brothers who meant most to Edward House were George, born in 1855, and Jimmie, born in 1852. George, his favorite, was "a gentle, refined, delicate boy, unlike any of the others." He was sent to Colorado for his health, and then to California, where he died at the age of twenty. Jimmie was the leader, a wild tearaway.[17] All the kids in Jimmie House's gang had guns and pistols and small catapults called "nigger shooters." Edward twice nearly killed one of his playmates with a firearm. But Jimmie House was the boldest and the wildest of his gang. At sixteen, he fell from a trapeze and died.

In 1866, two years before that calamity, Edward House, like his older brothers, was sent to England to school while his mother and father and their older children were traveling on the Continent. It was not a success. Victorian English boys were not used to the rough games to which the House boys tried to introduce them, and it was "a happy day when we took ship and turned our faces homewards."[18]

Edward nearly met the same fate as his brother Jimmie. One day he was swinging high when the rope broke. In falling, he hit his head against a carriage wheel. What he called "brain fever" followed—probably concussion—and it was many weeks before he had recovered enough to go out.[19] For the rest of his life House saw himself as a semi-invalid.

As a boy, House loved more than anywhere else his father's plantation at Arcola, a few miles south of Houston, famous for its prize-winning sugar. The local post office was in a town called House, Texas, after the family.

House remembered the game—deer, turkey, and wild duck—and the abundant fish in the lakes. He loved the melodious voices of the field hands as they went out singing to the cane fields at dawn. The frogs and the katydids made their music in the semi-tropical night, and the mockingbird sang at full moon. But Texas before antibiotics and air conditioning was not a healthy place. There was a yellow fever epidemic in Galveston during the Civil War in which 265 out of 2,500 inhabitants died.[20] Malaria was as rampant as in Africa for nine months of the year. Some were immune, but Ed House was not one of them. For the rest of his life, unless he dosed himself liberally with quinine—and sometimes even when he did—he came down with fever every three or four months.

One lasting consequence of House's fragile health was his annual exodus to avoid the Texas summer. Even on the North Shore of Massachusetts, with its sea breeze, he complained of the summer temperature. In New York and even more in Washington, before air conditioning he found it unbearable.

Although he gave many proofs of courage, House chose a semi-sedentary life. He saw himself as incapacitated for "out front" leadership and chose to channel his very considerable ambition into influencing people and politics indirectly. Nineteenth-century children were more used to loss than children are today. Even so, Edward House, by the end of his college education, had lost his mother, his father, and his two closest brothers. Several traits of House's character in later life, including his strong sense of family, his gift for friendship, and a highly self-disciplined approach to life, were perhaps caused by a heightened sense of paradise lost.

In 1872, after his mother's death, his father decided to send Edward east to school. At fourteen, Ed and his lifelong friend Paul Bremond Cruger set off for Mattoax, Virginia, in the back of beyond, thirty miles west of Richmond. The Harrison School, founded by a kinsman of President William Henry Harrison, was another fifteen miles on toward the Blue Ridge, and the boys were taken there in a farmer's cart. The very first night they got a taste of the hazing, ingenious and brutal, that awaited them. This was not child's play. Sometimes the rougher boys would tie a younger boy's hands behind his back and go through the pretence of hanging him until he went purple in the face.

The two friends stayed at this appalling place only from March to the fall, when their fathers sent them to another school, Verulam Academy, about nine miles west of Charlottesville. There the hazing was even more brutal, though House maintained that he protected himself with a large knife and a pistol. The teaching was useless. The food was scanty, and the boys supplemented their diet with pippin apples from the orchard and game they shot themselves.

T. W. House had hoped that one or another of these Virginia academies would prepare Edward for Yale, whose president, Dr. Noah Porter, was an acquaintance. Dr. Porter sent him to William Cushing, the head of the Hopkins Grammar School in New Haven, to see how much Latin and Greek he knew. House thought he was ready to become a Yale man, but Cushing, after asking him to translate one passage from Caesar's *Gallic Wars* and another from Xenophon's *Anabasis,* thought otherwise.

Edward House was always good at making friends, and at Hopkins his best friend was Oliver Morton, son of Oliver P. Morton, a U.S. senator from Indiana and a Republican candidate for president in 1876. They became inseparable friends who shared a fascination for politics. When the Republicans held their 1876 convention, the leading candidates were James G. Blaine, the "Plumed Knight," and the eventual winner, Rutherford B. Hayes of Ohio. House recalled his and his friend's bitter disappointment when the New Haven telegraph operator handed him the first slip with the news that Morton had thrown in the towel.

The 1876 presidential election was the closest until that of 2000. After weeks of political crisis, the result was decided only by the famous "Compromise of 1877," which ended Republican Reconstruction in the South. It was naturally a matter of fascination to the son of one of the actors and to his best friend. As a son of the South, House was, of course, a Democrat; Morton was a fanatical Republican. Both boys were in a state of continuous excitement. Whenever they could be, and sometimes when they should not have been, the two boys were in Washington. The Mortons lived at the Ebbitt House, a couple of blocks from the White House, and Senator Morton was the head of the opposition to the Democratic candidate, Samuel Tilden.[21] Politicians swarmed in and out of the Morton residence. When the fifteen-judge panel met in the Supreme Court chamber to elect the next president, there were few tickets, but young Morton and young House slipped in and out as they wanted. It was bitterly disappointing to House when Tilden finally lost, by a vote of seven to eight. There were rumors that a Democratic army might put Tilden in the White House by force. (The memory may have influenced House to invent in his only novel, *Philip Dru,* a successful military rebellion in the West against a corrupt Republican regime in Washington.)[22] As a boy in 1876, House already had entrée to the White House and met General and Mrs. Grant.

What he saw in Washington during the winter of 1876–1877, House speculated later, may have changed his whole career. "Fortunately or unfortunately for me," he saw, or thought he saw, that two or three men in the Senate and two or three men in the House, with the president, ran the government.[23] This ringside seat at one of the great dramas of American political history left the spectator with a lifelong craving to be a manager behind the scenes.

Impatient at the prospect of a long wait before he could go to Yale, House decided to go instead to Cornell, with an intention of going to law school once he had graduated. He quickly made friends again at Ithaca, many of them older than himself. He was pledged to Alpha Delta Phi, where he made more friends.

One less attractive side of House's character at this stage of his life, and indeed earlier, was his addiction to practical jokes and pranks, often of a faintly sadistic kind. As a boy, he tells proudly in his memoirs, a Swedish contractor by the name of Olsen came to paint the sugar house at Arcola. Olsen said he wanted to kill an alligator. Spotting that he was a poor rider, the House brothers found him a mount that was gentle but gun shy. Edward and his brother saw an alligator and motioned to Olsen to fire. The horse reared, throwing Olsen into some rushes. In New Haven, House and Oliver Morton tied another boy to a side rail when they knew an express was due on the nearby track. They pretended their fingers were all thumbs until the train sounded almost upon them. "Cruel sport," House admitted as a man of forty.

The carefree life of New Haven, then Ithaca, was abruptly interrupted by the news, in the fall of 1879, that Edward's father had suffered a stroke. House hurried back to Texas and nursed him until he died in early 1880. His estate was valued at $500,000, which made him in those days the third richest man in Texas.[24] His will enjoined the four surviving brothers to keep the estate together for five years. After that, the property was to be divided equally among his children. House considered going to Columbia Law School but decided in the end to help his oldest brother manage their father's estate. They shared out the assets, and House took the land, which was to be found in more than 60 of Texas's 250 counties.

House was keen to camp, hunt, and fish in what were still the wild, high tablelands of central Texas. He persuaded Paul Cruger, his schoolmate in the Virginia experiences, to go with him. As they headed west, the territory would become almost completely uninhabited and lawless. Looking like "uncivilized ruffians," they set out with a black servant, Sam, and his wagon, pulled by two mules. They fished and hunted in the daytime and camped near human habitations at night. As Sam was an expert fisherman, they ate like kings. Once they had entered country where there were no houses, no roads, and no fences, they were comprehensively lost, even with a map and a compass.

One day, pitching their camp near a shallow pool in the bed of a creek, they met Indians who had ridden south hoping to be hired by the cattlemen to work on the great drives north to Kansas. There were other adventures. Once they saw a magnificent saddle horse tied to a tree and learned later that it belonged to notorious bandits. Several times more they were lost, and once they ran out of water until they found they had camped in the dark almost on the banks of a creek.

After their return to San Marcos, House met a neighbor of his sister, Loulie Hunter. Her father, A. J. Hunter, who was related to the celebrated Scottish surgeon John Hunter, widely regarded as the founder of modern surgery, had moved from Louisiana to Texas before the Civil War.[25] The town of Hunter, Texas, near Waco, was named for the family. House's only mention of his marriage is contained in seventeen dry words in his *Reminiscences:* "I married Loulie Hunter, of Hunter, Texas, on August 4, 1881, and travelled Europe for a year."[26]

This laconic statement conceals what was one of the most formative years of his life.[27] So far as one can tell from House's papers and from the reminiscences of his family and friends, the marriage seems to have been one of unclouded happiness. Both husband and wife loved traveling in Europe. As soon as they could afford to, they visited Europe once a year; quiet as she was, Loulie House always went with her husband on his travels, even in wartime, when some of their journeys were seriously dangerous.

Loulie House was soon pregnant, and her daughter Mona was born in Naples. The birth was difficult, and it was some time before the Houses were able to travel. When they arrived home in Texas, House began to work with his brothers. His first, self-imposed task was to sort out the largest single landed property their father had left to them—ninety-seven sections, or some sixty-two thousand acres of land, surveyed by the Houston and Great Northern Railroad, in LaSalle County, around the town of Cotulla on the Nueces River, southwest of San Antonio and only sixty miles or so from Laredo and the border. The land had been granted, as Texas land law dictated, in a checkerboard pattern to the Houses and another family, the Dulls, absentee investors from Pennsylvania. The Dulls, like the Houses, wanted to consolidate their lands so that they could be fenced in with the newly invented barbed wire. Shrewdly, Ed House acted with generosity. He emerged from the complicated transactions, at the age of twenty-four, able to show his brothers a solid block of sixty-four thousand acres of ranch land.[28] William Sydney Porter, better known as O. Henry, lived for a time on the Dull ranch, and House knew him well later in Austin.

He also added to his deep knowledge of his native state. Even as a boy at Arcola, he made some penetrating observations. Unless you knew them well, he wrote in his memoirs, the white inhabitants of Brazos and Fort Bend Counties could be dangerous. Their gracious manners gave no sign of the fires burning beneath the surface. Brag and bluster were fatal with them. They shot quickly and accurately and held human life lightly. "An ill-considered word, an untimely jest, and the deed was done."[29]

Cotulla today is a remote little town of 3,500 inhabitants, mostly Spanish-speaking. The biggest building, in adobe, is the county seat, with a jail festooned with razor wire, and the only bright splash is a florist selling bouquets with silk ribbons for the faithful to take to the two Spanish churches, one Baptist and one Catholic. In the 1880s, it was equally simple, but the population was largely Anglo. The landscape has remained the same: flat, with shrubby trees and cattle every-where, and every few miles rough gates to huge ranches, Rancho Garza and the Lazy M.

In his day, in the plains around Cotulla, House came into contact with a breed of men rougher than the East Texans but at least as formidable. In the 1880s South Texas was full of "bad men," some of them former Confederate soldiers and officers who had drifted to a wild frontier, sparsely populated, terrorized by the Comanches not so long before, and still lawless in spite of brave sheriffs and the Texas Rangers. Wire cutting and range wars were common, and it was not uncommon for sheriffs, rangers, and indeed innocent bystanders to be shot down. "Almost every sheriff of LaSalle County was killed" at that period, House recorded.[30]

House himself had some hairy experiences. His journeys to and from the little station at Cotulla could plunge him into dramas that must have resembled the climax of the movie *High Noon,* with the dark smoke of the train announcing the onset of a duel. Once, as he left San Antonio on the train, a Cotulla merchant warned House that Sheriff Edwards and a man called Davenport were lying in wait at Cotulla station for House's neighbor, Bill Irvin, who was also on the train, and they meant to kill him. House did not forget the faces of the two men as the train pulled into Cotulla, the sheriff "as immobile as a graven image," the other young, small, dark, visibly nervous but wholly unafraid. Edwards had two six-shooters, and Davenport had a repeating Winchester rifle. Irvin, armed only with a six-shooter, would have had no chance. With difficulty House persuaded Irvin to leave the train on the side away from the station, and a shootout was avoided.[31]

House's most dangerous experience, according to his own account, came not in Texas but in Breckenridge, Colorado, where he went to visit a friend. House—it is a little hard to imagine—was in a saloon in a mining camp full of "rough men and rougher women, gambling, drinking and killing" when a "big brawny individual came into the room and began to abuse me in violent terms." House had a six-shooter in his overcoat pocket, cocked. If the owner of the saloon had not jumped over the bar, House would have killed the man. "It is a great satisfaction to me," House wrote in his "Reminiscences," "that I have never killed anyone and it is as much a matter of chance as anything else, for in those days in Texas anyone might be obliged to kill or be killed." Much later in life, he recalled with nostalgia the "reckless freedom" of the life. He loved the campfires at night and riding with a free rein "over the vast, undulating, flower strewn prairies."[32] He had shown his courage and his ability to handle tough hombres. But he suffered from the sultry summers. In 1886, he moved to Austin, which was to remain his home for thirty years and the first theatre for his political talents.

The ranch was for many years to come successfully managed by George Tarver. House visited fairly frequently but wisely left the operating decisions to him.[33] Tarver stocked the land with longhorn cattle, and once a year a dozen or more Mexican *vaqueros* would be hired to help drive the cattle north to San Antonio, Kansas City, or St. Louis.[34] As a very young man, House had consolidated the family holdings in LaSalle County, but it was many years before his own property was fully separated from that of his brothers.

There were two distinct agricultures in late-nineteenth-century Texas: ranching in the arid plains of the southwest and west of the state and farming to the east, with cotton and sugar being the principal crops. After he moved out of ranching—at a profit—at the end of the century, House continued to farm for the rest of his life. Loulie House inherited a large farm near Hunter, between Austin and Waco, and House also owned or leased farming land in Bastrop County, east of Austin. His most valuable property and the largest single source of his income was the plantation he called Monadale, after his elder daughter, Mona. It lay twenty-five miles northeast of Austin, at Hutto, Texas, where the Hill Country falls down from the Balcones escarpment to the famous black, waxy soil of central Texas.[35] For years after he inherited Monadale, it was "poisoned" by Johnson grass, which had been introduced from the Middle East sixty years earlier. In 1893 House ordered his foreman to exterminate it whatever the cost.[36] The job was done in a single year by repeated plowing, at a cost of between six and seven dollars an acre—roughly what the land was worth.

When the job was done, House was the owner of 1,200 acres of magnificent land. For many years, while the House family was living in Austin in the winter and moving to New York and Massachusetts in the summer, their milch cow would be sent to Monadale in April, and another would be ready when they returned in December. Similarly House's favorite dark bay riding horse, Sinbad, on whom he rode over the mesquite-covered plains (where the western suburbs of Austin are now), would go to the farm in the spring and would stay there unshod until his master returned to ride him again in the fall.[37]

Part of the acreage at Monadale was rented to Swedish families, part to "Mexicans," possibly American citizens of Mexican descent. The place was run by a resident manager—first Sam Sharp, and later E. J. Barkley, whose correspondence with House has been preserved and offers a detailed picture of an alert but fair absentee owner. Well over five hundred acres at Monadale was planted with cotton, though enough land was also set aside to produce corn and hay to feed the forty or fifty mules. The property grew an average of five hundred bales of cotton a year, of such quality that it commanded premium prices. That brought House an average income of $17,500 a year, the equivalent of perhaps $500,000 a year in modern money.[38]

House's letters show him to have been frugal, but not miserly, and notably scrupulous about his business dealings.[39] For example, House was concerned when he learned that Barkley was buying the cotton raised by his Mexican American tenants and reselling it. House wrote Barkley: "I do not doubt that you are perfectly fair with them; at the same time if I were in your place I would rather buy cotton from others rather than them for the reason that it would be so easy to have your motives misunderstood."[40]

The letters reveal House as a shrewd and careful businessman. At times, when he was established in New York as a mysterious Texan with political influence and still more when he was dealing with British gentlemen politicians and Parisian society hostesses, it suited him to present himself as a *rentier*, a man who could rely on a large inherited income from investments. This status was only part of the truth. From the time he moved to New York, House was financially independent, though not especially rich by the New York standards of the day. It is also true that he inherited from his father a very substantial fortune, and after about 1916 he did rely primarily on income from investments, if these include the notes on the money owed him by the purchasers of Monadale. For at least twenty years after 1885, though, he was actively and successfully involved in several businesses.

As well as a rancher and a cotton farmer, House was an active land dealer. For some time—from the 1880s at least until 1900—he bought and sold land through the land agency of Holmes and Bierschwale, at Mason, Texas.[41] As well as improving and selling on land he inherited, he also speculated in land bought from the state of Texas. His partner was T. F. Pinckney, who had worked in the General Land Office in Austin. In the 1880s, though most state land was in arid West Texas and of little value, it was still possible for a clever land man to buy what were known as "vacancies," small parcels in the farmlands of central Texas or timberlands in the east. Pinckney would find valuable vacancies, and Edward House would buy them.

As early as 1908 House considered selling Monadale at $125 an acre. These were years of financial panic and also of crisis brought to the cotton business in Texas by the boll weevil. In the end, between 1913 and 1916 House was able to split the property up into blocks of from 90 to 200 acres and sell them at from $160 to $180 an acre.[42]

By the end of the century, House already was generating substantial profits from his ranching, farming, and land-trading operations, and he was looking for new places to invest them. On December 27, 1899, Thomas Jefferson Coolidge Jr., of the Old Colony Trust Company in Boston, wrote to House confirming a purchase of five hundred shares in a stock called Planters Compress for a total cost of no less than $11,222.50.[43] The investment probably represented an ambition of House's to invest "downstream" from his cotton plantation. (At another time he showed interest in investing in a cottonseed oil mill.) It was not an outstandingly successful investment. Ten years later, Coolidge wrote, "I regret to have to report that the Planters Compress Company has been put in liquidation." House got $83.33. "You may get something more but I don't know how much."[44] The Coolidge connection, however, was to be valuable indeed for House, both in business and in his private life.

Thomas Jefferson Coolidge Jr. was the son of a Boston capitalist. The Coolidges, father and son, Yankees who were descended from Thomas Jefferson, made their Old Colony Trust a major investment house. By 1902, House had decided to invest in nothing less than a railroad, albeit admittedly a small one, and it was Coolidge who made it possible. On February 10, 1902, House wrote proudly to his friend Frank Andrews, a Houston lawyer-politico, that "my friends in Boston have decided to go in with us to the extent of a half million as a starter." He boasted that "We have with us the richest men in Boston and Chicago."[45]

In the early years of the twentieth century the great transcontinental trunk lines had been built, and now the fashion was for lines linking specific cities. The craze had reached Texas, and the big red cars of the Dallas-Fort Worth Electric Lines were the talk of the countryside. House and his friend Robert Homer Baker, an insurance man with a knack for putting together rights of way, decided to work together.[46] The idea eventually was to build a line from North Texas all the way south to Beaumont, where the great Spindletop gusher was attracting all attention.[47] In October 1902 the Trinity and Brazos Valley Railway Company came into existence, with E. M. House as chairman of the board, and his friend Baker as president of the board. By March 1903 a big steam shovel was at work. Three hundred and fifty teams of men were making the dirt fly, and the steel rails were arriving from Germany.

The first stretch of the line was opened before the end of 1903. The Boston financiers came through with $1,500,000. (It was a good deal for them as it included a commission of 10 percent, on top of the 10 percent interest they were paid.) The Boll Weevil Line, as it was called, however, suffered from the depredations of the insect. There was less cotton every year. All together only some seventy-eight miles were built, from Cleburne, south of Fort Worth, to Mexia, east of Waco. Before long, Coolidge was reporting on negotiations to sell the line to the Missouri, Kansas and Texas Line. The negotiations fell through, and so did efforts to interest E. H. Harriman of the Union Pacific.[48] In the end, Coolidge and House were able to sell out to B. F. Yoakum, from St. Louis, of the Frisco System. Coolidge made $17,000, and House, according to his "Reminiscences," $30,000.

It was enough for Coolidge. "I am off for a sixty day holiday on Tuesday," he wrote House on November 5, 1904, "and write to congratulate you on the work you have done in closing up the Trinity & Brazos Valley. . . . It is no amusement to you or to me to run a small railroad; it is a great nuisance and wastes much time. It is better for us to make a quick, fair profit and be ready for something new."[49]

The Jefferson Coolidges were to be important in House's life long after the Boll Weevil had hooted and puffed its last. From the 1890s on the Houses were in the habit of staying on the North Shore of Massachusetts, then at the height of its fashion. At first the Houses spent the summers either at the Oceanside Hotel or at one of its cottages, but later they seem to have rented cottages directly from the Coolidges, with whom they became close socially. On June 10, 1917, House wrote Coolidge, "I enclose my check for One Thousand ($1000) Dollars for the use of your cottage during the season."[50]

Like every man in Texas with money, and many without, House was excited by the Spindletop gusher.[51] Most of the hill was already bought up, but House had what seemed a clever idea. He proposed to buy the right to drill in the streets and alleys of the town site of Gladys, laid out by the promoters on the oil-bearing dome, and he and his friends, including Thomas Jefferson Coolidge, invested $90,000 in the scheme. But the courts finally held it was illegal to drill for oil in places dedicated to public use.

House was involved in a number of other business ventures in Texas, such as an insurance company, a proposed electric inter-urban line between Houston and Galveston, and an effort to rebuild the Austin dam on the Colorado River; the dam, which supplied water and power to the city, had been swept away by a flood in 1900.

By the turn of the century, House had been committed to a new career—politics—for the best part of a decade. He had also provided himself with a worthy base in Austin for his political adventures. It was in 1885 that he decided to move to Austin, at least in part for his health, and on September 17, 1886, he bought for $6,000 an entire city block on West Avenue, then the newest and most fashionable neighborhood in what was a city of twenty thousand inhabitants. The site was within walking distance of the giant state capitol, finished in 1888.

To build his home, House chose Frank Freeman, a disciple of one of the best-known architects in America, Henry Hobson Richardson, famous for his "Rich-ardson Romanesque" designs, with their strong arches and deeply etched shadows. By the early 1890s Freeman, Canadian born, had established himself as a designer of homes for wealthy people. Freeman had developed a version of Richardson's style that did not demand so much massive masonry. It was a variant of what was called the "shingle style." House commissioned Freeman in 1890, the cornerstone was laid in April 1891, and the Houses moved in by 1894.[52] The home was massive, impressive, comfortable, and well suited for the generous hospitality that was the background to House's remarkable influence in Texas politics. House preferred to talk business at home rather than in his office.

The Austin home was ideal for entertaining in style. It had seven bedrooms, where various visiting dignitaries came to stay, and spacious service areas, includ-ing a large kitchen, a big wine cellar, and a dining room for the servants.[53] (The family employed three Swedish maids, as well as an African American butler. There were cooks, yard boys, grooms in the stables, a coachman, and later a chauffeur.) Colonel House was not a heavy drinker himself, nor was he a "dry," and he served not only excellent wines, but also carefully chosen whiskeys and brandies. There was a humidor for the Havana cigars he offered his guests.

From the outside, the Austin house's strong horizontal lines were broken by sharp gables and a stone turret. Inside, there was a formal sequence of rooms, a hundred feet long, from the music room through the parlor into the library. There were two dining rooms, one for formal entertaining and the other for family meals, as well as a study for the master of the house. But the most striking feature was a huge porch, or veranda, wrapping around three sides of the building and overlooking the city in the background. "The large veranda to the south was the scene, perhaps, of more political conferences than any similar place in Texas. It was there that the clans congregated."[54]

3   *The Texas Kingmaker*   ⌒

Proud setter up and puller down of kings, Warwick.

—William Shakespeare, *Henry VI*

EDWARD HOUSE FIRST TOOK A HAND in Texas politics in 1892. The occasion was no trivial one. The contest between James Stephen Hogg and George Clark for the governorship was an epic encounter. Hogg, a genial, three-hundred-pound stump speaker who pulled his galluses off his shoulders to give better scope for his stomach and his oratory, was apt to present himself as a rougher diamond than his comfortable background warranted.[1] He had challenged "the interests"—insurance companies, absentee British land speculators, and above all the railroads—and in so doing, he had coopted for the Progressive wing of the Democratic Party much of the boiling populist discontent that was burning across Texas like wildfire.

First, in the 1870s, there was the Grange. Then came the Greenbackers. Then in the 1880s the Farmers' Alliance drew farmers to "speakings," which were more like revivals. Now, in the 1890s, a fourth wave of agrarian dissent, the People's Party, forged an alliance between hungry farmers and angry city workers.

The populist movement at times attained an almost revolutionary intensity. Lines of buckboards, miles long, would converge on the place chosen for "the speaking." There would be singing and speeches and entertainment, both sacred and profane. There would be barbecue pits for the hungry and lemonade and soda pop for the faithful. Alcoholic drinks were not allowed, but immediately outside the site beer and whiskey were easy to find. Thousands of populists, dry and wet, would stand for hours to hear the burning eloquence of James "Cyclone" Davis or H. S. R. "Stump" Ashby.

Jim Hogg could match these heroes in the passion of his oratory. But if Hogg was sympathetic to the farmers' grievances, he was an opponent of the populist leadership. His chosen path was the middle of the road, and his platform firmly occupied that ground.[2] It stated that "we are opposed to communism in any and all forms and pledge ourselves to the just and equitable protection of the interests of both capital and labor."[3] It was a position House would occupy all his life.

Hogg was a crusading attorney general in the 1880s and was elected governor in 1890—not as a spokesman for agrarian revolt, but as the Democratic Party's response to the rising tide of Farmers' Alliance support.[4] The Republicans had been a discredited minority in Texas, largely reliant on African American votes, since Democrat Richard Coke had defeated the carpetbagger governor, Edmund J. Davis, in 1873.[5] Texas had been reliably Democratic in all the presidential elections throughout the Gilded Age. But it was not in the usual sense a one-party state. Texas politics in 1890 were divided three ways. There were the populists. At the opposite extreme were the Bourbon Democrats, conservative men who cherished the memory of the war and resented the carpetbaggers. Seeing the South's future in social conservatism and industrial progress, they supported the corporations and the railroads and defended the big landowners, including big foreign landowners. It was against them that the rising tide of agrarian dissent was directed, and two-thirds of the working population in Texas in 1890 were farmers.[6]

In between were those Democrats, later sometimes called Progressives, who wanted to head off the populists by meeting at least some of their grievances. Jim Hogg was the candidate of this centrist tribe of Democrats; he was not truly, as he has often been portrayed, either a radical or a populist. In later life he abandoned politics and set himself, not altogether successfully, to make money as a businessman.[7]

It was in Hogg's second campaign for governor, in 1892, that Edward House first entered politics. Very quickly he showed exceptional gifts as an organizer and strategist. He was never a radical but a defender of the status quo, though a thoughtful and liberal one. The word "progressive" is a treacherous one and covers a multitude of positions. Some have seen the Progressive era as setting an agenda of change for American politics throughout the twentieth century. Richard Hofstadter defined it in terms of a desire on the part of Anglo-Saxon Americans to return to the virtues and simplicities of the days before America was changed by foreigners, radicals, and corporations. The radical historian Gabriel Kolko contended that what was "labeled the 'progressive' era by virtually all historians was really an era of conservatism."[8] That overstates the case, but it would be a mistake to see Colonel House in his Texas years as any kind of spearhead of radical change. Rather he was one of a generation of politicians who confronted a welling up of popular discontent that alarmed them and then watched with relief as it ebbed away after William Jennings Bryan's first defeat for the presidency in 1896.

When Edward House appeared as the right hand of Woodrow Wilson on the national stage, it was vaguely assumed that he was a leading Democrat from a safely Democratic state. Texas in the 1880s and 1890s, however, was not a safe fief for the one-party politics of the Democratic South.[9] In 1911, Governor Oscar B. Colquitt said, "We have only one political party in Texas, but there are enough political fights in that for half a dozen."[10] The same was true of Texas twenty years earlier. Parties and factions split, reunited, and split again. Individual politicians navigated these dangerous shoals as best they could, none more skilfully than Edward M. House.

Some Texans—House among them—were prospering as the resources of their huge state were developed and enjoying, as House himself put it, "the world and the fullness thereof."[11] Many were not. This was a frontier society. A lady only slightly older than House could remember a neighbor being scalped by Comanches.[12] The generation who ran Texas had fought in the Civil War, and military titles were de rigueur around the capitol in Austin.

Agrarian discontent was a constant. Farmers blamed falling prices on "the crime of 1873," as they called Congress's demonetizing of silver and the establishment of the gold standard. They denounced the dominance of the financial interests of New York and the City of London. In 1873 the financial panic after the collapse of Jay Cooke's bank triggered an agricultural depression that circled the world. Farm prices fell.[13] Texas farmers were heavily in debt. More and more were forced to sell their land and work as tenants: 37 percent in 1880 and 49 percent by 1900.[14] Most were in debt, and the only way they could pay out enough on their loans was to plant the cash crop, cotton, that merchants would accept in payment. To crown their misery, the boll weevil ravaged the cotton crop.

Above all, Texans resented the railroads. Many of them were "paper roads," built just to collect land grants or cash subsidies. They were all owned out of state. Regulating the railroads was not only an economic priority. It was a symbolic issue, and James Stephen Hogg understood that he must satisfy the average Texan's outrage at the railroads' power and greed if he were to stave off the populist challenge. The populists called for state ownership. Hogg and progressive Democrats were for regulation.

In Texas, as elsewhere, the populist platform had planks to appeal to ranchers—including a demand for an end to alien ownership (much of West and South Texas was being bought up by British cattle companies)—as well as to farmers, such as reform of the lien law, which kept so many of them in virtual peonage. It had strictly political elements, such as a call for fair elections and what was known as the "Australian ballot," and it bowed to the farmers' suspicions of city wickedness with its suggestion that children should be taught about the effects of alcohol.

To understand Edward House's career in Texas politics, it is essential to understand that his kind of progressivism was an alternative to populism, not an acceptance of its radical program. Silver was the litmus test. Hogg shared the populist enthusiasm for the free coinage of silver; House did not. Indeed, after his initial association with Jim Hogg, he became the leader of a rather conservative faction within the Texas Democratic Party.

Texas, when Edward House first stepped into its turbulent political waters, was not on the brink of surrendering to the populist fervor. It was preparing to reject it. (One reason for a rejection, most historians concur, was the underlying issue of race, whether felt as nostalgia for the lost cause of the Confederacy or as the raw racism of politicians like Senator Joseph Weldon Bailey.)

House ended up with extraordinary influence over the state's electoral process and the careers of its politicians. It was not that of a progressive, however, but that of an essentially conservative man with enough political acumen to recognize when something needed to be conceded to popular unhappiness. He possessed liberal instincts and a quite exceptional flair for making the system work for the distinctly mixed group of men he chose to consider his political friends—or, as he called them in his correspondence, "our crowd." Of the four governors House helped to elect, only the first, Jim Hogg—the least beholden to House's skills—could truly be described as a progressive. The second, Charles Culberson, reunited the Hogg Democrats with their Bourbon opponents, while the third and fourth, Joseph D. Sayers and S. W. T. Lanham, were not progressives at all. Moreover, in one instance, as we shall see, Colonel House actively defeated a promising progressive candidate.

In 1892 the forces of Bourbon democracy, energetically backed by the railroads, decided to challenge Hogg. They chose as their champion George Clark, a previous attorney general of the state. Hogg would have the fight of his life.

The chairman of the Hogg campaign was General W. R. Hamby, with House as his deputy. House himself implied, probably with truth, that it was he who chose Hamby in the first place. The general, an older man who was a member of the state legislature, a banker, and the publisher of the *Austin Statesman*, was something of a figurehead. House attended to the practicalities of the campaign. "I began at the top," House admitted bluntly.[15] House was Hogg's campaign manager and did the job so well that his reputation was established.

On April 21, 1892, "the banker, the merchant, the lawyer and the man with the hoe," not to mention the "boys from the forks of the creek," turned out in the thousands to hear Hogg deliver the expected stem-winder.[16] At great length, the Railroad Commission was praised, and the malfeasance of Jay Gould, the archetype of Robber Barons, did not escape reproof. "All of the railroads and most of the wealth of Texas were on the Clark side," House recalled, and so were most, though not all, of the newspapers.[17] The climax came at the state Democratic convention in Houston, which opened on August 16. It was to meet in the cavernous "car stable" of the Houston street railway, a brick structure 93 by 250 feet said to hold eight thousand people, but with one side open.[18]

When the convention met, the two sides could not agree on a chairman, and for a while the meeting was close to bloodshed. "Passions were at fever heat," House recalled, "and there were many who would have welcomed a chance to shoot and kill."[19] Two conventions, one for Clark and one for Hogg, tried to meet in the same hall and eventually adjourned until ten the next morning. At nine, when the Clark men arrived, they found that the open side of the car stable had been walled in. House's friend Captain Bill McDonald of the Texas Rangers had supervised the work, and he was there with armed guards to screen out the Clark delegates.

The Hogg Democrats, left in command of the car stable, nominated their slate of candidates: James S. Hogg for governor; M. M. Crane for lieutenant governor; and Charles A. Culberson, son of a congressman and Confederate general, for attorney general. They also adopted a platform, presented by John H. Reagan.[20] This was the text that denied any sympathy with "communism," but it was a fairly radical document just the same. It called for a state banking system, a graduated income tax, and regulation of securities. The People's Party met at Dallas in late June and adopted an even more radical program, too much so for the moderate majority. In the general election, Hogg received 190,486 votes; Clark, 133,395; and the Populist candidate, Thomas L. Nugent, 108,483.[21]

House had won a reputation for efficiency and sagacity that was to stay with him as long as he was active in Texas politics. In the second Hogg administration, as in the Wilson administration, he was "the man to see."[22]

The economic depression that began in 1893 strengthened the People's Party. Hogg's great achievement had been the creation of the Texas Railroad Commission, but until the eve of the 1894 primaries, it was not even certain that the Supreme Court of the United States would allow the commission to continue.[23] The depression also guaranteed that the "currency question" would continue to divide Texas Democrats. The People's Party campaigned for free and unlimited coinage of silver at sixteen to one against gold, and Jim Hogg and his mentor Reagan were free silver men too. Their enthusiasm for silver was strengthened by their need to compete with the Populists for farmer support.

After the 1892 election, House was approached by Charles Culberson, who asked him to manage his campaign for governor in 1894, and House agreed. There was a crowded field of candidates.[24] House, with some courage, opposed both his friend and patron Hogg and the "Old Roman," as the politicos called Reagan, because he did not buy the case for the free issue of silver. House advised Culberson to avoid the currency question, but Reagan's entry into the race, to take the silver question away from the People's Party, made that impossible.[25]

House, helped by his close friend Frank Andrews, previously one of Culberson's assistant attorney generals, wrote endless letters to line up delegates. In August 1894 the Culberson men, led by Colonel House, chartered a special train to take them from Austin to Dallas for the state convention in the Sam Jones Tabernacle. This was an even vaster arena than the Houston car stable, but the convention was an altogether less frenzied occasion. The weather was unbearably hot, so much so that the *Dallas News* said two questions preoccupied the delegates: "whether Texas will pull through and whether the beer will hold out."[26] Reagan spoke at excessive length and eventually withdrew. Culberson overwhelmed his opponent on the first ballot. Culberson won the general election easily: Culberson, Democrat, 216,373 votes; Nugent, People's Party, 159,676; W. K. Makeson, "Regular Republican," 57,147; J. M. Dunn, Prohibition (a cloud still no bigger than a man's hand), 21,295.[27]

The *Dallas Morning News* commented that "Mr. Culberson attributes a large share of his success to the skilfull work and untiring industry of Col. House, who organized the Culberson campaign and directed it." The same reporter noted "the equanimous figure of Charles Allen Culberson and in his shadow the smiling, silent Colonel House."[28]

Two years later, the state convention was in Fort Worth, and Colonel House was second only to Joseph Weldon Bailey as a celebrity at the convention headquarters. The *Dallas Morning News* judged that "the hand of the Austin Warwick"—that is, of the kingmaker—"has not lost its cunning."[29] That year again, at the high tide of populism, Culberson wrote to House that the contest would be close. "There is a general condition of unrest among the people, the hard times aggravate it, and lying newspapers propagate untruths. . . . You are badly needed at the helm."[30] He was not wrong. Even with House's firm hand on the tiller Culberson beat the candidate of the People's Party for governor by only sixty thousand votes.[31]

In 1899 Culberson was anxious to move to the Senate. Again, House was his counsellor. He set out to remove Culberson's rivals, one by one. In the end, House's candidate was elected unanimously in the Texas Senate and with only two votes against in the House.

The attorney generalship in Texas was the traditional stepping stone to the office of governor. Hogg had made that progression, and so had Culberson. The attorney general who might be expected to move up to governor in 1898 was Martin McNulty Crane, a man of first-class ability and the highest integrity. Instead, House opted to support Congressman Joseph D. Sayers, a Confederate war hero.[32] Technically, House's success in putting over Sayers against Crane was perhaps his most brilliant achievement as a political manager. From another point of view, it can be said to have deprived the state of Texas of a public servant of the highest quality.[33] Once nominated, Sayers was quite content to give House a free hand with running the campaign. "Whatever you do will be satisfactory to me," he wrote House in early 1897.[34] House first made the strategic observation that while Crane was ahead in far more counties than Sayers, there was no single county he could clearly call his own, whereas there were many counties that could not be taken from Sayers. So House got his friends in the Sayers counties to call their primaries early.[35] (At that time, counties could schedule their primaries more or less as they chose.) County after county declared for Sayers. Crane, in desperation, withdrew, and House easily disposed of the remaining candidates. This episode led directly to the passage of the Terrell election law, introduced specifically to block the use of early primaries by both House and Joseph Weldon Bailey.

Long before Sayers's second term was over, House was looking around for another candidate. His subsequent moves make it plain that his interest was not so much in policy as in finding a governor likely to be amenable to his influence. They also show how far he had moved from his commitment to the progressive cause. He was looking for a moderate conservative to challenge the candidate of the progressive wing of the Democratic Party, Thomas M. Campbell. He first maneuvered to elect his conservative friend from South Texas, James B. Wells, whose power derived in part from his hold over the Mexican vote along the Rio Grande. When that proved impossible, House fell back on Fort Worth congressman Lanham. "I believe that we can win with Lanham," he wrote Andrews, "although I think it would be a joyless and fruitless victory." While he did not anticipate "any great amount of pleasure out of Lanham's administration," he wrote in another letter that "we may control him about as much as we have controlled the present incumbent [Sayers] and by about the same methods."[36]

In 1902 Campbell accused House of being one of the "political idlers" who were the instrument of the railroads and the monopolies. But House's confidence was undented. "The truth of it is," he told Frank Andrews, "the prestige of our crowd in Texas is such that anyone with normal intelligence hesitates to run up against the inevitable."[37]

House was not excited by Governor Lanham's victory, nor by his governorship. "He made a colorless Governor," he wrote later. "Most of the legislative matters that I had in mind had been enacted into law and there was nothing in particular that excited my interest, so I did not press him hard. I wrote the platform as usual, but it was rather innocuous." House wanted Texas to copy the reform of land title in Australia, but, he complained contemptuously, Lanham "understood so little about it that it was a hopeless undertaking."[38]

House never accepted any executive responsibility in Texas, but his contribution to "his" governors was not limited to getting them elected. He was an adviser as well as a campaign manager. Though he was a staunch defender of property and hostile to the silver interests, in general his influence was deployed on behalf of moderately progressive causes.[39]

House was personally close to Jim Hogg, whom he held in high esteem. With Hogg, he was the younger man, the lieutenant. Between the two men there was no question as to who was the leader. With Culberson it was different. During his term of office, House said, he devoted himself as totally to public affairs as he was later to do under Woodrow Wilson. He went to Culberson's office in the capitol nearly every day, went over the governor's mail with him, and sometimes stayed there working until night. House admired Culberson's brains, but he did not respect his lack of decisiveness.

Governor Sayers, having used House as his campaign manager, tried to free himself from House's domination, or so it seemed to House. Sayers was beset by office seekers. House claimed he received more than twenty thousand letters, few of which he so much as opened. One day he gave in and asked House if they could meet. House was going through one of his periodic bouts of ill health, so he received Sayers in his own home, lying on a chaise longue in his sitting room.[40] By six o'clock, with Frank Andrews working as his secretary, House had filled up his slate of offices with suggestions, all but one of which Sayers accepted. It is clear that for all Sayers's efforts to break free, House controlled him. If anything, he controlled S. W. T. Lanham, the last of the candidates he steered into the governor's office, even more completely.

In 1902 the influence of House's crowd was very great.[41] It was almost that of a "machine," and some people called it that, though its style was very different from that of the typical urban machine of that age. House himself did not like the expression and corrected Governor Sayers when he used it. His friends were certainly not the partisans of any particular political doctrine, though they all— with the exception of Jim Wells—stood for clean government. Although they came to be identified as Texas progressives, in truth they represented one of several centrist factions among Democrats.

The inner circle of House's political friends was composed of Charles Culberson; Congressman Albert Burleson; Thomas Watt Gregory, an Austin trial lawyer; Frank Andrews; James B. Wells of Brownsville, the *caudillo* of the South Texas Mexicans; Thomas B. Love, a Dallas lawyer who published the militant prohibitionist paper *Home and State;* Robert H. Baker of Dallas, insurance man and railroad investor; and Joe Lee Jameson, often described as an "aide" of House's and even by less complimentary terms.[42] This group gave House intelligence about, and influence with, many different political worlds. His friends were not the ultra-conservative Democrats, men like Senator Joe Bailey. Nor could they be called the most progressive members of the democracy in Texas—those who carried on the tradition established by Hogg, such as M. M. Crane or Thomas M. Campbell. Of course even these genuinely progressive Democrats were a moderate alternative to the leaders of populism.

Already by 1896, according to his own account—and it is largely corroborated from other sources—House felt ready to take part in national politics.[43] But the nomination of William Jennings Bryan and the salience of the free silver issue made him feel it would be unwise to go national yet. He and Governor Hogg decided to get in touch with Bryan and try to wean him away from his passionate silver crusade. They had a stroke of luck. As noted in chapter 1, the Bryans' daughter Grace had not been well, and the Great Commoner wanted to spend the winter somewhere warmer than Lincoln, Nebraska. Hogg and House offered to find a home for the Bryans in Austin, and they rented a place next door to the Houses on West Avenue for the winter of 1898–1899. Thereafter there was "much visiting back and forth through the hedge."[44] Both the colonel and Mrs. House got on very easily with Mary Bryan, but they found the Great Commoner difficult. "I have never met a more self-opinionated man," House wrote later. "I believe he feels that his ideas are God-given and are not susceptible to the mutability of those of the ordinary human. He often told me that a man that did not believe in 'the free and unlimited coinage of silver at 16 to 1 was either a fool or a knave.' "[45]

House kept his opinion to himself because before the winter was over Bryan, who was already the front-runner for the Democratic presidential nomination again in 1900, asked House to "take a leading part in the management of the campaign" with Senator James Kimborough Jones of Arkansas, chairman of the Democratic National Committee in 1896, as his associate.[46] House—by his own account—told Bryan to get rid of Jones, but Bryan refused. So House declined the invitation and confined his interest in the campaign to wondering how easily Bryan would be beaten. They remained good friends, however. The Bryans came to Austin again the following winter and in several subsequent years.[47]

In 1904, the Democrats chose a conservative New York judge, Alton B. Parker, as their candidate. Parker made overtures to House through B. F. Yoakum, the St. Louis railroad man who had bought the Boll Weevil Line, to manage his campaign, but House pleaded poor health and went to Europe for the summer.[48]

When Bryan came to Texas in the winter of 1904–1905, House met him at the station early in the morning and took him home to have breakfast with the governor, then Thomas Campbell. On the way from the station to the house, the colonel ventured to tell Bryan he hoped he would not be the candidate in 1908. House advised Bryan to support another candidate and accept a high cabinet office under him. If he did the job well, nothing could keep him from succeeding as president. After Bryan did indeed become secretary of state, Bryan asked him whether it had been House's own advice or whether the president agreed. "Much to his disappointment," House recalled, "I told him the observation was mine alone."[49] The friendship, first made possible by Grace Bryan's illness, was to come in useful for both men in 1912.

House's greatest influence in Texas politics ran from 1892 to 1906. In later years, as he put it himself, "the political outlook was as quiet as a mill pond."[50] Of Governor Lanham's second term, from 1904 to 1906, House said, "He walked through his second term with practically no accomplishment, neither for good nor for evil."[51]

After 1906, in the judgment of the historian of progressivism in Texas, Lewis L. Gould, "House lacked a secure base in state affairs."[52] He was bored, for one thing. He was excited by business propositions like the Boll Weevil and Spindletop. The state was now in the hands of Campbell, who had earlier been denied the office by House's clever use of early primaries.

Texas was changing. Agrarian revolt was being sidelined into a new crusade against the demon rum. By 1905–1908 the "dries" were on top in North, Central, and East Texas. Only in the German-settled, beer-drinking Hill Country and in Mexican South Texas did the "wets" hold out. There was a new demand for white supremacy. Where the Populists of the 1890s had sought an alliance between poor white people and blacks, in the new century "the ideology of white supremacy permeated social customs."[53]

House, by his own account, flirted with the idea of running for governor more than once. "In 1898," he wrote in his "Memories," "I might have succeeded Culberson had I so desired. . . . The machinery was in my hands." And he might have won even if there was opposition, which there was not. In 1902 too, the colonel thought in later years, he could easily have become governor. Indeed, "had I become U.S. Senator, which would not have been very difficult to achieve from the Governor's chair, I should have tried for the Presidency."[54]

These were an old man's imaginings. House might perhaps have been able to make himself governor. His chances of striding from the Austin capitol to the Senate in Washington, let alone to the White House, would have been problematic. The national ambitions that had been awakened when he went to stay with his friend Oliver Morton in the heady days of the Hayes-Tilden election revived during the kingmaker years in Austin. But whatever House may have believed later, the opportunity for a national political career did not exist between the end of Governor Lanham's term in 1906 and the first glimmerings of a split in the Republican Party in 1910–1911.

In 1908, the presidential nomination was Bryan's again. House liked Bryan. But he simply did not believe that Bryan could be elected president. Moreover, House was quietly stubborn in opposing Bryan's obsession with silver.

So he busied himself with other things. He tried to make money, with some success. He interested himself in the affairs of the state mental health system and the university. He devoted some energy to getting a biography written of one of his heroes, Captain Bill McDonald of the Texas Rangers. He first tried to get O. Henry (William Sydney Porter) to undertake the job. When Porter refused, he turned to Albert Bigelow Paine, who dedicated his book to House. Later House dictated his recollections of Captain Bill to Tyler Mason, who published them as *Riding for Texas.*[55] Captain Bill, of whom it was said that he shot from the lip as well as from the hip, was as brave as a lion. He was not, however, as wholly admirable a character as House thought: he was blamed for racially prejudiced conduct in the notorious Brownsville affray.[56]

"I was never at any time," House wrote, "a boss or a near boss."[57] It was true. Nonetheless, he was well known in the inner circles of Texas politics, and Texas journalists treated him—as national journalists were to do later—as good copy. His wealth, his indifferent health, his avoiding of the hustings—all built up his aura of mystery. He was a kingmaker.

From 1906, however, House had lost much of his influence in Texas. The political wheel was turning away from him and his crowd. Wealthy, bored, and conscious of rare political talents, he was frustrated by his inability to put them to use. He was a kingmaker in search of a king.

4 *Going National* ॐ

IN 1908 COLONEL HOUSE OF AUSTIN was still a man with a regional reputation only. Five years later, his chance on the national stage came, and he took it with the silent efficiency of a pike swallowing a chick.

Between a first career as the kingmaker of Austin and a second as the president's political confidant, he tried his hand at political theory. As noted in chapter 1, in 1912 he published, anonymously, a novel called *Philip Dru: Administrator.* As a novel, it had limited appeal even then, and now it seems hopelessly dated. As a political dystopia, of a kind then much in vogue, it is more interesting. It reveals much about the preoccupations of an experienced observer of politics at that moment in American history. It is a master key to the political beliefs of the Progressive movement and of House in particular.

Philip Dru was written, very fast, immediately after House met Woodrow Wilson for the first time. By then Wilson's own political philosophy, contradictory as it was in certain respects, had already set hard. Edward House's credo, as set forth in his novel, was forged between the hammer of the prevailing unrest and the anvil of House's essentially conservative instincts.

The five years between the Panic of 1907 and the presidential election of 1912 had a mood of their own. The boisterous, brass band years from 1896 to 1906 were over. In the electrifying period of his "Cross of Gold" speech William Jennings

Bryan had given a silver tongue to the rage of the hinterland. William Randolph Hearst had caught the macho mood and egged the nation on into a victorious war with Cuba, all to push the circulation of the *New York Journal* past that of Joseph Pulitzer's *World*.[1] Theodore Roosevelt caught that same wind. He launched the nation into international politics and sketched the shape of the modern presidency. When he encountered the resistance of Congress and the financial interests it sustained, he turned his oratory against the trusts. The new journalism, in its daily yellow and its weekly muckraking manifestations, endlessly exposed the price Americans were paying for the unholy alliance between Republican corporations and Democratic machines.

For a few years—partly because of the new journalism—the nation lived on the edge of its seat, battered by one intense emotion after another. But by 1908, that breathless excitement was over.

The two-party system had failed. Bryan had been defeated for the third time. He himself joked that he was like the drunk who, three times ejected from a saloon, picked himself up, dusted himself down, and said, "They don't seem to want me in there." The Republicans settled with a sigh of relief on the massively reassuring figure of William H. Taft. Congress was discredited. Insurgency and third-party movements were in the air. William Randolph Hearst showed up the depths of discontent when he came close to carrying New York state as an Independent candidate for governor in 1906. Even that European import, socialism, began to make electoral inroads, especially in cities and states with high numbers of immigrants—Germans in Milwaukee, Scandinavians in Minneapolis, Russian Jews in the Lower East Side of Manhattan.[2]

Everywhere the cry was for reform, though there was no agreement on what that would mean. Sometimes reformers yearned for a vanished Currier and Ives America; sometimes they wanted to move forward into the new world of large-scale organization and social change. Populism and its urban version, anarchism, were replaced by an ambiguous amalgam, progressivism.[3]

What did progressivism mean? At one level, it meant sweeping away corruption in the body politic and society. At another, there was a veiled conservatism behind an eagerness for modernity. Many Americans were nostalgic for a lost Jeffersonian world of independent farmers; in reality farmers were being forced precisely into dependence—on lenders, landlords, railroads, and banks. Labor, as led by Samuel Gompers, cherished an equally vanished world of independent craftsmen, just when the new mass production was regimenting armies of workers.

The parties were divided and uncomfortably aware of how unpopular they had become. In the South, where they ruled, the Democrats had ended Reconstruction without creating the New South they had promised. They had absorbed the Populist energy but achieved few of the Populist goals. In the North, the Republicans had presided over the Gilded Age but also over fifteen years of inequality and impoverishment.

From the point of view of the disillusioned but still idealistic and ambitious Colonel House, fifty years old when his winter neighbor, William Jennings Bryan, was defeated for the third time, the prospects of the Democratic Party must have looked dismal. Yet House was enough of a Southerner that the Republican Party would have seemed a discreditable, unthinkable alternative. Only gradually did the alluring opportunity presented by the impending crisis of the Republicans become plain.

In 1908, what was called the "social question" invaded politics. In January, the Supreme Court struck down the Employers Liability Act, on which President Roosevelt had staked much of his credibility. Roosevelt responded with a message to Congress in which he denounced "malefactors of great wealth." Taft's nomination in July opened the possibility of a damaging split in Republican ranks.

In November Taft won 321 electoral college votes and Bryan only 162. Taft won the popular vote by only 1.27 million votes, less than Roosevelt's margin in 1904. The Republicans seemed to have become unashamedly the party of the corporations, while the Democrats were leaderless.

At this point House began to read everything he could lay his hands on about politics. Much of it confirmed a sense that the system was running down like an unwound clock. The most influential writers of his own generation, and many of the new crop coming along, were casting about for fundamental reform in the political and social structure of the country.

Samuel S. McClure founded the magazine that bore his name in 1893. For nearly a decade, it published the best in popular fiction, including Rudyard Kipling and Arthur Conan Doyle. But in 1902 McClure stumbled onto the discovery that made his fortune: it was not just that businessmen and politicians habitually broke the law; it was also that Americans loved to read about such scandals. In *McClure's* and other magazines, such as *Collier's,* a whole new school of journalists flourished: Lincoln Steffens exposed municipal corruption, Ida Tarbell attacked Standard Oil, and Jacob Riis explored the New York slums. Teddy Roosevelt half approved of what they were doing, but he called them the muckrakers, after the man in John Bunyan's *Pilgrim's Progress* who was so busy raking up the muck that he could not see the stars. The new journalism provided American reform politics with a new agenda. The reform impulse was not wholly free from nativist and racial undertones. Churchgoing, middle-class Protestants did not like what they learned about Jewish sweatshops and Irish ward bosses. They blamed foreigners. But the impulse for reform also came from healthy political instincts.

This journalistic craze for the social and political scandal burst on the nation in the first years of the new century. But for more than twenty years many serious and talented critics of American politics and society had been writing in a vein, sometimes caustic, sometimes apocalyptic, about the Gilded Age's stampede for wealth. In 1879 Henry George put his bitterness into a book whose reputation at the time rivaled that of Marx's *Das Kapital*. It was called *Progress and Poverty*, and it became a best seller. So did *Looking Backward*, the 1888 fantasy in which Edward Bellamy denounced the corruption of society.

Two years later, in a book called *Caesar's Column*, Ignatius Donnelly, one of the firebrands of the agrarian revolt, predicted an impending apocalypse due to the unequal distribution of wealth. An economist like Thorstein Veblen, whose biting *Theory of the Leisure Class* came out in 1899; a patrician like Henry Adams; and countless labor organizers reinforced the message. In fiction and in factual analysis, in journalism and cartoons, Colonel House's contemporaries whaled away at the same theses: the bitter contrast between wealth and poverty, the cruelty and cynicism of the rich, and the way the once pristine American democracy had been corrupted.

These were some of the influences to which House was exposed when, during what he later called his "twilight years," he embarked on a course of study of economics and politics.[4] Much of those years was spent in Austin. It was a time when House gave the impression of a man who was conscious of great abilities and frustrated that he had no suitable outlet for them. (As early as 1901, like many of his contemporaries, unimpressed by conventional religion, House showed an interest in the newly fashionable cult of spiritualism.)[5] Now, however, a new social relationship that was to have a lasting impact on the Houses opened up. Thomas Jefferson Coolidge Jr., as we have seen, had invested in the Boll Weevil railroad and acted as House's stockbroker, and he was to become a summer neighbor, occasional landlord, and friend. Through the Coolidge connection on the Massachusetts North Shore, House gained entrée to a powerful, cultivated, and in the main Republican milieu. It is possible that his wife, frustrated by the provincial limitations of Austin and always more interested in "society" than he was, encouraged her husband to look for new social worlds to conquer.

Later, as noted in chapter 1, the Houses took an apartment in the Gotham Hotel in New York City, the first of a series of apartments on the Upper East Side. They went to the theatre often and entertained modestly, and House himself read enormously. When William F. McCombs first went to House's apartment to interest him in the Wilson campaign, "a number of books lay upon his table. There were novels, books on current events, books of essays and books on psychology."[6] McCombs had interrupted the gestation of *Philip Dru.*

House was looking for a man to whom he could pledge his allegiance and offer his skills.[7] The first potential candidate to arouse his interest was the able, bad-tempered mayor of New York, William J. Gaynor. He was a strange hybrid. Promoted by Tammany, he was given to quoting ancient philosophers such as Marcus Aurelius. Famous as a judge for the quick disposal of his docket, he had a genuine sympathy for litigants. His instinctive distrust of bullying policemen and naïve do-gooders alike made him an attractive figure, and he has become a hero to modern libertarians. But he could be rude and unreasonable—especially after he was shot by a disgruntled ex-employee of the city—and he ended up mired in scandal.[8]

Bryan himself suggested that Gaynor was the only man in the East who could make a Progressive president. House calculated that the nomination must go to the East but that it would be impossible to nominate anyone opposed to Bryan. He met Gaynor at dinner and was impressed. So he followed up by taking Senator Culberson and another Texas friend to meet Gaynor. The Texans asked Gaynor to address the state legislature. Gaynor agreed. But when one of the Texas papers asked Gaynor to confirm his acceptance, Gaynor telegraphed back that he had no intention of coming. "I wiped Gaynor from my political slate," House recorded, "for I saw he was impossible."[9]

A better option was opening up. But on December 6, 1911, just after meeting Woodrow Wilson for the first time, House went to Texas and immediately fell ill with one of his fevers. He continued to be "up and down, but down mostly" for many weeks.[10] He had already discussed with his brother-in-law, Dr. Sidney Mezes, and with David F. Houston, who had just moved from the University of Texas to the University of Washington at St. Louis, the idea of writing a novel to air his economic and political theories. Houston advised him to write a serious economic text, but Mezes agreed with House that he should write a novel. House and Houston traveled west together on the train and talked the idea over. As soon as he was convalescent, in no more than thirty days House wrote the first draft. Mezes liked it, and House sent the manuscript to Houston in St. Louis for an expert opinion on the economic arguments. Houston said the economics was sound but still felt it would be better as a serious work of political economy. On Mezes's advice, House sent it at the beginning of April 1912 to Doubleday.

That summer, House was absorbed with the Wilson campaign. In July, however, as the climactic convention was due to get under way in Baltimore, the Houses were due to sail for Europe. House thought Doubleday's editor had made a carelessly written book worse, so he decided to rewrite the book himself on the ship. In Europe (where the Houses went to Sweden, Finland, and Russia, as well as to the more familiar England and France), there was no time to work on the manuscript.

House had heard of Wilson's nomination a day out from Liverpool. Now the campaign was taking up every moment of his time, but the publisher wanted the manuscript so that it could be advertised for the fall list. So he sent the book off, half rewritten as it was. House later wrote that "most of it I stand upon as being both my ethical and political faith."[11]

Philip Dru begins with an epigraph that expresses House's essentially centrist political philosophy and indeed echoes James Stephen Hogg's manifesto for the 1892 campaign. It is a quotation from the Italian liberal hero Giuseppe Mazzini: "No war of classes, no hostility to existing wealth, no wanton or unjust violation of the rights of property, but a constant disposition to ameliorate the condition of the classes least favored by fortune."

The book is indeed an odd mixture of fairly cautious liberal or Progressive policies, Southern resentment of Republican rule, generous if patronizing feminism, and military narrative of a kind that came naturally to a man who had grown up in the age of Grant, Lee, and Moltke, all rather awkwardly stuffed into the carcass of a Victorian love story. It is a novel of ideas, in the manner of George Meredith or William Dean Howells, dressed in the petticoats of Victorian lady novelists like Mrs. Hemans or Ouida.

House took his time to introduce his hero, Philip Dru, and his heroine, Gloria. In a leisurely way he approached his main theme, presenting a time when the politics of the republic were dominated by "masterful and arrogant wealth," largely created by government protection of its profits.[12] Once House has reached the political tract that is his real purpose, the story of Philip and Gloria drops out from sight. Every now and again, as he suddenly remembers he is supposed to be writing a novel, he interrupts his political analysis with an update on their doings, but his heart is hardly in it.

House's target is the "malefactors of great wealth," as Theodore Roosevelt called them.[13] Their representatives use the primary system to ensure that no candidates can be nominated by either party whose views do not coincide with theirs. Their chief political manipulator is none other than Gloria's father, Senator Selwyn, largely modeled on Marcus A. Hanna of Ohio. He is originally a sinister figure, though later House attempts to make him more sympathetic by reciting the misadventures of his early life. Behind him, massive and wholly unsympathetic, stands the mighty financial power of John Thor, based on J. P. Morgan (there is no hint here that House will soon be on friendly terms with many of Morgan's men): "Thor's influence throughout commercial America was absolute. His wealth, his ability and even more the sum of the capital he could control through the banks, trust companies and industrial organizations which he dominated, made his word as potent as that of a monarch."[14]

Selwyn offers the presidency, over dinner, to Senator Rockland, the model for whom is not so clear. Perhaps House had William McKinley in mind. Selwyn and Thor mean to control politics with the help of a "blind pool." This is a corruption fund of $10 million raised by contributions of $10,000 from each of one thousand hand-picked rich men. Nothing is to be left to chance. Selwyn will corrupt all three branches of the government (executive, legislative, and judiciary) so as to block all adverse legislation.

Selwyn's electoral method is simple. He will concentrate on some dozen un-decided states. In each neighborhood of each state, he will do the same. So he has to reach only a manageable number of blocs of voters, which he does with carefully targeted literature and, if necessary, with unconcealed corruption.

This fiendish scheme, however (similar as it is to standard modern electoral procedure!) is derailed by a somewhat unwieldy plot device. A dictagraph on which Thor has recorded messages to Selwyn is in a public spirit taken to a newspaper by his secretary. This somewhat creaky idea sets off the central action of the book. "A crisis had come and . . . revolution was imminent. Men at once divided themselves into groups. Now, as it has ever been, the very poor largely aligned themselves with the rich and powerful. The reason for this may be partly from fear and partly from habit. They had seen the struggle going on for centuries and with but one result."[15]

Philip Dru makes a speech at a mass meeting. He is chosen to head an action committee. He counsels against violence, though he himself begins to drill a militia. (As a West Point graduate, he knows how to go about it.) He urges citizens throughout the United States to organize. The conscience of the people is now aroused, he says. "There would be no halting until the Government was again within their hands to be administered for the good of the many instead of for the good of a rapacious few."[16]

The decision between war and peace is taken from Philip Dru. The forces of organized wealth—it is tempting to drop House's careful veil of party neutrality and call them simply "the Republicans"—deny a free ballot. There are troops at the polls. Eventually Philip decides to make his stand in the West. The South is slower to move. House explains why: "In some states sixty percent of the population were Negroes, and they were as helpless as children. . . . Of necessity, separate schools had to be maintained. The humane, the wise, the patriotic thing to have done was for the nation to have assumed the responsibility of the education of the Negroes for at least one generation."[17]

At this point House draws what seems to us a strange contrast between what he saw as the Union's foolish attempt to "reconstruct" the defeated Confederacy and Britain's conduct after the war in South Africa less than a decade earlier: "What a contrast we see in England's treatment of the Boers. After a long and bloody war . . . England's first act was to make an enormous grant to the conquered Boers."[18] British generosity, of course, was toward the defeated white Afrikaners, not the Africans.

Now, in the novel, the country is hurtling toward a new civil war. Dru raises an army in the Midwest and the South.[19] After a masterly campaign of maneuver, he defeats General Newton in a great battle in western New York State. At bayonet point Dru proclaims himself Administrator of the Republic. Dru knows some will be "affrighted" by the change from constitutional government to despotism, but dangerous times justify stern measures.[20]

By now Gloria's parents have accepted Dru as their future son-in-law. They move into the White House, while the austere administrator lives in the Washington barracks when he is not riding about the city on his "seal brown gelding."

The book then sketches, through the device of Philip Dru's actions, House's own program for Progressive reform. A commission of five great lawyers, none of them with objectionable corporate practices, is set up.[21] They introduce land title reform from Australia, which House had vainly tried to persuade Governor Lanham to adopt.[22] They visit Europe for the latest ideas on law reform. Dru does the same with tax reform.

Now at last House reaches the kernel of his political thinking: the financial system must be reformed.[23] "In the past the railroads and a few industrial monopolies had come in for the greatest amount of abuse and prejudice. This feeling, while largely just in his opinion, had done much harm. The railroads were the offenders in the first instance, he knew, and then people retaliated, and in the end both the capitalists . . . and the people suffered." (Interestingly the former railroad chairman deleted the word "largely" in a handwritten correction of his typescript.) He also addresses the problem of debt, which underlay the discontent of the South and West. He prohibits loan sharks. He calls attention to the "lesser, though serious evil, of . . . employers of ignorant labor making advances of food, clothing and similar necessities to their tenants or workmen and charging them extortionate prices." Dru/House also shared contemporary Populist prejudices against "stock, cotton and produce exchanges": both short- and long-selling were to be banned.[24]

More boldly, Dru was some years ahead of his time in deciding to give the suffrage to women and bolder still, for his time and culture, in his reasons: "It had long seemed to Dru absurd that the ignorant and, as a rule, more immoral male, should have such an advantage [as the franchise] over the educated, refined and intelligent female." Dru had "an infinite pity for the dependent and submerged life of the generality of women." To Selwyn Dru says, "In your propaganda for good, do not overlook the education of mothers to the importance of sex hygiene, so that they may impart to their daughters the truth, and not let them gather their knowledge from the streets."[25]

House puts into Dru's mouth a clear statement of that somewhat exaggerated gloom that was characteristic of the years between Theodore Roosevelt's departure and Woodrow Wilson's picking up of the Progressive torch. (Many writers guessed that *Philip Dru*'s anonymous author was none other than Roosevelt.)[26] "Our government is, perhaps, less responsive to the will of the people than that of almost any of the civilized nations. Our Constitution and our laws served us well for the first hundred years of our existence, but under the conditions of today they are not only obsolete, but even grotesque."[27] House cited as an example of unresponsive government the bill for an income tax, passed by both houses of Congress but blocked by the Supreme Court in 1895.

Toward the end of the book, House turns back to what was to be his own preoccupation for the next seven years: international affairs. The British government was being recruited to a plot against America with Germany and Japan. Dru forces the British to abandon this plan and successfully negotiates an alliance between England and America in a worldwide policy of peace and commercial freedom. Disarmament would take place. Customs barriers were to be torn down, zones of influence defined, and an era of friendly commercial rivalry established. Dru offers Germany and Japan a wide vista of commercial and territorial expansion. (This was the carrot with which House hoped to tempt Germany into abandoning its military dreams in 1914.) Germany was to have commercial access to South America. Japan and China, in alliance, were to have all Eastern Asia as their sphere of influence. If it pleased them to drive Russia back into Europe, no one would interfere.[28]

Then, eerily anticipating Wilsonian policy, Dru invades Mexico. "It had become no longer possible for the United States to ignore the disorder that prevailed in Mexico . . . for if the United States had not taken action, Europe would have done so."[29] Dru conquers Mexico and unites it with the other countries of Central America. His work done, he retires into private life, handing power back to a restored and reformed constitutional government.

There are still, however, new worlds to conquer. At the end, his reforming task at home done (and his creator perhaps in a hurry to get the manuscript to the publisher and get on with the winning of an election!), Dru and his Gloria sail off into the setting sun to bring the benefits of clean government and progressive thought to the teeming masses of Asia.

Whatever else it is, *Philip Dru* is a profoundly authoritarian vision, not of a democratic leader but of an "administrator." Not that such visions were rare in the age of imperial democracy. Such more or less progressive Republicans as Theodore Roosevelt, Henry Stimson, and Taft were not afraid of robust speech and action. We should avoid anachronism. In 1912, the world had not been reminded of what disasters dictators could perpetrate. House's hero is a dictator in the original Roman sense, a strong man who knocks heads together when the constitutional government is incapable of responding to deep-seated social problems. Still, it is interesting to note how little House looked to Congress to address what he saw as a crisis brought on by a Constitution and laws that were "not only obsolete, but even grotesque." House, almost like a Marxist of his generation, sees political institutions as little more than the "superstructure" upon underlying realities of business power. House was perhaps reflecting, in 1912, the mood of 1896, when President McKinley was shown by cartoonists as bounced on the knee of Mark Hanna. The Senate was described as "a Senate of the Monopolists, by the Monopolists and for the Monopolists" and dismissed by a Russian scholar as filled with multimillionaires, wire pullers, and "state bosses of mediocre intelligence," while the Supreme Court interpreted the Constitution to accommodate the interests of the railroads.[30]

There is also, in House's picture of a Southern military despot wreaking his revenge on a corrupt Republican administration, something of the resentment his generation of Southerners, who had experienced carpetbagger government, felt toward Republican Washington; something too, perhaps, of the fantasy of the boy who had once dreamed of military glory. Philip Dru, like his creator, had been denied a career in the military by ill health.

There was little truly original about Philip Dru's administration. Reform of land title and tax law, an attack on the pernicious consequences of the crop lien system and farm debt, even women's suffrage and sex education—these were all part of the welter of new ideas that were flying about in the first years of a new century. It is even possible to interpret them as alternatives to more radical upheaval and acceptable to middle-class Americans.

All these criticism of *Philip Dru* can be justly made. As a novel, it fails totally. Yet it is profoundly interesting in what it tells us about Edward Mandell House, on the brink of his extraordinary career in national and international politics.

One theme that runs through the book is that the constitutional checks and balances have limited the government to a "negative" role. House—like Woodrow Wilson at least at some stages of his life—was attracted by the idea of nudging the constitutional arrangements in the direction of a parliamentary system. House made Dru set up a board to work out a tariff law to abolish "the theory of protection as a governmental policy." He brought in a graduated income tax. And he introduced a new banking law, "affording a flexible currency bottomed largely upon commercial assets, the real wealth of the nation, instead of upon debt." This, House hoped, "would completely destroy the credit trust, the greatest, the most far-reaching and under evil direction the most pernicious trust of all."[31] He proposed a tax on corporate income; an old-age pension; a workers' compensation insurance to cover illness, incapacity, and death; and even workers' representatives on corporate boards (what the new Germany brought in after 1945). Unions were to be denied the right to strike but must accept compulsory arbitration of grievances. Most of these measures were advocated by Progressives in general. Some of them, the Wilson administration would carry out. Others are still considered daring today.

Only a few months after he had sent the manuscript off to the publisher, Colonel House would have an almost unique opportunity to put some of his ideas into effect, through his new friend the president. We know from chapter 1 that immediately after his election, Wilson took a copy of the book with him when he went on vacation in Bermuda. Few novelists of ideas have had such a chance.

5 Making Woodrow Wilson President ❧

My dear Governor Wilson,

I am pleased to tell you that we now have everything in good shape in Texas
and that you may confidently rely upon the delegates from this State.

—E. M. House

Colonel House played a minor, almost inconsequential role in the Texas campaign.

—Arthur S. Link

THE YEAR AND A DAY BETWEEN Edward House's first meeting with Woodrow
Wilson on September 24, 1911, and September 25, 1912, when the colonel began to
dictate an account of each day's doings to his secretary, Fanny Denton, was the
most critical period of his whole life. At the beginning of that time, he was a man
with an interesting political past, casting around for a new role. At its end, he was
"the man to see," the most influential counsellor of the candidate who was all but
certain to be president of the United States.

How did he make that crucial traverse from obscurity to influence? As inti-
mated in chapter 1, the historians' explanations divide sharply into two schools.
One school, founded by the guardian and editor of House's papers, Charles Sey-

mour (later president of Yale), puts House's elevation down simply to his disinterested wisdom. Wilson's election, Seymour wrote, was a triumph for Colonel House, "whose share in the campaign only a few of the more keen-sighted realized. . . . There was no thread in the campaign pattern which he had not touched, no symptom of party discord which had not evoked his genius for pacification. The new Wilson Administration might have been wrecked at the moment of victory. This the President elect understood and his gratitude to House was unfeigned."[1]

Seymour did not claim that House was the masterful manager of the whole campaign. He was crediting House specifically with having prevented the disaster that might have come to the Wilson campaign from the feuding of its two managers, William F. McCombs and William Gibbs McAdoo.[2] House made other valuable contributions to the Wilson campaign, Seymour claimed. Delivering Texas, bound hand and foot, to Wilson was not one of them.

Thirty years later, Arthur S. Link, the editor of the Wilson papers at Princeton, took pains to demolish the claim that Seymour had not made. In an article he went out of his way to minimize Colonel House's role in Wilson's capture of the Texas delegation.[3] "After a thorough examination of the House papers, the Burleson papers and the Woodrow Wilson papers, in addition to the outstanding Texas newspapers," Link concluded that "House played a minor, almost inconsequential role in the Texas campaign."[4]

A movement for Wilson in Texas was indeed well under way before House became seriously involved, but House was nevertheless influential in the campaign to carry the state for Wilson in several significant ways. Some, though not all, of those who did most of the work in Texas—including Albert S. Burleson, Thomas W. Gregory, and Thomas B. Love—were friends and protégés of House, though both Burleson and Love were later annoyed by the claims made by him and on his behalf. In 1928 Love, for example, told Ray Stannard Baker (who disliked House intensely) that House's "influence and contribution were in no way decisive."[5] But in 1912 Love wrote House, "It was certainly a great victory, and in my judgment there are very few men in the United States who contributed more to bring it about than yourself."[6]

This controversy over House's contribution to the campaign in Texas has obscured two more interesting questions: what was House's contribution to the campaign as a whole, and—of intense interest to a biographer of Colonel House—what was it that transformed House, in a year or so, from a complete stranger to Woodrow Wilson to his most intimate friend?

As soon as Woodrow Wilson was elected governor of New Jersey, in November 1910, a number of politicians wrote offering their services to help him win the Democratic presidential nomination. One of these was Thomas B. Love. Love had been speaker of the Texas legislature and was a friendly acquaintance of Colonel House. On November 15 Love wrote Wilson, saying he was advocating Wilson's nomination.[7] Almost immediately, however, Love became involved in the campaign for a Texas constitutional amendment prohibiting the sale of alcohol. It was not until the following August that he was free to organize on Wilson's behalf in Texas. By that stage, Colonel House had taken favorable notice of Wilson, though he had not yet taken any part in his campaign. "I think Woodrow Wilson's remark that the money trust is the most pernicious of all trusts is eminently correct," he wrote to his friend Senator Culberson.[8]

House's nose was somewhat put out of joint by Love's speed in coming out for Wilson. In his 1928 "Reminiscences" he played down Love's part in getting Texas to go for Wilson and played up the role of others, including himself. In the winter of 1910–1911, he wrote, he had a conversation with Judge W. F. Ramsey of the Texas Supreme Court, an enthusiastic Wilson booster, and decided "to do what I could to further Governor Wilson's fortunes." He said he spoke to all his political friends and "lined them up one after another for him." Later, he said, Love claimed to have put the idea into Judge Ramsey's head, but "I doubt it," House said with a sniff, "because sometimes men remember things that never happened."[9]

House went on to claim that Thomas Watt Gregory came east to consult him about the Wilson campaign in September 1911. Gregory, according to this account, first wanted House to go and see Wilson in Trenton, New Jersey, then went himself. House wrote that he planned to have Gregory become president of the Woodrow Wilson Club in Texas, "but Tom Love anticipated the move and called a meeting to put himself forward. House said he urged Gregory to go home and prevent this because "I did not consider Love strong enough politically to head the movement [so] we selected Cato Sells to open headquarters in Dallas." House said he personally guaranteed the headquarters' expenses but concealed this from Sells so he would not waste money.[10]

In 1921 House responded scornfully to the publication of a memoir by William F. McCombs in the Hearst newspapers. "The truth is, the direction of the campaign was almost wholly in my hands and I financially backed it. Texas headquarters would have closed if I had not sent Gregory to Cato Sells, who was the nominal manager, to tell him that he, Gregory, would guarantee Sells the expenses."[11]

Men, as House put it, sometimes remember things that never happened, and

House's 1928 version exaggerates both the early date and the extent of his role in the Wilson campaign in Texas. However, the papers of Thomas Gregory do show that Wilson's future attorney general, with House's knowledge, told Wilson that he and House were working for him in Texas, perhaps as early as 1910. Gregory wrote to Wilson on September 4, 1911, that he and House, whom he regarded as "the most influential private citizen" in Texas, "have been earnestly discussing your probable candidacy for the Presidency for almost a year."[12] They were organizing Wilson clubs in the state and intended to give Wilson a great reception at the Dallas state fair.

While House was in the East—and incidentally telling at least some of his correspondents, for whatever reason, that he was not sure he was for Wilson—Love launched the Wilson campaign in Texas with some éclat. It is likely that this was done with House's knowledge and approval. A few days later the principal Texas papers carried a stirring appeal to the Democrats of Texas written by House's friend Gregory. The Wilson movement in Texas was under way.

On September 30, 1911, Colonel House took a hand publicly for the first time. He wrote Culberson that "the friends of Woodrow Wilson very much desire that you introduce him" at the Dallas fair on October 28.[13] House had not yet definitively made up his mind to back Wilson. On October 10, 1911, he wrote Culberson that "Wilson does not altogether satisfy me as a candidate but as between him and Harmon I am for Wilson. It is among the possibilities that you or Underwood or some men not now mentioned may get the nomination and that would please me best of all."[14] Perhaps this was merely an elaborate way of flattering Culberson. Culberson's reply, however, handed House his opportunity. "There is a good deal of talk now as to Governor Wilson's attitude to the party in the past," Culberson wrote from Washington, "and it is not doing him any good. A member of Congress told me a few days ago that it is circulated in the East that Wilson refused to support Bryan in 1896, 1900 and 1908, and even voted against Judge Parker in 1904. This is a very important matter and ought to be cleared up at once. I take it for granted that he voted against Bryan in 1896 on the money question, as did Harmon, but the other cases, if true, are entirely too much for me.[15]

This was dangerous stuff, Culberson knew, and Wilson must correct it swiftly. He could understand anyone voting against Bryan in 1896, when many sensible middle-of-the-road Democrats (including Colonel House) thought Bryan was wrong on the silver issue. But if Wilson had failed to vote the Democratic ticket in the other three years, that was another matter.

House knew exactly what to do. On October 16, he wrote to Wilson. He had, he said, been so earnestly advocating Wilson's nomination for president that "in a way my friends look to me for information concerning you."[16] He then passed on the question Culberson had raised and suggested to Wilson that it would be a good thing to come up with an answer before he spoke in Dallas in less than two weeks' time. Two days later, Wilson answered: "It is very provoking how lies frame themselves and run current and I despair of keeping up with them. . . . The facts are that I voted for Palmer and Buckner in 1896 [in a primary election], but I have never supported at any time a Republican ticket. My difference with Mr. Bryan was over the money question."[17]

House replied immediately: "Your letter to me of October 18th supplemented by your verbal message to Mr. McCombs is very clear and will destroy one line of attack." That might seem to have disposed of the issue. But House cleverly raised another question that would give him credentials for further involvement with the campaign. And he dropped two useful names: "Mr. McCombs and perhaps Mr. McAdoo will dine with me Monday and among other things I want particularly to discus[s] with them the feasibility of asking the people when they select delegates to the next National Convention to also pass upon the question of majority rule."[18] (The existing two-thirds majority rule might have blocked Wilson's nomination.)

House advised Culberson to make Wilson's clarification public himself, if he did indeed favor Wilson's candidacy. House duly wrote both Culberson and Love, thanking them for publicizing his query to Wilson and reporting that it had received good play in the New York newspapers. To Love he added that the undemocratic two-thirds rule should be abrogated at the next convention. The impression that House's letter to Love leaves is that House was neither a self-important busybody nor the head of a political organization, but a political veteran handing on advice to a younger man who would value it.

In the meantime, House had received a very gratifying response from the candidate. "I feel very strongly," Wilson wrote, "that the two-thirds rule is a most un-Democratic regulation" that put the Democrats at a disadvantage against the Republicans, who had no such rule. He felt, though, with a characteristic blend of morality and calculation, that there would be "a certain impropriety in my urging a change because it would be so manifestly in my interest."[19] He would be delighted if the two-thirds rule were abolished, in other words, but he did not want his own fingerprints on the change.

On October 28, Wilson appeared in Texas and spoke to a big rally at the state fairgrounds in Dallas. He was introduced by Culberson, and House promptly wrote to congratulate his friend and protégé, noting that no one did such things better than he.

In the meantime, House had been active in another sector of the front. "I have been with Mr. Bryan a good part of the morning," he wrote Wilson, "and I am pleased to tell you that I think you will have his support. The fact that you did not vote for him in '96 was on his mind, but I offered an explanation which seemed satisfactory."[20] House explained that his main effort had been aimed at dissuading Bryan from coming out for Champ Clark, the Speaker of the House. House went so far as to congratulate Wilson on all but buttoning up the nomination. In fact, Champ Clark was to prove a far more formidable opponent than House or anyone else had spotted, and the race between him and Wilson went down to the wire. But getting Bryan on Wilson's side, if that was what House had indeed done, was a major coup. After Bryan's three defeats, the party had reluctantly decided to look for new leadership. But there were still many active Democrats, especially in the South and West, who loved the Great Commoner. His endorsement would decide many of their votes. House closed his letter by saying Bryan had sent several messages that House would be glad to deliver in person. Once again, he had provided a reason for his relationship with Wilson to grow.

House was pleased with his meeting with Bryan and reported on it to Culberson. He thought Bryan was coming around to the idea of supporting Wilson. House added that "the more I see of Governor Wilson the more I like him and I think he is going to be a man that one can advise with some degree of satisfaction. This you could never do with Mr. Bryan."[21] He was beginning to glimpse a possible relationship he could never have had with Bryan, in spite of the Houses' and Bryans's easy family relationship on West Avenue in Austin.

House had been planning to go home to Austin on December 1, but his interest in Wilson made him postpone his departure. He invited the candidate to dine at his apartment in New York to meet his friend David F. Houston. This was another clever move. Houston was an economist and an expert on the tariff. House believed that Wilson should come out strongly against a protective tariff, and he counted on Houston, who had made a lifelong study of the subject, to convince Wilson. The dinner took place on December 7 and was a great success. In addition to House, Wilson, and Houston, the guests were McCombs, Walter Hines Page (a partner in Doubleday, Page and later ambassador to the Court of St. James), and Edward S. Martin, the editor of *Life* magazine.[22] Houston remembered later that the talk was indeed largely about the tariff and the currency issue, but it was also about Wilson's meeting, earlier that same day, with Colonel George Harvey and "Marse Henry"

Watterson, at which Wilson in effect emphasized his preference for Western Bryan Democrats over the Wall Street variety.[23] Perhaps House's suggestion that Bryan might be there for the taking emboldened Wilson to take this line as brusquely as he did.

House too had touched base with Colonel Harvey, as he reported to William Jennings Bryan, then pursuing his need for winter sunshine in Jamaica. House had lunched with Harvey himself the day before the Wilson dinner. He reported too that he had been approached by none other than William Randolph Hearst, who was keen to get House to work for him as a candidate. House now said he was "thoroughly committed" to Wilson.[24]

Colonel Harvey, true to his reputation as a Wall Street man, told House that "everyone south of Canal Street was in a frenzy against Wilson," especially J. P. Morgan, because of something Wilson had said about bankers that Morgan had taken personally. There would be no shortage of money, Harvey said, to beat Wilson. This was indiscreet of Colonel Harvey, because House immediately formed a plan to turn Wall Street opposition to Wilson to the latter's advantage.[25]

The editor of House's "intimate papers," Charles Seymour, later parsed House's letter to Bryan, pointing out how cleverly House was going about recruiting Bryan to the Wilson cause.[26] House let Bryan know that Hearst, who was anathema to Bryan because of the Hearst papers' treatment of his campaigns, preferred Champ Clark to Wilson. He reported how keenly Bryan's enemies on Wall Street were trying to defeat Wilson and left Bryan to calculate that Wilson, as the enemy of his enemies, might be his friend.

In early December, House set out for Texas.[27] That was when he fell ill. Over Christmas 1911 he was too sick to get out of bed, and on the second to the last day of the year Woodrow Wilson received a "strictly confidential" letter, not from his new friend but from House's secretary, Fanny Denton: "Mr. House asks me to quote the following from a letter he has just received from Mr. W. J. Bryan. Mr. House is still in bed but thinks it important for this information to reach you at once. 'Am anxious to get back and find out more of the political situation. I shall attend the Washington banquet on the 8th of January and will have a chance to learn how things are shaping up. I am glad Governor Wilson recognizes that he has the opposition of Morgan and the rest of Wall Street. If he is nominated it must be by the Progressive Democrats and the more progressive he is the better.' "[28]

In Austin, House was first on his sickbed, then rapidly scribbling the fable of *Philip Dru*. He was neither too ill nor too preoccupied, however, to address the task that he now saw as the key to his relationship with Woodrow Wilson: bringing

Bryan on board. Wilson did indeed take the opportunity of the Jackson Day banquet on January 8, 1912, to appeal to Bryan, and Bryan accepted the offer, in spite of a shrewd attempt by his opponents to drive a wedge between him and Wilson. Some five years earlier, Wilson had written a letter in which he was indiscreet enough to have alluded to "knocking Bryan into a cocked hat." The letter was exhumed and published by Bryan's opponents. Bryan, who might well have sulked, ignored it in his most expansive and generous manner.

In the new year, Wilson sent House a letter whose affectionate tone went beyond a politician's routine gratitude for favors received: "I am so glad to hear through Mr. McCombs that you are at last about to get out and feel like yourself again, physically. . . . Pray, take care of yourself. If you will permit me to say so, I have come to have a very warm feeling for you, and hope that in years to come our friendship will ripen."[29]

House replied in kind. He was deeply touched, he said, "for I have come to have a regard for you that is akin to affection." He apologized for the fact that his illness had made him "lag behind in endeavor" but promised that he would soon be doing his full share. He told Wilson that he would be seeing Bryan and asked if there was anything Wilson wanted him to raise with Bryan, "for there can be no better place to do this than by the quiet fireside."[30]

House wrote McCombs that Bryan's support was absolutely essential, not only for Wilson's nomination, but also for the election. "I shall make it my particular province," he added, "to keep in touch with him. . . . He has evolved considerably in our direction, for when I first talked to him in October he did not have Governor Wilson much in mind."[31]

It was not until March 6 that House wrote Wilson again. His letter certainly did exaggerate, at least by implication, his part in lining up the Texas delegation for Wilson, as is clear from the passage quoted in the epigraph above. There might or might not be a Texas Democratic presidential primary, House explained, but it would make no difference. In two or three weeks, he said, "our organization will be perfected." Then House would leave for the East, "where I shall have the pleasure of meeting you."[32]

The fact is that House had less influence over the campaign in Texas than his letter seems to imply, though more than Arthur Link was subsequently prepared to admit. House was slow to come out for Wilson, and by the time he did so Thomas Love had taken the initiative. Then House's illness from December 1911 to March 1912 kept him from a major organizational role. However, those who were running the Wilson campaign, including Love, sought House's advice and deferred to his judgment, and at a crucial moment in the campaign House was able to keep a faltering effort afloat with financial guarantees. House did not deliver the Texas delegation to Wilson. That was done by others. But those who ran the Wilson campaign there, even if they were sometimes irritated by House's claims (both at the time and later), were House's friends, and in spite of his illness he was a major figure in the background.

House and his friends were all unduly complacent about Wilson's prospects in Texas. At first, their attention was fixed on the two arch-conservatives, Judson Harmon and Oscar Underwood. They all underestimated the strength of the compromise candidate, Champ Clark. On April 9 Clark countered Wilson's success in Wisconsin with a crushing victory in Illinois. Two days later he carried New York, then Nebraska and Massachusetts. Wilson's friends were not prepared for the impact of a speaking tour by Senator Joe Bailey, who barnstormed Texas in late April. Finally, Gregory warned House, and House implored Culberson to come into the state and counter Bailey's attack or at least send a strong election address, which he did.

By the end of April, the Wilson campaign was shaken in morale and running out of money. On April 19 House wrote Culberson that Cato Sells, the manager Love and House had put in to run the campaign, was so short of money that he had started closing down state headquarters. As noted, House had to guarantee expenses such as rent and stenographers. The Wilson campaign had raised no more than $1,000 where $5,000 was needed.

May 1912 was one of the darkest months in Woodrow Wilson's political career. On the first of the month, Oscar Underwood won in Georgia, with the help of a faked document linking Wilson to the black leader Booker T. Washington. On May 14 Clark won in California, New Hampshire, and Nevada; on May 16 he won in Iowa and the District of Columbia. "By mid-May . . . " wrote McAdoo's biographer, "many of the Wilsonites of a few weeks before seemed to be disappearing into the swollen ranks of Clark."[33]

Champ Clark was running like a prairie fire. Within five weeks he had gained 324 instructed delegates, and there were probably another 150 votes for him in uninstructed delegations. It looked as though Champ Clark might simply rush Wilson's position before Wilson and his managers could stop him. House himself was discouraged. On April 30 he reported to Love that he had just come from a conference with McCombs, Albert Burleson, and Congressman William Hughes of New Jersey. The consensus was that if Wilson could carry Georgia, Florida, and Texas, "everything will come our way from now on."[34]

Wilson lost Georgia, but in Texas things were more promising. Thomas Love was called away on law business to St. Louis and Indianapolis, but he scrawled a long note to House beginning "Hurrah for Texas."[35] He had got hold of some damaging intelligence on a maneuver by the Clark camp to inject racism into the campaign. Cato Sells, Love urged, should be instructed immediately to send the damaging evidence of Clark's use of a smear about Wilson's closeness to Booker T. Washington to national magazines. The letter is evidence that Love did sometimes defer to House, at least on questions of strategy.

On May 7, once it was clear from the primary results that Wilson was going to carry Texas, House wrote Love about the composition of the Texas delegation at the national convention, to be held at Baltimore at the end of June: "You should come as a delegate and so should [Attorney] General [M. M.] Crane, Tom Ball, Governor Campbell and Mr. Gregory. . . . If there is any suggestion of sending me please say that I desire Mr. Gregory to go and under no circumstances would I take the place."[36]

By May 28 and 29, when the state Democratic convention met in Houston, the Wilson supporters were in complete control. They elected a Texas delegation of forty for Baltimore, all staunch Wilson men.

The correspondence between House and Love in 1912—and it is supported by other letters (from Culberson and Gregory, for example)—shows Love operating as a day-to-day manager but both making suggestions to House to be passed on to national headquarters and accepting House's advice. After the convention, Love wrote House a long letter sharing political intelligence and making practical suggestions for the more efficient running of the campaign. He was careful, however, to write tentatively, "for what it may be worth, and not with the idea of trespassing on your time."[37]

The House-Love correspondence makes the relationship clear. Love was an old friend of House, and, as noted, he had said very few had done more to elect Wilson. Love might be the manager for Texas, but he deferred to House as a powerful party chieftain whose support and advice were valuable. But the relationship was something short of that in an organized machine, in which the chieftain had the power to reward and punish lieutenants as he wished.

House's most important contributions to the Wilson campaign were at the national and strategic level. Two were crucial. The first—as we sketched above for 1911—was House's patient courtship of William Jennings Bryan. (The second, to which we will come below, was his role as a peace maker in a bitterly divided campaign headquarters.) Wilson might have Southern roots. But as far as politicians in the South and West were concerned, he was an Easterner, a president of Princeton who had been elected governor of New Jersey and whose initial backing, furthermore, had come from men, like George Harvey, who were close to Wall Street. Bryan was idolized throughout the South and the West as the arch-enemy of the "money trust." While most Democrats had accepted that the nomination must go to someone else, many hearts were still with Bryan. If Bryan endorsed another candidate, then it would be hard for Wilson to win the nomination and probably impossible for him to be elected. If, on the other hand, Bryan could be persuaded to endorse Wilson whole-heartedly and to campaign for him actively, Wilson's prospects would be immeasurably brighter.

Colonel House was almost uniquely in a position to bring off the ticklish task of wooing Bryan.[38] For one thing, the Bryans had been the Houses' neighbors for more than a decade. For another, Mary Bryan, a forthright, strong-minded woman whom House respected, wanted her Will to come out for Wilson.

As discussed above, House's tact smoothed over the difficulty that Wilson had not supported Bryan. Nor, indeed, had House. His friendship with Bryan had survived open disagreement on the currency question. House was inclined to favor the Aldrich currency reform bill, which Bryan regarded as anathema (see chapter 7).

As soon as House reached New York in April 1912, he saw Bryan and persuaded him to say that either Wilson or Clark would be an acceptable candidate. This, from Wilson's point of view, was a minimum position since it ruled out Harmon and Underwood, whose challenges were fading, but Clark was emerging as the more dangerous threat. For the time being, House could not get Bryan to go further, but he did not give up.[39] He argued that the combination against Wilson was a league of all Bryan's old enemies. Mary Bryan backed up every argument he used to persuade her husband to come out for Wilson.

On June 7, House was able to report a message of encouragement he had received from Mary Bryan. "I have a letter this morning from her containing this most significant sentence: 'I found Mr. B. well and quite in accord with the talk we had.'"[40]

House was not the only Wilson supporter who realized the importance of extracting an endorsement from Bryan. In mid-June, discovering that Bryan would be attending the Republican convention in Chicago as a newspaperman, McAdoo jumped on a train and rushed to try his own powers of persuasion. Catching Bryan in a hotel room crowded with his admirers, McAdoo argued that Wilson was the only dependable Progressive in the race and that Champ Clark's links with Tammany Hall would mean defeat for the Democrats in November. Bryan said he felt "very friendly" toward Wilson, but as a Nebraska delegate, he must vote for Clark on the first ballot. After that he would act as his conscience should dictate. The Great Commoner had avoided being pinned down. But his sympathy for Wilson had clearly grown.

On June 20, as the delegates gathered in Baltimore, House wrote to Wilson that he would not be there. The Houses would be sailing for Europe on the *Laconia* on June 25, the day the convention opened. "Both my inclination and my deep interest in your success calls me there," he assured Wilson, "but I am physically unequal to the effort." However, he added, to emphasize his influence over the delegates, "I have done everything that I could do up to now to advise and to anticipate every contingency. . . . Some of my warm personal friends on the Texas Delegation will be here tomorrow in order to have a final word. Colonel Ball, who is perhaps the most forceful man on the Texas Delegation and the one best equipped for floor tactics, has wired me that he will be in Baltimore today."[41] If Wilson did win the nomination, House added, he recommended Senator James O'Gorman of New York, Albert S. Burleson of Texas, and McCombs to manage the campaign. It was an odd list. O'Gorman was a stalwart of Tammany, Burleson was House's old friend, but McCombs was unstable to the verge of insanity.

At the beginning of June, House invited McCombs to stay with him on the North Shore and "patiently began to teach McCombs the fundamentals of convention strategy."[42] In his memoirs, which bubble with malice, McCombs quoted House as saying, "If you will turn the present forces of Woodrow Wilson to Senator Culberson of Texas, you and I will control the United States for the next four years."[43]

It is hard to know what to make of this mischievous anecdote. In 1921, House dismissed it with contempt in his diary. "Poor fellow, he took both drink and drugs most of the time which largely accounts for what he says and for the wreckage of his career."[44] It is possible, given McCombs's distinctly paranoid personality, that he simply made the conversation up out of whole cloth. More likely, he misunderstood what the colonel was saying. All along, House had liked the idea that his friend Charles Culberson might squeeze through at the last minute as a compromise candidate. In cherishing this hope, he did not appreciate that Culberson's reputation in Washington was no longer (if it had ever been) one that would make him a plausible candidate.

House's friends thought he was wrong to sail off to Europe at the most critical moment of the campaign, and it is easy to see why. Charles Culberson scrawled him a note on Senate letterhead. "I regret exceedingly that you will leave June 25th. It is my opinion that you ought to postpone your trip, for you can unquestionably be of real service to Wilson at Baltimore. Do it!"[45]

Three days later, he tried again: "Put off your trip to Europe and take me with you *next year* when no Wilson campaign is on. Your friend, C. A. Culberson."[46]

Why did House not go to Baltimore? He maintained—both at the time and years later, when he wrote his "Reminiscences"—that the steamy summer heat would have been too much for his health.[47] The decision was certainly an extreme example of House's preference for the backstage role. On balance, though, there is no compelling reason to reject his well-established fear of hot weather as the main reason.

The Houses sailed on the evening of June 25 from Boston. The colonel worked on his *Philip Dru* as best he could on the voyage. At ten o'clock at night, one day out from Liverpool, he got a wireless telegram from a Texas friend. It read, "Wilson wins."

The Houses returned at the end of August and drove to Beverly. Almost immediately the colonel found himself in the middle of a furious row between the joint Wilson managers, McAdoo and McCombs. As soon as he arrived, House wrote, "messengers began to come telling of discord and demoralization at Democratic Headquarters."[48] These first arrivals told a version of events sympathetic to McCombs, and House began by seeing him as the victim and McAdoo as the villain. Soon McCombs himself arrived with a story of "perfidy that was hardly believable."[49] House went to New York and reported the McCombs version. Wilson asked him not to make up his mind until he had heard the other side of the story and asked him to investigate. It was not long before House saw that the row was "almost wholly McCombs's fault." McCombs, House decided, was jealous, dictatorial, and egotistical. He was not well enough to run the campaign, but he could not bear to see McAdoo run it.[50]

After the convention the bad blood between the two Wilson campaign managers became even more acute. McCombs fell sick, and McAdoo stepped in as acting chairman. But on September 5 McCombs came back from the Adirondacks, where he had been convalescing, to meet Wilson. McAdoo wrote later that "no human being . . . could even approximate McCombs in his insane jealousy and envy."[51] House found him "simply impossible and quite crazy on the subject of McAdoo."[52] McAdoo felt that "for the last two weeks of the campaign we all lived over a volcano."[53] House had done what he could to keep the peace, but there was no knowing when McCombs might explode.

There was one brief flurry of fear of a quite different kind. On October 15 Theodore Roosevelt was shot in Milwaukee. McAdoo was suddenly made aware of his responsibility for the candidate's safety. Where could he find a bodyguard for Wilson? House instantly put forward the name of his old friend Captain Bill McDonald of the Texas Rangers. House wired Captain Bill: "Come immediately. Important. Bring your artillery."[54] McDonald was on his little ranch in the Panhandle. He rode into town, read the telegram, and wired back that he was coming. He jumped on the first train, packing only a Stetson, a shirt, and two blue steel .45 revolvers. Woodrow Wilson and his wife and daughters took a great liking to Captain Bill, but McDonald was glad to quit walking on "these rocks," as he called the New York sidewalks, and went back to Texas as soon as the campaign was over.

On September 25, while the tension between McCombs and McAdoo was still threatening the Wilson campaign, Colonel House dictated to Fanny Denton the first entry of what was to run to some four thousand pages of diary.[55] He was already at Woodrow Wilson's elbow. The first item of business was what position Wilson should take on New York politics. The break between Tammany Hall, led by the formidable Charles Francis Murphy, and national Democratic headquarters was becoming wider every day, fed by constant newspaper speculation. "My dislike of Tammany and its leaders is perhaps stronger than that of Governor Wilson," House told his diary, "yet, having had more political experience, I am always ready to work with the best material at hand."[56]

Behind the intense personal hostility between McCombs and McAdoo, which McAdoo suppressed and McCombs allowed to break out in wild, sometimes drunken outbursts, there was a serious political issue. McCombs, as a Princeton-educated Southern Protestant, was by no means a typical Tammany brave. But he was in fact a member of Tammany Hall, and he turned to Murphy for help. McCombs's friends made House nervous. "McCombs is in conference most of the time with old-style politicians. . . . I fear Governor Wilson will have trouble on account of connections made at this time."[57]

For all these misgivings, the result was not in doubt. The election of 1912 had already been decided by the split in Republican ranks between Roosevelt and Taft.

On election day, November 5, House and his wife dined at the Plaza. The returns came in slowly, but by half past six it was clear that Wilson had already won, and House sent off a telegram of congratulations. By seven, it was a landslide. House went to the Waldorf, where McCombs had invited guests to listen to the returns. He had taken nearly half of the hotel, but there were no more than twenty-five people there. McCombs was talking in a wild and crazy way, boasting that

Wilson would make him secretary of state, but he would refuse the position and make a million dollars in his law practice. House went home to bed.

The result was beyond the Democrats' hopes. Wilson received 6.3 million votes. Roosevelt came second, with 4.1 million, and Taft was third with 3.5 million. Eugene Victor Debs, the socialist candidate, won the highest number of votes his party was ever to reach—just over 900,000. Wilson carried 40 states and received 435 electoral college votes. Roosevelt carried 6 states with 88 electoral college votes, and Taft carried only Utah and Vermont.[58]

Politicians at the time and historians subsequently have disagreed about the value of Colonel House's contribution to that result, and there is scope for some disagreement. What mattered was that the president-elect meant to rely on him as his most trusted adviser.

6 *The Hungry Horde* ॐ

ON NOVEMBER 5, 1912, Colonel House wrote to his friend Senator Culberson that "we expect to remain [in New York] until about Christmas and then go to Texas."[1] President-elect Wilson too would leave in ten days' time for four weeks of absolute rest in Bermuda. In those days there was none of the elaborate "transition process" of a later generation, when a "lame duck" president continued in office for nearly four months.

One vital process, however, would not wait for Inauguration Day. House soon realized that Woodrow Wilson had neither the experience nor the temperament to take on the selection of personnel, even for his cabinet. A burden fell on House that was also a supreme opportunity. Overnight he moved from being a mysterious figure occasionally glimpsed closeted with the candidate to "the man to see" for everyone who had a job to claim or a project to push. His diary from election day to the inauguration is one long record of a determined siege by the "hungry horde" of office seekers and of his efforts to equip the Wilson administration with the ablest servants he could find.

He started with one high trump card. Wilson offered him any cabinet office he wanted except the State Department. (That was reserved for William Jennings Bryan.) House, as ever, preferred to be the gray eminence. By putting himself above the rancor of personal rivalry, he made the job of fitting the men into the slots easier. Later, it was safe to deride House's influence. In 1913, if one wanted a job, it was not wise to ignore it.

In 1913 there were only nine cabinet posts: Attorney General; Postmaster General; and the secretaryships of State, Treasury, War, the Navy, the Interior, Commerce, and Labor. But there were literally hundreds of other jobs in the administration of an incoming president, some of them very well paid by the standards of the day. The secretaryship of the Senate, to take an example at random, paid $6,000 a year, the equivalent of some $150,000 a year in modern money. (The president wanted that post for his brother, Joseph.) The Collector of the Port of New York was paid $12,000 a year. His was one of the most sought-after jobs, and not just because of the salary. The collector's political patronage helped Chester Arthur to climb from the Custom House to the presidency itself.

"To the victors," the New York senator William Learned Marcy had proclaimed in the 1830s, "belong the spoils."[2] As the two-party system developed in the United States, so too did the spoils system, the idea that federal jobs should go to the new president's followers. The leaders would reward, in the hard coin of public salaries, the work their followers had done to get them elected. Although the Civil Service Commission had been created in 1871, when Woodrow Wilson entered the White House, the spoils system was still alive in most corners of federal, state, and local government.

The task of putting together a new administration was all the harder because the Democrats had essentially been out of power since the Civil War. There was of course one massive exception: the South. Only there had Democrats been in power enough to have bred a political class. As a result, a disproportionately large share of the important jobs in the Wilson administration went to Southerners, and in particular to transplanted Southerners—like the president himself and now House. Wilson himself called House's attention to the fact that nearly all the men they were discussing for cabinet office were Southerners. He listed Walter Hines Page and Secretary of the Navy Josephus Daniels from North Carolina; McAdoo, born in Georgia, and McCombs, originally from Arkansas; David F. Houston and T. W. Gregory from Texas; Newton D. Baker; and many others, such as James McReynolds, originally from Tennessee.[3]

The Democratic Party in the early years of the twentieth century largely recruited from two sources: Northern urban machines—especially Tammany Hall—and the South. Both Wilson and House were determined to break the power of Tammany if they could. To find men with specialist experience of international affairs from outside Tammany's web of influence in New York would not be easy.

House was keen to find talent among Democrats elsewhere, but a distinctive flavor was imparted to the Wilson administration by the Southerners who occupied so many of the seats of power.[4]

From the moment Wilson was elected until well after the inauguration on March 4, scarcely a day went by when House was not discussing the cabinet with Wilson, with aspirants to it, and with friends who could give him opinions about the talents and shortcomings of potential cabinet members. The process cemented House's personal relationship with Wilson, and indeed the House family's relationship with the Wilson family. By early 1913 the Wilsons and the Houses were seeing each other frequently and informally. For example, on January 17 House took a box at the Cort Theater for the Houses and the Wilsons to see *Peg o' my Heart,* a hit comedy of the moment. After the play, they went back to the House apartment and talked again over some sandwiches.

One of the issues they discussed was whether Wilson should bring men into his cabinet from Congress. House thought he should. The two men he had in mind were his Texan friend Albert S. Burleson and A. Mitchell Palmer of Pennsylvania, much later (in 1919) Wilson's third attorney general and the man who ordered the notorious "Palmer raids" on suspected radicals. House's position was not a casual one. In *Philip Dru* he had stressed the importance of bringing congressional leaders into the cabinet to break down the dislocation he thought was caused by the constitutional separation of powers. Wilson thought instead that he should spend time on Capitol Hill. House conceded in his diary that Wilson was correct in theory. But in the end Wilson took both of the congressmen into his cabinet, Burleson from the start and Palmer later.

In accordance with political tradition, the three men whose services in the campaign gave them the strongest claims to cabinet rank were William Jennings Bryan, William Gibbs McAdoo, and William F. McCombs. McAdoo was easy. There was never much doubt that he would go to the Department of the Treasury.[5] He had just finished lathering his face on the morning of February 1, he recalled in his memoirs, when his servant came to the bathroom door and said that Wilson was staying at the University Club and would like McAdoo to go over right away. When he arrived, Wilson offered him the Treasury.[6]

More ticklish was the question of what to do with William Jennings Bryan. It had always been understood that Bryan would be made secretary of state, though many felt that he was not ideally qualified to be the head of American diplomacy.[7] On November 16, 1912, Wilson asked House, not for the first time, whether he should offer Bryan the State Department or the London embassy.[8] House was for making him secretary of state, and Wilson agreed. But Bryan had not given up his ambition to be president, even after three defeats. Indeed, one of House's arguments to get him to come out for Wilson had been that he would have a better chance of being elected president if he served as secretary of state first. On January 18, 1913, House told Wilson he wanted to go to Florida to talk to Bryan about the cabinet and also about Bryan's obsession with silver and "currency reform."[9] Wilson authorized House to talk freely but "not to ask his advice."[10] On January 29 House duly reported that Bryan was "in a delightful humor." He had urged that "a Catholic and perhaps a Jew be taken into the family." Bryan's only serious objection was to Wilson's intention of appointing Charles W. Eliot, the former president of Harvard, as ambassador to China. Eliot, as a Unitarian, "did not believe in the divinity of Christ."[11]

In the end, McCombs got nothing at all. This was entirely his fault. He was, after all, the successful campaign manager. But Wilson did not want to trust him with a major responsibility, and McCombs behaved in such a way that it would have been impossible to do so. On November 16, 1912, Wilson said he would make McCombs Collector of the Port of New York were it not that he would build up a formidable political machine there. House tried to get him to accept an embassy. By January 15, 1913, Ellen Wilson was telling House that McCombs had "the strangest effect" on her husband. If he had to spend time with the man, "he felt as if he had been sucked by a vampire."[12]

It would be wearisome to recount all of McCombs's neurotic twists and turns. As late as May 1 House was writing in his diary, with a sigh, "McCombs came this morning and talked about himself for an hour." McCombs bitterly resented House's failure to fix him up with a worthy job and later attacked him in a chapter in his memoirs called "Colonel House—The Intriguer."[13]

Another unsuccessful candidate for the Wilson cabinet was to have a far more brilliant future. Louis D. Brandeis had made a name for himself in Boston as the "People's Attorney."[14] From 1905 to 1914 he fought J. P. Morgan's attempts to consolidate the New York, New Haven, and Hartford railroad with the Boston and Maine. He loved to represent small business against the rising trusts, and he wrote a classic of what has been called "serious muckraking," *Other People's Money and How the Bankers Use It,* which did not endear him to the financial community. He transformed the style and technique of legal practice with what came to be called the "Brandeis brief." First deployed in 1908 in *Muller v. Oregon,* over the regulation of the number of hours women might be made to work, his approach involved supplementing a technical legal argument with an analysis of the long-term social and economic consequences of a judicial decision. It was Wilson who appointed him to the Supreme Court, the first Jew to sit on the court.

House's diary reveals an uncharacteristically timid willingness to allow Brandeis's immense qualities to be canceled out by the anger of the comfortable classes at his attacks. Before Christmas 1912 the question of appointing him attorney general came up. House told Wilson that he had "run down all the material" and checked with law school deans, but it was with much regret that he had to advise against Brandeis. At that stage House preferred James McReynolds, later a notably reactionary Supreme Court Justice. At dinner on January 17, 1913, Wilson brought up Brandeis again, but House recorded that "we practically eliminated Brandeis from any cabinet place." Wilson persisted. He said he had investigated Brandeis's record and did not believe he had done anything to deserve the virulent criticism he was getting.[15] Indeed, Boston's enmity, House felt, had made Wilson stubborn over his appointment.

In August, Wilson and Brandeis lunched at Wilson's summer residence, Sea Girt, on the New Jersey coast. Brandeis was "very favorably impressed," while Wilson, as one of Brandeis's biographers put it, accepted Brandeis as his tutor.[16]

House wanted to appoint a Jew to the court, but he passed on to Wilson the unreasoning hostility of the Boston Brahmins. House spoke to Abbott Lawrence Lowell, the president of Harvard, who took it upon himself to tell Wilson that Brandeis "did not stand very high in the opinion of the best judges in Massachusetts."[17] The best judges, there and elsewhere, have come to a different view.

The question arises whether the opposition to Brandeis was anti-Semitic in nature. Brandeis thought so. "The Massachusetts opposition to my going into the cabinet," he wrote the Progressive journalist Norman Hapgood, "was not in its essence political."[18] Some anti-Semitism there undoubtedly was. President Lowell suggested introducing a quota for Jews at Harvard in 1922. Allon Gal writes that "in the Boston of 1912, anti-Semitism in Brahmin circles clearly affected Brandeis's political prospects."[19] That does not mean, however, that House's opposition to putting Brandeis in the cabinet was due to anti-Semitism on his part. For one thing, several of those whom House consulted were themselves Jews—men like Jacob Schiff, who did not think of Brandeis as a "representative" Jew, probably because they disliked his determined opposition to railroads and bankers like themselves. Gal agrees that "certain powerful Jews . . . opposed Brandeis as being too radical in economic matters."[20] At the same time, one petition against

Brandeis's appointment was signed by people named Adams, Coolidge, Gardner, Grew, Lowell, Peabody, and Putnam.[21]

Many Progressives, on the other hand, pressed Brandeis's claims. Wilson himself wrote to William Jennings Bryan that "Brandeis has been very grossly aspersed but of course I am looking into the matter very carefully."[22]

House's attitude seems to have been simple caution: "I argued against putting him in the cabinet for the reason that so many of the respectable people of New England think ill of him. It does not matter whether they are right or wrong, they believe he is dishonest and his value of service would be minimized."[23]

The two candidates House preferred at the time—Palmer and McReynolds—both later acquired reputations for extreme reactionary views. As late as February 14, 1913, Wilson and House agreed that Palmer should get the Justice Department, and the next day Wilson authorized House to offer the solicitor generalship to McReynolds, leaving the attorney general's position open to Palmer. A week later Wilson, at House's apartment, offered the War Department to Palmer, who was very disappointed. (He frankly admitted that he was interested in being attorney general because it would allow him to build up a lucrative law practice afterwards.) House tried in vain to persuade him that secretaries of war, such as Elihu Root and Henry Stimson, had done pretty well in the law. With Wilson, Palmer used a different argument. He was a Quaker, he proclaimed, and the job would go against his conscience. The day after Palmer's meeting with Wilson, McReynolds accepted the attorney generalship. When McReynolds resigned, he was succeeded by Colonel House's friend from Austin, Thomas W. Gregory. It was not until Gregory retired in 1919 that Palmer came in.

Whatever the merits of his doubts about Brandeis, House gave sound advice on the overall personnel strategy of the administration. More than once he warned Wilson against choosing too high a proportion of Progressives without strong ties to the Democratic Party. On January 14, 1913, for example, House told Walter Hines Page that he was afraid Wilson was appointing too many Independents and not enough "rock-ribbed Democrats."[24] To get great measures into law, he argued, it would be necessary for the president to be on good terms with his party in the Congress. It was a prescient remark in view of the shipwreck Wilson encountered when he underestimated congressional objections to the League of Nations.

House was shocked by the amateurish way in which Wilson went about what every professional knows is the absolute heart of the game of politics: patronage. "The thing that impresses me most is the casual way in which the President-elect is making up his Cabinet. I can see no end of trouble for him in the future unless he proceeds with more care."[25] Wilson himself seems to have had the same thought. On March 31 he gave House lunch at the White House and afterwards took him upstairs to the library in the new electric elevator, which Wilson enjoyed operating. They went over the whole list of foreign appointments. Then they talked about the tariff, and House filled Wilson in on the sugar growers in the South and the beetroot growers out West and what they wanted.

Wilson asked if House would act as the chairman of a committee to make out lists of federal appointments in every state; it would consist of McAdoo, McCombs, Senator Gore of Oklahoma, Burleson, and Joe Tumulty. House had a better idea. He volunteered to do whatever he could to help. After a moment's discussion, Wilson said it would be better if House did the whole job himself. House commented, "I wondered whether he realized that he was practically placing the entire patronage of the Government in my hands."[26]

That moment was, perhaps, the absolute apogee of Wilson's trust in his adviser and of House's influence over the Wilson administration. House enjoyed his influence over appointments immensely, but he disliked it when the flattery became excessive. At one dinner at the French Embassy a guest said that House had the president, the cabinet, and the Democratic Party in his pocket. He was sorry such nonsense was said, House commented to his diary, as it tended to make mischief. Indeed it did.

The knottiest of all the problems with which House was called upon to help the president, however, had nothing whatever to do with the New Freedom or the New Diplomacy. It was a classic constitutional confrontation between an idealistic new president and a doughty exponent of the old politics, Senator James Aloysius O'Gorman of New York. The issue was the lushest of all the honeypots at the president's disposal: the collectorship of the Port of New York. In the end, as was perhaps inevitable, the president won, but not before his authority had been sharply challenged by a politician who had the power of Tammany at his back.[27]

Wilson and House deliberated long and hard about who should be the collector of the port, precisely because it was so strong a potential node of patronage. On March 7, House recorded that he and Wilson shared a "keen desire to revamp New York politics."[28] That was one of the main priorities of the middle-class Progressives who had made Wilson president. It was also precisely what the sachems of Tammany feared. On April 1 Senator O'Gorman threw down his gauntlet.

My dear Mr. President,

I beg to offer for your consideration, in connection with the office of
Collector of the Port of New York, the following names:

> John G. O'Keefe,
> Michael J. Drummond,
> Thomas Mulry, and
> John Jerome Rooney.

All of these gentlemen are residents of The City of New York, have had
large and varied business experience and are well qualified for the
position.[29]

All, O'Gorman might also have added, were Irish Catholics. And all were in a state
of grace with the Society of St. Tammany.

House and Wilson had agreed that the right man for the job "should not be
affiliated with Tammany, but should be an independent Democrat." Where was
this paragon to be found? House met the lawyer Frank Lyon Polk and commented
that he was "a handsome and attractive gentleman but I doubt whether he is fitted
for a place."[30] Polk was indeed a matinee idol. He was also a successful lawyer. He
was later to be connected with House's life in several ways. As counsellor of the
State Department, he aided the career of House's son-in-law, Gordon Auchincloss.
He rose through the State Department to be acting secretary of state during Robert
Lansing's absence, when Lansing was House's colleague at the Paris peace conference. (Polk was later one of the name partners, with John W. Davis, of the great
New York law firm Davis Polk.)[31]

By April 11, 1913, House and McAdoo had decided—largely, said House, on his
own recommendation—that Polk should be offered the appointment. By May 1 the
matter had become critical. House cut short a meeting with McAdoo to dash to
Penn Station to meet Wilson's special train. With a "great tooting of horns, stop-
page of traffic and a staring public" he and Wilson dashed back to his apartment
and talked over sandwiches for more than an hour about O'Gorman's challenge.[32]
Wilson admitted he was afraid that if he antagonized O'Gorman, it would jeopar-
dize his entire legislative program. House argued that he must make a stand against
O'Gorman's contention that a senator had the right to suggest a list of names and
that the president must not go outside that list. Such a contention would virtually
strip the president of his right to appoint.

There was another dimension to the question too. House called to the president's attention "the necessity of keeping on good terms with England." Wilson replied that "there again O'Gorman was opposing him, and would oppose him in the Senate." House replied, "The more reason for a fight now."[33] House and Wilson had already been irritated by O'Gorman's stance on the issue of the Panama Canal tolls.[34]

So on grounds of high constitutional principle and practical politics alike, battle was joined. House urged Wilson to take a firm stand: "If I were you I would name Polk. . . . Your mastery of Congress depends largely upon your maintaining that unflinching courage which our people rightly appreciate. . . . You are clearly within your rights and I would not temporize with a situation that must be met either now or later."[35]

Wilson took House's advice. He wrote O'Gorman a long and courteous letter that frontally challenged the senator's interpretation of "senatorial courtesy." "I cannot accept the interpretation you put," Wilson wrote, "upon the constitutional relationship between the President and individual Senators in the matter of appointments." The solution, he proposed, "is not clash or contest, but frank and frequent conference." He would accept O'Gorman's compromise suggestion and give the appointment to Lawson Purdy. But he could not do that because Purdy, "whatever his personal character and quality," would be regarded as representing a recognition of Tammany, "now more than ever discredited in the eyes of the country."[36]

That was frank enough. On the same day that Wilson wrote the letter to O'Gorman, House sent an emissary to John Purroy Mitchel to ask him to accept the job of collector of the port.[37] Within a couple of days McAdoo was able to announce that Mitchel had been appointed. On May 7 McAdoo called House and asked him to break the news to Frank Polk. House did so, and Polk took the news well. McAdoo also reported that O'Gorman had already been to see the president and had suggested Mitchel's name himself. The president smiled and promised to appoint him at once. House thought that O'Gorman had little fight in him and would have accepted Polk. House's emissary explained what had happened: the "foxy senator," to save face, seized on Mitchel's name as a compromise, not knowing Wilson had already chosen him.[38] O'Gorman got away with some undeserved glory.

For months after the inauguration, House was kept busy with patronage. He developed a fairly thick skin in dealing with the office seekers. "A colonel who would be a brigadier general," he wrote in his diary in April, "and a secretary of legation who would be transferred from Japan to France caught me at breakfast.

The diplomat is wealthy so I requisitioned his motor and had him take me from place to place until lunchtime."[39] Wilson wanted to appoint the best men for the work, unlike Bryan (whom Wilson called "a spoilsman").[40] House was entirely in sympathy with that aspiration but far more aware of the practical inconvenience of ignoring the calls of party.

For several months, House's diary is one long record of lunches, meetings, phone calls, and dinners at the Metropolitan and Cosmos Clubs in Washington and the Century and other men's clubs in New York to discuss appointments. He was busy acting as the president's eyes and ears in relation to the administration's early preoccupations, which included the tariff and currency legislation, Mexico, and the potential row over the Panama Canal tolls with Britain. But by far the largest slice of House's time in 1913 was consumed with the endlessly delicate matter of appointments, especially to American embassies abroad.

Wilson was anxious to appoint a new kind of ambassador, cultivated and progressive, in place of the wealthy, socially well-connected but often pompous Republicans who had represented America in the nineteenth century.[41] House sincerely tried to take the New Freedom to American embassies overseas, but it was hard at a time when ambassadors were expected to pay for their upkeep out of their own pockets. The results of his efforts were not, perhaps, so very different from their predecessors. Wilson was keen that America should be represented abroad by men of solid reputation and dignity. He tried to persuade a former secretary of state, Richard Olney, to go to London, but Olney, who was seventy-eight, refused. He wanted Charles W. Eliot, the outgoing president of Harvard, to go to China, where the age-old empire had just been overthrown by Sun Yat-sen's revolution, but Eliot too said no. House was able to put forward the claims of friends and acquaintances to several embassies: the romantic Southern novelist Thomas Nelson Page to Rome, for example. House recommended Henry Morgenthau for Constantinople (as it then was). Wilson, better informed than House about the condition of the Ottoman Empire, said, "There ain't going to be no Turkey," but Morgenthau got the job. His reporting of the Armenian massacres in 1915 did him honor.[42]

The three most important ambassadorships were London, Berlin, and Mexico, and in each decision House exerted considerable influence. Samuel Untermyer, a wealthy Wall Street lawyer of German Jewish extraction, wanted the Berlin job.[43] Wilson merely smiled and said dismissively he was glad to know that Untermyer would be pleased if he were sent.

James Watson Gerard, an equally successful corporation lawyer and justice of the Supreme Court of New York, had always wanted to be an ambassador.[44] Wilson told House that he would not appoint any man who was conspicuously money-oriented. House said that too many major appointments were going to New Yorkers. In his notably conceited memoirs, Gerard said Wilson's mind was changed "by the friendly intervention of a combination of Tammany, Senator James A. O'Gorman of New York, William G. McAdoo, William F. McCombs, and William Jennings Bryan." Then he added, rather nastily, "For a while Colonel E. M. House, the Harry Hopkins of the Wilson Administration, very cleverly succeeded in persuading me that he had been the principal factor in my appointment, but this conviction wore off."[45]

Walter Hines Page became American ambassador to the Court of St. James in London. Page, a North Carolinian, was another Progressive Southerner actively involved in lobbying for improved (though segregated) education in the South. House's first, though perhaps not altogether serious, thought was that Wilson should send William Jennings Bryan to London.[46] He suggested as much to Mrs. Bryan, who was pleased because her daughter Ruth was married to a British army officer and lived in England. But in March 1913 Wilson delighted the colonel by saying he thought "Walter Page was about the best man left for Ambassador to Great Britain."[47] Page had serious money worries about taking the post, and in the event he was right to worry. Nonetheless, one morning Page's telephone rang.

"Good morning, Your Excellency!" came the colonel's well-modulated voice.

"What the devil are you talking about?" asked Page.[48]

House was keen to help his friend T. W. Gregory, the Dallas attorney who was a member of "our crowd" in Texas. He tried to keep Gregory's hat in the ring as a possible attorney general. In January 1913, over breakfast in the White House (Wilson's breakfast was a cereal with two raw eggs, on which lemon juice had been squeezed), House tried to help his friend in another way. Gregory wanted to be ambassador to Mexico. Bryan argued that a Texan, because of ancient resentments, would not be acceptable in Mexico. McReynolds offered Gregory the solicitor generalship instead. Gregory, who had a hearing defect, could not take it. (The solicitor general is "the government's lawyer" and appears for it in court frequently.) House had to accept defeat. But his luck held. After no more than a year, McReynolds went to the Supreme Court. Gregory could go to Justice after all.

On the whole, House brilliantly balanced the demands put on him by the president's confidence. Patronage could not be extended without enemies being made. Some of those who got the jobs they wanted resented their dependence on House's help. Some of those resentments came home to roost later. Still, House had done well by "the fortunes of four or five warm personal friends," as he put it.[49] He placed two of his friends in the cabinet right away (Houston at Agriculture and Franklin K. Lane at Commerce), and a third, Gregory, would join them before long.[50] He had got his publisher friend, Page, sent to the Court of St. James. The secretaries of state and the treasury were friends and political allies. House was annoyed when people said, as someone did at a dinner party, that no one had ever had a position such as his in any administration in the history of the republic.[51] Yet it was true.

In the summer of 1913, House's friend Mrs. Borden Harriman told him the president had said he had more confidence in his judgment than in any other man in the world. Ten days later he had confirmation in Wilson's own hand. "I cannot tell you how often I think of you," he wrote to House at his summer residence at Beverly Farms, Massachusetts, "or how often I feel the need as well as the desire for your advice upon many a complicated and difficult matter. I am impatient for the cool weather to come back chiefly because it will bring us together."[52]

Even with such an endorsement from the president, House had to choose where to throw his weight. He first focused on the currency question and the complex processes leading to the passage of the Federal Reserve Act of 1913. Abroad, he could not avoid the consequences of the Mexican Revolution. But already he was stalking bigger game. He was beginning to dream of an intervention in international politics. What if he could export the Progressive dream of morality and modernity to the world?

7   *Wall Street and Mexico*   ❧

ONCE WOODROW WILSON WAS IN the White House, three tasks demanded attention. He must carry through some major measure of banking reform. He must persuade Congress to lower the tariff. And he must tackle the crisis presented by the sudden onset of what would be ten years of bloody revolution in Mexico.

Colonel House had little to do with lowering the tariff, though he had urged Wilson to make it a priority. On Mexico, he was able to act as a sort of intelligence officer. This experience led to other tasks in foreign policy, and in particular to smoothing relations with Great Britain over the Panama Canal tolls.

The events of 1913 taken together were a formative experience for House's career. His involvement with the Federal Reserve Act reinforced his reputation for sagacity with the president. It also provided him with valuable contacts on Wall Street. The affair of the Panama tolls made him reliable friends in London. And revolutionary Mexico was a rehearsal for the questions of war and peace that would be the great work of House's life.

House's first major concern was with currency reform. This meant helping to steer through Congress the Federal Reserve system.[1] Since the Jefferson administration, the nation's banking system had caused political as well as economic problems. Under the wartime National Banking Act of 1863 (amended in 1864 and 1865) national banknote currency was secured by government bonds held by national banks. The amount of currency in circulation therefore depended on the value of bonds held by banks, not on the amount needed at any time by farmers or businessmen. This system caused serious shortages of currency at harvest time in what was still a predominantly agricultural country. It also caused the economy to gyrate wildly between booms and busts.

By 1896 much of the West had worked itself up into a passionate crusade, led by William Jennings Bryan, against the iniquities of the banking system. The Panic of 1907 offered the unedifying spectacle of J. P. Morgan dealing with President Roosevelt as with another sovereign power, and the Aldrich-Vreeland Law of the following year, which set up a National Monetary Commission composed entirely of bankers, only made things worse for the Bryanites.[2]

In January 1911 Senator Nelson Aldrich of Rhode Island, whose credentials west of the Hudson River were not enhanced by the fact that his daughter was married to John D. Rockefeller, presented his plan for banking reform. It was promptly denounced by Bryan. In 1912, legislation based on the plan was drafted (in the course of a vacation trip to the Georgia Sea Islands) by Senator Aldrich and Paul M. Warburg (a partner in the Wall Street investment banking firm of Kuhn, Loeb). The legislation was never passed because control of the Congress passed to the Democrats, but the Aldrich-Warburg draft became a cherished point in the Populist indictment of Wall Street. In the meantime, the House of Representatives' Banking and Currency Committee, chaired by Congressman Arsène Pujo of Louisiana, set up hearings to investigate the banks. In July 1912 the Democratic National Convention at Baltimore called for the establishment of a central bank to protect the nation from panics and for revision of the banking laws to control the money trust.

Thus the political temperature of the banking reform was hot when, on the day after Christmas in 1912, Woodrow Wilson received in Trenton two visitors from Washington, D.C. One was a Virginia newspaper publisher, Congressman Carter Glass. The other, a young economist in rimless glasses and a four-in-hand tie, was Glass's assistant, Henry Parker Willis.

The House Banking and Currency Committee had been split into two subcommittees. Pujo retained the chair of the investigative subcommittee, with alluring opportunities for publicity. The other subcommittee, charged with drafting legislation, was chaired by Glass.[3] By the time Wilson was elected, Glass and Willis had finished drafting a banking reform bill.

On December 16, 1912, there was a highly revealing flap. Wilson was supposed to speak at the Southern Society dinner. Suddenly the news flew around the Wilson circle that J. P. Morgan would be at the dinner.[4] J. P. Morgan! What would New York's yellow papers—Hearst's *Journal* and Pulitzer's *World*—make of the new Progressive president sitting down with the emblematic bogeyman of the money trust! The moment of horror passed; Mr. Morgan could not attend the dinner. But nothing could give a clearer picture of the political climate than the consternation caused by the prospect of the president dining with the head of the House of Morgan.

Wilson liked the Glass bill. He had only one modification to propose, and it horrified Glass. Wilson wanted a supervisory federal reserve board to oversee the new banking system Glass proposed. For Glass and Willis that smacked too much of the centralized system Aldrich had offered: "Centralized" meant "New York." For Democrats the very essence of banking reform was that it must take power over credit away from the money trust in New York.

Meanwhile House was talking to Paul Warburg on the phone, apparently unaware, until Warburg told him, that Warburg had helped Aldrich write the bill that was anathema to Bryanites. On January 8, 1913, House was asked by Wilson to work with Glass on another bill.[5]

At the end of February, House was nervous about accepting an invitation to a dinner with the chosen elite of Wall Street. He declined to go to the dinner but agreed to talk to the guests after the meal. He records in his diary that the guests represented "five billions of capital."[6] They included Henry Clay Frick, Henry P. Davison, and Otto Kahn.[7] "All the guests gathered round me in a circle, and I talked to them in a general and conversational way. . . . The main thought running through my talk was that they were the victims of their own fears; that it was astonishing to me that they should 'cry before they were hit.'"[8]

House thought these champions of big business were like children who needed to be told there were no bears around to hurt them. But he was undeniably impressed. Young Jack Morgan, son of J. P., he told his diary, "seems to be a fine fellow." Paul Warburg "is a fine man and I have confidence in him."[9]

Most potentially embarrassing were the attentions House received from Henry Clay Frick, an authentic survivor from the Robber Barons. Frick wanted to get House to use his influence to settle the government's suit against U.S. Steel. He invited House to dine at his mansion. House was uncomfortable with the way Frick was using their acquaintance. "It is a difficult task to steer oneself in the uncertain seas where politics and finance meet."[10]

On February 2, 1913, the final report of the Pujo subcommittee was published.

It adopted the Bryanite thesis of a money trust and made a few proposals for reform. The main task was left to the Glass subcommittee and to its "legislative expert," Henry Parker Willis, who had little sympathy with the Bryan men and "soft money."

On May 11 President Wilson called in Colonel House, who warned Wilson that Bryan was beginning to realize the the bill was not to his liking and advised Wilson to have a word with Bryan alone. If he did so, House believed, the president could bring him around. Even if Bryan left the cabinet, House assured Wilson that his reelection was probable.

In June Senator Robert L. Owen of Oklahoma agreed to introduce the Glass bill into the Senate. The moment the bill was printed, however, it was shown (almost certainly by Owen himself) to Bryan, who immediately spotted points to be criticized. He demanded changes, with major political implications. The Federal Reserve Board must be a purely governmental body appointed by the president and confirmed by the Senate, not one that represented only the bankers. The president consulted Brandeis, who agreed with Bryan.[11]

On June 17, 1913, Wilson met with Glass, McAdoo, and Senator Owen. Wilson insisted that four members of the Federal Reserve Board must be directly appointed by the president. McAdoo agreed, and so did Owen. But Glass resisted furiously, and when he got home at midnight, he wrote Willis a passionate letter saying, "It is wrong, totally wrong!"[12] Glass's argument, which he had sustained that evening for three hours, was that Wilson could not expect a powerful Republican minority in the Senate to permit the creation of a banking system controlled by Democrats.[13]

Enter Colonel House. He set up a dinner, after which the banking situation was discussed.[14] A copy of the new bill was read over and discussed by Secretary McAdoo, Colonel House, and Congressman Glass. At the end of the evening, House asked for a copy, but Glass refused, saying it was the only one in his possession.

A few days later Glass received a request from the president for a summary of the essential features of his bill. Willis duly prepared the summary, and Glass gave it to the president. But Willis was angry when he was later told by McAdoo that House had passed the summary on to Paul Warburg, who used it to write a memorandum criticizing the bill.[15] Warburg subsequently used the memo as the basis for a well-informed attack on the Glass-Willis proposals. House seems to have chosen Warburg as the most reasonable of the champions of "Wall Street."

By late May the president had three bills from which to choose. There was the

Glass-Willis draft. There was a compromise draft written by Secretary McAdoo with the aim of appealing both to Glass's supporters and to the Bryanites. And Senator Owen had his own version. The choice for Wilson was delicate. Glass's bill might upset the American Bankers' Association. But the whole vast agrarian movement would rise in wrath if too much was conceded to the bankers.

Wilson set himself to push an acceptable measure through Congress. On June 20, 1913, he asked the House Committee on Banking and Currency to support his bill.[16] (That move was unusual in itself and demonstrated just how much the president had at stake.) On June 23 Wilson presented the bill to Congress as a whole. Control was to be vested in the government, he proclaimed, "so that the banks may be the instruments, not the masters, of business and of individual enterprise and initiative."[17]

Two days later Bryan wrote for the *Philadelphia Public Ledger* a letter approving the president's bill. "One at once realizes that it is written from the standpoint of the people rather than from the standpoint of the financiers." The same day, Wilson, flanked by McAdoo, Glass, and Owen, met with four leading bankers forming the "currency committee" of the American Bankers' Association.[18] The president blinked. He proposed a modest compromise: there should be a politically appointed Federal Reserve Board in Washington, but regional banks in the principal centers would be run by bankers.

So suspicious were agrarian politicians, in and out of Congress, of anything that smacked of compromise with the hated bankers that a passionate revolt flared. It was led by an acquaintance of Colonel House: Congressman Robert L. Henry from Texas. "He knew as much about banking," said Carter Glass, "as a child about astronomy."[19] What Henry did know, however, was how Texas farmers felt about bankers.

The bill as now written, Henry said in July, "is wholly in the interests of the creditor classes, the banking fraternity, and the commercial world, without proper provision for the debtor classes and those who toil, produce and sustain the country."[20] Henry introduced a series of amendments, and for a time it looked as if they might be able to kill the bill as a whole. The president quickly invited agrarian leaders to the White House and partially mollified them. In early August, the Banking and Currency Committee reversed itself and approved the bill. Once again Bryan proved his value to the Wilson administration. He asked his friends to stand by the president, and so great was his prestige that they did, with the result that the Democratic caucus in the House of Representatives approved the bill at the end of August.

Public opinion as a whole was coming around to support it. But the bankers remained unappeased. Now Wilson and Carter Glass took on the banking lobby openly. On September 18 Glass pushed his bill through the House by a vote of 287 to 85. That left the Senate banking committee. Three of the seven Democrats seemed intent on joining the Republican opposition. Hearings dragged on. In early October, the American Bankers' Association passed a series of resolutions condemning the Federal Reserve bill as "socialistic." Democratic senators invited a prominent banker, Frank Vanderlip of the National City Bank of New York, to write an entirely new bill. Vanderlip's draft appealed both to Progressives, who liked its insistence on government control, and to conservatives, who were pleased that it proposed a single central bank.

Once again, President Wilson put his office and his popularity on the line. On December 19 the Senate chose the original Federal Reserve bill over the Vanderlip plan by only 44 to 41 and gave it final passage by 54 to 34. On December 23, the struggle finally ended. President Wilson signed the Federal Reserve Act, saying, with truth, that it would prove of lasting benefit to the business of the country.

On February 22, 1913, just ten days before Woodrow Wilson was inaugurated, the president of Mexico, Francisco Madero, and his vice president were murdered by an officer called Major Cárdenas. Precisely whose orders Cárdenas was obeying is unclear. But responsibility for Madero's assassination clearly lay with the tough old fighter from the Indian wars, General Victoriano Huerta, whom Madero had called in to put down a rebellion.

Madero's own arrival in power in 1910 was the beginning of ten years of revolutionary upheaval. Madero, owner of a copper smelter that competed with the Guggenheims' American Smelting and Refining Company, was a liberal. His presidency marked the end of thirty-four years of rule by the dictator Porfirio Díaz. Diaz and his technocrats—*científicos,* as they were known—had begun to bring Mexico into the late-nineteenth-century global economy but at the cost of cruel inequality. They wanted Mexico to join the world's progressive, white nations.[21] They had encouraged foreign investment by Americans and also increasingly by British, German, and other European investors, especially in railroads and the fast-growing oil industry. By 1912 British investment in Mexico, once far behind American investment, had become "about equal."[22] This parity was largely due to the massive enterprises of the British engineer Weetman Pearson, later Lord Cowdray, in railroad building and oil.

Washington could not be indifferent to what happened in Mexico. There were over fifty thousand American residents there by 1911.[23] These included *haciendados*—i.e., those with vast feudal estates—among them the most powerful newspaper publisher in the United States, William Randolph Hearst, who, with his mother, owned more than a million acres in Chihuahua.[24]

An even more urgent reason was the behavior of the U.S. ambassador in Mexico City, Henry Lane Wilson. Like some European proconsul, he had taken it upon himself to tell members of the Mexican Congress that they need not fear the landing of the American troops President Taft had sent to Mexican waters "if the President [Madero] resigns and order is restored."[25] That was not all. Ambassador Wilson summoned the diplomatic corps to the U.S. embassy and urged the assembled envoys to recognize Huerta. He had personally presided at a secret meeting—the so-called Pact of the Embassy—between Huerta and the rebel Félix Díaz (nephew of former President Porfirio Díaz) at which it was decided that Huerta would become provisional president and that Félix Díaz would succeed him.[26] Henry Lane Wilson had been appointed ambassador in large part through the influence of the Guggenheim copper interests, which were hostile to Madero;[27] and here he was, deeply involved in a plot to overthrow Madero and one in which, intentionally or not as far as H. L. Wilson was concerned, Madero was assassinated.

The British government recognized the Huerta administration as the de facto government of Mexico. Britain, like most European powers, did not see recognition as a conferral of moral approval. Sir Edward Grey, the British foreign secretary, said simply, "Our interests in Mexico are so big that I think we should take our own line," independent of Washington.[28] American diplomats believed that British recognition of Huerta was motivated by the wish to promote the Cowdray interests.[29]

As early as April 1, 1913, Wilson discussed with Colonal House whether or not to recognize Huerta. House was annoyed that William Randolph Hearst was circulating rumors about House's alleged vast interests in Mexico. "I not only have not a dollar invested there," House wrote in his diary, "but never had further than a few hundred dollars of worthless silver mining stock."[30]

Throughout 1913 there were issues to be resolved about Mexico. One was recognition. Another was how long to leave Henry Lane Wilson as ambassador. On the one hand, he was tarnished by his involvement with Huerta, the Pact of the Embassy, and the murder of Madero. On the other hand, to replace him too hastily might weaken American influence. Finally, there was the question of intervention.

President Taft had sent military and naval forces capable of intervening effectively. But President Wilson was reluctant to give the order.

Wilson's attitude was both confusing and confused. Progressive and idealist he might be. But he had none of the philosophical objections to intervention that were axiomatic to later generations of American liberals. An admirer of Edmund Burke, who had endorsed the American but opposed the French Revolution, Wilson feared the influence of French radicalism. He distinguished between European imperialism, which was bad, and American expansion, which he saw as extending the area of freedom.

Wilson seems at first to have seen Mexico as a dangerous distraction from the domestic issues. From the start House saw international politics as an opportunity to make the world a peaceful and more prosperous place by exporting American ideas of democratic governance. Specifically, he saw the Mexican crisis as an opportunity to replace the negative principle of the Monroe Doctrine, widely resented by some Latin Americans as imposing gringo dominance, with a more equal partnership. He made a determined, though ultimately unsuccessful, attempt to create such a Pan-American relationship and later even saw it as a potential model for postwar cooperation in Europe. "It was my idea," he wrote in late 1914, "to formulate a plan . . . as a model for the European nations when peace is at last brought about."[31]

Wilson was especially suspicious of Lord Cowdray, whose Mexican Eagle Company first hit a spectacular gusher at Potrero del Llano in November 1910. Wilson was convinced that Huerta would favor British interests if he came out on top.[32]

Even so, Wilson could not make up his mind. He did not replace Henry Lane Wilson as ambassador, but instead sent a series of presidential special agents to keep himself informed. On October 27, 1913, in a major speech at Mobile, Alabama, he put the Mexican situation into the context of his fight against "special interests" in America. That was a hit at British and other European interests in Mexico, not at the American business interests, toward which Wilson's attitude was so ambiguous. Sometimes, for him, American businessmen abroad were selfish predators; sometimes he saw them as bearers of American ideals.

Wilson may have had moral scruples about intervention, but in fact he did intervene militarily in Mexico twice.[33] For the first intervention he used as a pretext a trivial incident at Tampico in the spring of 1914. Mexican officials arrested some American bluejackets at the port of Tampico, and the local authorities ignored an order from the American admiral to apologize. Two years later Wilson sent General

John J. Pershing across the border with a flying column after Pancho Villa had invaded New Mexico and murdered seventeen Americans at Columbus.

In 1901 potential friction between the United States and Britain had been avoided by a treaty negotiated by Theodore Roosevelt's secretary of state, John Hay, and the British ambassador, Sir Julian Pauncefote. It laid down that tolls in the Panama Canal would be the same for all nations. By the time Woodrow Wilson became president, however, Congress had made American shipping exempt from the tolls, and the British government, prompted by British shipping interests, was displeased.

In July 1913 Colonel House, at the lunch where he first made friends with Sir Edward Grey, found the conversation drifting to the question of Panama tolls. Grey said he would have no objection to American vessels having free passage so long as there was no discrimination against British shipping. House replied frankly that the president was preoccupied with the tariff and the Federal Reserve legislation. Grey said he was happy to leave the Panama tolls question until later.[34] In November, Grey sent one of his most trusted officials, Sir William Tyrrell (later a close friend of House), to Washington. House arranged for Tyrrell to see the president, who spontaneously brought up the Panama tolls. Wilson said he shared Grey's feeling that treaties must be kept. He even explained that the problem in the Congress was "Hibernian patriots [who] always desired a fling at England."[35] He singled out Senator O'Gorman of New York, of whom the president had said (to House earlier) that he "constantly regards himself as an Irishman contending against England rather than as a United States Senator upholding the dignity and welfare of this country."[36] Sir William commented to House that "if some of the veteran diplomats could have heard us they would have fallen in a faint."[37]

A few days later House had a talk with Senator O'Gorman's son-in-law, Dudley Malone, who left him in no doubt of O'Gorman's determination. The president and the colonel decided not to beard O'Gorman alone but to invite the whole Senate Foreign Relations Committee for a briefing on the canal tolls. It was not until March 1914 that the president sent a message to Congress asking that the exemption from the tolls for American shipping be repealed, and in June Congress complied. Wilson's firm stand on a principle, that treaties must be kept, was lubricated by House's tact and political antennae.

Repeatedly in the winter of 1914, House urged Wilson to pay more attention to foreign affairs. He said so in a conversation, and he repeated it in a letter.[38] He had in fact another plan up his sleeve. It was an opportunity to edge Bryan out of an important piece of foreign business. House wanted to take advantage of the warring European powers' preoccupation to reinforce the Monroe Doctrine. But he was also sketching the outline of a great idea. He was foreshadowing the League of Nations, and in particular Article X, the contentious rock on which American consensus would split and defeat the league: nothing less than the idea that the United States should guarantee the territorial integrity of other nations.

House's idea was to get the "ABC powers"—Argentina, Brazil, and Chile—to reach a Pan-American accord under American auspices. He kept at this doggedly for years. Only in 1917, when the United States was at war, did he finally give up.

Thwarted where they thought it would be easiest to succeed, in the Western Hemisphere, House and Wilson pressed on with an even harder task: to use the growing strength of the United States to persuade the whole world to accept their vision of a negotiated peace and a League of Nations.

8   *The Schrippenfest Affair*   ᢙ

The situation is extraordinary. It is militarism run stark mad. . . .
There is some day to be an awful cataclysm.
> —Colonel House to President Wilson, May 29, 1914

LONG AFTER WORLD WAR I WAS OVER, the deposed kaiser, Wilhelm II, in exile in Holland, told the German American journalist George Sylvester Viereck that "the visit of Colonel House to Berlin and London in the spring of 1914 almost prevented the World War."[1] The visit was nothing less than a semi-official attempt on the part of an American private citizen, Colonel House, to save Europe from the war that cost millions of European lives, overthrew four empires, and—for better and for worse—destroyed the old European civilization for ever.

The colonel found the kaiser surprisingly receptive to a scheme that would cure Germany's dangerous sense of encirclement by creating an understanding among what were then called the three "Anglo-Saxon" powers—the United States, Britain, and Germany—to prevent the war whose shadow was looming over Europe. This extraordinary diplomatic intervention took place with Woodrow Wilson's full knowledge, but it was House's own idea. Perhaps it never had any chance of success. But even as a failure, it had immense consequences for Colonel House and for the Wilson administration.

Roughly half way between Woodrow Wilson's election and his inauguration, on January 22, 1913, House lunched with his friend Edward S. Martin (the editor of the old, pre-Luce *Life* magazine) and told him of his ambition to persuade Wilson to let him "bring about an understanding between Great Britain, this country and Germany in regard to the Monroe Doctrine." House had no intention of bringing the Senate Foreign Relations Committee or even the secretary of state into the secret. His plan was simple. He would take messages in person from the president to the British Liberal foreign secretary, Sir Edward Grey, and to the German emperor. He wanted to bring about a better understanding between Britain and Germany. "If England were less intolerant of Germany's aspirations for expansion," he thought, "good feeling could be brought about between them. I thought we could encourage Germany to exploit South America in a legitimate way, that is by development of its resources and by sending her surplus population there."[2]

House's mention of the Monroe Doctrine requires some explanation. President James Monroe formally promulgated the doctrine in his State of the Union message to the Congress in 1823. The context was the independence movements against Spain and Portugal in Latin America after the end of the Napoleonic Wars in Europe and the possibility that Austria, Russia, and Prussia, after defeating Napoleon and in alliance with the restored monarchy in France, might intervene in Latin America to reverse the result of the wars of independence. Mexico's uprising against Spanish rule in 1810 followed Napoleon's capture of Madrid in 1808. The uprisings of Simón Bolívar in the north of South America, of José de San Martín in the south, and in Brazil were all aided by the British. The Holy Alliance actually authorized France to intervene in Spain, and there was talk of recapturing Spain's American colonies before this was prevented by the British foreign minister, George Canning.[3]

Europe was still unsettled, Monroe told Congress, and American policy in Europe remained unchanged. It was not to interfere in the internal politics of any European power. In the Caribbean and South America, however, the United States could not be indifferent to European politics. The policy of the United States should be "to leave the parties to themselves."

By the early twentieth century, much had changed. The United States had become, in economic though not yet in military terms, a great world power. American forces had intervened repeatedly in Mexico, Haiti, the Dominican Republic, Nicaragua, and Cuba and had helped the Republic of Panama secede from Colombia. The United States had taken over the Philippines, a Spanish colony. In 1904 Theodore Roosevelt introduced Congress to what became known as the "Roosevelt Corollary." The Monroe Doctrine told the European powers to keep their hands off the American continent. The corollary must be that if intervention was needed—for example, if Latin American governments failed to pay the interests on foreign bonds—then the United States would do it.

The Monroe Doctrine, needless to say, looked very different when viewed from Europe or Latin America. To contemporary Europeans, it often seemed a cynical excuse for developing an exclusive American sphere of interest at the very time when the United States was calling for an "open door" in China and elsewhere many Americans were loudly denouncing European imperialism. To many in Latin America, it was a fig leaf to hide dollar diplomacy. Poor Mexico, they said: "so far from God, so close to the United States." But to Americans, it was a noble idea: the United States would protect its poor neighbors to the south from the depredations of European imperialists.

House and Wilson both returned at important moments in the formation of their foreign policy to the idea of extending the Monroe Doctrine in this enlightened sense to all parts of the world. So in 1913 House thought in terms of sharing with the British and the Germans the burdens and benefits of developing Latin America and other undeveloped parts of the world, including Persia and China.

The recent history of relations between Britain and Germany, however, was not encouraging. There was a serious danger of war in Europe. The two countries seemed locked in reciprocal paranoia. British business circles were thoroughly shaken by the aggressivity, not to mention the skill and success, of German competition. British naval and political circles were equally horrified by Germany's evident intention of challenging the Royal Navy's supremacy at sea.

Germans too were nervous, as well as truculent. They saw the Entente Cordiale, the 1904 reconciliation of Britain and France, as directed against them. When Britain made friends with Russia, the Germans felt they were being deliberately encircled. They feared that, allied with Britain and France, Russia could thrust into the Balkans, taking advantage of the disintegrating Ottoman Empire. That would put an end to Germany's ambitions of finding oil, markets, and allies in the Middle East—ambitions made concrete in the plan for a Berlin-to-Baghdad railway. And they were afraid that Russian influence and power in the Balkans would weaken Germany's ally, the Austro-Hungarian Empire.

The Germans did their best to free themselves from the tightening noose by robust, even arrogant, diplomacy and by rearmament. They already had the most formidable army in Europe. Now they were going all out to acquire the best navy as well. In 1905–1906 and again in the Agadir crisis of 1911 the tensions between the two alliance systems—Britain, France, and Russia on the one side, known as the Entente, and Germany, Austria-Hungary, and Turkey, known as the Central Powers, on the other—nearly broke out into open warfare.

The Balkans were on fire with a new nationalism. There were Balkan wars in 1912 and again in 1913. There were fears and resentments, ambitions and conspiracies, in Belgrade and St. Petersburg, Vienna and Paris. But House, as a rank amateur, and Grey, as the consummate professional, were both right. The heart of the problem lay in the mutual suspicion between Berlin and London.

This suspicion was the iron knot House had, almost casually, set himself to untie. Either he was not altogether serious at first, however, or he was very patient. There is no mention of this plan in his diary for three months. He was preoccupied with patronage, with Mexico, and with the Federal Reserve. Still, he had many long talks with Woodrow Wilson during the early months of the new administration, and if he brought up the subject of his ambition to bring about better relations among the United States, Britain, and Germany, he did not mention doing so in his diary.[4]

Then, out of a clear blue sky, on April 23, 1913, the German American banker James Speyer wrote inviting House to lunch downtown to meet the German ambassador, Count Johann von Bernstorff. House noted that he never went downtown. He was anxious to avoid appearing to Progressives as too close to Wall Street. So when, two days later, Speyer telephoned to ask him to lunch uptown, he readily agreed. The lunch took place at Delmonico's on May 9.

After lunch, his work as link man done, Speyer left House and Bernstorff, and they walked up Fifth Avenue together. House came to the point. It would be a great thing if there could be a sympathetic understanding among England, Germany, and the United States, and House added Japan. Together, House suggested, these four industrial countries could wield an influence for good. They could keep the peace and ensure the proper development of what House called "the waste places of the earth." To House's surprise, Bernstorff agreed. Relations between England and Germany had improved, he said, and if they could find a field of common endeavor, they would be better still. He mentioned China as a promising field for common action.[5]

Twelve days later, Edward and Loulie House sailed for Europe on the *Mauretania*. Ambassador Walter Hines Page was full of the perils of London society and of the costs of diplomatic living. Page was keen for House to meet politicians and for him and Loulie to be presented to the king and queen, but House would have none of it. House met with Sir Horace Plunkett, the Irish patriot and agricultural expert who was to become one of House's closest friends. The Houses also met a number of American women who had married British aristocrats, such as the Duchess of Marlborough (the former Consuelo Vanderbilt) and Lady Paget (the American Minnie Stevens), as well as the Labour Party leader and prominent pacifist, George Lansbury.

On July 3 came the most important meeting. That was the day House met Sir Edward Grey. Grey was a tall, cool man, desolated by the loss of his beloved wife in a carriage accident seven years earlier. His two passions were trout fishing and birds; once he and Theodore Roosevelt had hiked for miles through the New Forest in southern England, together listening to birdsong.[6] Though he was one of Britain's greatest foreign secretaries, Grey traveled in continental Europe only once in his life. Whenever he had a moment to spare, he went either to his family estate near the bleakly magnificent Northumberland coast, three hundred miles north of London, or to a beloved cabin on a Hampshire trout stream, where he loved to fly fish and watch birds. Colleagues saw him as both an idealist and a pessimist.[7]

There were only four present for the July 3 lunch meeting: House, Grey, Page, and the Earl of Crewe, secretary of state for India. House impressed Grey and Crewe, members of the Liberal government, by telling them something he had learned from Lansbury: the coal miners' union wanted state ownership of the mines. Then House brought up the subject he had come to Europe to discuss: relations between Britain and Germany and the danger of war.

House told Grey about his lunch with Bernstorff and the latter's belief that good feelings would soon come between Britain and Germany. They talked about Japan, about Mexico, and about the Panama Canal tolls. After lunch (lobster followed by lamb cutlets) the men went to the library. Grey said the industrial problems that afflicted all the civilized nations were more pressing than the Balkan situation. How wrong he was! House brought up the tension between Britain and Germany. Grey said the great cause of the antagonism between nations was the distrust each felt for the other's motives. No more was said. But an important contact had been made—the key contact, in fact, that launched House as a diplomat. House was impressed by Grey's liberal attitudes and his tact over Panama. Grey for his part was impressed by House's knowledge and friendliness.

Over the next eleven months, House prepared his visit to Berlin carefully. In early December 1913 the senior official at the Foreign Office, Sir William Tyrrell, "came informally to dinner" with House in New York. "I told him the next thing I wished to do was to bring about an understanding between France, Germany, England and the United States, regarding a reduction of armament, both military and navy. I said it was an ambitious undertaking but was so well worth while that I intended to try it."[8]

Tyrrell thought House had a "good sporting chance of success."[9] House asked him about procedure. Tyrrell suggested that he go to Berlin and see the kaiser first and afterwards the ministers of foreign affairs and finance. They would be responsive. The difficulty would come with Admiral Alfred von Tirpitz, the minister of the navy, whom Tyrrell called a reactionary. House should tell the kaiser that Germany should show its good feelings by agreeing to stop building an "extravagant" navy.

Ten days after Tyrrell's visit House discussed his scheme with the president, who gave his approval. On New Year's Day 1914 he wrote to Ambassador James Gerard in Berlin, asking him to find out the kaiser's plans. Gerard wrote back with the kaiser's schedule. Wilhelm would go first to his private palace on the Greek island of Corfu in the spring. He would return to Potsdam for a short while, then go to Kiel for the yachting regatta. After that he would go on a cruise in Norwegian waters.

That same day, House had lunch with educator Benjamin Ide Wheeler, the president of the University of California, who had been educated in Germany and had recently met the kaiser several times. Wheeler, like Tyrrell, warned House that the obstacle to his plans would be Tirpitz.[10] The coming antagonism, as the kaiser saw things, was not among the European nations but between the Western peoples as a whole and the Asians.

House spent the winter in Texas as usual, but soon after his return to the East Coast he had more briefings, first from Irwin Laughlin, now counsellor at the American Embassy in London but previously first secretary in Berlin, where he had discussed disarmament with the kaiser.[11] Laughlin did not believe there was one chance in a million of persuading Germany to agree to a naval building "holiday." House explained that he advocated disarmament, not from an ethical standpoint but on grounds of the material advantages it could bring to Germany: "I went into some detail as to giving Germany a zone of influence in Asia Minor and Persia, and also lending a hope that they might be given a free hand commercially in the Central and South American Republics."[12] The next day House used Laughlin as a stand-in for the kaiser, trying out on him the arguments he would use if he could gain access to the emperor.[13]

On April 28, House had another word with the president and asked whether Wilson was certain he wanted House to go to Europe. The president replied, according to House, "The object you have in mind is too important to neglect."[14] So it was a proposal for a benevolent directorate of Britons, Germans, and Americans—and the French too if they wanted to cut themselves in—to prevent war and develop what a generation later was called the Third World that House took to present to the German emperor at Potsdam. And he took it only weeks before, as Grey put it, the lights went out all over Europe.

The colonel and his wife sailed on a German liner, the *Imperator,* and arrived in Berlin on May 23, 1914. At an embassy dinner the colonel met the richly bewhiskered Admiral Tirpitz, who evinced for the British, House found, "a dislike that almost amounted to hatred."[15] In a corner of the drawing room, they talked armaments for an hour. House pleaded for limitation. Tirpitz said Germany wanted peace, but the best way to maintain it was to put fear into the hearts of its enemies.

Thanks to a diplomatic bluff by Ambassador Gerard, who insisted that House would leave if he could not see the kaiser alone, the colonel was finally invited to meet the emperor at Potsdam. The occasion was an annual military festival (started by Frederick the Great's father, Elector Friedrich Wilhelm) known as the Schrippenfest, or the Feast of White Rolls. These rolls were served instead of the usual black bread to the common soldiers of a *Lehrbataillon,* a training battalion, on this day alone, while the emperor sat among them and drank beer from a glass already used by one of his men. The event was one of the high points of the Prussian religion of military glory and sacrifice. The kaiser showed his princely condescension by bonding with the common soldiers on whom the Hohezollerns had relied as they fought their way from the Brandenburg marshes to be the terror of Europe.

House and Gerard lunched in the famous (and hideous) Shell Hall of the New Palace with the imperial party, which included Field Marshal Erich von Falkenhayn, soon to be commander on the Western Front, and Arthur Zimmermann, the acting foreign secretary. There was comic relief in the shape of a Saxon general who, assuming from House's Texas rank that he was a brother in arms, engaged him in an erudite discussion of infantry tactics. Trying with characteristic insensitivity to be funny, the emperor looked across the table at House and Gerard, who were wearing plain black dress suits amid the brilliant uniforms of some sixty officers, and said they looked like a couple of undertakers or a pair of crows.

The lunch menu and musical program are preserved among House's papers.

The meal began with salmon; then smoked beef, with a Schwartzhofberger Auslese Rhine wine; then crayfish tails in jelly, with Heidsieck champagne; pheasant with an 1878 Chateau Margaux; an ice bombe; and cheese *vol-au-vents*. Digestion, though not conversation, was helped by the accompanying music of a military band playing pieces by Suppé, Gounod, and Weber. After lunch House was presented to the empress, who talked politely about Corfu and the beauties of the German spring flowers.

At last the moment came.[16] The emperor sent for House. Zimmermann and Gerard accompanied him to the terrace, then left the two men alone, the resplendent sovereign and the quiet Texan in black. Wilhelm spoke without courtly protocol but had a disagreeable habit, House told Wilson, of pushing his face close to the colonel's in the heat of conversation. They spoke first about the character-building qualities of military service and about Mexico. Wilhelm praised the former president of Mexico, Porfirio Díaz. House boldly disagreed; Díaz, he said, had left conditions in Mexico as bad as they were in Russia.

Now, House wrote in his diary, came the interesting part: "the European situation as it affected the Anglo Saxon race." The kaiser "spoke of the folly of England forming an alliance with the Latins and the 'semi-barbarous' Slavs." England, Germany, and America were the only hope for advancing Christian civilization. In the long run, they would have to stand together against the Oriental races.

House went along with the kaiser's known obsession with the "Yellow Peril," agreeing that Japan was trying to proselytize the other "Asiatic" peoples. The kaiser ranted on about the demographic strength of Asia. House countered that Russia was a greater threat to Britain than Germany was and that the British ought to see Germany as the barrier between Europe and the Slavs. The kaiser said it was impossible to rely on alliance with either France or Russia, and this gave House his opening.

There was a community of interests among England, Germany, and the United States, he said. If only they stood together, the peace of the world could be kept. The kaiser readily agreed.

House said the English were troubled by Germany's ever-growing navy. There might come a time when they would have to decide whether they faced more danger from a German invasion than they did from the possibility of losing their Asian colonies to Russia. If that time came, he said, the decision would go against Germany.

The kaiser said Germany must have a big navy to protect its trade and to defend itself against a combined threat from Russia and France. But when would Germany's naval building program end, House asked. Britain had nothing to fear from Germany, Wilhelm replied. He was a friend of England (he was after all a grandson of Queen Victoria) and was doing it a great service by holding the balance of power against Russia.

At this point House felt he had got as far as he was likely to get at a first meeting. He said that President Wilson and he had thought that perhaps an American might be better able to compose the difficulties that arose among Europeans because of their distrust and dislike of each other. Once again, the emperor agreed. So House moved on to practicalities. He was heading for London, he explained. (Diplomatically, he did not point out that he had already gone over his whole plan in great detail with the British.) He would keep the German emperor informed if the emperor wished. Wilhelm approved and said they could communicate through Zimmermann.

For some minutes there had been comic opera efforts to end the conversation. The empress was afraid her husband would miss his train. First, she sent two of her sons out to the terrace to remind their father. The emperor, unused to being chivied, ignored them. Then she went herself. Finally she sent the great chamberlain, who was curtly dismissed. The emperor had not finished. Finally, House himself stopped talking in order to indicate "that I at least was through." The conversation had lasted thirty minutes. Gerard told House later that all Berlin was wondering "what the devil we had to say to each other for so long."

House, exhausted and perhaps too cagey to give more than a vague sketch of his interview with the kaiser even to Gerard, left at eleven o'clock that same night for Paris. There, however, he found it impossible to interest the politicians in his quest. They were far too excited about a juicy *crime passionel,* the murder of the editor of the *Figaro* newspaper, Gaston Calmette, by the second wife of Joseph Caillaux, the minister of finance. Calmette had threatened to publish Madame Caillaux's love letters to Caillaux before they were married. Madame Caillaux had gone to Calmette's office, pulled out a pistol, and shot him dead. All Paris was agog.

In London, there were other distractions. In London, House wrote to Wilson, "they have their thoughts on Ascot, garden parties, etc. etc." They also had their thoughts on Ireland. This was the summer of near-rebellion by the Unionists in Ulster. "In Germany," by contrast, House went on, "their one thought is to advance industrially and to glorify war."

From London, on June 13, while waiting to see British officials, House reported to William Jennings Bryan: "I had a most interesting visit to Germany and will tell you of it when I return. I have never seen the war spirit so nurtured and so glorified as it is there. The situation is dangerous in the extreme and I am doing what I can in a quiet way to bring about better conditions."[17]

On June 16 the president sat down and wrote his dear friend a note of "deep pleasure" about his achievement in Berlin. "You have, I hope and believe, begun a great thing and I rejoice with all my heart."[18] It was not until June 17 that House had lunch with Grey, Tyrrell, and Ambassador Page. Sir Edward, House thought, was "visibly impressed" by his account of his meeting with the kaiser.

House found Grey "very fair concerning the necessity for Germany to maintain a navy commensurate with her commerce and to protect herself against Russia and France." House thought the kaiser and most of his immediate advisers did not want war, but the army was militaristic and aggressive. He feared "some spark might be fanned into a blaze." He suggested that Britain might allow Germany to share in the development of Persia. Grey's "old diplomacy" response was that it might be a good idea to play Germany off against Russia there, but then again, "the Germans were so aggressive it might be dangerous." House also attempted to persuade Sir Edward that Britain could no longer rely on being an island protected by a navy. He talked about Germany's aerial strength and said the Germans believed Britain would soon be within striking distance for German bombers. "The idea, then," asked Sir Edward, "is that England will be in the same situation as the Continental Powers?" "Quite so," said Colonel House.[19]

That night House reported eagerly to Wilson that he had found Grey "a willing listener and very frank and sympathetic."[20] Grey's problem was how to broach House's plan to his existing allies, especially the French, without offending them. Meanwhile, House continued his penetration of British society and politics: dinner with a company including Theodore Roosevelt, Lord Curzon, the novelist Henry James, and the historian G. M. Trevelyan; breakfast with the chancellor of the exchequer, David Lloyd George; and lunch with the prime minister, H. H. Asquith, and his amusing, socially ambitious wife, Margot.

House had a second, two-hour conversation over lunch on June 26 with Grey and the lord chancellor, Richard, Viscount Haldane, a well-known friend of Germany, at which he pushed his idea that "America, England, France, Germany and the other money-lending and developing nations [should] develop, under favorable terms, the waste places of the earth."[21] He wanted loans at low interest rates to poor countries, an idea he developed in front of a log fire one cool evening at Sir William Tyrrell's country house in Sussex. House was able to report to Wilson on July 3 that Grey wanted him to convey to the kaiser London's positive reception of his proposals. On July 9, House sent the president copies of letters he had written to the kaiser and to Zimmermann. Gerard reported that he had dined with the emperor at Kiel, that the emperor had spoken pleasantly of his meeting with House, and that even Tirpitz had thanked Gerard for bringing them together. To the kaiser, House wrote of the British government's hope of a response that might permit another step forward.[22]

But that was all, it turned out, House was able to do. Substantive progress would take time, and time was what the world did not have. House's letter to Wilson reporting the British response to his proposals was on the Atlantic when Gerard watched from a yacht as "launches darted like dragonflies over the waters" at Kiel. They were bringing the news that the heir to the Austrian throne had been assassinated at Sarajevo.[23]

A countdown had begun.

What are we to make of this intriguing episode? Why did Wilhelm II agree to meet House in the first place? The emperor, like all European statesmen, had been made aware by Theodore Roosevelt of the arrival of the United States in the ranks of the Great Powers. In the spring of 1914, however, Woodrow Wilson was an unknown quantity. European diplomats regarded William Jennings Bryan, the secretary of state, as a wild man from the hinterlands. The word had gone out from Washington that the little colonel was more *salonfähig* (more fit for the drawing room) and also closer to Wilson, and if there is one thing on which diplomats pride themselves— even more than journalists—it is judging who is in and who is out. So it was natural that the kaiser should want to know what House had to say.

One of the few recent historians to have studied the meeting, the biographer of Wilhelm II, Ragnhild Fiebig von Hase, is inclined to see the kaiser's after-the-fall assessment of the opportunity that was missed as merely one of his many excuses to divert attention from the fact that Germany started the war. But she does not think that the episode is without all importance.[24]

How much influence did the emperor actually have over German policy? Could he have set a process of mediation in motion, even if he had wanted to, in the face of the bellicosity of Admiral Tirpitz and the generals? Certainly many in military circles in Berlin were so alarmed by the growing strength of Russia that they had made up their minds to attack when an opportunity offered itself, before Russia became too strong. Most historians now accept the judgment of Fritz Fischer that "the German government was determined from early July onwards to use this favourable opportunity for a war against France and Russia."[25]

Was Grey serious in his interest in House's move? Probably, though he did not mention the episode at all in his memoirs. He may have thought he had more time to talk the French around than he did. Could he have brought his Liberal colleagues with him on a venture that must have seemed to many of them a dangerous reversal of alliances that was bound to upset the French?

House and his admirers have had an interest in exaggerating the importance of his attempt at shuttle diplomacy. He dreamed of being a peacemaker, and he also knew that if he could make Wilson the man who saved Europe from its own furies, he would earn the gratitude not only of the president, but also of an American people always keen to show themselves wiser and more virtuous than the stuffed shirts and cocked hats of Europe.

David Lloyd George, who came to respect Colonel House, shrewdly summed up the chances of House's mission: "The affable Colonel's visit to Europe was, through no fault of his own, fruitless. Wisdom expressed in gentle tones could not be heard above the roar of the nearing cataract. He found hearty sympathy for his ideas in England, a trumpeting militarism in Germany, and political chaos in France. The mass of the American public was as remote in its thoughts and interests from these things as though they were happenings on another planet."[26]

It was, after all, a long shot. House himself had few illusions. Shortly after the war began, he wrote to President Wilson with far-seeing pessimism: "There is no good outcome to look forward to. If the Allies win, it means largely the domination of Russia on the Continent of Europe; and if Germany wins, it means the unspeakable tyranny of militarism for generations to come."[27]

Still, House's mission, if it had been followed up before the murder in Sarajevo, might just have come off. If House had planted a "seed of peace," he might have prevented the whole chain of horrors—war leading to communism and inflation, then slump leading to fascism and war, then to Cold War—that made up the tragic history of what Eric Hobsbawm has called the "short twentieth century."[28] House's plan for British-German-American investment at low rates of interest to develop the "waste places of the earth" could have saved untold misery. At the very least, the Schrippenfest incident deserves to count among the more tantalizing examples of the idea of the great Austrian novelist Robert Musil: in history the things that might have happened but did not are as interesting as those that did.[29]

9 *Trying to End the War in Europe* ∾

America would have come into the War in the spring of 1916, instead of twelve months later. The world would have been saved a whole year of ruin, havoc and devastation.

—David Lloyd George

COLONEL HOUSE HAD TRIED TO PREVENT the war before it began, and he had failed. As soon as war was declared, on August 4, 1914, he started trying to stop it. On September 5 he wrote to Zimmermann, flattering the kaiser. "Now that His Majesty has so brilliantly shown the power of his army, would it not be consistent with his lifelong endeavor to maintain peace to consent to overtures being made in that direction?"[1] House was not to know that the very same day the French, led by General Joseph Gallieni and a division mounted in Paris taxis, launched the counterattack that saved Paris. The Germans had suffered a strategic defeat.[2]

The Wilson administration started the war more or less neutral between the two alliances. It was at first more concerned with British efforts to impose a blockade on Germany than with the struggles of the armies. Wilson gave his opinion, in an off-the-record interview in the *New York Times*, that the best outcome to the war would be a deadlock.

Not until January 30, 1915, almost six months after the guns of August, did House set sail for London in the first of repeated efforts to mediate between the Entente, or the Allies (Britain, France, Russia, and soon Italy) and the Central Powers (Germany, Austria-Hungary, and the Ottoman Empire).[3] Fifty years of Cold War assumptions about "the alliance" between the United States and Western Europe against the Soviet Union make it hard to understand how different American attitudes were in 1914. Both House and Wilson believed that the war's immediate cause was what they called German "militarism." But they also held the view— widely held in America—that all European governments were more or less undemocratic. At times, Wilson drew a distinction between the relatively democratic countries—Britain, France, and Italy—and the autocratic Central Powers. In his Flag Day speech on June 14, 1917, for example, he contrasted German autocracy with "a government accountable to the people" of the kind that existed "in England, in the United States, but not in Germany." But sometimes he thought all the European countries were pretty much equally bad.

Both House and Wilson were shocked by the Allies' war aims. They took it for granted that Germany and Austria hoped to make territorial gains out of the war. They found it harder to forgive the Allies for wanting to do the same. They knew that secret treaties pledged the Allies to reward France with Alsace-Lorraine (seized by Germany in 1871), Italy with territories in the Alps and on the eastern side of the Adriatic, and Russia with control of Constantinople.

In part because of the secret treaties Wilson refused to allow the United States, after it finally entered the war, to be called an "ally" of Britain and France, but only an "associated power." Indeed Wilson developed something of an obsession with the Allies' war aims. In late 1918 he told three journalists that the Allied statesmen "are evidently planning to take what they can get frankly as a matter of spoils, regardless of either the ethics or the practical aspects of the proceedings."[4] Wilson ceaselessly repeated that the United States had no territorial ambitions; it was true, though—given the vast territory and resources of the continental United States— not particularly relevant.

The truth was that Wilson had the most ambitious peace aim of all. He wanted the United States to emerge from the war as the arbiter of world politics. He wanted to use the war, if possible without fighting in it, to impose American ideas. House later told a British member of Parliament, "The President is going into this war to fight against Junkerism in every country. . . . He has a profound disbelief in secret diplomacy and in the way it had been practiced in Europe by all countries including England."[5]

Several historians—among them Arno J. Mayer, N. Gordon Levin, and Arthur S. Link—have stressed Wilson's commitment to a more transparent "new diplomacy." The truer view, to my mind, is that of John Reinertson, who wrote the following: "Wilson and House were not fighting to defeat Germany; they were not fighting to create a League of Nations; they were not fighting to establish a . . . New Diplomacy; they were fighting an ideological struggle, to further the democratic revolution."[6]

Wilson himself made no secret of his ambitions. America, he said, "seeks no material profit or aggrandizement of any kind. She is fighting for no advantage or selfish object of her own but for the liberation of people everywhere from the aggressions of autocratic forces."[7]

To achieve this ambitious goal, Wilson was prepared to play tough. "England and France have not the same views with regard to peace that we have by any means. When the war is over we can force them to our way of thinking, because by that time they will, among other things, be financially in our hands; but we cannot force them now. . . . Our real peace terms—those upon which we shall undoubtedly insist—are not now acceptable to either France or Italy (leaving Great Britain for the moment out of consideration)."[8]

At Paris, Wilson used financial pressure in an attempt to get the Italian government to give way over its claim to Fiume in Dalmatia.[9] In December 1916 Wilson interfered with a loan to Britain that was being raised by J. P. Morgan to demonstrate that he could destroy the credit of any nation.[10]

At different times both Wilson and House contemplated building a navy even bigger than Britain's so that the United States would be free to do what it wanted in the world. On May 17, 1916, House wrote to Wilson, "Why not come out for a strong Navy? We have the money and if we have the will, the world will recognize that we are to be reckoned with. . . . It will give us the influence desired in the settlement of European affairs."[11]

On shipboard on his way to the Paris peace conference Wilson repeatedly threatened to use American naval power to compel the Allies to go along with his proposals.[12] European democratic politicians who had recently won massive electoral and parliamentary endorsements, like Georges Clemenceau and Lloyd George, resented Wilson's assumption that his democratic mandate was more legitimate than theirs.[13]

Both Wilson and House proclaimed their belief in the self-determination of peoples or of nations. There is a vital difference between those two principles. What the Russian nation might want under the czar might well be different from what the Russian people would want. Wilson did not seem to grasp an even greater difficulty: which populations should qualify as "nations" for self-determination? The subsequent history of Eastern and Central Europe is full of examples of the distinction between the self-determination of nations and the self-determination of peoples. If Yugoslavia was to be independent, what of the Bosnians? If Bosnia was to be independent, what of the Croats, Serbs, or Muslims within Bosnia? Each of the European nations that acquired independence as a result of the application of Wilson's principle of self-determination—Poland, Czechoslovakia, Yugoslavia, Hungary, Romania, Bulgaria, and Finland among them—contained national minorities, most of which would have preferred to determine their own political status. In practice, both Wilson and House were willing to bargain territories and populations for the particular peace they wanted.

Throughout the war, Colonel House maintained close contact with British pacifists and radicals through unofficial agents. Several of these agents were journalists—among them Walter Lippmann of the *New Republic,* Lincoln Colcord and William C. Bullitt of the *Philadelphia Public Ledger,* and Lincoln Steffens.

The closest connection with liberal and Left thinking in Europe was the link between the British pacifist pressure group, the Union for Democratic Control (UDC), and the *New Republic,* backed by House's friend Willard Straight and his wife Dorothy and edited by Wilson's chief journalistic champion, Herbert Croly. Wilson was impressed by UDC members like Norman Angell, author of *The Lost Illusion,* and H. N. Brailsford, who wrote a powerful 1914 tract against war, *The War of Steel and Gold.*

Both Wilson and House systematically underestimated the way in which, once the war had started, all nationalisms were strengthened. With almost every family in Britain and France mourning a father or a son killed in battle, pacifism seemed closer to treason than to idealism. Yet both Wilson and House were conservative in their instincts. Neither had much sympathy for European socialism, for Russian revolutionists, or even in practice for Irish nationalism. Wilson saw his support for democratic movements in Europe as an alternative to revolution.[14]

Both were instinctively Anglophile, House more so than Wilson. House found the British annoyingly cautious. But he got on very well at a personal level with Grey; with the British agent Sir William Wiseman; and with both liberal politicians and Tory aristocrats, as well as with British journalists such as C. P. Scott, A. G. Gardiner, and Henry Wickham Steed and Foreign Office officials like Sir William Tyrrell and Sir Eric Drummond. He and his wife plunged happily into London political society. In France they were much less interested, no doubt in part because

House spoke little French. House did talk, in English or through interpreters, with many leading French figures—with the great philosopher Henri Bergson and the leading defender of Alfred Dreyfus, Joseph Reinach.[15]

House was better informed about Europe and more realistic than Wilson. But when the British government proved cool to his offers of mediation and Grey spurned his offer of a peace conference, House's response was almost petulant. He even spoke of war between the United States and Britain. Such fears, however, may have been intended to reassure the president and others that he had not, like Walter Hines Page, "gone over to the British." It is clear that a "special relationship" with the British was part of House's international vision.

On January 30, 1915, Colonel and Mrs. House boarded the *Lusitania*, bound for Liverpool. The colonel left with such personal encouragement as few presidential agents have ever enjoyed. "Your unselfish and intelligent friendship has meant much to me," Wilson said; House was the only one in all the world to whom he could open his entire mind. House asked if he remembered their first meeting, and Wilson replied, "Yes but we had known one another always."[16]

House had volunteered to travel to Europe at his own expense, but the president promised to pay the Houses' expenses and in addition to pay for Fanny Denton, to whom House continued to dictate his invaluable diary. So the Houses set off, in their fifties, through winter storms and submarine-infested waters, to try to arrange the one thing about which no one in Europe was yet ready to talk seriously: peace. As the *Lusitania* approached the Irish coast, the captain was so alarmed by rumors that the ship was about to be torpedoed that he flew the Stars and Stripes to protect it.[17]

House reached London safely in great secrecy. (One friend, asked what the colonel was up to, explained that he had come to see his Savile Row tailor; his trousers had worn out a little early this year.) At eleven on the day after arrival, Sunday, House was ushered into Grey's drawing room at Eccleston Square. They talked for three and a half hours. House felt complimented that Grey talked to him as if to a member of his own government, and Grey said, "Here I am helping to direct the affairs of a nation at war, and yet I have been talking like a neutral."[18]

House remained in London for over a month, and he and his wife were, if anything, even greater social lions than the previous year. There was a lunch with Henry James and a "notable gathering" at Lady Paget's, where the Houses met that "most superior person," Lord Curzon, classical scholar and former viceroy of India.[19] House found Curzon "the worst jingo I have met," though King George V, with whom he had an hour's audience at Buckingham Palace, ran him close. Possibly he was misled by King George's German family connections into imagining that the king might be sympathetic to House's peace moves. The king was cordial but spoke "rather viciously" of the kaiser and was by no means receptive to peace talk.[20]

House got on as well as ever with Sir Edward Grey, with whom he had one of those intensely personal conversations he had had with Woodrow Wilson in the early days of their friendship. Grey talked of the wildness of the Northumberland shore, and House reminisced about long winter rides in the Texas hills. They spoke of "the hereafter, and of our belief in the wisdom and mercy of the Almighty," and Grey even allowed himself to speculate about reincarnation.[21]

On March 11 the Houses left London for Paris. The ferry "ran as if the hounds were after it," escorted by a destroyer, and en route from Folkestone to Boulogne they passed a floating mine. House met the minister for foreign affairs, Théophile Delcassé, "a small, polite, shrewd-looking man."[22] But essentially House met with no response in Paris. The French were too preoccupied by the war and too confident of victory to think of peace.

On March 19, having traveled by train through neutral Switzerland, the Houses arrived in Berlin in a snowstorm, and within two and a half hours House was closeted with the top official of the German foreign office, Arthur Zimmermann. House had to report to Wilson that there was nothing doing. The plain fact was that he had now been told by the British, the French, and the Germans that peace negotiations were not on the agenda.

House's next idea was to draw Britain and Germany together first by agreement on the freedom of the seas. (The phrase "freedom of the seas" could be traced back to Hugo Grotius's *Mare Liberum* of 1609 and to the beginnings of American foreign diplomacy in 1776. House made it a slogan for American policy.) Britain naturally wanted to use its naval superiority to blockade Germany, and since the United States was the biggest neutral exporter, a quarrel between Britain and the United States was almost inevitable. House thought that only weapons of war should be contraband. He believed his proposal would favor the British. They would lose their power to blockade Germany, but their sea lanes to the United States and to their empire, which guaranteed supplies of food and munitions, would be safeguarded.

After an agreement on the freedom of the seas had unlocked the possibility of an armistice, House hoped that belligerents and neutrals, including the United States, would meet in a second convention to outlaw war. But in the back of his mind he was already shaping a different idea: a single conference, at which the American president would act as the decisive peace giver.

On April 30 he reported to Wilson that he had outlined his plan for freedom of the seas to Grey and told Grey he believed the Germans were interested. By May 1 he was ready to try to draw Zimmermann into his net. He told the German diplomat that he had mentioned to Grey the interest of both America and Germany in the freedom of the seas.

Once the Germans and the Allies had fortified formidable defensive positions from the Alps to the English Channel, there were those in both high commands who argued that decisive strategic victory on the Western Front was impossible. In both Paris and London, therefore, some turned their eyes to Germany's southeast front in the hope of splitting off Germany from Turkey. The plan finally chosen was Winston Churchill's. He argued for an attack on Gallipoli, the flat tongue of land that closes the Aegean end of the Dardanelles. The strategic instinct was correct. If the Royal Navy had put in enough troops with tactical surprise, Turkey might have been forced from the war.

As it was, the operation was botched. There were too few troops and no surprise. The Turks fought better than the Allies expected. The operation lingered on until the end of 1915, costing unjustifiably heavy casualties.[23] The only strategic effect was to convince the Germans that they were winning the war and did not need to listen to peace proposals, from Colonel House or anyone else.

Another event of early May reinforced German confidence. On the morning of May 7, House and Grey drove out to the Royal Botanical Gardens at Kew to look at the flowers. "We spoke," House said, "of the probability of an ocean liner being sunk."[24] Later that day at Buckingham Palace the king asked House, "Suppose they should sink the *Lusitania* with American passengers on board?"[25] That evening House was dining at the American Embassy when a message came in. A German submarine had torpedoed the *Lusitania.* Just under 1,200 men, women, and children, the great majority civilians, were drowned, 124 of them American citizens.

House's first reaction was that war must now come for the United States. On May 9 he sent Wilson a telegram that the president read out to his cabinet: "America has come to the parting of the ways, when she must determine whether she stands for civilized or uncivilized warfare. We can no longer remain neutral spectators."[26]

Wilson, however, immediately threw himself into an effort to avoid war. On May 11 House dictated to Miss Fanny that "Page and all of us are distressed by the President's speech at Philadelphia, in which he is reported to have said, 'There is such a thing as being too proud to fight.' "[27] Wilson's first "*Lusitania* Note" carefully avoided the tone of an ultimatum. House privately thought the Germans needed tougher talk, and he wrote presciently to William Gibbs McAdoo on May 18: "The German mind seems not to understand anything except hard knocks, and they have a curious idea that we will not fight under any circumstances. As a matter of fact, this idea is prevalent through Europe and will sooner or later involve us in war."[28]

Two weeks later, House still concluded in his diary that he felt war was inevitable.[29] In the meantime he had seen Grey again, on May 13, and their conversation suggested another possible avenue to peace. Grey asked House what he thought Berlin's reply to Wilson's *Lusitania* Note would be. House said if he were writing it, he would say that if England would lift the embargo on foodstuffs for Germany, Germany would stop sinking merchantmen. Grey said if the Germans would do that and stop using poison gas, Britain would lift the embargo.

House was excited about the possibility of a deal. But on May 25 Foreign Minister Gottlieb von Jagow turned it down flat, saying that Germany was in no need of food. When on May 30 House decided that war with Germany was inevitable, he did not waste time. He decided to leave for home just six days later. After a last dazzling round of meetings with everyone who counted in London, he set sail. When he reached Washington, a development had taken place—less violent than the sinking of the *Lusitania*, but in the end more fatal for Edward House's hopes: Woodrow Wilson had fallen in love.

The first Mrs. Wilson, Ellen, died of kidney disease on August 6, 1914, just two days after the outbreak of war in Europe. Wilson was prostrated by Ellen's death, bursting into floods of tears and reading detective stories to forget his loss "as a man might get drunk."[30] Surprisingly soon, however, he found consolation in the person of a Washington woman, Edith Bolling Galt.

Forty-one years old, tall and stately, Mrs. Galt, the widow of a fashionable Washington jeweller, came from an old Virginia family. Her grandfather was a judge, but like many another, in Virginia and elsewhere, she tended to exaggerate the grandeur of her ancestry.[31] Described by Irwin Hood Hoover, the chief White House usher, as an "interesting widow, living alone, with admirers too numerous for her comfort," Mrs. Galt liked orchids, Paris dresses, and feather boas.[32] "Who is that beautiful woman?" asked Woodrow Wilson when on March 15 he first saw her on Connecticut Avenue.

By April 28 the lovelorn chief executive, not quite nine months widowed, sent Mrs. Galt a book of poems. On May 4 he proposed marriage. On May 28, the day he received the cool German response to his first *Lusitania* Note, he wrote to her in anguish, "For God's sake try to find out whether you really love me or not."[33] The very next day, she accepted.

The intimate friendship between Edward House and Woodrow Wilson was based in many compatibilities: they were both liberal Southern gentlemen of the same generation, both animated by an aspiration to do good in the world. The special intensity of the relationship, after early 1914, when Ellen Wilson first fell ill, however, owed much to Wilson's loneliness. Now Wilson's emotional horizon was full again. He hoped that Edith would like his best friend. But from the start she was cool toward House.

There are some misunderstandings that cannot quite be cleared up because there is truth in the suspicion that underlies them. Edith Wilson suspected House of stooping to dirty tricks to prevent her marriage because he disapproved of it. She was wrong about the dirty tricks (see chapter 15). But she was right that House disapproved of the marriage. In fact he declined Wilson's invitation to his wedding to Edith "due to the hurt feelings it would engender," as he recorded in his diary.[34] He may not have been aware that his refusal too engendered hurt feelings. Edith's enmity was not openly declared, and House continued to be the president's closest friend. But after Wilson's marriage to Edith, the friendship was never quite the same.

While House was still on the high seas, the German admiralty announced that all the waters around Britain were a war zone where all enemy and neutral merchant ships would be destroyed. On March 28, 1915, the dilemma for Washington became acute. An American citizen was drowned when a German submarine sank the British ship *Falaba*. Just over a week later the *Lusitania* went down.

On May 15, Wilson sent off his first note to Berlin, demanding that the German government disavow the sinking of the *Lusitania*. On May 28, as Wilson waited in anguish for Edith's reply, the Germans answered. *Lusitania* was an armed ship and therefore fair game. There would be no apology and no promises of good behavior.

Bryan, the lifelong pacifist, clung to American neutrality like a torpedoed sailor to a raft. He equated the British blockade to the sinking of the liner. The guilt on both sides, he thought, was equal. In cabinet, Bryan, showing "some heat," said some members of the cabinet were not neutral. Wilson turned to him—so House's friend Gregory told House later—"with a steely glitter in his eyes. 'Mr. Bryan,' he said, 'you are not warranted in making such an assertion.' "[35] Bryan apologized, but on June 9, he resigned.

That same day the president sent a second note to Germany, jointly drafted by himself and the new secretary of state, Robert Lansing, but sounding Wilson's characteristic trumpet note: "The Government of the United States is contending for something much greater than mere rights of property. . . . It is contending for nothing less high and sacred than the rights of humanity."[36]

Colonel House was at sea when Bryan resigned. He was met at Ambrose Light by Dudley Field Malone, collector of the Port of New York, in a revenue cutter. According to House's diary, Malone said House could have Bryan's job if he wanted it. House brushed it aside. He had far more useful work to do.[37]

On June 16 House sent Wilson a "despatch" from Long Island that sealed the fate of his own peace initiatives for the time being. "I think we shall find ourselves drifting into war with Germany."[38]

Wilson did not agree. It is impossible to say how much his decision was influenced by a conviction that he must keep the country out of war if he were to be reelected in 1916 and how much he was motivated simply by hatred of war. In any case, he was willing to let the Germans get away with the clear breach of international law that was the sinking of the *Lusitania*.

"If war comes with Germany because of this submarine controversy," House wrote, "it will be because we are totally unprepared and Germany feels we are impotent."[39] He made the same point in a letter to the president.

Wilson's third note was strong in tone but it did not propose any sanction that would give the Germans second thoughts. Bernstorff in Washington, like Gerard in Berlin, felt it was only a matter of time before an incident brought matters to a head.

It came on August 19. The British liner *Arabic,* outward bound for New York and therefore carrying no contraband, was sunk without warning off the coast of Cornwall. Two Americans were killed. Once again, Wilson turned to House for advice. House confided in his diary what he would do if he were president: "I would send Bernstorff home and recall Gerard. I would let the matter rest there for the moment, with the intimation that the next offense would bring us actively in on the side of the Allies. In the meantime I would begin preparations for defense and for war. . . . I would measurably exonerate the Germans as a whole, but I would blister the militant party in Germany."[40]

House was clear that the United States could not go on like this without the means of self-defense. In late August, while he was still up at Manchester, Massachusetts, he had a visit from Josephus Daniels, the navy secretary. House urged the secretary to ask for whatever would be needed to make the U.S. Navy second only to the British navy and easily superior to all others. House told him it did not matter if it cost $300 million or $400 million. "The country demanded it and it should be done."[41]

While the president dreamed of saving the world, House was beginning to contemplate the implications for the American state of being a world power. In his activity between 1915 and 1917 it is not fanciful to see a first, sketchy draft of what would become the national security state.

House preached "preparedness." There must be a great navy and a great army too. There must be security for such vulnerable places as New York harbor. House wanted a regiment, at least, posted at Governor's Island.[42] Early in 1915 the German government began to infiltrate secret agents, led by the German naval and military attachés, the oddly named navy captain Karl Boy-Ed and Captain Franz von Papen (later chancellor of Germany and a leading Nazi), for espionage and sabotage.[43] They tried to slow the American munitions flowing toward Britain and France. In July 1916 their agents blew up the Lehigh Railroad's pier at Black Tom, New Jersey (across the Hudson River from Manhattan), where munitions were loaded for Europe. The explosion "scarred the Statue of Liberty with shrapnel, shattered windows in Times Square, rocked the Brooklyn Bridge, and woke sleepers as far away as Maryland."[44] There was no Central Intelligence Agency in 1915 and no Federal Bureau of Investigation. House took it upon himself to liaise with the agencies to whom it fell to check these hostile activities: the bomb squad of the New York police department, the tiny Military Intelligence Department in the War Department, and the Treasury's Secret Service.

House never gave up on his central effort: to bring about a negotiated end to the war. In a talk late in the summer of 1915, the president surprised him by saying "he had never been sure that we ought not to take part in the conflict."[45] This surprising break from Wilson's usual attitude encouraged House to come up with a peace plan. He should ask the Allies unofficially whether it would be helpful for the United States to demand an end to hostilities. "If the Central Powers refused to acquiesce, we could then push our insistence to a point where diplomatic relations could first be broken off." The president was startled, according to House, but "seemed to acquiesce by silence."[46]

By October 17 House had put his proposal into a letter to Sir Edward Grey, "one of the most important letters I ever wrote"[47]—so important that he and his secretary, Fanny Denton, took unusual precautions to keep it secret. They sent it as a "split message," and House wrote Sir Edward to tell him how to put the two halves of the message together. On November 9 Grey replied that the split letter had been received. "The time may soon come," House wrote, "when this Government should intervene . . . and demand that peace parleys begin upon the broad basis of the elimination of militarism and navalism."[48]

House told Grey that when he thought the time was right for U.S. intervention, he would propose it to the president. Grey asked what House meant by "the elimination of militarism and navalism." Was he thinking of the language of Grey's own letter to House of September 22, which read as follows? "To me the great object of securing the elimination of militarism and navalism is to get security for the future against aggressive war. How much are the United States prepared to do in this direction? Would the President propose that there should be a League of Nations binding themselves to side against any Power that broke a Treaty, which broke certain rules of warfare on sea or land . . . or which refused, in case of dispute, to adopt some other method of settlement than that of war?"[49]

Grey wrote House that his personal fear was that the United States "might now strike the weapon of sea power from our hands, and thereby ensure a German victory"[50] House was irritated by Grey's response. "The offer which I made in my letter—which was practically to ensure victory for the Allies—should have met with a warmer reception." The British, he added, "are in many ways dull." The richer America grew by selling them munitions, the more unpopular it became. "I loathe the idea of our making money out of their misfortune," he said, "but nevertheless it is inevitable."[51] Indeed, huge British and French orders for munitions of all kinds were creating a boom in manufacturing. House thought he was doing the British and the Allies a huge favor that would not merely end the war, but also end it to their advantage. The Allies did not see it quite like that.

The relationship, difficult enough in any case, suffered because of the personalities of the ambassadors formally charged with nurturing it. Walter Hines Page in London had become more British than the British. Sir Cecil Spring-Rice, the British ambassador in Washington, was eccentric. He said he could not talk to House because of the Logan Act of 1800, which prohibited private diplomacy. Meanwhile, Bernstorff, the German ambassador, was suspected of covering up for spies in his embassy. All the more reason for House to take a hand at personal diplomacy again.

By January 6, 1916, House was back in London. His plan was simply that the president of the United States would call the powers to a conference that would end the war. The conference would also plan a new postwar international regime whose first principle would be a commitment to end militarism and "navalism" through disarmament. All nations would accept the principle of the freedom of the seas,

Peace conference in the Clock Room at the Quai d'Orsay; group painting by Sir William
Orpen. Bridgeman Art Library, London.

Kaiser Wilhelm II as the devil in a sketch by Sir William Orpen. Bridgeman Art Library, London.

David Lloyd George. Bridgeman Art Library, London.

Georges Clemenceau. Bridgeman Art Library, London.

The House family in the 1880s. Edward and Loulie
House with their daughters, Mona and Janet;
Loulie's sister, "Aunt Mezes"; and an Italian nurse
(top right). Courtesy of Edward Auchincloss.

House residence at 1704 West Avenue, Austin, designed by Frank Freeman in the "shingle
style" and completed in 1892. Yale University Library, Manuscripts and Archives.

"The strangest friendship in history":
Colonel House with Woodrow Wilson.
Yale University Library, Manuscripts and
Archives.

President Wilson (at the head of the table) with his cabinet, including, to his right, William
Jennings Bryan (Secretary of State) and, to his left, William Gibbs McAdoo (Treasury
Secretary). Corbis.

House loved to ride. Here (in 1923) he is riding Old Joe, the horse of his nephew, T. W. House III. Yale University Library, Manuscripts and Archives.

Colonel House on board SS *Rotterdam* en route to Europe in 1916 with (left to right) Dudley Field Malone, C. N. Carver, Sidney Mezes, and Cary T. Grayson. Yale University Library, Manuscripts and Archives.

Colonel House at Chesterfield House, the London mansion lent him in 1917. Yale University Library, Manuscripts and Archives.

House's devoted secretary, "Miss Fanny" Denton. She carried a revolver in her bag to protect his papers. Yale University Library, Manuscripts and Archives.

House's best friend in England, Sir Edward Grey, foreign secretary and later Viscount Grey of Fallodon. Portrait by John Singer Sargent. National Portrait Gallery, London.

House's wife, Loulie. Portrait by Sir Philip de Laszlo. Courtesy of Edward Auchincloss.

Colonel House in his New York apartment on
East 53rd Street. Yale University Library,
Manuscripts and Archives.

Leaders of the Inquiry. The five seated are (from left) Charles Homer
Haskins, Isaiah Bowman, Sidney Mezes, James Brown Scott, and
David Hunter Miller. Standing (farthest left) is Charles Seymour. Yale
University Library, Manuscripts and Archives.

Sir William Wiseman, head of British intelligence in the United States. Yale University Library, Manuscripts and Archives.

Porch of the Jefferson Coolidge mansion at Coolidge Point, Massachusetts, where President Wilson and Colonel House drafted the covenant of the League of Nations. Manchester Historical Society.

Bust of Colonel House by Jo Davidson.
Courtesy of Edward Auchincloss.

and this new world would be regulated by a league of nations. The president would propel the warring powers to the conference table by announcing that the United States would intervene on the side of the Allies if the Germans would not attend.

The first opportunity to test the British cabinet's response to this plan came on January 11. Ambassador Page gave a dinner for House to meet Lloyd George. House was asked what the United States wanted Britain to do. He replied: "The United States would like Great Britain to do those things which would enable the United States to help Great Britain win the war."[52] A reasonable interpretation of this sibylline exchange is that the United States would continue to arm the Allies but would not enter the war unless circumstances changed.

On January 14 House judged the circumstances were right to be more specific in another talk with Lloyd George. They discussed how President Wilson could dictate peace terms, which might include, for example, the restoration of Alsace-Lorraine to France, the creation of an independent Poland, and the partition of the Ottoman Empire. They also discussed, in a highly non-Wilsonian spirit, such matters as the German colonies in the Pacific, southern Africa, and the Baghdad railway. Lloyd George said Britain would never even discuss the German idea of the freedom of the seas. House corrected him; it was not a German idea but had been put forward by himself, with the president's approval, in Berlin the previous year.[53]

On January 20 the Houses set out again for Berlin. House soon plunged into a round of conversations with many of the same personages he had met in 1914 and 1915. He did not see Tirpitz, whom he blamed for the torpedoings. Nor did he see the kaiser, but Ambassador Gerard had good stories to tell. The kaiser thought that "I and my cousins, George and Nicholas, will make peace when the time comes."[54] House had an earnest talk with Zimmermann of the Foreign Office, who spoke eagerly of his hope that the "white races" (by which he meant America, Germany, and Britain) would get together one day.[55]

House was followed everywhere in Germany by plainclothesmen, and it was not until he got to Switzerland that he felt free to report to the president. There was a great controversy in Germany, he wrote, about the submarine campaign, not about its ethics, but about its effectiveness. The navy, backed more or less by the army, believed that Britain could be effectively blockaded if the German navy could use its new big submarines unhampered by law.[56]

Meetings in Paris somewhat altered House's thinking about his great project. On February 3 and 4 he met separately with the prime minister, Aristide Briand, and Jules Cambon, head of the foreign ministry. He told Cambon that in spite of all he was doing, a break with Germany could not be averted but only deferred. He warned Cambon, as he had warned Lloyd George, of his fear that Germany might reach a separate peace with Russia.

Cambon's account of the conversation was rather different. After House had briefly recounted his talks in Berlin, Cambon reported that House said the French had no idea of the strength of American sentiment in favor of the Allies. "Inevitably America will enter the war," House said, "before the end of the year, and would align herself on the side of the Allies." However, it would be necessary for an incident to happen that would cause the American people to rally behind the president. "This statement from Colonel House astonished me," Cambon wrote in a memorandum of the conversation. "I had him repeat it and after having noted it in English, I had him read it. He said to me: 'exactly.' "[57]

House saw Briand and Cambon again, this time together, on February 7 and felt he had achieved a significant diplomatic triumph. It had been, he cabled Wilson, the most important conference he had had in Europe. So far, he told the president two days later, he had taken only the British into his confidence, but he had been struck by their slowness and lack of initiative. So he had decided to "take the risk and talk plainly to the French." The result was "surprisingly satisfactory." House told Wilson he had outlined to the two Frenchmen the circumstances in which Wilson would intervene. He added a jeremiad, calculated to appeal to the president's view of European governments, about the "stubbornness, determination, selfishness and cant" he had found in London, Berlin, and Paris. "A great opportunity is yours, my friend," House wrote, "the greatest perhaps that has ever come to any man."[58]

Again, Jules Cambon's account of the meeting was fuller. House "assured us anew of the profound sympathies of the United States for the Allies. The intention of the American government is to intervene, either peaceably or even, according to the circumstances, militarily, in order to produce for the world a peace favorable to the Allied cause."[59]

Not surprisingly the Frenchmen asked what House thought of Alsace-Lorraine. "I believe [Cambon recorded House as replying] that Germany could be led to envisage the restitution of Alsace-Lorraine to France, but in return it would be necessary for her to receive compensation, in Asia Minor, for example, where one could award her Anatolia. Thus . . . Russia, which would take Armenia, would become Germany's neighbor. We asked Mr. House what, in his conception, he would do with Turkey. He replied to us that she must disappear."[60]

The willingness to swap provinces and compensate one power for the loss of provinces at the expense of another reads oddly in the light of Woodrow Wilson's dislike of secret diplomacy and his proclaimed commitment to the self-determination of peoples. House was behaving in precisely the way Wilson most deplored. Yet House confirmed Cambon's account. In his diary he underlined the following sentence: "In the event the Allies are successful during the next few months I promised that the President would not intervene. In the event they were losing ground, I promised the President would intervene."[61] Could France regain Alsace-Lorraine? House said he thought it might be accomplished by giving Germany a part of Asia Minor and compensating Russia in the same way. Cambon exclaimed, in House's version, "Then you would wipe out Turkey?" "This, I said, was in my mind."[62] It was a bold proposition for an unofficial diplomat.

On his way back to England, House had promised to visit Albert, King of the Belgians, who was holding out in a corner of his country that could just be reached by a road threatened by German positions. The Houses went by rail as far as Boulogne. From there the colonel was driven to Calais "at a terrific pace, estimated . . . at 75 to 80 miles an hour."[63] They saw trenches, forts, barbed wire entanglements, and buildings destroyed by shells. When House finally reached the royal headquarters at La Panne, he had an audience of an hour and a half. Would the king let Germany have the Belgian Congo if it paid for it? If the Germans could buy the Belgian Congo and Portuguese Africa and Germany could get a sphere of influence in Asia Minor, peace might be arranged. The king said he could not justify letting go the Congo, which had been created (some might say seized and brutally oppressed) by his uncle. The conversation was largely a waste from House's point of view. But once again he had been willing to talk the language of the old diplomacy.

The day after his audience with King Albert, the colonel and his wife crossed on a British troop ship. Five or six miles out of Dover a British secret serviceman, whose presence they had not suspected, told them to go up on deck and stand by one of the lifeboats with their life jackets on. A tramp steamer had been torpedoed close by, and two German seaplanes were dropping bombs along the English coast, while a British airship was overhead, hunting the U-boat.

House's equanimity, untroubled by a combat zone, was disturbed by Ambassador Page, who told him that the United States was in bad odor everywhere. House "flayed" him for his lack of patriotism. House talked to Grey "with the bark off."[64] He said the Allies were in trouble and Britain might find itself alone. But Grey was pleased by House's account of his talk with Briand and Cambon. House persuaded Grey, he reported to Wilson, that his idea for a peace conference would be better than American intervention in the war on the submarine issue. The Allies, House told the president, would agree to the conference, and if Germany did not, "I have promised for you that we will throw in all our weight in order to bring her to terms."[65]

House had to submit to a press conference at the Ritz Hotel, and he handled it with deadpan humor. He was, one British reporter noted, "a little active man, with iron grey hair and moustache—the perfection of courtesy, but the dumbest of diplomats." (He used the word "dumb" in the British sense, meaning not stupid but uncommunicative. "Did you hear any discussion on the possibilities of peace?" "I have not heard peace discussions anywhere because I purposely avoided them.")[66]

The day after the press conference, like an old sheepdog nudging his flock toward the pen, House had lunch with Grey, Asquith, and Balfour and dinner with Lloyd George and Lord Reading, a close friend of Lloyd George and a brilliant lawyer. Both groups were cautious.[67] They would prefer for the United States to enter the war unconditionally on the submarine issue. Perhaps they feared Wilson would not keep House's promise that he would fight if Germany refused a settlement on reasonable terms. Those terms, it seems, would have meant German withdrawal from Belgium, Serbia, and France; and the ceding of Alsace-Lorraine to France; Constantinople to Russia, and Italian-speaking Austrian territories to Italy; Germany would be compensated with territories in Anatolia and perhaps Africa.[68] If those were the terms House had in mind, they left vast and dangerous questions unresolved, not least about the future of the Balkans and the Near East.

At lunch with Grey, Asquith, and Balfour, House again played the Russian card: What if Russia collapsed? Asquith thought he was too pessimistic. House replied that he thought Russia "would stick," but why take chances? Balfour asked House directly what message he wanted to take back from London. A definite understanding, House replied, that the British government would welcome a U.S. proposal to end the fighting and a conference to thrash out the terms of peace.[69]

"The thing I fear most," House added with prescience, "is that Germany will break loose in an unrestricted undersea warfare."[70] The president might then be unable to keep the United States out of the war. House's own dream, of placing the president as the arbiter of Europe by convening a peace conference, would then go up in smoke.

The evening meeting was no less important. It was vital to have Lloyd George on board because his was now the strongest voice calling for total victory. If the Asquith government collapsed, he might well become prime minister (as in fact he did).

At half past eight on February 14 House sat down to dine with Asquith,

Balfour, Grey, Lloyd George, and Reading.[71] It was, House felt, the supreme test of his diplomacy. It was Asquith who asked the crucial question, which both demonstrated his serious interest in the House plan and showed up its difficulty. When should the president be involved? The psychological moment would come, House answered, if the Allies could make a sufficient impression militarily to discourage the Germans. What, though, House added, if the Allied success were so great that public opinion thought victory was in sight? Asquith admitted that was not likely.[72] To get Lloyd George, Balfour, and Asquith, political rivals and temperamentally very different, even to talk about peace was a great achievement. But the British public was doggedly committed to victory. Grey told House a mob would break the windows of his house if he came out for a negotiated settlement.[73]

It was agreed, to House's great satisfaction, that he should work out the details of an agreement with Grey. On February 23, the day the Houses left Falmouth for New York on the *Rotterdam*, House asked Grey, if he cabled the request, to send Lord Reading to America to see the president and confirm there was no change in the agreement.[74] House made this request for his own protection. He was afraid that something might happen to make the president change his mind. He and Grey parted with genuine affection. Grey looked forward to the day when they could greet each other with the words, "The war is over."

Grey had the previous day initialed what came to be called the House-Grey Memorandum.

> *(Confidential)* Colonel House told me that President Wilson was ready, on hearing from France and England that the moment was opportune, to propose that a Conference should be summoned to put an end to the war. Should the Allies accept this proposal and should Germany refuse it, the United States would probably enter the war against Germany.
>
> Colonel House expressed the opinion that, if such a Conference were held, it would secure peace on terms not unfavourable to the Allies; and, if it failed to secure peace, the United States would leave the Conference as a belligerent on the side of the Allies, if Germany was unreasonable. Colonel House expressed an opinion decidedly favourable to the restoration of Belgium, the transfer of Alsace and Lorraine to France, and the acquisition by Russia of an outlet to the sea. . . . The loss of territory incurred by Germany . . . would have to be compensated by concessions to her in other places outside Europe.[75]

In Washington, House showed Wilson the memorandum. "The President accepted *in toto,*" House noted, but added the word "probably." House wrote Grey that this made no difference. "He inserted the word 'probably' which, of course, was merely overlooked in our original draft as it occurs in the sentences above and with the same meaning."[76]

Some historians have accepted House's view. Experience suggests, however, that if one is closing an important agreement with a customer or partner and his only comment is to add the word "probably" to qualify the verb that commits him to his side of the deal, to say the least one's confidence in him must be weakened. Certainly Lloyd George did not think it was unimportant. Was the problem Sir Edward Grey's reluctance to press the idea on the French, he wondered: "Or was it attributable to the insertion by President Wilson of one fatal word in the gentleman's agreement suggested by Colonel House? The document as cabled by Colonel House definitely committed the President (subject of course to the assent of Congress) in the event of rejection by Germany of a conference into which he was prepared to enter with a pledge to the Allies of support for minimum terms. The President in his reply inserted the word 'Probably' in front of the undertaking. Sir Edward Grey's view was that this completely changed the character of the proposal."[77] The future British prime minister could not imagine going into a commitment that would depend on the good faith of a man whose only response to a position reached after earnest negotiation was to add the word "probably," in effect removing his own commitment to carry out his side of a bargain that might mean life or death to the Allies.

Grey focused more on the "extreme delicacy" (mentioned by Lloyd George too) of communicating Wilson's offer to intervene to the French. To recommend the deal to the French might suggest that Britain was weakening in its support for them. Grey solved this dilemma by informing Briand of the deal without recommending it. Perhaps Wilson failed to understand the sheer size of the stake the British and French had riding on the proposed agreement. If he did understand it, one must assume that he cared more about bringing the warring nations together than he did about the Allies' survival.

After some discussion, Wilson noted in shorthand the substance of a reply to Grey and then went to his typewriter and typed it out. In the event, the House-Grey Memorandum was a dead letter. It was overtaken by the German decision to resume submarine warfare, and in the end the United States entered the war in other circumstances. Probably the Allies, in both London and Paris, saw House's commitment as a get-out-of-jail card to be used only in extremis. One hard-headed historian dismissed the agreement: "Grey may have been deceiving House. House was certainly deceiving both Grey and Wilson. He dangled war before the one, peace before the other, and in reality achieved neither."[78]

Another scholar speaks of "the subtle but steady process through which Sir Edward Grey, while appearing to encourage Wilsonian mediation efforts, was in reality working to enlist American influence and power behind the achievement of allied war aims."[79] One could point with equal truth to the subtle but steady process by which House, while appearing to encourage Britain and France in their struggle, was in reality working to commit the Allies to American war aims.

The House-Grey Memorandum was not a corrupt bargain between two poker players, each trying to bluff the other. It was a genuine attempt by two men who respected one another to stop the slaughter of Verdun and the Somme. The combatants dared not dismiss it out of hand. The tragedy was that none of them dared seize it for fear of betraying the sacrifice of their soldiers and the hope of victory.

House was thrilled when the president put his hand on his shoulder and said, "You should be proud of yourself and not of me, since you have done it all."[80] But exhilaration soon gave way to bitter disillusion, not so much with the Germans, who destroyed House's hopes, as with the British, who failed to take advantage of what House saw as the unrepeatable opportunity he had given them.

On March 24, 1916, the English Channel ferry *Sussex* was cut in half by a torpedo, without warning, with heavy loss of life. By early April, House was telling Wilson again that a break with Germany was inevitable.[81] But on April 18, nearly a month after the *Sussex* sinking, Wilson sent a note to Berlin saying merely that unless Germany abandoned its submarine attacks on civilian ships, the United States would sever diplomatic relations. Berlin answered sarcastically that it was a pity that Washington's sympathy for the victims of German submarines was not also given to the children the British wanted to starve.

President Wilson prompted House to ask Grey if he was prepared to take up the president's offer of intervention. Grey responded coolly. The president's peace conference, he replied, would look as if it had been instigated by the Germans.[82] By May 16 Wilson was writing to his "dearest friend" a characteristic letter in which he moved effortlessly from tough *realpolitik* to protestations of his own disinterestedness:

We should get down to hard pan. . . . The at least temporary removal of the acute German question has concentrated attention here on the altogether indefensible course Great Britain is pursuing with regard to trade . . . and her quite intolerable interception of mails on the high seas. . . . Recently there has been added the great shock opinion in this country has received from the course of the British government towards some of the Irish rebels. . . . The United States must either make a decided move for peace . . . or . . . must insist to the limit upon . . . [the] freedom of the seas. . . . Which does Great Britain prefer? She cannot escape both. To do nothing is now, for us, impossible. . . . We have nothing material of any kind to ask for ourselves.[83]

House, too, was getting impatient. Within a week he was writing to Grey in a distinctly cooler tone: "Your seeming lack of desire to cooperate with us will chill the enthusiasm here—never, I am afraid, to come again, at least in our day. . . . If it is [lost], the fault will not lie with us."[84]

In late May House helped Wilson with the preparation of an important speech in Washington to the League to Enforce Peace. The speech casts light on how House worked with his friend on this and other major pronouncements. There is always the suspicion that House in his diary exaggerated his role in Wilson's major decisions and speeches, but in this case (and in many others) there is corroboration.[85] On May 20 House wrote, at Wilson's request, a memorandum making suggestions for the speech.[86] Wilson himself drafted the speech in shorthand. At one point Wilson's draft reads, "House's first two paragraphs," and his speech does indeed follow House's text closely in calling for "a new and more wholesome diplomacy."[87] This cardinal and characteristic thought, which would surface in the Fourteen Points and in Wilson's commitment to "open covenants, openly arrived at," can thus be directly traced to a suggestion of House's. At three other points in the speech Wilson indicates that he is to take in language from House's memorandum.

Unfortunately—and House himself commented more than once on Wilson's tendency to do this—Wilson gratuitously offended the Europeans. Speaking of the war, in the speech Wilson said, "With its causes and its objects we are not concerned." House predicted that the Allies would pick on this one sentence, and he was right. It was not long before Jules Jusserand, the French ambassador in Washington, was telling House of "the distress naturally caused in France and England by the President's proclaimed indifference to the causes and objects of the war."[88]

If Allied opinion was inflamed by Wilson's lofty indifference to the causes of the war, American opinion, not least in Congress, was infuriated by Allied tactlessness in interfering with neutral mail and blacklisting American firms trading with the Germans. By July House was writing Wilson that "a crisis has arisen with Great Britain and the Allies."[89] One direct consequence was the passage by Congress of the "largest naval appropriation ever passed by any legislative body of a state not at war."[90] This appropriation provided for the building of 137 new ships of all sizes, with emphasis on the huge battleships then deemed the ultimate measure of naval power. That made and would make the U.S. Navy, for the first time, almost equal to the British Royal Navy.

From early June House fled New York's heat and humidity as usual, this time to Sunapee, New Hampshire, and stayed there until September 16. He spent some time in late June dictating sixty pages of reminiscences to Fanny Denton, and to the extent that he was in contact with his political friends by letter and telephone all summer, he was preoccupied with the presidential election. He remained irritated by the failure of the Allies to take up his proposal. "I believe the French and English are prolonging the war unnecessarily," he wrote in his diary. "It is stupid to refuse our proffered intervention."[91]

In late September House went to stay with Wilson at his summer home, Shadow Lawn, in Long Branch, New Jersey. House said the real reason for difficulty with Britain now was that the United States was building a great navy, its trade was expanding beyond all belief, and the United States looked as dangerous to British interests as Germany had looked before the war. Wilson replied, "Let us build a navy bigger than hers and do what we please."[92]

The two friends fell back into their old habits of easy philosophical speculation. Wilson read out loud Browning's poem about an Arab physician who visits Jerusalem just after the time of Christ and is told that Jesus has raised Lazarus from the dead.[93] House asked if Wilson thought Christ's teachings had made much progress in two thousand years. Wilson said they had not, but they did act as a moral balance. "We knew what was wrong," Wilson thought, "even though we did wrong, and our conscience held us in check."[94]

By November 14, the election was over. Wilson was back in the White House, and House was staying there again, grappling once again with the question of peace or war. House seemed for a moment to be contemplating a complete reversal of alliances. If the United States proposed peace, the Germans would accept and the Allies would refuse. If the Germans did not begin unrestricted U-boat warfare, the United States would drift into a "sympathetic alliance" with Germany, and England and France might declare war on the United States. House said Britain could

conceivably destroy the U.S. Navy and land troops from Japan in sufficient numbers to hold certain parts of the United States, perhaps as far as the Gulf of
Mexico.[95]

Was House attempting to convince Wilson that, unlike Page, he was not a
partisan of the Allies? Was he just irritated by what he saw as their stubborn
foolishness? Or was he simply assembling arguments for preparedness? He did not
seriously contemplate an alliance with Germany against Britain. He saw only too
clearly that the Allies were trying to push the United States into war with Germany.
But he was irritated by the president's tendency to offend the Allies to avoid war
with Germany. "If we are to have war, let it be with Germany by all means."[96]

10 *America Drifts into the War* ◡

Blockade of Germany was essential to the victory of the Allies, but the ill-will of the United States meant their certain defeat. It was better therefore to carry on the war without blockade, if need be, than to incur a break with the United States about contraband. . . . The object of diplomacy, therefore, was to secure the maximum of blockade that could be enforced without a rupture with the United States.

—Grey, *Twenty-Five Years*

AS EARLY AS MAY 30, 1915, House wrote in his diary, "I have concluded that war with Germany is inevitable."[1] Yet it took almost two whole years before the United States entered the war. Woodrow Wilson was absolutely determined to keep the United States out of it if it was humanly possible.

The German reply to Wilson's third note on the *Lusitania* sinking finally conceded the essence of what Wilson wanted. War had been averted. But now American neutrality lay in the German government's hands. If ever it decided to resume attacks on merchant shipping, Wilson's hand would be forced.

In the second half of 1916 House spoke frequently with Count Bernstorff, the German ambassador in Washington. The truth, which House was quicker than

Wilson to acknowledge, was that the German government was not serious about a negotiated peace so long as it believed it could win the war.

In the meantime, Wilson had to be reelected. He took remarkably little interest in the tactical details of the campaign, delegating those to professionals like Daniel C. Roper, first assistant to the postmaster general; to Vance McCormick, a Harrisburg newspaper publisher who was chairman of the Democratic National Committee; and to House. Wilson understood that he had been elected in 1912 only because the Republicans had been divided by the Bull Moose insurgency. He would need to attract as many Progressives as he could by pressing a number of progressive measures. In the end, Wilson may have won one-fifth of the 1912 Progressive vote in 1916. In a close election, that was enough.

After the Republicans nominated Charles Evans Hughes as their candidate, Wilson, according to House, showed some signs of panic.[2] He asked House to take over as national chairman, but House, as always, preferred to work behind the scenes. From early July to early August, summering at Lake Sunapee, he saw no visitors. Before that, however, he played a significant part in the election preparation. It was typical that House had no official role in the campaign, yet he planned its structure; set its tone; guided its finance; chose speakers, tactics, and strategy; and, not least, handled the campaign's greatest asset and greatest potential liability: its brilliant but temperamental candidate.

Vance McCormick came to House's summer home, and House gave him an outline of the organization that would be needed. The president should stay at his summer home. House took the old-fashioned view that the candidate should not campaign. It was "bad form and poor politics."[3]

McCormick visited again in the second week in August to discuss, among other campaign issues, the question of the vote for women. (Both Wilson and Hughes had come out for women's suffrage.) House suggested that McCormick read the riot act to the suffragists for coming out for the Republican Party. They would risk antagonizing the Democrats to the point where they would not get a two-thirds vote in Congress for a constitutional amendment.

William Gibbs McAdoo came to complain that he was shut out of Wilson's confidence. House took it for granted that McAdoo wanted to be president, in spite of his denials, and thought he might make a great president. The nation was deprived of these talents when McAdoo withdrew from contention at the Democratic convention of 1924 at the 102nd ballot.[4]

The campaign manager, Roper, came to urge House to return to New York, as he was the only man who could harmonize the differences among the men around

Wilson. "While I have planned the campaign in general," House noted, "I have tried to lay the burden of detail on other shoulders." On September 16 he yielded. Within the week the colonel could write that every waking hour of the last two days had been occupied with the campaign.[5]

One troublesome problem was the Wilson campaign's relations with Tammany Hall, then a mighty power in Democratic politics. House always had an unholy dread of dealing with Charles F. Murphy and his Tammany lieutenants. His suspicion of Catholic politicians amounted to prejudice. (It extended to Joseph Tumulty, President Wilson's secretary.) House thought Catholics always tried to put a fellow Catholic into every job that came open. House hated to deal with the men of Tammany and did so only through third parties.[6]

By mid-October, with election day only three weeks away, House considered that the campaign strategy outlined at Sunapee was working. If the election were held that day, he was sure of victory. He was irritated the next day when the Republican candidate made House personally a target. We have a government, Hughes said several times, pleased with his own wit, of "two houses, and not of three."[7]

House was worried about what would happen to foreign policy over the four months that elapsed in those days between election day and the inauguration. Who would decide matters of war and peace if Wilson should by any unhappy chance be beaten? Wilson's campaign slogan, after all, had been "He kept us out of the war." If, for example, the Germans restarted submarine warfare, the outgoing president would not want to take any action that might commit his successor, yet such action might be urgently needed. In deepest secrecy, House suggested to Robert Lansing an ingenious constitutional solution. The president, in the event of his defeat, should ask both Vice President Thomas R. Marshall (best known for his opinion that what the country needed was a good five cent cigar) and Lansing, third in succession as secretary of state, to resign.[8] Wilson would then appoint Charles Evans Hughes, the president-elect, as secretary of state, who would succeed immediately as president. A couple of nights later House startled the attorney general, his old friend Gregory, by telling him he had already made this suggestion to Wilson. Gregory was silent for five minutes, then said he approved.

House reminded Roper of what he had said at Sunapee—that Wilson should run not for president, but for justice of the peace. What he meant was that they should forget the intimidating presence of the 16 or 17 million voters in the national electorate and focus on individual precincts. House felt the Democrats' weakness lay in the machinery for getting out the vote. Of course, if he could have overcome his fastidiousness about Charles F. Murphy, there would have been no lack of expertise in that department.

By the end of October House was complaining that his days were "a mad whirl of telephone talks and visitors," and on November 1 he felt he had to abandon his reclusive style and appear at headquarters for the first time. He was studied with curiosity by the campaign workers, who had heard of him as a man of mystery. After the election, House was one of those who sat down to deal with the bills for election expenses. The party was half a million dollars in debt thanks to its efforts to match Republican spending.[9]

The great culminating event of the campaign was to be the president's speech at Madison Square Garden on November 2. The planning was meticulous. The head of a parade would reach 34th Street and Fifth Avenue at half past eight. Ten minutes later, the president would leave the Waldorf Hotel on his way to the Garden. The chairman of the meeting was to deliver a ten-minute speech at precisely fifteen minutes of nine and allow five minutes for applause.

Wilson was not in a happy mood. House met him on the presidential yacht *Mayflower*, moored in the East River. They talked for an hour and a half, and it was the most acrimonious talk they had had in a long while. Wilson did not like the plans for New York. He did not like the amount of Republican advertising in the New York papers. Come to that, he did not like New York. He thought the city was "rotten to the core." He accused the Texan House and the Pennsylvanian McCormick of "New Yorkitis" and thought the campaign should have been run from elsewhere.[10]

House had heard that story from candidates so often—notably from William Jennings Bryan—that it made him tired. Wilson, House told his diary crossly, thought that the people decided elections themselves. "If he had been in politics as long as I have, and knew from the point of view of a worker rather than as a candidate, he would understand how easy it is to change the vote of a state one way or another."[11]

In his diary House likened Wilson to a spoiled boy whose mother had to tell him it was another boy's turn to ride the hobby horse. To his face, of course, he said nothing of the kind, and tact worked. The president put his arms around both House and McCormick and said they must not mind his disagreement over the tactics. The Madison Square Garden speech went off well. House poked his nose in and went home well content with the volume of cheering.

The election was close. For forty-eight hours, House was steadily on the telephone or meeting party managers. He retired to bed at eleven on election night, leaving Gordon and Janet Auchincloss to monitor the returns until three. By five o'clock the next morning he was "into the game" again, still in bed, but with the telephone at his bedside. For a time it looked as though Hughes had been elected, and the New York papers actually reported that he had. House called his friends at the *World,* and the United Press, as well as other journalists, for fear the Far West would go by default. Finally, he went down to headquarters to find "a motley mob" running about in a disorganized frenzy. "I never permit myself," he commented, "to worry about matters over which I have no control." In the end, the East and Midwest went for Hughes, but Wilson was brought safely home by the South and the West.[12]

After the election House knew that his own position was unassailable. The president had not been worried about the outcome of the campaign, Wilson's cousin Helen Bones told him, because House had been directing it.[13]

Wilson confirmed that he had been prepared to act on House's suggestion that he hand over to Hughes if he had been defeated. He also confided in House another bold constitutional plan to allow members of Congress to join the cabinet, a step in the direction of British practice and a distinct break with the American tradition of the separation of powers. As both men turned back toward the greatest test of their strength and wisdom, House could feel that his position was buttressed by a friendship that could survive disagreement. But disagreement there would be.

The president must now turn his attention to foreign affairs. New U-boat raids made it impossible to ignore the growing danger that the Germans, with their big new boats, would resume unrestricted submarine warfare, ending the suspension of torpedo attacks on merchant ships into which they had reluctantly entered on May 4, 1916. The president tried over and over again to postpone a decision to declare war. House had two goals in mind: to persuade the president of the inevitability of war and to do what he could to make the country ready, or less utterly unready, when it came.

The day after Wilson's triumphal reception at Madison Square Garden, Albert Burleson, the postmaster general, and his first assistant, Daniel Roper, lunched with House, and so did the secretary of state. The two politicians came to talk about the campaign, but after Burleson and Roper left, Lansing stayed behind to talk about the darkening international sky. For House, this was the moment when domestic and international politics came together. The previous day, House had told the president he was glad that the news of a German submarine sinking an American ship, the *Marina,* had not come sooner. *Marina* was only the last of a worrying sequence of merchantmen sunk by submarines.

The inescapable question was whether the Germans had decided to abandon their self-denying concession of May 4, and—if they had—what the United States should do about it. House and McCormick had both been astonished when Wilson had earlier told them, "I do not believe the American people would want me to go to war no matter how many Americans were lost at sea."[14] He went on to argue that sinking merchant ships was somehow less serious than sinking passenger liners. Lansing was appalled. American sailors deserved protection just as much as civilian passengers. He and House briefly discussed whether to send Count Bernstorff home. In spite of his personal liking for the German, House argued that he should go.

Johann von Bernstorff, blond, long-haired, and personable, had been one of the House's visitors at Sunapee in early December, accompanied by his countess, who had just arrived from Germany with a message from the chancellor, Bethmann-Hollweg. (In the countess's absence, many rumors had circulated about Bernstorff's women friends. A British agent even had a photograph of the ambassador, in a bathing suit, his arms round two similarly clad beauties, surreptitiously thrust into his hand.) The message Countess von Bernstorff had been given was that since Field Marshal Paul von Hindenburg had taken over as chief of staff from von Falkenhayn, the chancellor might no longer be able to prevent unbridled submarine warfare. While Countess Bernstorff was on the seas, Bethmann-Hollweg sent her husband a cable telling him to ignore the message.

House and Bernstorff talked for two hours about a wide range of subjects. Although House liked Bernstorff, his trust in him had been abused, not by Bernstorff himself, but by his masters in Berlin.

When war had broken out in August 1914, the five submarine cables that linked Germany to the United States all ran through the English Channel.[15] In the very first hours of the war a British cable ship cut them. The Russians had handed the British the German naval code book, recovered from the body of a drowned sailor. As a result, the British navy cryptographers in the Admiralty in London were able to read some German codes.[16] The Germans could communicate only with their own embassies in the Americas, either by radio from Nauen (near Berlin) to Sayville (on Long Island) or by a circuitous route passing from Stockholm to Buenos Aires and back again, known as the "Swedish roundabout."[17]

In September 1916 Ambassador Bernstorff, keen to maintain his secret contact for peace negotiations through Colonel House, persuaded the colonel to let him have access to American cable facilities. House agreed, so the Germans found themselves using American cables to transmit messages in codes the Americans could not read. The consequences were not at all what either House or Bernstorff had anticipated.

One week after the election, as we have seen, House went to stay at the White House to thrash out the leading issues of the second term. Wilson said he would like to break off diplomatic relations with Germany but wanted to make a peace move first. House said that would look like rewarding Germany for breaking its promise to halt submarine warfare. Wilson asked if House thought he should return to Europe. House said he was willing to go.

Wilson wondered aloud whether he could not have an agreement with the Allies to throw the weight of the United States on their side once they agreed to mediation. House argued that they would only ask what peace terms America favored. When Wilson showed House a draft of his note on peace terms, the colonel found that the president had returned to his favorite theme. He wanted to say that the causes and objects of the war were obscure. House noted that "would have made the Allies frantic with rage" and succeeded in getting the phrase cut out.[18]

On December 20 Wilson sent another note to the belligerents, asking what their peace terms would be. House, still hoping to be able to deliver the peace agreement the president craved, got Bernstorff in mid-January 1917 to say his government was willing to make four certain concessions.

Wilson was still determined to keep out of war and to press for a peace settlement brokered by himself. By the end of 1916 House thought that aim unrealistic. The situation was deadlocked, and the two friends were at loggerheads, when a new player entered the stage, one who was to become House's close friend and ally.

This was Sir William Wiseman, the new head of British intelligence in America.[19] He was thirty-two years old, an investment banker with the firm of Kuhn, Loeb before the war. He had fought as an artillery officer and been gassed in Flanders in 1915. Wiseman could trace his ancestry to one of Henry VIII's courtiers in the sixteenth century, and his title was a hereditary knighthood awarded to an ancestor in 1628. A plump man with a military moustache and an adventurous streak, he had been orphaned at the age of eight. Now married with two young children, Wiseman had represented Cambridge University against Oxford at boxing, written an unsuccessful play, and worked as a reporter on the London *Daily Express* before coming to the United States to speculate in Canadian real estate and Mexican meat.

Wiseman had been sent across the Atlantic with a double mission. As head of British intelligence in the United States, his brief was to investigate activities directed against British interests by German, Irish, and Indian groups, among others. But he was also in effect London's ambassador to Colonel House and through him a back channel to the president; this unofficial position reflected the widespread irritation felt in both London and Washington with the official British ambassador, the charming but difficult Sir Cecil Spring-Rice. On December 17 House recorded in his diary that "Sir William Wiseman came with a letter of introduction from the British ambassador. He proved to be the most important caller I have had for some time." Wiseman had been asked to find out what Germany's peace terms were. House told him that he would find out from Bernstorff. By January 15, 1917, House and Wiseman were having a remarkably frank conversation in which Wiseman criticized his own ambassador while House pressed his favorite topic, the freedom of the seas.

Very quickly Wiseman became a great favorite of House. The Asquith Liberal government in Britain had fallen in early December 1916, replaced by a bipartisan government headed by David Lloyd George. House's closest political friend in London, Sir Edward Grey, had left office and was replaced by the Conservative, Arthur James Balfour. Wiseman, a Conservative with decidedly liberal views, was a providential conduit to Balfour.

On December 20 Wilson sent House a draft of the note he proposed to send to Berlin. Once again it contained a sentence claiming ignorance of what the Allies were fighting for. House said it would "enrage" the Allies. "He seems obsessed with that thought," was House's comment, "and he cannot write or talk on the subject of the war without voicing it." House added that Wilson "has nearly destroyed all the work I have done in Europe."[20]

In the meantime House was receiving upbeat reports from his pacifist friends and agents in Britain stressing how much sympathy there was for Wilsonian intervention. But these were the views of the liberal Left. Other informants stressed how unpopular the president was. Music hall comedians in London got a big laugh when they called an unexploded shell a "Wilson." House's pro-American Irish friend, Sir Horace Plunkett, pointed out that British working men, speaking through their union leaders, were clear about what they were fighting for: there could be no liberty in Europe until German autocracy had been shown to fail.[21] Wiseman too reported strong demands in England for British propaganda in America to explain why Britain was fighting.

On January 3, 1917, House went down to Washington for what he subsequently called the pleasantest and certainly one of the most important of his long series of meetings with Wilson. The president asked him what he thought of the idea of outlining in a speech the general terms of what he thought a postwar settlement should be. The keynote would be the future security of the world against war, and "territorial adjustments" would be subordinate. Wilson would start by stating the principle that nations had the right to determine under what government they should continue to live. Then House and Wilson sat down to cases, for all the world like two old European diplomats trading provinces. Belgium and Serbia should be restored. Poland should be free. "Alsace and Lorraine we were not quite certain of, but we agreed that Turkey should cease to exist." House said Russia should have a warm seaport. In such ways were the fates of empires determined in the upstairs sitting room of the White House. House was delighted, all the more so because he felt that Wilson's idea of putting forward terms was his own suggestion, made a week earlier to Wilson and to Bernstorff.[22]

Before Wilson could make his speech, William "Billy" Phillips at the State Department phoned to say that Bernstorff had asked permission to use American facilities to send a 1000-group coded message. That was exceptionally long, and it was as fateful as it was long.[23] The secretary of state, who did not believe in the possibility of peace negotiations at this late stage, disapproved. On several occasions Lansing refused to allow the Germans to use the U.S. transmission facility, only to be ordered to do so by House or Wilson. On January 24 Wilson wrote House that if the State Department continued to forward Bernstorff's messages to Berlin, Germany would know that he was working for peace. It does not seem to have occurred to either man that the channel could be used for messages in the other direction—from Berlin to the Americas—and that those messages were not necessarily in the cause of peace. Less than a week later, Berlin used that very method to send a message that was the ominous sound of approaching war for the United States.

Both Wilson and House were taken so completely by surprise in the winter of 1916–1917 partly because they misinterpreted the political meaning of changes in the German military and political command. On August 29, 1916, General Paul von Hindenburg and General Erich von Ludendorff replaced von Falkenhayn at the head of the general staff. On November 22 Arthur Zimmermann became foreign secretary. Zimmermann was not an aristocrat but a hard-working middle-class man who had made his way up through the consular service. American journalists assumed he was a liberal and covered him with praise. Colonel House told Wilson he had always liked Zimmermann, and even the acerbic Gerard called him a warm personal friend. House went so far as to extrapolate to Wilson from Zimmermann's nonaristocratic origins that "the whole government of Germany is now completely in the hands of the liberals."[24] In fact, Zimmermann was no liberal. If his bourgeois origins had any effect on his policies, they made him "more Hohenzollern than the Kaiser,"[25] and incidentally strongly anti-American.

The president and his adviser, meanwhile, were still desperate to reach over the heads of princes and Prussians to tap the supposed pacific instincts of the German people, although as 1916 gave way to 1917 Colonel House was considerably less confident about the prospects for a negotiated peace than the president. House was fully in sympathy with the aim of Wilson's speech to the Senate, given on January 22, 1917, and indeed he saw drafts of it and gave the president his comments and his compliments. There must be, Wilson proclaimed, "not a balance of power, but a community of power. . . . The freedom of the seas is the *sine qua non* of peace." He wanted to extend the Monroe Doctrine to the whole world, so that "every people should be left free to determine its own polity, its own way of development, unhindered, unthreatened, unafraid, the little along with the great and powerful." In the phrase that was to be remembered, he stressed that it must be "a peace without victory."[26]

It was a brave vision, eloquently set forth. But Wilson did not, then or later, attempt to define what he meant by a nation, or a people. Nor did he attempt to reconcile his vision of a concert of nations or peoples, free from what he called "selfishness," with the rather hard-headed dispositions he and Colonel House were already beginning to discuss with both sides in the war.

House continued to share Wilson's dreams. But he was losing faith in the possibility of a negotiated peace. He was losing faith in the Germans and in his friend, their ambassador in Washington. Three days before Wilson's Senate speech, House warned the president that the Germans were "slippery customers." The English might be "stubborn and stupid," but they were reliable. Specifically, he warned Wilson that "the Germans may be manoeuvring to put the Allies in the wrong while they resume unbridled submarine warfare."[27]

House was exactly right. Wilson might reply that "if she will but confide in me and let me have a chance," Germany could have peace.[28] He continued to insist that the German people were peace loving. (Some of them were and some were not.) He refused to accept that the German government was now in the hands of military reactionaries who thought they were winning and saw no reason to give up their gains.

On January 20 Bernstorff changed his tune abruptly. "I am afraid the situation in Berlin is getting out of our hands," he wrote to House. "The exorbitant demands of our enemies, and the insolent language of their note to the President seem to have infuriated public opinion in Germany to such an extent, that the result may be anything but favourable to our peace plans. . . . The answer of our enemies to the President has finished the whole peace movement for a long time to come. . . . My Government may be forced to act accordingly in a very short time."[29]

These might appear to be the ambassador's own thoughts about the situation. There was more to them, however, than met the eye. The previous day Bernstorff had received a telegram from Bethmann-Hollweg informing him in strict confidence that on February 1 German submarines would begin unrestricted warfare against all shipping in a broad zone around Britain and France.[30]

On January 26 House reported to Wilson that Bernstorff had just left him. He said the military now had complete control in Germany, with Hindenburg and Ludendorff at the head. House had asked Bernstorff directly how much power and influence the kaiser had. Bernstorff said he thought the emperor had deliberately left things in Hindenburg's hands. House asked him directly to find out what Germany's terms were. The same day House saw Wiseman, who was cheerful about Wilson's speech. But Wiseman also cabled back to the Foreign Office (unknown to Spring-Rice) the substance of his conversations with House. "A. [House] says the information that he gives me is extremely confidential and comes direct from J. [Wilson]. He may suspect that I cable to you, but I doubt it." He reported that Wilson was ready "to back practically all the Allies' terms, including compensation for invaded factories; expulsion of the Turks from Europe; and a warm seaport, presumably Constantinople, for Russia; also, of course, a really independent Poland."[31]

The next day Wiseman tipped House off that the German and Austrian consulates had been busy all night and that the Germans were "planning to do something with the interned ships," presumably to try to take them to sea. House, on his way to a dinner at the Plaza, telephoned Dudley Field Malone in time for him to order precautions.[32] Bernstorff meanwhile passed on to Arthur Zimmermann the gist of his talks with House. Wilson still hoped that Germany would declare its peace conditions, the ambassador thought. But "if submarine warfare is now begun without further ado, the President will take this as a slap in the face and war with the United States cannot be avoided."[33]

On February 1, in spite of Bernstorff's direct warning, the submarine war began again. In the meantime Bernstorff had come up with a letter which said only what terms the German government would have been willing to accept as a basis for entering negotiations if "our enemies had accepted our offer of December 12." The terms were miserly.[34] Even Wilson agreed that the offer was "perfectly shallow." He spoke of Germany as "a madman that should be curbed."[35] House, now openly in favor of war, asked if it was fair to the Allies to ask them to do the curbing without the United States doing its share. The president winced. But he still insisted that the United States must keep out of the war.

Robert Lansing described how Bernstorff had entered his office at ten past four on the afternoon of February 4: "Though he moved with his usual springy step, he did not smile with his customary assurance." After shaking hands, he fished out three papers from an envelope. He asked whether Lansing wanted him to read them out loud. No, said Lansing, he would read them himself. As he read, he realized the message would bring on the gravest crisis the government had had to face. Lansing sent Wilson a blunt memo that spoke of "deceit" and suggested the president should sever diplomatic relations with Germany.[36]

Now, after all Wilson's dreams of peace and all House's patient efforts to seek common ground, the United States and Germany were sailing toward war. House wrote what sounded like a final letter to Bernstorff. Bernstorff wrote thanking House for his friendship.

Yet even at this last minute, when House and Lansing—not to mention many in the press and on Capitol Hill—could see no alternative but war, Wilson stepped back. On February 3 he addressed a joint session of Congress. He made the fairly astonishing statement that "I refuse to believe that it is the intention of the German authorities to do in fact what they have warned us they will feel at liberty to do."[37] Once again, he distinguished between the German government and the German people. And once again he repeated that the United States had no selfish ends. He did not declare war.

On February 26 Frank Lyon Polk telephoned House to say that the State Department had "obtained a dispatch which Zimmermann had sent to Bernstorff on January 19."

When Secretary Lansing returned from a long weekend out of town on Tuesday, February 27, William Phillips handed him a confidential telegram received from London the day before. It was the English translation of a telegram from Arthur Zimmermann, the German state secretary for foreign affairs, to the German minister at Mexico City. The message had been intercepted by British naval intelligence and decoded in Admiral Sir Reginald "Blinker" Hall's Room 40 code-breaking section. Hall took the cable to Balfour, and Balfour gave it to American ambassador Page.

Lansing went to the White House, where the president doubted the telegram's authenticity on the grounds that secret communications between Berlin and its Washington embassy were closed. Lansing explained that when Bernstorff was trying at Colonel House's insistence to find out Germany's peace terms, the State Department had reluctantly allowed him to use the American embassy's line. On January 17 a long message arrived from Berlin and was delivered to the ambassador on January 18. On January 19 it was sent on to Mexico. Wilson several times during Lansing's explanation exclaimed, "Good Lord!"

Any doubt as to the message's authenticity was removed when Zimmermann, foolishly, acknowledged that it was genuine. On the evening of February 28 Lansing briefed the Associated Press on the content of the intercepted message. The next morning, March 1, the message was published in the papers and created a sensation. The secretary of state fielded the journalists' queries and, in order to protect the British Admiralty's code-breaking secret, contrived to give the impression that the document had been obtained from a spy. The text, thus decoded, translated, and authenticated, was short but devastating.

> Berlin, January 19, 1917
>
> We intend to begin on the first of February unrestricted submarine warfare. We shall endeavor in spite of this to keep the United States of America neutral. In the event of this not succeeding, we make Mexico a proposal of alliance on the following basis: Make war together, make peace together, generous financial support and an understanding on our part that Mexico is to reconquer the lost territory in Texas, New Mexico and Arizona. The settlement in detail is left to you. You will inform the President [of Mexico] of the above most secretly as soon as the outbreak of war with the United States is certain and add the suggestion that he should, on his own initiative, invite Japan to immediate adherence and at the same time mediate between Japan and ourselves. Please call the President's attention to the fact that the ruthless employment of our submarines now offers the prospect of compelling England in a few months to make peace.
>
> Zimmermann

Here was something! The German government was offering to help Mexico recover the territories—including Texas, New Mexico, and Arizona, and by implication presumably California—signed away after the Mexican War in 1846. And asking Japan, the Yellow Peril of the kaiser's fears, to help Mexico do the deed!

It was not quite so fantastic as it sounds to our ears now. Mexico was in turmoil and had come close to war with the United States on more than one occasion since 1913. German investments and influence in Mexico were considerable. Some leaders in Japan resented perceived slurs on Japanese immigrants in the West and dreamed of replacing American power in the Pacific. American military forces were a fraction of what they would become even a year later, and the former Mexican territories in the Southwest were still sparsely populated. It was a low blow and a shocking breach of international comity. But it was not entirely irrational.

The day after the Associated Press carried the text of the telegram, House was inundated with callers, many of them journalists. Roy Howard of the United Press was upset that the Associated Press had been give a "beat," and House wrote to the president, asking that the United Press be given the next big exclusive. So did the colonel water his relationships with influential journalists: one never knew when one might need them.

On March 3 the Houses were back at the White House for the inauguration. The colonel had a confidential talk with Mrs. Wilson, who said how much she disliked McAdoo, the president's son-in-law as well as his treasury secretary. She alluded to the malicious joke we noted in chapter 1: the new way to spell Lansing was H-o-u-s-e. House said Lansing was unaffected by such talk: he was "a pretty big fellow in that way and does not seem to be disturbed by jealousy."[38]

Inauguration Day, March 4, was dark and gloomy, with floods of rain. The following day Wilson suggested that they drive through the streets to see the illuminations. House thought this rather a risky adventure. There were Secret Service men in a following car, but none in the president's own car. House sat "with my automatic in my hands ready to act if the occasion arose."[39]

In mid-March, House was greatly concerned by the news from Russia, where the first revolution was taking place. The czar abdicated on March 16 (by the Western calendar). House confessed in his diary that ever since the war had begun, he had been afraid of the consequences if "bureaucratic Russia and autocratic Germany" were to join up together. He admitted that throughout the war he had been afraid of the consequences if "Prussia" won. He was sure that the pendulum would swing back and that the people would finally rule, but he feared that the world would have to go down a long and bloody road first. "Now that Russia bids fair to be free," he said, "one sees more hope for democracy and human liberty than ever before."[40]

House's (short-lived) optimism about Russia set off a rare reflection on his own political philosophy in his diary. It reveals that he thought of himself as not merely President Wilson's helper, but also to some degree his guide.

> My whole life work has been directed toward the unfortunate many without equal opportunity, and their bitter struggle for existence. Everything I have done, or have tried to do, has been with this end in view. I stood back of every liberal movement, both in Texas and in the Nation, which seemed rational and headed in the right direction. Sometimes I have feared that other zealous friends of progress might go too fast and cause a reaction which would be difficult to overcome. I have advised moderation, but have always pushed in the same direction.
>
> *Philip Dru* expresses my thought and aspirations and, at every opportunity, I have tried to press rulers, public men and those influencing public opinion in that direction. Perhaps the most valuable work I have done in this direction has been in influencing the President. I began with him before he became President and I have never relaxed my efforts. At every turn, I have stirred his ambition to become the great liberal leader of the world.[41]

Events were in the saddle now with a vengeance. On March 27 House took the 11:08 a.m. train to Washington. It was now, even for Wilson, only a question of how the thing should be done. As soon as House arrived, Wilson asked him whether he should ask Congress to declare war or tell Congress that a state of war existed and ask for the means to carry it on. House advised the latter. He was afraid of an acrimonious debate if the issue was left to Congress. Thinking ahead as ever, House told Wilson that the worst crisis of his administration had arrived. He should meet it in such a creditable way that his influence would not be lessened when he came to do the great work he would have to do after the war. Wilson said he did not think he was fit for the presidency in war. House privately agreed, as he put it in his diary, that Wilson was "too refined, too civilized, too intellectual, too cultivated not to see the incongruity and absurdity of war" and that it needed a man of "coarser fiber and one less of a philosopher than he."[42] He did not say so, of course. Instead he tried—and Edith Wilson told him later that he had succeeded—to persuade the uncertain chief executive that he had met tougher tests in the past.

House and Wilson went on to discuss the organization of the White House and the personalities of the administration. House argued that the president needed a second secretary. House tried to use the coming of war to get rid of Josephus Daniels, at Navy, whom he had never liked, and Newton D. Baker at the War Department. House was surprised by the president's animus against Lansing. House also tried, through Mrs. Wilson, to persuade the president to reach out to the Republicans, arguing that it would have a good effect if he were seen to be consulting the likes of Elihu Root, Charles Evans Hughes, and Henry Cabot Lodge.

House went back to New York for a few days. By April 2 he was back at the White House. Neither Lansing nor Polk nor any cabinet member knew what the president would say in a scheduled address. House knew, but he was keen to hide the fact that he knew. House wondered in his diary how much of his speech the president thought he, House, had suggested. "I think it is quite possible," he commented "that he forgets from what source he receives ideas and suggestions."[43]

At twenty to nine on the evening of April 2 Woodrow Wilson finally reached the point he had never wanted to reach. With "a profound sense of the solemn and even tragical character of the step I am taking," he called on the Congress to declare that "the course of the German government was nothing less than war against the government and people of the United States." Neutrality was no longer either feasible or desirable. But the United States had no quarrel, Wilson insisted yet again, with the German people. He returned to his twin favorite themes, the incompatibility of war with democracy and the purity of American motives. In a famous phrase he proclaimed that "the world must be made safe for democracy."[44]

Now the drift was over. Wilson and House still hoped that the war might lead to the building of a better world. But first it had to be won.

11   1917   ∾

THE YEAR 1917 WAS the supreme test for Europe. Of the seven European "Great Powers," four—Russia, Austria/Hungary, the Ottoman Empire, and Germany—were under such strain that their regimes, economies, and military capability eventually collapsed, though at first Germany seemed strengthened by the Russian Revolution. The three Western and relatively democratic societies—Britain, France, and Italy—were each grievously tried.

Collapse was most dramatic in Russia, where the czar abdicated in March and the parliamentary Kerensky government was swept away by the October Revolution. Imperial Germany still looked formidable, though in reality both the military machine and the society that sustained it were close to cracking. The "betrayed revolution" of 1918–1919 was just ahead.[1] Turkey was as much on the brink of dissolution as Russia.[2] The Ottoman dynasty was on the eve of being overthrown. The Austro-Hungarian dual monarchy, the great Habsburg empire whose historic achievement had been to save Europe from Islam, was tottering to its fall.[3] The Poles in Galicia; the Czechs and Slovaks in Bohemia, Moravia, and Slovakia; and the South Slavs in Croatia and Slovenia were all on the verge of open mutiny.

The great cities of northern Italy were shaken by industrial strife, and the Italian government was in crisis.[4] Just before the Russian Revolution, the thin crust of the Italian front in the northeastern Alps cracked at Caporetto in a defeat as total as any in the war. After the great but savagely costly victory at Verdun, mutinies in the French army meant that France might drop out of the line at any time, while Britain risked being slowly throttled by German submarine warfare. Britain's Indian empire was on fire with dreams of independence, and Ireland was on the point of seizing its freedom. Only America was growing stronger as the Wilson administration decided at last to build a great navy and then to recruit and train an army that grew from one hundred thousand to 4 million in eighteen months.[5]

Structures that had lasted for centuries had been softened by the hammering and shaking of modern war to the point where anything could happen. The volcanic bubbling and cracking the war created was not confined to Europe. British and German soldiers fought in remote corners of Africa, while British Indian armies marched through what are now Iraq and Palestine and others shivered in trenches in France. In the Near East, the Ottoman Empire crumbled like baked brick into dust, but Islam was alive again with the caliphate movement and the Arab revolt. The Zionists won the opportunity to create a national home for the Jewish people. Britain and France each tried to build new client states in the Middle East. China and Mexico were separately in the grip of revolution. The whole world seemed simultaneously on fire.

The impact of these cataclysms was felt nowhere more incongruously than in a small apartment on East 53rd Street in Manhattan, in the crowded study of the quiet amateur who had gathered so many of the threads of revolutionary change in his hands. In the intervals of dangerous voyages through seas infested with German submarines and conferences with the mighty, the Houses lived the cosy domesticity of a comfortable middle-aged couple with a taste for dining out and attending undemanding comedies of manners at the theatre. Yet Colonel House's life in the war years was mobilized. The little apartment was the headquarters of one of the most remarkable intelligence services ever put together by a private individual.

Years later, after the war, House told a visitor about some of the practical implications of the part he had been asked by the president to play.[6] Details that could easily be settled, he said, were left to be dealt with in the State Department, and House had his friends and agents there, including the department's counsellor, Frank Lyon Polk; his own son-in-law, Gordon Auchincloss; and Auchincloss's law partner, David Hunter Miller. House in effect had his own diplomatic service, with friends reporting informally to him from Paris, London, and Petrograd. A whole corps of newspaper men kept him in touch with radical and revolutionary politics.[7]

From them, House learned of what Pancho Villa and his men felt along the Rio Grande and of the state of mind of Social Democrat members of the Reichstag in Berlin and shop stewards in Glasgow.[8]

Through his friend Wiseman, House had a direct channel to the British foreign secretary, A. J. Balfour.[9] House had excellent sources on Wall Street who could keep him in touch with the financial straits of the Allies, while through his friend Dudley Malone and others he could reach out in the direction of Tammany Hall, the Roman Catholic Church in America, and the more secretive elements in the New York police department. New York publishers, Democratic politicians across the United States, hostesses in London and Paris, neutral diplomats, and occasional windfalls (like the kaiser's dentist who came to lunch, to be treated with polite suspicion)—all added their grains to the colonel's hoard of miscellaneous information. There was no one who knew better how to mine such rich deposits of human intelligence, even though there were vital areas, such as the internal politics of Germany or Russia, where the colonel's grasp of fast-moving realities was shaky.

House's correspondence, in the days when letters had either to be dictated and typed or written in longhand by the colonel himself, was indeed "excessively large."[10] Yet there were no filing cabinets in the little apartment and no safes to store even the most confidential documents, and House daily received cables and letters whose disclosure could affect the course of the war. So every evening Fanny Denton took the most sensitive documents to a bank vault; they were hidden in a large muff, which also concealed a revolver she had learned to use in Texas.

House had two private telephone wires from Washington, one to midtown Manhattan and the other to his summer home in Magnolia, Massachusetts. He took certain cloak-and-dagger precautions. When he went to Washington, he was carefully shadowed by agents of the Secret Service. On his trips to Europe both American G-men and British Secret Service men watched his back, except in the German Reich, when very visible plainclothesmen would take over. The British were especially careful about covering their tracks. The British naval attaché, Commodore Guy Gaunt, would take the subway, then a cab, then the elevated, and would never go to House's apartment if, at any station where he got off, anyone else got off too. It was not the British, however, but Justice's Bureau of Investigation that (to House's annoyance) had recording machines installed in his apartment and in a cottage at Magnolia. The conversations House had with his friend Count Bernstorff, for example, were regularly recorded.

Wilson had found two vital jobs for House: to maintain contact with the British and to organize American thinking about how the war's ending might fit in with Wilson's and House's dream of lasting world peace.

Immediately after Wilson called on Congress to declare war, both the British and the French sent high-level missions to Washington. The British delegation was led by the foreign secretary, the former Conservative prime minister A. J. Balfour. The French delegation was headed by Marshal Joseph Joffre, accompanied by another former prime minister, René Viviani. As Balfour put it, "America had just entered the war. This raised innumerable questions of the first importance, and of the utmost variety—naval, military, financial and international. Opportunity for personal intercourse had become necessary if they were to be successfully solved."[11]

On April 22 in New York, House advised Balfour not to minimize the Allies' difficulties, but if anything to exaggerate them. He urged him not to discuss peace terms; the first order of business was to win the war. House also maintained contact with the French delegation, through Henri Bergson, the famous philosopher, who spoke good English.[12]

Wilson was absolutely determined that the peace would be something utterly different from what he saw as the cynical deal making of traditional diplomacy. But both House and Wilson understood that any peace settlement would have to satisfy the very concrete interests for which the nations were fighting. There was no point in telling the French to give up their hope of recovering Alsace-Lorraine; too many Frenchmen had died for that.

The discussions placed at the very center of the table the delicate matter of the "secret treaties" between Britain, France, Italy, Russia, Romania, and Japan. House knew of their existence and had a good idea of their content, and so did other well-informed American diplomats and journalists. House insisted in his talks with Balfour that he should let Washington see the secret treaties, and—perhaps to House's surprise—Balfour agreed.

On April 28 House settled down with Balfour in front of a large map of Europe and Asia Minor at the Washington home of Breckinridge Long, the assistant secretary of state, to talk business in detail.[13] They quickly agreed that Alsace-Lorraine must go to France and that the territories of France, Belgium, and Serbia must be restored. Poland (which had been divided between Russia, Prussia, and Austria since the Partitions in the late eighteenth century) must be united. They saw no difficulty in rewarding Romania for joining the Allies with a small portion of Russian and a larger slice of Hungarian territory, both supposedly inhabited by ethnic Romanians. Then they talked about Italy's ambitions in Dalmatia, on the eastern side of the Adriatic.

This gave House his opportunity to ask for copies of the treaties. Balfour thought the request reasonable, though he was not sure whether or not copies were in the mission's baggage. He promised to make sure that House got copies. Finally, they discussed the postwar fate of the Ottoman Empire beyond the Straits. Balfour admitted that the British had Mesopotamia (Iraq) and its oil in their sights; the French wanted Syria and Lebanon, while the Italians and also the Greeks wanted territory in Anatolia, or Turkey proper. "It is all bad," House commented in his diary, "and I told Balfour so. They are making it a breeding place for future wars."[14] He was right.

The British foreign secretary stayed in Washington until mid-May, and on May 13, on his way to Canada, he came to lunch with House, who showed he had been thinking ahead. How would Balfour react, he asked, if the Germans made an offer of peace on the basis of the status quo? Balfour thought this would happen only if Germany was failing. House pointed out that the same might be true of Russia, Italy, and even France.

When he reported on the meeting to Wilson, he said little of their discussion of the specifics of the postwar settlement.[15] Already it was clear that House was more willing than Wilson to get into the details of what the victorious Allies would want to get out of the war. House said nothing at all of an even more delicate matter that had arisen in the conversation and that Balfour immediately reported to Lloyd George. The United States, Balfour had pointed out, was building battleships that would be of no use against Germany at the expense of the destroyers that were needed to protect merchant shipping against U-boats. How would the British respond, House asked, if the United States were to stop building capital ships (battleships and battle cruisers) in return for a guarantee that the British would let them have capital ships in case of need? House then suggested a defensive alliance at sea between Britain and the United States. Of course the Japanese would be annoyed, Lloyd George said when he heard of the proposal, but personally he rather liked the idea.

A couple of days later Balfour's diplomat colleague, Sir Eric Drummond, came to spend two days with Colonel House to nail down the matters raised in the Balfour talks. Even now House "tried to pin him and Balfour down" on the Allies' minimum terms for ending the war. House urged on Drummond the idea, long cherished by House and Wilson alike, that the United States and Britain should help the German liberals against their own government by announcing that they would not deal with "a military caste that is in no way representative of the German people." They would, however, exclude the kaiser from this ban because of his strong personal following in Germany.[16] Already high ideals and practical political considerations were getting awkwardly confused.

Later the question was raised whether Balfour had been frank about the secret treaties. Ray Stannard Baker, in his biography of Wilson, stated that Wilson was kept in ignorance of them by Colonel House.[17] Both Balfour and House denied this allegation. In a private letter to House on July 17, 1922, Balfour stated that Baker "was certainly wrong in his statement that Mr. Wilson was kept in ignorance by me of the secret treaties."[18] In fact on January 30, 1918, Balfour wrote to the president as follows:

> My dear Mr. President:
>
> I gather from a message sent by Wiseman that you would like to know my thoughts on the Italian territorial claims under the Treaty of London. . . . That Treaty . . . bears on the face of it evident proof of the anxiety of the Allies to get Italy into the war. . . . But a treaty is a treaty and we . . . are bound to uphold it in letter and in spirit. The objections to it indeed are obvious enough: It assigns to Italy territories on the Adriatic which are not Italian but Slav; and the arrangement is justified not on grounds of nationality but on grounds of strategy.
>
> Now I do not suggest that we should rule out such arguments with a pedantic consistency. Strong frontiers make for peace. . . . Personally, however I am in doubt whether Italy would really be strengthened by the acquisition of all her Adriatic claims; and in any case it does not seem probable that she will endeavor to prolong the war in order to obtain them.[19]

In 1928, less than two years before his death, Balfour told his niece and biographer, Blanche Dugdale, that House had "blown to pieces" the story that he had never told Wilson about the secret treaties. "I was bound to tell him. But it was a very delicate business, for of course they *were* secret. The way I got over it was to tell him about them *as* a secret—as man to man. I told him personally."[20] In fact, on May 18 Balfour did send Wilson the texts of what he called "the various agreements which Great Britain has come to with the Allied Powers."[21]

By the end of May, House was taking a more militant line toward Germany. "It is, I think, evident that the German Military Clique have no intention of making peace upon any other basis than that of conquest." He advised Wilson to say so.[22] Wilson agreed that the present military masters of Germany "meant to take a gambler's chance, stand pat if they win, yield a parliamentary government if they lose."[23] He wanted to say just that in a speech, perhaps on Flag Day. He asked House, as one who was closer in touch with Europe, for his advice. On June 5, House sent it. He thought a Flag Day speech would be right and suggested that Wilson "get the world on tip-toe beforehand, and then arrange to have what you say cabled to the ends of the earth."[24] House had a far stronger grasp than Wilson of public relations. He advised Wilson to ignore the kaiser, to accelerate liberalism in Germany, and to take care that the French and the Italians did not see a threat to their hopes of recovering Alsace-Lorraine and the Trentino. The two main points Wilson should stress were imperial Prussia's purpose of conquest and the unwillingness of the democracies to negotiate with a military autocracy.

Some historians have portrayed House as little more than a courtier, ever avid to say what he thought Wilson wanted to hear. The Flag Day speech, given on a rain-soaked mall in Washington on June 14, 1917, is evidence that this view underestimates Wilson's need for House's intellectual support and his willingness to follow House's advice. The speech took House's suggestions and clothed them in Wilson's inimitable prose, at once eloquent and grandiloquent. House could not have written, let alone delivered, such a speech. But Wilson, on this and other important occasions, turned to House to be told what he should say.

The British government sent to Washington, as head of the British war mission, the brilliant but exceedingly difficult newspaper publisher Alfred Harmsworth, ennobled as Lord Northcliffe. He owned *The Times* of London and the *Daily Mail,* among many other publications. House had been opposed to Northcliffe's appointment, but with his usual gift for personal relations, he got on better with him than he had expected. House invited Spring-Rice and Wiseman up to Magnolia to discuss how to deal with Northcliffe. Almost immediately Northcliffe panicked over the British financial situation. On June 29 Balfour, spooked by the horror stories he was hearing, sent House a message that "we seem to be on the verge of a financial disaster."[25] Wiseman, on House's prompting, reassured Balfour through the head of the Foreign Office, Sir Eric Drummond, and House calmed down President Wilson.[26] It turned out that the British needed to pay "$35,000,000 on Monday, $100,000,000 on Thursday and $185,000,000 a month for two months beginning ten days from next Thursday." This was, as House said, "a staggering amount and indicates the load Great Britain has been carrying for her allies."[27]

The financial mess went back to the day after the United States entered the war. That day the House of Morgan, which had advanced just under half of the total of $400 million advanced to Britain by a syndicate of New York and Philadelphia banks, suggested the loan should be taken over by a public sector purchasing agency. The British government was slow to do so, in part because President Wilson used the loan to emphasize to the British how dependent they were. In the first three and a half months after the United States entered the war, it advanced £139 million (roughly $700 million) to Britain and £90 million ($450 million) to the other Allies, mainly France and Russia. Britain had lent £193 million (almost $1 billion with the British pound worth roughly $5) to the other Allies.

On June 30 House confided to his diary that Britain and France should have let the United States know how desperate they were.[28] Given the lofty indifference the president had shown to the Allies' cause, the comment was perhaps naïve. But House certainly made up for it by the energy with which he tried to help the British, assisted by his friend Sir William Wiseman. Nothing in House's wartime role is more remarkable than the way he coolly used Wiseman, who was after all the head of the British Secret Service in America, as his personal agent.

By the late summer, Northcliffe was still close to panic about money. "If loan stops," he cabled Balfour, "war stops."[29] House had given him a stern lecture on the realities of congressional politics. "House said," Northcliffe cabled Lloyd George, "that the whole forthcoming winter would be spent in congressional wrangling about finance, and for this reason McAdoo must be in a position to make perfectly clear that the money of the people of the United States was not being used for the benefit of . . . Wall Street and the Money Power to which the Democracy so strongly objects."[30]

House would have preferred to spend the summer mounting a diplomatic campaign to appeal over the heads of the German government to the German people. Instead he spent a good deal of time and energy on the alarming financial relations between the Allies and the new associated power. He spent five hours with the treasury secretary, McAdoo, at Magnolia in the last week in July, and then four days with Northcliffe there in the second week of August. He also arranged for Northcliffe to meet Benjamin Strong, the governor of the Federal Reserve. By July 11 he was able to tell the president "everything seems on the road to an amicable adjustment."[31]

This assessment was perhaps premature. It was not until late August that an inter-allied purchasing commission was set up in Washington to take over the functions previously carried out by the J. P. Morgan firm as the British government's agent in the United States. The commission ironed out most of the difficulties in the purchase of American munitions. At the same time the British government sent Lord Reading, a close friend of Lloyd George and a respected financial expert, with authority to negotiate financial arrangements. Colonel House, at the direct request of the British government and without consulting President Wilson, urged the immediate dispatch of Reading. After the war Sir William Wiseman commented that it was "a truly remarkable tribute to both the wisdom and discretion of Colonel House, that a foreign government should seek his advice upon so important and delicate a problem."[32]

House still found time to promote one diplomatic venture and to advise the president about another. On July 15 he wrote to his friend Frank Cobb, editor of the *New York World,* reminding him that he had already suggested through Wiseman that the *World* should challenge the leading Berlin newspaper, the *Tageblatt,* to a debate. Twice a week the *World* would allow the *Tageblatt* to present "the German side of the controversy" if in return the *Tageblatt* would publish a piece twice a week from the *World.* The idea, of course, was right in line with Wilson's, and House's, conviction that if only America's position were explained to the German people, the war could end. Cobb was willing, but Wilson pointed out that it would amount to the beginning of peace parleys.

In the summer of 1917 peace moves of various kinds were in the air. Neither Wilson nor House fully understood what was going on, though House's view, even if it wobbled somewhat, was clearer than Wilson's. House, after all, had some knowledge of European politics and some of the players. Wilson had, and apparently wanted to have, none.

Even in Germany, there were stirrings for peace. In July 1917 the Reichstag voted 212 to 126 for a resolution, promoted by Matthias Erzberger of the Roman Catholic Center Party, that "the Reichstag strives for a peace of understanding and the permanent reconciliation of the peoples. With such a peace forced acquisitions of territory and political, economic or financial oppressions are inconsistent."[33] Neither Wilson nor House seems to have understood that the Reichstag was not an independent component of a democratic constitutional system, like Congress, nor a sovereign body, like the British Parliament. It might sometimes be allowed to express discontent with the government's policies. That was all. The government of Germany was in the hands of Ludendorff, Hindenburg, and Tirpitz.

The principal significance of the Reichstag's peace resolution was as a move in

German domestic politics. It was also part of the feeble attempts of the new Austrian emperor, Karl, and his minister, Count Ottokar Czernin, to free themselves from German domination. Czernin had written as early as April 2 that by autumn an end had to be put to the war at all costs. Czernin wanted to put pressure on the Germans for a general peace. That was what Erzberger and the parliamentarians who voted for his resolution had in mind. The principal consequence of the Reichstag resolution was the dismissal of the German chancellor, Bethmann-Hollweg, and his replacement by a nonpolitical civil servant, Georg Michaelis, who was even more totally controlled by Ludendorff than Bethmann.

Wilson and House believed that the war had been imposed on the peoples of Europe by the monarchies and their aristocracies. Now by a supreme irony they were suddenly confronted by a conspiracy for peace, mounted by the proudest of European monarchs, working through the very heart of the European aristocracy.

On November 21, 1916, the emperor Franz-Josef had died after sixty-eight years on the throne. His successor, Karl, issued a proclamation that he would do everything to give back to his peoples the lost blessings of peace. The emperor's motives were mixed. He hated war, but he also disliked the House of Hohenzollern, who had destroyed his family's primacy in Germany at Sadowa in 1866. He also saw that peace might be the only hope of hanging on to some of the Habsburg possessions that were peeling away with every passing month. So he set about using his family's extraordinary network of contacts among the rulers of Europe to do something rather similar, in the hope of preserving the old regime, to what Woodrow Wilson wanted to do in order to destroy it.

The new emperor's mother, sister of the last king of Saxony, was a pious Catholic and disliked the Hohenzollern emperors of Germany because they were Lutherans. His wife, Empress Zita, was the sister of the princes of Bourbon-Parma, who were fighting as officers in the Belgian army. From early December 1916, the new emperor of Austria contacted his brothers-in-law through their mother, the dowager duchess of Parma. On more than one occasion one of the brothers, Prince Sixte, met an emissary of the Austrian emperor secretly in Switzerland. He told the president of the French Republic, Raymond Poincaré, and the director of the foreign ministry, Jules Cambon, that the emperor was prepared to sign a separate peace treaty on four conditions. Sixte, however, as A. J. P. Taylor observed in a characteristically caustic account of this transaction, "like other amateur diplomats . . . misrepresented the position to both parties. He first drafted the terms which he thought the French likely to accept; submitted them to Poincaré, who did not object to them; and then communicated them to Charles [Emperor Karl] as official French demands. Thus both Charles and the allies thought they were faced with a 'peace offer.' . . . The specific promise of a separate peace was made only by Sixte, not by Charles."[34]

In this desperate effort to end the war before his vast and ancient possessions finally melted away, the Austrian emperor was able to deploy no lesser personages than the Pope and the king of Spain. On August 1, 1917, the Pope sent a note to the belligerents. It proposed an end to the war on the basis of the status quo ante. It also called for disarmament and international arbitration of future conflicts.

House thought it would be a mistake to dismiss the Pope's proposal out of hand. That would discourage the German liberals, of whom he still had exaggerated hopes. It might also tip Russia into suing for peace. It was more important, House wrote Wilson on August 15, "that Russia should weld herself into a virile republic than it is that Germany should be beaten to her knees." He was also keen to avoid the dismemberment of Turkey. He therefore advised Wilson to "throw the onus on Prussia."[35]

Three days later House passed on to Balfour Wilson's response: a flat refusal to consider the Pope's proposal. "The present government of Germany is morally bankrupt," he said, and . . . the world will be upon quicksand . . . until it can believe that it is dealing with a responsible government."[36] Wilson's instinct was simply to ignore the Pope's letter. (He was not free from traditional Presbyterian suspicions of Rome.) House thought this stance was a mistake. The Pope's letter, properly handled, was an opening for the president to press his own strategy: he should appeal to the German people—in this case the substantial Catholic minority in Germany—against their rulers.

Wilson now had an opportunity, House argued, to take the peace negotiations out of the Pope's hands into his own.[37] Things might be going badly for the Allies, but Germany was in a worse condition. Wilson ought to make a statement that would bring forth an upheaval in Germany and at the same time reassure moderate Germans that they had nothing to fear from an American peace. That would also strengthen the hands of the Russian liberals.

The liberal government in Russia already believed the Allies had made a mistake by refusing passports to British, French, and American pacifists to attend a Stockholm peace conference. If the Allies simply brushed aside the Pope's mediation, it would cause the downfall of the Russian government. House urged Wilson to say that he would deal with a representative government in Germany so that the Germans could "return to the brotherhood of nations."[38]

House also attempted to intervene, through Dudley Field Malone, with the

Roman Catholic Church. He asked Malone to suggest to the "Papal delegate at Washington that the Pope answer any inquiry concerning the President's reply to his peace message by saying that he did not believe the President had closed the door to peace, but rather had indicated a way by which it might be opened." His purpose, House explained in his diary, was "first to unite Austria and Catholic Germany in favor of the legislative reforms which the President made as a require-ment for peace negotiations. Second, to leave the door open for further discus-sion."[39] This démarche came to nothing because Malone, another amateur diplo-mat, who had been asked to make the suggestion as his own, presented it, to House's annoyance, as coming from the president.

Once again Wilson turned to House for advice on how to respond to the Pope's peace proposal. He sent a draft of his reply up to House at Magnolia, with the acknowledgment that "the many useful suggestions you have made were in my mind all the time I wrote," and he added a note of personal friendship: "I think of you every day with the deepest affection." Wilson refused to deal with the present government of Germany and promised instead to deal with "the great peoples of the Central Powers."[40] House managed to read Wilson's draft and return it by the overnight mail so that it would arrive in Washington by the next morning, thanks to the personal attention of the postmaster of Boston. House pointed out that the British and the French would not like Wilson's saying that "the dismemberment of empires . . . we deem childish."[41] House agreed that America ought not to fight for "the old, narrow and selfish order of things," but he stuck to his guns and sent another note the next day urging Wilson to take out "childish."[42] Wilson sub-stituted "inexpedient." House was careful to let Balfour know of this small but useful victory. The episode shows very clearly how much Wilson relied on House's judgment, to the extent of allowing him to pencil edit the state papers of a states-man not free from vanity about his style.

Early in September Wilson gave two further proofs of his reliance on House's counsel. On September 2 he wrote to House saying it was time "to go systematically to work" to find out what the belligerents would want in the final peace settlement so as to decide what the American position should be.[43] He asked House to get a group of men together for this purpose. This was the origin of what came to be known as the Inquiry, which warrants a chapter of its own. Second, Wilson came by sea on the presidential yacht *Mayflower* to House's seaside summer home to ask his advice about whether to get rid of his secretary of state. On September 8 two Secret Service men called at Magnolia to say that the president would be there the next day on the *Mayflower*.[44] No one knew of his visit, not even the White House. The president and Mrs. Wilson slipped out by the rear entrance, caught a train to New York, and boarded the *Mayflower* there. At eleven o'clock in the morning House had a phone call from the Boston navy yard: *Mayflower* would be in Gloucester harbor at two o'clock. Colonel and Mrs. House went over and took the Wilsons for a two-hour drive, then took them over to see Mrs. Jefferson Coolidge's treasures (inherited from Thomas Jefferson) and returned to dine on the *Mayflower*.

Wilson had come to ask House whether he should ask for Lansing's resignation. He said that every time he wrote a note or put out a statement, Lansing gave it a more conservative construction. The question was embarrassing for House, who was quite content to have Lansing do the department's work and leave House influence over high policy. So he argued against firing Lansing and asked who could do the job better. Wilson mentioned Newton D. Baker, but said he could not spare him from the War Department, and David F. Houston. House suggested making Baker secretary of state and replacing him at the War Department with Frank Polk. Wilson proposed sending Lansing to negotiate with Brazil. House countered by suggesting sending him to London as ambassador. In the end they left the subject with a tentative agreement that Wilson would offer Lansing London.

Wilson revealed one of his many prejudices when he and House were discussing who should be the new chief of staff. House mentioned a certain General Barry. Wilson said he thought well of him but "was unwilling to put an Irish Catholic in that place because his experience with them was that they never recommended anyone for office excepting fellow Catholics."[45]

The next day the two men lunched and talked again. At first they focused on planning for the peace conference. House urged Wilson not to tell Lansing about the Inquiry. He said it would be a mistake to fire Lansing. (House's son-in-law, Gordon Auchincloss, who worked closely with Lansing, defended his boss.)[46] All that was needed was a frank talk, ordering Lansing to leave press statements to others. If that made Lansing resign of his own volition, so much the better.

While the Wilsons enjoyed their brief vacation, House replied to a query from Lord Robert Cecil. "We are being pressed here," Lord Robert wrote House, and House passed the message on to the president on September 4, "for a declaration of sympathy with the Zionist movement, and I should be very grateful if you felt able to ascertain unofficially if the President favors such a declaration."[47]

The background to this deceptively simple inquiry was as complicated as the politics of the Middle East have always been. In the winter of 1915–1916 a British member of Parliament, Sir Mark Sykes, negotiated a secret agreement with a

French foreign ministry official, François Georges Picot; it was reached on January 16, 1916, but not made public for almost two years. The British administration in Cairo had been told that if only the British would strike north from Egypt, an Arab army led by the sheriff (ruler) of Mecca would join them and ignite an Arab revolt against Turkish rule in Palestine and Syria. The Lloyd George government in London saw how strategically important the Middle East would be after the Ottoman Empire had collapsed, both for its oil and as a bridge to British India. The British government had also become concerned about the influence of Zionism, which it considerably exaggerated, in Germany, Russia, and the United States. Key British officials had been persuaded—by Chaim Weizmann (later the first president of Israel) and other British Zionists—to look favorably on the Zionist ideal of a Jewish home in Palestine. One of these was Lord Robert Cecil. Another was Sir Mark Sykes. The Sykes-Picot agreement won French permission for a British offensive in support of the Arab revolt. Once the revolt had taken place, the Middle East was to be divided between Britain and France. The French would rule Lebanon, with Syria as a sphere of influence. Britain would control the Turkish provinces of Baghdad and Basra and have Arabia as a sphere of influence. Both Britain and France wanted Palestine. On February 7, 1917, Weizmann and other British Zionists met Sykes and said they wanted Palestine to be under British rule. The next day Sykes introduced François Georges Picot to Nahum Sokolow, an official of the world Zionist organization, who told Picot that Jews admired France but "had long in mind the suzerainty of the British government." In the end it was agreed that Palestine should be under international administration. Lloyd George, with his Welsh Bible Christian upbringing, was sympathetic to Zionism. He told Weizmann that Palestine "was to him the really interesting part of the war and that the future of Palestine was a matter for Britons and Jews. He ordered the British army in Egypt to launch an offensive northward into Turkish-held Palestine and sent Sykes with its commanding officer as the head of a political mission. At a meeting before Sykes left on April 3, Lloyd George told him to make Palestine part of the British territories in the Middle East after the war.[48]

On June 4 the director of the French foreign ministry, Jules Cambon, made a vague commitment of support for Zionism to Nahum Sokolow in return for the latter's promise to use his influence with Russian Jews to keep Russia in the war. In mid-June Balfour, who admitted to a social prejudice against Jews, was sufficiently convinced by his officials of the need to back the Zionists that he invited Chaim Weizmann to draft language for a written British commitment to a Jewish homeland in Palestine. The project ran into opposition from the three politically powerful Jews in the British cabinet: Rufus Isaacs (Lord Reading), Sir Herbert Samuels, and especially Samuels's cousin, Edwin Montagu. Their standpoint was assimilationist. All had been highly successful in British society. They had little empathy with the Jews of the Ottoman and Russian empires, who had experienced none of the opportunities that had allowed Isaacs and Samuels to succeed brilliantly as lawyers and Montagu's father to make a fortune as a banker. Few Jews anywhere were Zionists before the world war. Montagu, in particular, saw the Jewish homeland as a threat to the position of Jews in Britain; he had been striving all his life to escape from the ghetto, he said.

The Foreign Office and British politicians believed that Jews in Germany, Russia, and also America, were both more influential and more Zionist than in fact they were. So when Lord Robert Cecil inquired of House where Wilson stood on the question of a Jewish homeland in Palestine, it was true that he was personally sympathetic to the Zionist case. But powerful political colleagues did not share his sympathy. And in any case both his and his colleagues' attitudes to the Zionist question were not primarily determined by sympathy or antipathy to Zionism but as one important piece of the larger question of the future of the Middle East after the collapse of the Ottoman Empire. Lloyd George and Balfour were inclined to make a public declaration of their support for a Jewish homeland. But now they were dependent on the goodwill of the American president and of the person through whom they could ascertain his views, Colonel House.

On October 31 the British cabinet authorized Balfour to make his famous declaration, though in a watered down form that bitterly disappointed Weizmann.

> Dear Lord Rothschild [Balfour wrote to the leader of British Jews],
> I have much pleasure in conveying to you, on behalf of His Majesty's Government, the following declaration of sympathy with Jewish Zionist aspirations which has been . . . approved by the Cabinet: "His Majesty's Government view with favour the establishment in Palestine of a national home for the Jewish people, and will use their best endeavors to facilitate the achievement of this object, it being clearly understood that nothing shall be done which may prejudice the civil and religious rights of existing non-Jewish communities in Palestine, or the rights and political status enjoyed by Jews in any other country."

Colonel House understood British motives for supporting Zionism. "The English naturally want the road to Egypt and India blocked," he wrote Wilson in

September 18, "and Lloyd George is not above using us to further this plan."[49] (He meant that he thought London's motive for supporting Zionism was in part that a Jewish state in the Middle East would defend British communications with Egypt and India.) It was not until October 16 that House was able to write that he would let the British government know that the Balfour declaration met with the president's approval.

On September 22 House hurried back from seeing his baby granddaughter to keep an appointment with Justice Louis D. Brandeis and Rabbi Stephen Wise.[50] They had received a cable from Chaim Weizmann (which House had already seen, as it had been intercepted by British intelligence and passed to him by Sir William Wiseman!) asking about American attitudes to the Zionist question. House cautioned Brandeis and Wise against pressing the president for any public statement. He admitted that Wilson was prepared to go further than he, House, thought advisable. He advised the American Zionists to bring the governments of France, Italy, and Russia as close to the British position as they could and leave the matter there.

As it happened, Wilson himself took a long time to come out in favor of a Jewish homeland. He was not especially interested in the Middle East. British sponsorship of Zionism, to Wilson's mind, was yet another example of imperial machinations and the Sykes-Picot agreement just another secret deal of the kind he meant to stamp out.

It was not until the Jewish New Year in September 1918 that Wilson indicated his endorsement of the Balfour declaration in an open letter to the American Jewish community. By then, Colonel House had done many things. He had made another of his visits to wartime London. He had gathered the group of men for the Inquiry into the Allies' war aims and those of the United States. He had also played a crucial part, with the help of some of those men, in defining American aims in the most famous of all Woodrow Wilson's utterances, the Fourteen Points.

12 The Inquiry and the Fourteen Points ∾

Of all Wilson's advisers, Colonel House, armed with the Inquiry memorandum, played perhaps the central role in the conception and composing of the Fourteen Points Address, delivered on January 8, 1918.

—N. Gordon Levin

ON SEPTEMBER 2, 1917, as we saw in chapter 11, Woodrow Wilson wrote to Colonel House asking him to "quietly gather a group of men" to help him study the various powers' war aims.[1] This group was the inception of what came to be called the Inquiry.

To some extent the Inquiry shaped American policy at the peace conference, and it had a direct influence on the Fourteen Points. It also had a lasting influence on the way American foreign policy continues to be shaped—far more than in other democracies—outside both the legislature and the executive branch.

House had had a similar idea in mind for some time. On April 27, House had received a letter from William H. Buckler, who worked for Walter Hines Page in the London embassy: "My regular work having now ceased owing to our breaks with Austria and Turkey," Buckler wrote, "I am thinking of suggesting to Mr. Page that I should 'work up' either the Balkan question or the League of Nations proposals with a view to ultimately 'devilling' for some Delegate at the Peace Conference (say yourself) who might not wish to carry in his own head the multifarious details of these problems."[2]

House knew that in both London and Paris professional diplomats had been hard at work preparing their countries' positions for a peace conference. Some Americans too saw the need to do something of the kind. In May 1917, for example, William Phillips, first assistant secretary of state, had written to House that the United States was not adequately informed on the Balkans and the Near East ahead of a peace conference.[3] Felix Frankfurter, that ubiquitous suggester of innovative ideas in high places, recommended to House that since committees in France and Britain were preparing for the peace conference, something similar should be done in the United States.[4]

The Inquiry was not an open-ended analysis of how the peace treaty should deal with the problems that had caused the war. The motive, from the start, was suspicion in Wilson's, and to a lesser extent in House's, mind of the Allies' secret diplomacy.[5]

The Wilson/House strategy involved recruiting "liberal" and pacifist elements, especially within the elites, in both the Allied countries and Germany, to press Wilsonian policies on their own governments.[6] They must be assured that the United States was fighting for higher ideals than those of imperialism.[7]

Such concerns were made urgent by the obvious fragility of Russia, where the imperial government had been replaced by a liberal one in the spring, and the liberal government would be overthrown by the Bolsheviks within weeks (see chapter 13).

The first obstacle to be cleared was the delicate question of the Inquiry's relations with the State Department. On September 19 the president wrote House that "Lansing is not only content that you should undertake the preparation of the data for the peace conference but volunteered the opinion that you were the very one to do it." Wilson enclosed a memorandum Lansing had drafted with a list of perceptive questions, among them the following: How far should the United States take part in the determination of Europe boundaries? How far should the United States take part in the redistribution of colonial possessions? Should the basis of territorial distribution be race, language, religion, or previous political affiliation?[8]

House quickly began to find his own men to help him. He first consulted Abbott Lawrence Lowell, the president of Harvard, and Archibald Cary Coolidge, who was the first Harvard professor, back in the 1890s, to teach Russian history and who later developed a famous course on Turkey and the Balkans. He also talked to Herbert Croly, the founder of the *New Republic*.[9] As a result, House recruited Croly's colleague, Walter Lippmann, who was ecstatic. The project appealed both to his intellectual curiosity and to his yearning to be at the heart of things.

House's next move was to get his brother-in-law, Sidney Mezes, involved. He was worried that he might be criticized for nepotism, but Woodrow Wilson reassured him. "I don't think anyone could reasonably criticize your associating President Mezes with you," he wrote on September 24.[10] (Mezes, a philosopher of religion, previously president of the University of Texas, was now president of the City College of New York.)

Herbert Croly suggested James T. Shotwell, a Canadian-born historian of the British Empire at Columbia University.[11] Shotwell thought up the name, the Inquiry. Archibald Cary Coolidge realized that the Inquiry would need maps, so Shotwell approached Isaiah Bowman, director of the American Geographical Society.[12] The last member of the leadership team was David Hunter Miller, the law partner of House's son-in-law, Gordon Auchincloss.

The new organization first worked in rooms at the New York Public Library, then moved uptown to the American Geographical Society's rooms at 3755 Broadway. It was supposed to be extremely secret, but on September 25 its existence was revealed by House's protégé Lincoln Colcord of the *Philadelphia Public Ledger* in bold headlines. The Inquiry quickly sketched out a program of work that became more and more ambitious and hired the scholars to carry it out. In the summer of 1918 there was a spectacular clash of personalities involving Bowman, Lippmann, and Mezes. Colonel House had to intervene personally to sort it out.[13]

The Inquiry accumulated a working reference library to arm the president and other American delegates to the peace conference with facts, figures, and arguments at their fingertips. Lippmann found that in the State Department the Near Eastern Department consisted of a single official with maps that were two Balkan Wars out of date.[14] The Geographical Society was able to provide most of the maps required, though it was not long before Douglas Johnson, a special agent bound for Europe, was commissioned to buy missing maps from Stanford's map store, in Long Acre, London. The Inquiry also prepared detailed reports on matters likely to arise at the conference. It depended heavily on two groups of "experts," the Brahmins and the immigrants. The Inquiry often had to choose between information from established, sometimes very able, academics (mainly from Harvard, Yale, and Princeton), or from recent arrivals from Europe who knew the politics of

Europe all too well and had political or ethnic axes to grind. (One-third of all American diplomats who served in Europe between 1898 and 1914 were graduates of Harvard, and another third had graduated from Yale, Princeton, or foreign universities.)[15]

By January 1918 there were 51 scholars on the Inquiry's payroll, and at the peak that number had reached 126. Many of the Ivy League recruits were men who went on to careers of great distinction, such as Charles Homer Haskins and Samuel Eliot Morison of Harvard; Charles Seymour, later president of Yale; Wallace Notestein of Minnesota, a Yale PhD; and E. S. Corwin of Princeton.[16] These men were among the cream of American scholarship in their generation. But with a handful of exceptions—such as Robert J. Kerner, a Harvard PhD who had traveled and studied for two years in France, Germany, Austria, and Russia and was said to speak all the main Balkan languages—they were scarcely experts on the politics of Europe.[17] Few had any detailed knowledge of, for example, the disputed frontiers of Romania, Hungary, or Bulgaria, still less of the history and ethnography of Poland or the Ottoman Empire. One who was assigned to work on Italy confessed later that he was "handicapped by a lack of knowledge of Italian."[18]

The problem with the recent immigrants was the opposite. There were men like Henryk Arctowski and S. J. Zowski, who (as Gelfand puts it) "apparently thought there was nothing wrong in serving two masters."[19] They leaked information about the Inquiry's conclusions to Polish nationalist leaders, which enabled them to launch propaganda campaigns in the United States. Kerner might be a man of genuine erudition, but he used his voluminous Inquiry reports to make propaganda for a Yugoslav state.[20] Albert Lybyer got into trouble for his extreme pro-Bulgarian commitment, and Leon Dominian, a Turkish native of Greek descent, shocked his colleagues by his Greek bias.

If it was hard to find respectable scholars who were experts on the Balkans, when it came to what we would now call the Middle East, the Inquiry more or less gave up. It recruited professors of classics, like David Magie of Princeton or the great archaeologist Carl Blegen, experts in periods two or more millennia out of date.

In the end the Inquiry produced about two thousand reports of varying length and quality. But its most influential work was done before a single specialist report had been written. In November 1917 the new executive committee of the Inquiry (Mezes, Lippmann, Hunter Miller, Bowman, and Shotwell) was beginning to discuss work plans. Then, suddenly, a new urgency and a sharp focus were injected into the Inquiry's work. Colonel House was back from Europe. And the president was calling for his advice and that of his men.

The Allies called an Inter-Allied Supreme War Council for the fall of 1917. Sir William Wiseman, who had recently rented an apartment in the same building as the Houses, told House that Prime Minister Lloyd George wanted the colonel to be the American representative. By October 12 House had agreed to go at the head of a substantial delegation. From October 29 until December 15 House was first in London, then in Paris.

War aims and the secret treaties had provided the impetus to setting up the Inquiry. Now, in House's absence, its work began in earnest, especially thanks to the energy and intellectual clarity of Walter Lippmann. House and the core group of the Inquiry played a more decisive role in the formulation of Wilson's Fourteen Points than has been acknowledged by Wilson's admirers. The Fourteen Points, in turn, gave Wilson the master key he needed to unlock German surrender and to ensure that the peace conference would address Wilson's agenda, with its hopes of a new world order of lasting peace, and not merely ratify the secret treaties.

House landed at Falmouth on November 7, the very day when the Kerensky government fell in Russia. Lloyd George, meeting with the French and Italian prime ministers at Rapallo on Italy's Mediterranean coast, won their agreement to the creation of a Supreme War Council to direct the Allied war effort. Lloyd George, threatened with defeat in the House of Commons, was helped by a statement released by House that expressed President Wilson's support for the council.[21]

The former Conservative foreign secretary, Lord Lansdowne, encouraged the peace movement with his open letter, published in the *Daily Telegraph* on November 29. Lansdowne called for precisely what Wilson and House had been working for: definite, moderate war aims to appeal to men and women of goodwill in all countries.

All these efforts were put into shadow by the news that on November 7 the Kerensky government had fallen and the Bolshevik revolution had taken over in Russia. On December 3 House reported to Wilson that the new government in Russia had asked the Germans for an armistice. The prospect of the Germans being able to bring dozens of divisions from the east to mount a culminating offensive against the Anglo-French front in France threatened the Allies with calamity. And there was worse. On November 22 Leon Trotsky, the Bolsheviks' commissioner for foreign affairs, published the secret treaties, and on December 13 the liberal *Man-chester Guardian* published them in English.[22]

House was pleased with much that he had accomplished on this mission. But his successes were canceled by the one failure that to his mind threatened defeat for the entire Allied cause. The setting up of the Supreme War Council and the other machinery for cooperation among the Allies and between them and the United States was satisfactory. But the inter-Allied conference did not issue the clarion manifesto House and Wilson hoped for to keep Russia in the war and, by clothing the enemies of Germany in righteousness, shake Germany profoundly.

In return for his helping hand to Lloyd George, House got the British to back the resolution he planned to offer at the conference. It read: "The Allies and the United States declare that they are not waging war for the purpose of aggression or indemnity. The sacrifices they are making are in order that militarism shall not continue to cast its shadow over the world."[23]

House checked this text with the president, who cabled back that it was entirely in line with his thought. "Our people and Congress," he added, "will not fight for any selfish aims on the part of any belligerent, with the possible exception of Alsace-Lorraine."[24] House failed to get the Allies to agree to this text, how-ever. The Russian ambassador waded in with truculently anti-Bolshevik language. Lloyd George countered with an anodyne resolution that used language that agreed with House but neutralized it by saying it was too early to define war aims. The Allied governments were not yet ready, if they would ever be, to share the Wilsonian vision.

Back in the United States, as soon as he had finished his official reports on the mission, House saw Wilson in his study at the White House on December 18. He had tried, he said, to persuade the Allies to "join in a broad declaration of war aims that would unite the world against Germany, and would not only help to a solution of the Russian problem but would knit together the best and most unselfish opinions of the world. I could not persuade them to do this and now it will be done by the President."[25]

It was probably on this occasion that House told Wilson that at a dinner in London he had "pinned down" Lloyd George on British war aims. In a letter the day after the dinner he had told the president he was "afraid to write details but I have careful memoranda to go over with you when I return."[26] In his diary, House noted, "What Great Britain desires are the [former German] African colo-nies, both east and west, and an independent Arabia, under the sovereignty of Great Britain. Palestine to be given to the Zionists under Britain or, if desired by us, to be under American control. An independent Armenia and the internationalization of the Straits."[27]

Unlike France or Italy, in other words, Britain had no ambitions in Europe. But the British government did mean to be compensated for its efforts and its huge loans to the other Allies with territories in the Middle East and Africa. That was shocking enough to Wilson's mind, though Lloyd George had held back other ambitions, such as some Pacific islands for the Australians and British control of the Iraqi oil fields.

Wilson quickly made up his mind to supply the need for a manifesto by making a speech himself. House noted in his diary that their discussion of this lasted no more than ten to fifteen minutes. He returned to New York and set the Inquiry to work to produce the materials the president needed for what would be his most important speech, the Fourteen Points, delivered to a special session of Congress on January 8, 1918.

It is apparent from House's diary, his correspondence with Wilson, and other sources that the speech had multiple motivations. House and Wilson wanted to keep Russia in the war if they could. They needed to counter the effect of the publication of the secret treaties. In order to encourage both the neutrals and liberal opinion in France and Britain, they sought to emphasize America's unselfish motives. They hoped to strengthen opposition to the German government within Germany. And they wanted to seize the leadership of the coalition from Lloyd George, whom they distrusted.

Even before House got back from France, Walter Lippmann had sent him a memorandum on American priorities.[28] His most important contribution, however, was a paper he prepared with his colleagues on the Inquiry's executive committee, Isaiah Bowman, Sidney Mezes, and David Hunter Miller. The draft, which became the master plan for the Fourteen Points, was a direct response to the secret treaties, which Lippmann himself had been shown in October (by Secretary of War Baker) before the Bolsheviks leaked them. Lippmann's job, he explained, was "to take the secret treaties, analyze the parts which were tolerable, and separate them from those which we regarded as intolerable, and then develop a position which conceded as much to the Allies as it could, but took away the poison. . . . It was all keyed upon the secret treaties. That's what decided what went into the Fourteen Points."[29]

For three days, the Inquiry team worked furiously day and night.[30] They prepared charts showing the various national groups in different European countries. Lippmann coordinated the charts with national political movements to see how each group could be given national self-determination without exacerbating ethnic rivalries. By December 22, House received the first draft of a detailed document.[31] Almost before the ink was dry, the same authors came up with a revised and extended draft, completed on January 2, 1918.[32]

The first draft began with an analysis of how the Germans had created an axis from Berlin to Baghdad that, if successful, would make Germany the master of Europe and western Asia. In order to prevent this, the Inquiry paper suggested, the first objective must be "increased democratization of Germany, which means, no doubt, legal changes like the reform of the Prussian franchise, increased ministerial responsibility, control of the army and navy, of the war power and foreign policy. . . . It means the appointment to office of men who represent the interests of south and west Germany and the large cities of Prussia . . . the men who . . . forced through the Reichstag [peace] resolution."

It went on to propose various strategic objectives, such as control by friendly forces of the two ends of the Berlin-Baghdad axis and the neutralization of Constantinople and the Straits. Then it drew up a balance sheet of America's assets and liabilities. Among the assets it counted "the commercial control of the outer world" so that Germany could be excluded from both markets and sources of raw materials. This handed to America "a double weapon of fear and hope" to hold over the Germans. The memorandum went on to count, in the asset column, the fact that the Russian Revolution had three positive elements: hostility to capitalism, including German capitalism; a religious love of Russia; and nationalism. It took for granted that "with time the manpower and resources of this country, added to the present forces of the Entente, render a complete and crushing military victory over the Central Powers a certainty." It also listed "intangibles," among them the universal longing for peace, the feeling that the old diplomacy was bankrupt, the hope for a league of nations, and the fear on the part of the governing groups that the war debts would make revolution in Europe inevitable.

The Inquiry paper then proceeded to sketch what it called "a program for a diplomatic offensive." There should be, first of all, more explicit assertion that if the Germans failed to democratize, they would be excluded economically after the war. The reward for democratization, on the other hand, would be partnership. It then spelled out the details of a peace program under ten further headings. Belgium must be restored. Northern France must be evacuated. As to Alsace-Lorraine, "the wrong done in 1871 must be undone." Italy was entitled to rectification of its boundaries to meet its just demands "without [the allies'] yielding to those larger ambitions along the eastern shore of the Adriatic for which we can find no substantial justification." For the Balkans, it would be unwise to redraw frontiers just yet, but "economic considerations will outweigh nationalistic affiliations." There should be an independent and democratic Poland. Austria-Hungary should become a federal state, freed from German vassalage. "It is necessary to free the subject races of the Turkish empire from oppression and misrule," a statement that implied at the least "autonomy for Armenia and the protection of Palestine, Syria, Mesopotamia and Arabia by the civilized nations." Finally, the paper called for a league of nations.

House went down to Washington on Saturday, January 4, 1918. He brought with him so many maps and papers that he took an aide to help him with them. He spent a couple of hours in conference with Wilson that night. Wilson was now in a hurry. He was discouraged by news of a speech by Lloyd George to the Trades Union Congress at which he too had attempted to redefine British war aims in such a way as to "placate the moderate Left."[33] House was privately contemptuous of Wilson's concern on this point. "It is not so much general accomplishment that those in authority seem to desire," House reflected in his diary, "so much as accomplishment which may redound to their own personal advantage."[34] When he saw Wilson at the White House, however, House, with his usual blend of tact and flattery, persuaded Wilson that Lloyd George's speech offered an opportunity to Wilson to become the spokesman for the Entente as a whole.

On January 5 House and Wilson settled down to work at half past ten, and—as House later put it in his diary—"finished remaking the map of the world . . . at half past twelve o'clock."[35] House described in great detail the process of putting together what became the Fourteen Points. They began, he said, by outlining general concepts—open diplomacy, freedom of the seas, armaments reductions, a "general association of nations"—then proceeded to specific territorial adjustments. House made a strong argument for open diplomacy and for the removal of trade barriers. That would meet with opposition from the Senate, Wilson argued. The two causes of war were territorial and commercial greed, House countered, and it was just as important to get rid of one as the other.

Next House suggested they talk about the freedom of the seas. Wilson asked what he meant by the term, and House said he would go farther than anyone because he thought that in war or in peace a merchantman should sail the seas unmolested. They drafted language calling for "absolute freedom of navigation . . . alike in peace and in war." Then they wondered how this would be received in London, so House suggested they add a proviso that "the seas might be closed by international action in order to enforce international covenants."[36] House said the

British would be able to live with this. They discussed arms reduction and colonies before moving on to the various specific questions of national territory.

Belgium was swiftly disposed of, but they had a long discussion on Alsace-Lorraine. House's initial instinct was not to mention the disputed provinces at all. But Wilson persuaded House that they must say something specific. So House suggested the passage should read, "If Alsace and Lorraine were restored to France, Germany should be given an equal economic opportunity."[37]

On Poland, House said he showed Wilson the memoranda he had been given by the Polish national council in Paris. They drafted a paragraph that came "as near to [the memorandum] as we felt was wise and expedient."[38]

On the Ottoman Empire, Wilson thought Armenia, Mesopotamia, Syria, and other Ottoman territories to be separated from Turkey ought to be mentioned by name. House disagreed and won the point. Next they had to grapple with a paragraph dealing with Romania, Serbia, and Montenegro. Wilson asked House to show it to Milenko Vesnić, the Serbian minister to the United States who was in Washington with a delegation of Slav diplomats.[39] Vesnić was happy about the text House showed him, but he was unwilling to discuss peace until the war was over. He scrawled his position in strange, French-influenced English: "There cannot be in Europe any lasting peace with the conservation of the actual Austria-Hungary."[40]

The editor of the *Public Papers of Woodrow Wilson,* Arthur Link, is at some pains to minimize the influence of the Inquiry's drafts and of House in the drafting of the Fourteen Points. He concedes that House brought with him "a revision and enlargement of Part 3 of the first report"—that is, the January 2, 1918, memorandum titled "A Suggested Statement of Peace Terms." But he adds, "there is no evidence that Wilson ever read this long document," and he therefore decided not to print it.[41] This seems ungenerous. There is rarely evidence that a given diplomatic actor actually read any particular document. House may or may not have exaggerated in his diary his part in drafting the speech. What carries more weight than the claims in the diary is the close similarity between the Inquiry documents and the speech as the president delivered it.

Early on January 8 members of the House of Representatives' Committee on Foreign Affairs were startled when a courier arrived announcing that the president proposed to address a joint session of Congress that very afternoon. Several members of the cabinet did not get the news in time to be there.[42] It was in this way and to this audience that Wilson announced his Fourteen Points as the basis on which the United States was prepared to negotiate the peace.

The first five points dealt with general principles: open diplomacy, freedom of the seas, free trade, disarmament, and respect for the interests of colonial people.[43] The next eight points referred, often in quite general terms, to specific territorial questions in various areas: Russia; Belgium; Alsace-Lorraine; Italy's claims in the Trentino, Trieste, and Dalmatia; the Habsburg empire; the Balkans; Turkey; and Poland. This was a menu to give any international conference indigestion. The fourteenth point introduced Wilson's favorite project, a general association of nations—in other words, the League of Nations.

It is striking how closely the speech followed the outline provided by House and the Inquiry. There were, of course, verbal differences. For example, the Inquiry's memorandum spoke of a "league," whereas Wilson called it an "association." One scholar who analyzed the texts carefully concluded simply that "in the formulation of the Fourteen Points, the Inquiry's memorandum exerted much influence."[44]

Wilson's draft conspicuously ignored complexities the Inquiry had recognized. The Balkans were an example. The Inquiry report asserted that "The ultimate relationship of the different Balkan nations must be based upon a fair balance of nationalistic and economic considerations, applied in a generous and inventive spirit after impartial and scientific inquiry."[45]

That statement was vague enough and naïve enough. But Wilson (and House) went for a formula that was even vaguer and more naïve: Balkan boundaries should be "determined by friendly counsel along historically established lines of allegiance and nationality."[46] The phrase was meaningless.[47] "Historically established lines" in the Balkans did not exist. But in general Wilson, working with House under time pressure to prepare his speech, not only followed the Inquiry's outline, but also accepted most of its detailed suggestions.

The scope of the Inquiry expanded steadily. The first undated "preliminary brief outline of the subjects to be dealt with in the Inquiry" took up a bare two pages, beginning with "Suppressed, Oppressed and Backward Peoples etc." On December 15, just before the inner group broke off to prepare material for the Fourteen Points speech, the committee reported that it had laid out a plan of research divided into six fields: politics and government; economics and business; social science, including history; international law; geography; and strategy. By March 20 a new report listed fourteen geographical areas for discussion, from France to the Pacific. This list was eventually expanded to cover forty-nine geographical and many thematic topics. Virtually no geographical, demographic, historical, or political question was excluded from the Inquiry's work, and a formidable team of researchers was set to work.

Something of the scope of this extraordinary exercise is conveyed by looking at one of the most controversial topics with which the researchers dealt: Alsace-Lorraine. The following list of documents in the House papers is far from exhaustive, and an even larger mass of material is contained in the Inquiry collection in the National Archives. On March 2, 1918, E. B. Krehbiel handed in a 123-page historical paper dealing with the historical claims of France to the provinces, the probable results of a plebiscite, and the provinces' military importance to Germany. On April 27, Hetty Goldman produced a statistical report on emigration and immigration, showing that 534,000 people had emigrated from the two provinces, mostly to France or America. Three days later Edward C. Armstrong wrote a memo reporting that 77 percent of the inhabitants of the territories were German speakers. A Miss Jacoby reported on the iron and steel industry. On October 26 Wallace Notestein produced an ambitious memo on the "Solution of the Alsace-Lorraine Problem," in which he listed, no doubt tongue in cheek, no fewer than seventeen possible scenarios, including "XVI. The Pope!" And on November 14 Charles Homer Haskins wrote a 133-page report.[48]

The Inquiry's work went on until on October 18, when Colonel House sailed for Europe. Sidney Mezes drew up a list of some 75–80 members of the Inquiry to go to Paris. In the end, only twenty-three of them set sail with the president on his historic voyage. There were furious complaints from scholars who had been left behind.

13   *Russia*   ❧

FROM THE START OF WORLD WAR I in 1914, and even more as they saw the crisis of 1917 develop, Colonel House and President Wilson hoped that the very violence of the vortex into which Europe had been drawn by the war could be used to replace the political order there with a new system in accordance with their own liberal ideals. They failed, in large part because, like most Americans, they profoundly misunderstood the character of the Russian Revolution. It is hard to be precise about what they thought about the turbulent and confusing events they saw taking place in Russia—perhaps because most of the time even they were not very clear about what they thought. At first, they seemed to have underestimated how utterly different the Bolsheviks were from any other European politicians with whom they had had to deal.

President Wilson was delighted when the March 1917 revolution handed power in Russia to a government led by Alexander Kerensky. The "great, generous Russian people," he said, had been added "in all their naïve majesty and might" to the forces fighting for freedom. House wrote, more thoughtfully, that "the news from Russia concerns me greatly. I have been fearful lest bureaucratic Russia and autocratic Germany would link fortune and make trouble for the democracies of the world. Now that Russia bids fair to be free, one sees more hope for democracy and human liberty than ever before."[1]

It was natural for House and Wilson to be pleased. The members of the Kerensky government, after all, looked not so dissimilar from their own political friends. Academics and liberal businessmen, they believed in the same ideals that animated Wilsonians. Unfortunately these ideals were in Russia at best mere aspirations. Kerensky and his civilized friends had been put in power by revolutionaries. What American observers like Wilson and House, and their like in Britain and France, imagined they saw happening in Russia was an alliance between a liberal bourgeoisie and industrial workers and peasants. What was actually happening in the course of 1917 was a lethal struggle between liberals like Kerensky and a revolutionary conspiracy wedded to Marxist ideology and hardened by police persecution. In November, the revolutionaries won.

Woodrow Wilson's first reaction was to welcome the Bolshevik revolution too. He felt, as George F. Kennan has observed, that the Bolsheviks "could be introduced into the world balance of power as his own allies against the arrogant and reactionary forces predominant in the European governments, with whose narrow and selfish war aims he was so disgusted."[2] In a phrase that was either foolish or dissembling, he saw Russia as "a fit partner for a league of honor."[3]

Immediately after the October Revolution, Wilson included in the Fourteen Points speech of January 8, 1918, an eloquent appeal not to the Bolsheviks, but to the Russian people.[4] Like in so many of Wilson's speeches, this appeal was at once a noble vision and sheer self-deception. It was not that Woodrow Wilson shared the Bolshevik philosophy or approved of Bolshevik behavior. Not at all. It was simply that, confronted by the Russian Revolution, he reacted, as he did to so many other crises from Mexico onwards, by projecting onto reality his own feelings about how the world ought to be.

Woodrow Wilson's response to the Russian Revolution is a special case of his general tragedy. Gradually he was forced to acknowledge that his initial view was a fantasy. Generous instinct and idealism soured into defeatism and a reluctant agreement to go along, like the wicked old Europeans he so much despised, with the realities of blood and iron. He began by seeing Russia as the partner that would enable him to sweep away the unredeemed old Adam of the European chanceries. Point 6 of the Fourteen Points said "the treatment accorded to Russia by her sisternations in the months to come will be the acid test of their good will." He felt it was a tragedy that Russia was unrepresented at the peace conference. The Allies were virtually at war with the Bolsheviks, and—however reluctantly—Wilson had gone along with that policy. He was gradually induced to join in half-hearted military intervention in both north Russia and Vladivostok, and in the case of Siberia he was reduced to giving a pathetically inadequate excuse for intervention (see below). As in Mexico, he began by professing his sympathy for a people and his contempt for their rulers, and he ended by making war on both government and people. Finally he acknowledged that his real policy toward Russia was "to do nothing."[5]

As usual, House shared Wilson's basic attitudes, but his closeness to the realities of war, alliance politics, and power opened up gaps between his views and Wilson's. Halfway through his involvement with the Russian question he admitted to his diary that "I disagree almost entirely with the manner in which the President has handled the Russia situation, though I agree heartily with the objects he has in view."[6]

House believed that the German people, under liberal and socialist rule, might be brought to reject their militarist leaders and sue for a negotiated peace. He had made an earnest attempt to build up contacts with liberal and labor leaders in Europe through agents such as William Buckler in London and Arthur H. Frazier at the American embassy in Paris. He had sent a whole series of his friends, many of them journalists, to Europe to make contact with the European Left (among them William C. Bullitt, Lincoln Steffens, Ray Stannard Baker, Lincoln Colcord, Raymond Swing, and Carl Ackerman). House did not necessarily believe their sometimes excited analyses of European politics, which tended to predict that the bastions of European privilege were about to fall, like the walls of Jericho, at the blast of the ram's horn. But he did hope that a liberal uprising would chase the reactionaries from power.

The March revolution in Russia seemed at first to fit the view of House's friends that the Allied governments would soon be replaced by governments more representative of what House and Wilson thought of as ordinary citizens. It followed that the United States ought not to intervene militarily in Russia, as the French and, less unanimously, the British wanted to do. After the March revolution House wrote to the president: "I think this country should aid in every way the development of democracy in Russia for it will end the peril which a possible alliance between Germany, Russia and Japan might hold for us."[7] He was against military intervention and in favor of diplomatic contact with the Bolsheviks and food relief and economic aid to the Russian people.

The first decision was whether or not to recognize the Bolshevik government. Wilson's first instinct was that it should be recognized, and House agreed. So did the British prime minister, David Lloyd George. All of them came up against the granite hardness of Clemenceau's opposition. If the Bolsheviks were recognized, he would resign. In the circumstances, that amounted to an absolute veto.

Then came the question of intervention. The Russian army stopped fighting on December 2, 1917, but the issue became more acute after the Treaty of Brest-Litovsk in early March 1918, by which the Germans sheared off western Russia into a tier of states effectively under German control.[8] For the hard-pressed Western Allies, the point was that once Russia made peace, the Germans would have access to Russian food and oil and be able to switch perhaps as many as seventy divisions from the East to the Western Front; these troops might make the difference in the decisive battles that were shaping up in the spring of 1918.

Clemenceau and the French government, Marshal Ferdinand Foch, the French military, and a strong faction led by Winston Churchill in Britain thought it was vital to reconstitute an eastern front. Foch seemed desperate. One day he appeared suddenly at a British general's headquarters and barked, "There must be no more retreat, the line must be held at all costs," and stalked back to his car.[9] To impede German reinforcement of the Western Front from the East, they were willing to send small French and British forces, not to mention any American troops they could persuade General John Pershing to spare, to stiffen the anti-Bolshevik Russian forces that were beginning to take the field under General Anton Denikin, Admiral Alexander Kolchak, and other "White Russian" leaders. They were delighted to use the services of the tens of thousands of Czech prisoners and deserters from the Austro-Hungarian army who had formed themselves into the Czech Legion and were marching eastward along the Trans-Siberian Railway. And, though this was a matter of angry controversy, they looked forward to coopting the help of the Japanese.

What now constituted Russia? The Poles, the Finns, and the peoples of the Baltic provinces (Lithuanians, Letts, and Estonians) saw the revolution as an opportunity to win their national independence. The vast, potentially rich Ukraine, with a population approaching that of France or Britain, was largely occupied by the Germans and wavered between remaining attached to Russia and striving for independence. In the Caucasus the Turks regained their 1878 boundaries. All together Russia lost a million square miles of territory, a third of its population (about 55 million people), half its industry, three-quarters of its iron ore, and almost all its coal and oil.[10] Perversely, Woodrow Wilson, the high priest of the national self-determination of peoples, was in favor of keeping Russia intact. House, who was in contact with Polish and Czech nationalists like Ignazy Paderewski and Jan Masaryk, disagreed.[11]

The Brest-Litovsk treaty has generally been interpreted as an example of the ruthless terms the victors can impose on a beaten enemy. But the Bolsheviks were not fools. They had no intention of being bound by the treaty an inch more than they had to be. It recognized them as the rulers of Russia and enabled them to say they had ended the war. It also knocked on its head the idea, on which Wilson and House had both invested such hopes, of winning the war by detaching the German Center-Left from the imperial war effort. For the time being, all but the far Left in German politics (the "independent" antiwar socialists) sniffed the scent of victory and rallied round the government. Further opportunities to appeal to the socialists and liberals might arise, William C. Bullitt wrote to Colonel House, who had asked him to study the situation. "For the present, therefore, we had better fight and say nothing."[12]

By the middle of January 1918 the Japanese had sent four warships to Vladivostok and the British one, ostensibly to protect their citizens. Even before Brest-Litovsk, Colonel House discussed with the president at great length the question of Japanese intervention in Siberia, but they came to no conclusion.[13] There were arguments for and against it. Three days after their discussion, Wilson drafted but did not send a note to the Allied governments saying that it would not be wise for the United States to join in the Japanese invasion of Siberia but that he had no objection to the Allies doing so. House felt that going into Siberia would lower the American moral position, and Elihu Root agreed that Russian antipathy to the Japanese would throw the Russians "into the arms of Germany." House tried to persuade A. J. Balfour that the Japanese invasion of Siberia would be "the greatest misfortune that has yet befallen the Allies."[14] But House lost that argument.

On March 11 Wilson, still under the delusion that the Bolsheviks were essentially liberal allies who were linked with the United States by a shared distaste for monarchy, sent a message to the Soviet congress saying that "the whole heart of the people of the United States is with the people of Russia in the attempt to free themselves for ever from autocratic government." The Bolshevik snub was prompt. "The happy time is not far distant," Wilson was reminded, "when the labouring masses of all countries will throw off the yoke of capitalism and will establish a socialistic state of society, which alone is capable of securing just and lasting peace."[15] Nevertheless by the end of March Trotsky authorized acceptance of Western aid, and in late April he even suggested that the Czech Legion might be used to resist the Germans.

The situation in Russia was chaotic, and the discussions between the Americans and their allies were scarcely less so. On May 1 Sir William Wiseman reviewed the options and came down in favor of Allied intervention at the invitation of the Bolsheviks as the least bad alternative. British troops had already landed at

Murmansk, on an inlet leading south from the Barents Sea in the Russian Arctic. After meeting the new Japanese ambassador to Washington, Viscount Kikujiro Ishii, President Wilson was confirmed in his view that Japanese intervention would only make the Russians even more anti-Japanese, but Tokyo was taking an ever harder line. A spokesman for the Japanese general staff warned that if German influence spread eastward to Siberia, Japan would have to intervene alone.

Wilson was more willing to send U.S. troops to the Northern Front, where the Japanese were not involved, and in fact he authorized the transfer of a couple of U.S. battalions there in mid-June. Even in Siberia, against all his instincts, he finally gave in. In late July he allowed himself to be persuaded that the Czech Legion was threatened by armed German and Austrian prisoners of war in Siberia and allowed a small American force to be sent to Vladivostok. He may have imagined that an American presence would restrain the Japanese. The U.S. Army was not to exceed seven thousand, and the original understanding was that the Japanese force would be no larger. Ultimately the Japanese forces grew to more than sixty thousand. The people of Russia were assured "in the most public and solemn manner" that the United States had no intention of interfering with the political sovereignty of Russia. By this stage, with Russia in the grip of a civil war, with foreign armies wandering almost at will across its territory, with huge gobbets torn away by newly independent nations, and with a massive German army in control of large areas, Wilson's protestation was genteelly unrealistic to the point of absurdity.

Colonel House's liberal friends were horrified by Wilson's decision. William Bullitt wrote that the policy seemed to be to give encouragement and supplies to anyone in Russia who fought the Bolsheviks. Either the United States should decide that the Bolsheviks were German agents, in which case they should invite the Japanese to send in five hundred thousand men, or they should withdraw the Czech Legion and open diplomatic relations with them.

Bullitt and House's other friends believed that the war could not be won until late 1919. By that time, they calculated, the American contribution to the fight against Germany would be so preponderant that President Wilson would be able to dictate terms to the "reactionary" European governments whether they liked it or not. But in the summer of 1918, it was the Germans, not the Allies, who lost.

On August 8, at Amiens, the British, with air superiority and a far higher complement of heavy weapons than on the Somme in 1916, inflicted what General Ludendorff himself called "the black day of the German army." From then on the Allies—the British, French, Americans, Canadians, and Belgians—rolled forward. By the end of September they had punctured the formidable fixed defenses of the

Hindenburg Line. Ludendorff was so shocked that he fell to the ground at the news and, according to some accounts, foamed at the mouth. From then on, the German high command was more concerned with avoiding revolution than with victory. The leaders of the Entente were more determined than ever not to be bounced into a Wilsonian settlement.

House's friends began to fear that the opportunity to which they had looked forward, when the United States could dictate its peace settlement to the Allies, might be passing. Lippmann, Colcord, and Bullitt all wrote House in August and September urging that it was time for the president to call openly for the support of the European Left.[16] On September 3, 1918, House passed this thought on to the president.

> Dear Governor,
>
> Do you not think the time has come for you to consider whether it would not be wise to try to commit the Allies to some of the things for which we are fighting?
>
> As the Allies succeed your influence will diminish. . . . While the liberals are largely with you at present I have a feeling that you are not so strong among labor circles of either France or Britain as you were a few months ago. . . . I do not believe [such support] will be powerful or steadfast enough to compel the reactionaries in authority to yield at the peace conference to American aims.[17]

Wilson was preoccupied with the peace feelers from Austria and Germany. The peace conference, from which he expected so much, could not be far away. House himself departed for Europe. One of his tasks was to try to commit the Allies to agreed war aims. In this he was unsuccessful. His hopes of seeing a democratic Russia sitting at the table with the victorious powers had long disappeared. The absence of Russia from the conference was one of the two chief reasons why it was impossible to build the foundations of a lasting peace there. It was as serious as the absence of Germany. Nevertheless, the victors did make five attempts, during the conference though not at it, to seek a solution to the problems of Russia.[18]

The first attempt, in January 1919, was an invitation to the Bolsheviks and their various enemies to send delegates to discuss their differences. The location chosen for this sub-conference was remote, not to say bizarre: the island of Prinkipo in the Sea of Marmara, near Istanbul in the Straits. The anti-Bolsheviks refused to attend.

The Bolsheviks did not quite refuse. Sarcastically, they professed willingness to discuss demands for concessions, such as mineral rights, that the West had not made.

Next Winston Churchill made a dramatic last plea for serious Allied military intervention in Russia, not now to forestall German power, but to overthrow the Bolsheviks. Churchill was still a Liberal and had not completed his transformation into a die-hard Tory. But he had a deep, visceral loathing of communism. He pictured Russia under the Bolsheviks in almost hysterical language: "not a wounded Russia only, but a poisoned Russia, an infected Russia, a plague-bearing Russia; a Russia of armed hordes . . . preceded by swarms of typhus-bearing vermin which slew the bodies of men, and political doctrines which destroyed the health and even the souls of nations."[19]

On February 14, 1919, just as President Wilson was about to leave Paris to return to Washington, Churchill appeared without warning and demanded an audience before the Supreme Council.[20] He announced that at a cabinet meeting the previous day in London great anxiety had been expressed about the Russian situation, in view of the apparent failure of the Prinkipo meeting. There were still five hundred thousand men in the White Armies, and British troops were still being killed fighting against the Red Army. Lloyd George wanted to know what the policy was.

Clemenceau said such a large question could not be answered at a short and unexpected meeting, but Woodrow Wilson said that given that Churchill had come to Paris specially to catch him before he left for Washington, he was prepared to give his view. He had two clear opinions, he said. First, the troops of the Allied and associated powers were doing no good in Russia. Second, the Prinkipo meeting might not end the civil war but might be an opportunity to find out what the Bolsheviks wanted.

Churchill replied that if the White Armies were not reinforced by the Allies and America, they would collapse, leaving "an interminable vista of misery and violence."[21] Wilson countered that the Allies were not willing to reinforce their troops in Russia. Churchill pleaded passionately for volunteers, but Wilson shrugged the matter off, saying he would go along with whatever the council decided.

The next day, with Colonel House replacing the president, Churchill proposed that the conference set up a council for Russian affairs. He then pleaded with all his eloquence for some policy to be adopted. The alternatives were either to take military action in Russia or to face the consequences of abandoning Russia to its fate. "Russia was the key to the whole situation, and unless she formed a living part of Europe . . . there would be neither peace nor victory."[22] Colonel House evoked a more immediate danger. Unless tact were used, all the peoples east of the Rhine might be thrown by an alliance between Germany and Russia against England, the United States, and France. In essence, the council had heard Winston Churchill predict Hitler's invasion of Russia in 1941 and Colonel House anticipate the Nazi-Soviet pact of 1939. Even so, the council decided to do nothing. There was in truth little it could do.

House's friend Lincoln Steffens suggested sending a private mission to Moscow to sniff out what the Bolsheviks might accept. House liked the idea and persuaded President Wilson to authorize sending Steffens and Bullitt. The British agreed. The French were not consulted.

Bullitt was received in a friendly way by Lenin, who gave him a document that took the form of an Allied proposal to the Soviet government. Lenin told Bullitt that if the Allied governments made such a proposal to the Bolsheviks, they would accept it. It offered an end to hostilities, raising of the Allied blockade, withdrawal of Allied troops, and a general amnesty for the White Russians.

Bullitt reached Paris at the end of March 1919 in triumph, only to find that the statesmen were now locked in conflict over how to treat Germany. Wilson told Bullitt he had a headache and could not see him. Bullitt was deeply offended. Years later he teamed up with no less an ally than Sigmund Freud to analyze Wilson's mental problems in no friendly spirit. In reality Wilson was seriously ill.

From Bullitt's point of view, things went from bad to worse. Wilson passed him back to Colonel House, who—unknown to Bullitt—was already at odds with Wilson and handed Bullitt over to colleagues who were unsympathetic to his proposals. Lloyd George, under heavy attack from Conservative members of his coalition and from the *Daily Mail* over Russia, pretended he had vaguely heard of the mission of "a young American." Bullitt himself was so disillusioned that he later told reporters he was going to go down to the Riviera and lie on the sand and watch the world go to hell.

House saw Bullitt the night he got back from Russia. The next day he put a plan he had been thinking over to the Italian prime minister Vittorio Emmanuele Orlando. The Allies should draw up a peace treaty "practically upon our own terms, provided they were just," and send it to Moscow for signature.[23] Orlando said House could count on his cooperation. But Wilson said he had too much else on his mind to think about Russia.

Two days later House brought Russia up with the president again. Wilson asked him to work with Herbert Hoover and see whether it would be possible to get ships to carry food to Russia if it was decided to do so.[24]

The leaders in Paris were tired of Russia. They were preoccupied with Germany and with their own rivalries and quarrels. Wilson's and House's dream of bringing in a democratic Russia (led by Lenin and Trotsky!) to restrain the "annexationist" instincts of Britain and France was long dead. Churchill's dream of an anti-Bolshevik crusade was dead too; neither the Americans nor the Allies were willing to send hundreds of thousands of troops to fight in confused but bloody battles in the Russian Arctic or Siberia.

There remained the option of offering food to save Russian lives and Western consciences. Hoover had done impressive work as head of the commission for relief in Belgium and after the war ended in other parts of Europe. If Hoover offered the Bolsheviks food, it occurred to many in Paris, they would have to choose between denying food to their own people, many of whom were starving, and moderating their behavior.

To turn over the pages of House's diary for the next week or two is to realize how hopeless it was to imagine that the Council of Four—the United States, Britain, France, and Italy—would address the problems of Russia and its abrasive revolutionary government in an imaginative or generous way. The president was sick with a precursor of his later vascular collapse. Lloyd George was not well. Clemenceau was injecting one intractable issue after another—the Saarland, the Rhineland, reparations—into the discussions. Orlando was about to create the biggest crisis in the entire history of the conference over an obscure town in Dalmatia, Fiume. House spent much time soothing Admiral William S. Benson, the first American chief of naval operations, who was angrily insisting that the United States must never have fewer warships than Britain. The statesmen to whom the world had looked for peace with justice were all but at each other's throats. High hopes and lofty ideals were on hold. The last chance of bringing Russia into the society of nations before Stalin's time, and Stalin's crimes, had been missed.

President Wilson arrives at the Place de la Concorde, Paris, on December 14, 1918, for the peace conference. Yale University Library, Manuscripts and Archives.

Hotel Crillon, Place de la Concorde, where the American delegation had its offices. There were complaints that Colonel House had the best rooms. Corbis.

Colonel and Mrs. House stepping out in Paris. Yale University Library, Manuscripts and Archives.

House with Georges Clemenceau and Stephen Bonsal after the war. Yale University Library, Manuscripts and Archives.

A. J. Balfour, British foreign secretary, golfer, and philosopher. Yale University Library, Manuscripts and Archives.

Vittorio Emmanuele Orlando, prime
minister of Italy. Yale University Library,
Manuscripts and Archives.

Ignazy Jan Paderewski, piano virtuoso and first
president of an independent Poland. Yale University
Library, Manuscripts and Archives.

Lord Robert Cecil, Christian Tory whose
life was devoted to world peace. Yale
University Library, Manuscripts and
Archives.

André Tardieu, journalist and French delegate. Yale
University Library, Manuscripts and Archives.

To The Colonel,
Who wrought not for himself but for The Thing,
Who strove in silence, and, in silence strong,
Never laments that any did him wrong
Knowing full well what cheer the years will bring

Xmas 1921   Wickham Steed

(above) Henry Wickham Steed, editor of *The Times* and the Paris *Daily Mail*. Yale University Library, Manuscripts and Archives.

(opposite, top) Allied officers who could not get tickets to the signing of the peace treaty stood on tables to peek at the ceremony. Corbis.

(opposite, bottom) Colonel House, sick with gallstones, is helped down the gangplank from the SS *Northern Pacific* on his return to New York in October 1919. Yale University Library, Manuscripts and Archives.

George Sylvester Viereck, poet, German agent,
and Nazi sympathizer. Corbis.

Colonel House with Franklin D. Roosevelt. Corbis.

14 *Armistice* ❧

I have the most profound respect for Colonel House . . . yet I confess that a most undesirable obscurity hangs over his "interpretation."

—Harold Nicolson

BY THE FALL OF 1918 General Ludendorff, the most successful of German commanders and for at least a year virtually the dictator of Germany, was suddenly desperately anxious for peace.[1] Why was this? He may have wished cynically to give his armies time to regroup and rearm. No doubt he realized that his great gamble, to end the war before American reinforcements arrived in force, had failed: American troops were now arriving at the rate of three hundred thousand a month. The most plausible explanation is that his essential aim was to save the army and its reputation in order to defeat revolution in Germany. To do that, he was prepared to hand power to the Social Democratic parliamentarians so that they would inherit the disgrace of defeat.[2] In any event, the German request for an armistice offered Woodrow Wilson and Edward House the opportunity for their greatest diplomatic achievement.

By offering the Germans peace on the basis of the Fourteen Points, Wilson and House outflanked the Allies' hard-purchased war aims and took control of the agenda for the peace. Not that they deceived the Allies. (To most of the specific geographic provisions in the Fourteen Points, in any case, Britain at least had no objections.) The Americans did keep their associated powers informed. They even allowed them to make important qualifications: Britain would interpret the freedom of the seas so as not to exclude naval blockade and France would insist on reparations. But Wilson's whole strategy had been to use the war to replace the self-aggrandizement of the Entente powers with an unselfish American agenda of popular sovereignty. He meant to achieve this agenda by offering peace on the basis of the Fourteen Points—that is, on American terms.

In this way, Wilson and House made it hard for the Allies to ask for more. Certainly the Allies were free to press for territorial gains and for reparations, and in Paris they did. But if they pressed too hard, they ran the risk that the Germans would stick to the terms they had already been offered, and the United States might not back the Allies up. The military terms of the pre-armistice agreement, in any case, amounted to surrender; in practice, they deprived the German generals of any hope of renewing the war.

From an Allied point of view, the American negotiation on the basis of the Fourteen Points looked like uncomradely behavior. For many Americans too, it came to look as though a settlement resulting from decisive victory had been sacrificed on the altar of Woodrow Wilson's naïve belief in such favorite slogans as "open diplomacy" and "the freedom of the seas" and his pet project for a league of nations. From the German point of view, the transaction came to seem like a shabby trick, whereby Germany's weakness, which to many Germans seemed only a temporary disadvantage, like a fencer's short breath, was turned into humiliation. On the foundation of these differing perceptions, menacing structures of fear, suspicion, and resentment were built.

The fact remains that Wilson did seize his opportunity. Cleverly, he used German acceptance of the Fourteen Points as a way of imposing his conception of how peace should be made. Edward House was the essential collaborator in this diplomatic victory.

The image of Woodrow Wilson has been frozen for many by the unkind portrait penned by an opponent who also happened to be a genius, John Maynard Keynes.[3] If Wilson was, as Keynes portrayed him, a Presbyterian minister, firm in self-righteous conviction of what must be done, that is not how it felt to Wilson himself. Wilson was far from self-confident. He felt the need to summon House to Washington to help him respond to the first German note, and when he sought advice about how to reply to the second, House "never saw him more disturbed." Finding the right answer, Wilson said, reminded him of a maze. "If one went in at the right entrance, he reached the center, but if one took the wrong turning, it was necessary to go out again and do it over."[4] It is hardly the image of a prophet armed with adamantine certainty.

A bitter historical irony mocks Wilson's hopes. Wilson believed that behind the bristling mustachios of imperial Germany and its military masters there was a people's Germany that was "liberal." In his very first reply to Germany Wilson demanded to be assured that the request did not come from the same "constituted authorities of the empire" who had been in charge of the war all along.[5] The Germans did their best to assure the American president that the old order had passed away, and it was true. Since September 29 the old regime had handed over power to the previous Socialist parliamentary opposition—to the Scheidemanns and Eberts and Noskes, working-class leaders of the Social Democratic Party.[6] What no one realized, least of all Wilson, was that it was the old regime itself, in the person of Ludendorff, the hardest of the hard, who had forced through the constitutional revolution from above for its own reasons. This is only one example of Woodrow Wilson's limited understanding of a Europe in the grip of revolutionary turbulence.

Colonel House learned on Sunday, October 6, that the chancellor, Prince Max of Baden, had sent a note, delivered through the Swiss embassy. In it the German government accepted the Fourteen Points and other Wilson speeches as the basis for an armistice.

House had been waiting for just this happening for four years. Yet when Adolph Ochs of the *New York Times* and Frank Cobb of the *World,* among others, called for his response, it was not triumphant. "These are momentous days," he wrote in his diary. "A misstep means so much. It is an hour in which to be calm, in which to be unselfish, in which to be just." He sent off a cool telegram suggesting that the president make no direct reply to the Germans yet. He asked the president to send him to Paris to confer with the Allies. He also sent a cautious personal message. It was stirring news, of course, but an armistice seemed impossible; a refusal must leave the advantage with the president. "Our position, I think, should be one of delay without seeming so."[7]

On October 7 House was summoned by telephone to Washington. This was the opportunity he and Wilson had dreamed of since 1915, when they could bring the war to an end, not by the sort of ruthless "Carthaginian" peace terms the Allies might impose, but by a peace that would reflect their own high ideals. At the same time they were at a loss how to reply to Prince Max's note. Was it a trick? House went straight to Wilson's study, where Lansing joined them. Wilson read a draft reply to the German note, but House uncharacteristically expressed his disapproval. (This *was* unusual because House tells us frequently in his diary that if he disagreed with the president, he would usually show his dissent by silence.) They argued for half an hour, and the two of them worked on the draft until nearly one o'clock in the morning.

Wilson had planned to play golf in the morning, but instead he retreated to his study with House, who persuaded him to make a tougher response than he had originally intended.

Wilson did not reject Prince Max's request for an armistice out of hand. He replied by asking whether the Germans accepted three conditions. First, Germany must accept the Fourteen Points. Second, Prince Max must give credible assurance that he spoke for the German people, not for those who had been responsible for war. Third, the Germans must agree to evacuate all the territories they had occupied, in Poland and the East, as well as in Belgium and northern France.

The Germans accepted all three conditions but said they would want preliminary negotiations about evacuation. Such negotiations, House thought, might be a catch. Under the cover of talks, perhaps Ludendorff hoped to disengage his bloodied legions, regroup, rearm, replenish them with drafts (including the eighteen-year-old class of conscripts), and live to fight again. "I want to save the army," said Ludendorff's chief of operations, Colonel Wilhelm Heye, "so that we can use it as a means of pressure during the peace negotiations."[8]

The German reply was signed by the state secretary for foreign affairs, Wilhelm Solf, not by Prince Max. Solf assured Wilson that the chancellor did indeed speak in the name of the German government and people.[9]

On October 11 President Wilson arrived in New York, where he was due to attend an Italian fête at the Metropolitan Opera. He arrived in a bad mood. As usual, House managed to calm him down. It was then that Tumulty came in with news of the German reply.

Two things had changed in the interval between the first and second German notes. Most of the important newspapers agreed that Wilson's answer, by giving the Germans not so much an answer as a questionnaire, had been clever. But now the press was afraid that the German reply was a trick to gain time. Some now began to call for unconditional surrender. Meanwhile, in the Senate opposition to an armistice was hardening.[10]

House wrote in his diary that Monday, October 14, was "one of the most stirring days of my life." Immediately after breakfast he and Wilson sat down to draft a reply to the German note. House suggested that Wilson make it an absolute condition of an armistice that the Germans renounce "atrocities" such as submarine attacks on passenger liners and the retreating army's attacks on French towns and villages. Both points duly appeared in their reply and were in turn rejected in the German reply.[11]

Wilson suggested that he should use what he had said about autocracy in his July 4 speech at Mount Vernon, and that too found its way into the note in direct quotation: the United States supported "the suppression of all arbitrary power wherever it might be, which could secretly and by its own will disturb the peace of the world." Wilson's note (signed for reasons of protocol by Lansing as secretary of state) tightened the screw on the Germans. It left no doubt that Wilson wanted regime change in Germany.

After dinner on October 14 Wilson wrote out a letter of credentials in his own hand. House left for New York on the midnight train, and when he arrived, he had numerous affairs to settle before he left for Europe, including a last-minute visit to the dentist. There was a family reunion with his daughter Mona and son-in-law Randolph, who came down from Boston, and with Gordon and (daughter) Janet Auchincloss and their little daughter, Louise. Then the Houses took a boat out through the fog to their ship, the *Northern Pacific,* anchored off Staten Island.[12] They did not get under way until four o'clock in the morning. The party consisted of Edward and Loulie House; Miss Denton and her assistant, Miss Tomlinson; Gordon Auchincloss; Joseph Grew from the State Department; Admiral Benson and Commander Worrall R. Carter from the U.S. Navy; Frank Cobb from the *New York World;* a Navy surgeon (Frank McLean); and clerks and stenographers.[13]

House kept in touch with Wilson on the crossing, which was so rough that House and the admiral decided to send their destroyer escorts home. He had doubts about the wisdom of the president's handling of the armistice process. He was pleased with the German reply to the president's second note of October 14. On October 22 the Swiss chargé d'affaires had transmitted to Lansing the third German note. It stressed the "fundamental change" in the German constitution. The new government had been formed in accordance with the wishes of the people's representatives and elected by universal suffrage, and the heads of the major parties in the Reichstag were members of the government. The guarantee of the survival of the new democratic system, however, Solf said, lay in the "unshakable will of the German people, the immense majority of whom support the new reforms." (Within weeks Germans from Right and Left were shooting at one another in the streets.)

House's first reaction, nonetheless, was that "it means the beginning of peace for a war-torn world." He wanted to wireless the president, advising him simply to give out a statement that "The President will immediately confer with the Allies regarding the German reply."[14] On October 23, without input from House, Wilson sent his third note to Berlin. It was lengthy, not to say verbose, and in it, Wilson laid down his ace of trumps. He had informed the associated powers of the exchange of notes, he said. He had received a reply containing the Allied governments' response. They professed themselves ready to make peace with Germany on the basis of the Fourteen Points, though they had qualifications. Point 2 (the freedom of the seas) was "susceptible to various interpretations." (That was a tactful way of conveying the depth of British horror at Wilson's pressure on Britain's traditional weapon of defense.) And they opened the door to damaging haggling about reparations by specifying that Wilson's language about "restoration" should be extended to cover "all damage done to the civilian population of the Allies and to their property."[15]

An armistice, Wilson made plain, would have to "make a renewal of hostilities on the part of Germany impossible." Wilson would consult the Allies' military leaders to work out how they could enforce the peace. But then he reverted to his concern with eliminating the militarists. The government of the United States could deal only with "veritable representatives of the German people," not the "military masters and monarchical autocrats of Germany."[16] Wilson was calling for the end of the Hohenzollern dynasty, for regime change.

House was not happy with this text, the first in which he had had no hand. "The Germans have accepted his terms. . . . He should then have communicated them to the Allies and gotten them to agree to his terms. . . . Instead . . . he has gone into a long and offensive discussion which may have the effect of . . . welding the people together back of their military leaders."[17]

In this particular instance, House was wrong. It was either too late or too early for German unity. The country was on the verge of civil war. It was the army, in the shape of General Ludendorff and his political allies in the military, such as his successor, General Wilhelm Groener, who were using the Socialists as human shields to take the blame for defeat.[18] It would be the army, in the irregular shape of *Freikorps* led by officers like General Ludwig von Maercker, who would put down the revolutionaries in 1919–1920.[19] House knew nothing of these violent political currents. On the general principle, however, House was surely right, and Wilson was wrong. House understood that political success depended on analyzing what one's opponents wanted and what they could be persuaded to settle for.

Wilson saw politics not as a map, with stubborn irremovable features—rivers and mountains—but as a theorem inscribed with luminous simplicity on a sheet of white paper. House saw political leadership as a matter of dealing with people as they were. Wilson saw it as a matter of a being superior in wisdom and virtue—i.e., himself—leading weaker brethren toward the higher plane he inhabited. House's admiration for his friend remained undiminished to the end. But by the end of 1918, his diary reveals that he was beginning to understand the political limitations that went with Wilson's gifts of intellect and rhetoric.

For the time being, Wilson was launched on the trajectory of a diplomatic operation that has been rightly admired. It was, at the high-minded level at which Wilson's mind always worked, a version of the old salesman's trick of "bait and switch." He invited the Germans to deal on the basis of the Fourteen Points and his later speeches of explanation. When they accepted, he piled on further demands. The Germans, once on the hook, had no option but to pay these additions to the price they had agreed.

In the short run, Wilson was successful. He had responded to the first German inquiry about an armistice in such a way that both the Germans and the Allies were trapped into following his plan. He then tightened the screw, turn by painful turn.

Later, many critics, especially but not only in France, accused Wilson of cutting the Allies out of the crucial negotiation with Germany. That is not fair. The Allies were aware in general terms of what was going on.[20] On October 5, before the German note even reached Washington, the prime ministers of Great Britain, France, and Italy met in Paris, and on October 6 they agreed on principles for an armistice; the principles roughly followed the lines of the Fourteen Points but specified that the Germans would "retire behind the Rhine into Germany." General Tasker Bliss, the U.S. military representative, declined to take part in the discussions. Since the Supreme War Council acted only with unanimity, Bliss was correct in his judgment that the document did not have the full council's authority but issued only from the prime ministers of Britain, France, and Italy. While formally the Allies were brought into the negotiation between the United States and Germany only on October 23, both the Allies' political leadership and military commanders were aware that a negotiation was taking place, and the actual terms were worked out by their military representatives.

The reality of the transaction, however, as Wilson was aware, was a little different. Wilson took advantage of the opportunity offered by Prince Max's note to hook the German government on the Fourteen Points. Those points included at least one—freedom of the seas—that Wilson well knew was intensely unpalatable to one of the Allies, Britain. He was presenting the Allies with a fait accompli: he was asking the Allies to buy into his peace terms, not those the Allies would have offered themselves. The Allies were free to refuse but only if they were prepared to go on fighting a Germany that still had 8 million men under arms and without American help in men or munitions, not to mention money.[21] Wilson felt fully justified in acting as he did. He felt he was destroying "militarism" and "navalism." House supported him. But he was unhappy with his friend's high-handed approach.

While House was still on the high seas, Wilson did something else that disturbed House and has generally been accounted one of the most serious blunders of his political career.[22] The midterm elections were now only days away, and they threatened all that Wilson, and House, had dreamed of achieving.

On May 27, 1918, President Wilson had proclaimed, hopefully, that politics was adjourned. Of course nothing of the kind happened. The Wilson administration had not only taken the country to war, something that remained deeply unpopular in many quarters. In an effort to head off war inflation, it had also fixed the price of wheat at $2.20 a bushel for 1917 and kept the same price level for 1918.[23] But it had not fixed the price of cotton, which promptly soared by 400 percent. That not only infuriated millions of wheat farmers and their neighbors from Ohio to the state of Washington, but, coming from a government packed with Southerners, it also struck the Midwest as an act of base sectional favoritism. There were other burning issues that risked losing valuable votes. On September 30 the president addressed the Senate in favor of women's suffrage, but the Senate voted against his wishes. Moreover, Southern agitation for prohibition was beginning to annoy voters. The issue on which the Democrats were most vulnerable, though, was the war itself and what struck many Republicans as the president's naïve idealism about his league of nations.

In late August, Henry Cabot Lodge came out with an attack on the Fourteen Points, with not a word about a league.[24] In late September Theodore Roosevelt set off to barnstorm through the West, ostensibly to support the Liberty loan, but in reality to denounce the president's peace notes as "war by correspondence."

By October the administration was in trouble. The Democrats had a majority of ten in the Senate but of only three in the House. Wilson might seem a pacifist by comparison with the Rough Riders, Roosevelt and General Leonard Wood. But he was a fighter in his way, and his Scots Irish blood was up. On October 10 he summoned his advisers, including the deputy chairman of the Democratic National Committee, Homer Cummings of Connecticut, and Senator Key Pitman, chairman of the Senate Foreign Relations Committee. He decided to put his own reputation on the line.

After several drafts and careful consideration with Joseph Tumulty, his closest political adviser while the colonel was away, Wilson appealed to the American people to vote for Democratic candidates. To modern eyes, there was nothing strange about the appeal. At the time, though, it was thought wrong for the president to put his authority, and the international crisis, so nakedly in the service of partisan advantage. "If you have approved of my leadership," Wilson's statement read, "and wish me to continue to be your unembarrassed spokesman in affairs at home and abroad I earnestly beg that you will express yourself unmistakably to that effect by returning a Democratic majority to both the Senate and the House of Representatives."[25] Most of the cabinet thought this was plain bad politics. T. W. Gregory thought that without it, the Democrats would have won the midterm elections easily.[26]

The voters declined to accept the president's invitation. On November 5 the Republicans won a majority of forty-four seats in the House of Representatives and a one-vote margin in the Senate. Wheat prices counted for something in these results: Democrats lost twenty-one seats in the farm belt. The president's war aims, his style, and his ill-judged appeal to the voters all contributed to a catastrophic defeat.[27] Henry Cabot Lodge, a personal enemy, would be both Senate majority leader and chairman of the Foreign Relations Committee.

The Houses went straight on to Paris and by midnight were settled into the Crillon on the Place de la Concorde, next to the American embassy.[28] (Later they found a handsome house on the rue de l'Université in the aristocratic faubourg St. Germain neighborhood.) On October 26, his first day in Paris, House was so busy that he "didn't know how he lived through the day." He met Henry P. Davison of the American Red Cross (formerly of the House of Morgan), Ambassador William Sharp, and others in the morning; gave a press conference for the American correspondents at noon; then lunched with Field Marshal Sir Douglas Haig, the British commander, and Lord Milner, the British war minister. Then at six he was received "with open arms" by Clemenceau, who lost no time before sticking conversational darts into Lloyd George and General Pershing.[29]

Seeds of doubt about Woodrow Wilson's judgment had entered House's mind, but the two men still worked closely together. Throughout these hectic weeks leading up to the armistice, they exchanged as many as half a dozen telegrams a day. (Amazingly, the president sometimes decoded them himself.) On his second day in

Paris, October 27, House recorded laconically that he had lunch with Frank Cobb and gave him some work. House realized that if the armistice was to be based on the Fourteen Points, it would be as well to be clear about what precisely the points meant. So he asked Frank Cobb to put his colleague, Walter Lippmann, to work. House told Lippmann, "You helped write these points. Now you must give me a precise definition of each one," and he wanted it by ten o'clock the next morning. Lippmann left House's office slightly dazed. He did not even have a copy of the Fourteen Points but managed to track one down at the Paris *Herald.* Then he sat down and proceeded to gloss the points, one by one. In the course of the night, Frank Cobb dropped by to help with the article about the League of Nations. Exhausted, Lippmann finished at 3 a.m. and rushed the copy to the decoding room to be cabled to the president. Wilson's approval arrived just in time for House's meeting with the Allies.[30]

Lippmann's glosses had been skillfully drafted. On the freedom of the seas, for example, there was no mention of the British Royal Navy, blockade, or naval building programs. All the president was saying was that the rights of neutrals against belligerents must be precisely defined. Again, point 5 specified that all colonial claims must be adjusted in accordance with the principle that the interests of the populations concerned must be given equal weight with those of the colonial powers. Fear had been expressed in France that this meant all colonial issues would be reopened. Obviously, wrote Lippmann, this was not intended. The colonial powers should act as trustees for the natives, and the peace conference would write a code of conduct for such trustees of territories detached from German rule.

House's strategy was to jolly the Allies along to agree to an armistice as quickly as possible. On October 29, for example, he cabled that there "can be no real difficulty about peace terms and interpretation of fourteen points as Entente statesmen will be perfectly frank with us and have no selfish aims of their own which would in any case alienate us from them altogether. It is the fourteen points that Germany has accepted. England cannot dispense with us in the future and the other allies cannot without our assistance get their rights as against England."[31] Again, on October 30, House first sent a telegram saying, "The English I think will accept your fourteen points with some modification such as . . . making of the freedom of the seas conditional upon the formation of the League of Nations. The French are inclined not to accept your terms but to formulate their own."[32] Later that same day, after lunch with Lloyd George, Balfour, and Lord Reading, House had to admit that the British were taking a rather more stubborn line. If the Allies accepted an armistice based on the Fourteen Points, Lloyd George argued, then the

Germans would assume that the Allies had simply accepted the Fourteen Points and Wilson's other speeches without qualification. But Britain could not accept point 2, on the freedom of the seas, without qualification. If it was simply made part of point 14, the league covenant, then Britain could not agree to the covenant.

Later still House sent a longer telegram after a conference at the French foreign ministry with Clemenceau and the Italian foreign minister, Baron Sidney Sonnino. House now reported that Lloyd George "reversed his position taken a short time before with me privately" and said "we cannot accept this [point 2] under any circumstances. It takes away from us the power of blockade."[33] House then got tough. The president would have to tell the Germans that the negotiations were at an end. The president would decide whether the United States should fight for the principles laid down by the Allies. That might mean a separate peace between the United States and the Central Powers.

His statement, he told Wilson, "had a very exciting effect upon those present."[34] Wilson promptly cabled back: "I cannot consent to take part in the negotiation of a peace which does not include freedom of the seas because we are pledged to fight not only to do away with Prussian militarism but with militarism everywhere."[35]

House cabled Wilson that he intended to tell the prime ministers that if their conditions of peace were essentially different from the Fourteen Points, for which the American people had been fighting, then Wilson would probably have to go before Congress and ask whether the United States should fight for the aims of Britain, France, and Italy. He had told the British privately that Wilson anticipated that their policy would lead to the greatest naval building program the world had ever seen.

Lloyd George handed House a memo saying that the Allies were willing to make peace on the basis of the Fourteen Points and Wilson's subsequent speeches. But the freedom of the seas was open to several interpretations, "some of which they could not accept."[36] The Allies wanted to be clear that when President Wilson in his Fourteen Points speech said that invaded territories must be restored, they understood that to mean that Germany would make compensation for all damage done.

The president sent House a more understanding message about the British and the freedom of the seas. He insisted that Congress would not want "American life and property . . . sacrificed for British naval control." But while blockade would have to be redefined, it would not be abolished. He added that he was "proud of the way you are handling the situation."[37] House wrote in his diary that he appreciated this recognition, "for he is not given to much praise."[38]

Soon the Colonel could report that "everything is changing for the better." "Assure you," he wrote in cablese, "that nothing will be done to embarrass you or to compromise any of your peace principles." He specifically asked permission not to use Wilson's suggested threat that the United States "would build up the strongest navy our resources permit."[39]

Later, the British writer Harold Nicolson zeroed in on the "fundamental misunderstanding" papered over by the manner in which House, with the help of Walter Lippmann's supple pen, successfully procured the Allies' agreement to Wilson's negotiations with the Germans:

> I have the most profound respect for Colonel House—considering him
> to be the best diplomatic brain that America has yet produced, yet I con-
> fess that a most undesirable obscurity hangs over his 'interpretation.'
> Was it on the basis of that interpretation that the Allies accepted the
> Fourteen Points, the Four Principles and the Five Particulars, as the basis
> of the eventual Treaty of Peace? . . . It is difficult to resist the impression
> that the Enemy Powers accepted the Fourteen Points as they stood;
> whereas the Allied Powers accepted them only as interpreted by Colonel
> House. . . . Somewhere, amid the hurried and anxious imprecisions of
> those October days, lurks the explanation of the fundamental misunder-
> standing which has since arisen.[40]

While the Allies wrangled over the interpretation of Wilson's speeches in Paris, Europe was in flames. Austria surrendered. A mixed French, British, and Serbian army pushed up from Macedonia to the Danube. On November 4 House chaired a meeting that approved an invasion of Germany from the south by these forces; they were ordered to find airfields from which to bomb Germany.[41] The German admirals, desperate to preserve the honor of their navy, planned a suicidal sortie against the British navy in the North Sea. The enlisted men, aware that they were being sent to futile deaths, mutinied. There was rioting under the red flag in Munich, Stuttgart, Nuremberg, and Berlin and artillery battles in the streets of Hamburg.[42] House's young assistant, William C. Bullitt, reported to Secretary of State Lansing that Bolshevik activity was spreading everywhere from Bulgaria to the Baltic.

While chaos raged from the North Sea to the Ukraine, most of House's time was occupied with the obstinate British resistance to Wilson's insistence on the freedom of the seas. The critical meeting of the Supreme War Council was held in House's quarters on November 3. Lloyd George said he was quite willing to discuss the matter. "Why do you not say so?" House asked and extracted a letter from the British prime minister.[43] It was a "fudge," committing Lloyd George to nothing specific. But it was enough. House called it in his diary a "red letter day." He added that he felt the British were "so wholly in the wrong that I have been confident that they would eventually give way."[44]

As the meeting broke up, the news came through that the Austrians had accepted the terms of an armistice. House had the presence of mind to say to the Italian prime minister, Orlando, "Bravo, Italy!," which brought Orlando close to tears. By November 5, House was able to send a telegram to the president blaming "that mischievous and reactionary blue water school" of British Conservatives for Lloyd George's obstinacy and concluding that "we have won a great diplomatic victory."[45] But that same day in the midterm elections, Wilson had suffered a great political defeat.

On November 8 the Allies sent their terms for an armistice to the Germans, and at 3 a.m. on November 11 Colonel House was able to pass on the German acceptance, which he had received from Clemenceau.

House added his personal message: "Autocracy is dead. Advance democracy and its immortal leader. In this great hour my heart goes out to you in pride, admiration and love." Wilson issued his own characteristically biblical statement: "A supreme moment of history has come. The eyes of the people have been opened and they see. The hand of God is laid upon the nations. He will show them favor, I devoutly believe, only if they rise to the clear heights of His own justice and mercy."[46]

It was indeed a great moment, and the culmination of years of work for both House and Wilson. Together they had drafted the Fourteen Points as a practical expression of their ideals. Together they had played the German government as a skillful angler plays a fish that was gasping with exhaustion but still big enough and strong enough to break its line. While Wilson stuck to his principles, it fell to House to bring the Allies, balky and resentful, along. He managed those tough and temperamental politicians, Lloyd George and Clemenceau, with tact, but also when necessary with firmness. He knew how to use the strength of the United States to bring them to heel. And he did it without causing personal offense.[47]

If the achievement of the armistice was a brilliant feat in which the qualities of both men played a necessary part, the management of the peace process was less successful, and here it is Woodrow Wilson, not Edward House, who must bear the larger share of the responsibility. House shared Wilson's ideals. Like Wilson, he hoped that a new and better world would rise from the war. Like Wilson, he believed American liberals must reach over the heads of the militarists to enlist the peoples of Europe in a crusade for peace.

Unlike Wilson's, though, House's ideals, as we have noted, were steeped in an instinctive understanding that politics is the art of the possible. Thanks to Wilson's high-handed style, the negotiations over the armistice turned into a conflict, not between German militarists and the democratic countries, but between the United States and those countries whom Wilson refused to call his allies.[48] It was left to House to bring the Allies along, by a judicious mix of bonhomie and veiled threats.

It would have been simple—given the Allies' predominance and the Germans' desire for an end to the fighting—to arrange a German surrender, followed by swift negotiation of a peace treaty that would deal with the unresolved issues.[49] Instead, an armistice was arranged for one month, then renewed for another, and then for a third. Suddenly, as their armies demobilized, the Allies' great strength melted away.[50] Traumatized by their casualties and half-ruined by the struggle, they wanted peace and security. It was not wise for the president of the United States to lecture them relentlessly about their selfishness. Colonel House understood this and tried to move forward to a realistic settlement before the Wilsonian vision had been tarnished. His reward was to be accused of betraying a vision he shared and a strategy he had helped to develop.

For the time being, House remained the president's lieutenant in Europe. He was the man to whom everyone turned who wanted a knot untied or a conflict resolved. In the meantime, the leaders of the victorious nations had to deal with tiresome practical questions. Where would the peace conference be held? How many delegates, from which countries, would attend it? Who would be the American delegates?

Gradually it became apparent that the peace conference would be held in Paris. (The treaty was signed in Versailles, less than an hour from Paris, in deference to the French wish to avenge the humiliation of France's 1871 surrender, signed at Versailles.) Wilson's early enthusiasm for Lausanne had waned; he now thought, for reasons that are unclear, that it was "saturated with every poisonous element and open to every hostile influence in Europe."[51] House loyally came out for Paris, though he personally felt the conference should be held in a neutral country. Wilson accepted House's advice that the United States, Britain, France, Italy, and also

Germany should each have five representatives at the peace table and the other belligerents from three to one, according to their importance.

The president had already made it plain that he himself, Colonel House, and Secretary of State Lansing would be three of the American delegates. In November Wilson added General Bliss, the American military representative, and Henry White, a veteran diplomat, a Republican but with no active political involvement.[52] House realized how useful it would be to have distinguished Republicans on the peace commission. He tried to interest Wilson in Governor Samuel W. McCall of Massachusetts and later urged Wilson to appoint William Howard Taft or Elihu Root, as well as Wilson's son-in-law, William McAdoo, who as secretary of the treasury would have been "a tower of strength."[53] Wilson's decision not to appoint Republican delegates of the first flight, such as Taft or Root, who approved of the League of Nations, has been widely blamed, at the time and since, for the failure of the treaty to pass the Senate.[54] House shared this view but loyally limited himself to remarking that except from a political point of view, Wilson made no mistake. It was a large exception.

Most difficult of all for House was the question of whether the president should be the active leader of the delegation. Wilson himself simply assumed that he would sit in the conference. He cabled to House that he assumed that he would be selected to preside. House replied, "If the Peace Congress assembles in France, Clemenceau will be presiding officer. If a neutral country had been chosen, you would have been asked to preside." He then bravely went on: "Americans here whose opinions are of value are practically unanimous in the belief that it would be unwise for you to sit in the Peace Conference. They fear it would involve a loss of dignity and your commanding position."[55] Frank Cobb sent the colonel a memorandum to that effect. Secretary Lansing advised the president not to go to Paris. Wilson ignored him, and Lansing wrote a prophetic note: "I am convinced he is making one of the greatest mistakes of his career and will imperil his reputation. . . . I prophesy trouble in Paris, and worse than trouble here."[56]

House, knowing his man so much better, was even more acutely aware that his motives would be misconstrued, and they were. Wilson replied crossly that they were "pocketing" him.[57] House did not argue the point any further.

Two days later the president announced that he would leaving for Paris immediately after the convening of the U.S. Congress on December 2. House remained convinced that it was a mistake. Days before he fell sick and died, young Willard Straight, in Paris as an aide to House, wrote in his diary, "I think [Wilson] wants to come. It's obvious the others don't want him to. They're afraid of him."[58] In point of fact, not all of the European statesmen were against Wilson's presence. Arthur Balfour said the conference "would not have run at all" if Wilson had not been there.[59] But there was general nervousness about how Wilson would behave.

In the summer of 1919, House reflected on the question in his diary. As far as Wilson's reputation was concerned, he was sure that attending the conference had been a mistake. As to whether it was a good thing or not on balance, "some think one way and some another." And then House made a rather notable admission. "What I should have preferred," he wrote, "would have been to have had the chairmanship of the delegation and to have had as my colleagues Taft, Root, McAdoo and Bryan. I could have driven that team successfully if I had been in charge."[60] That is, House would have opted for two Republicans and two potential Democratic presidential candidates at a time when Wilson had not yet given up on running for a third term. It was perhaps precisely because he guessed that his friend had thoughts along those lines that Wilson was so determined to make the journey himself.

The president did not fully appreciate that the situation had changed once the United States became a belligerent. In 1916, he saw himself as the disinterested arbiter, trusted by both sides, brokering a "peace without victory." Now that more than a million doughboys had been shooting at Germans on the Western Front, he could hardly claim that Olympian posture. But in his own mind he had not abandoned that aspiration. Certainly that is what Secretary Lansing thought: "In December 1916 . . . he had an idea that he might, as a friend of both parties, preside over such a conference and exert his personal influence to bring the belligerents into agreement. A service of this sort undoubtedly appealed to the President's humanitarian instinct . . . while the novelty of the position . . . would not have been displeasing to one who . . . seemed to find satisfaction in departing from the established paths marked out by custom and usage."[61]

On December 7 Woodrow Wilson sailed for Europe on the *George Washington*, the first president of the United States to make that journey in office. New York saw him off in style. There was a twenty-one-gun salute, and as the former German liner swung out into the East River, the dock was jammed with movie cameras. Battery Park was black with people, all waving handkerchiefs and flags, as airplanes did stunts over the masts and funnels of the liner. One young official who was traveling to Europe with the president wrote his family that "it almost made the tears come to my eyes to realize what a tremendous grip on the hopes and affections, not only of America but of the world, this one man has."[62]

Wilson was accompanied by 113 officials, technicians, and advisers, including the 23 members of the Inquiry who had been allowed to travel to Paris. At first the president kept to his cabin with a cold and a cough, but he responded to the sea air and the ministrations of his doctor, Admiral Cary T. Grayson. The members of the Inquiry were not happy about the cabins they had been assigned and the way they were being ignored. William C. Bullitt, then charged with relations between the State Department and the Inquiry, brashly sat down next to the president as one evening's movie was about to start and said the members of the Inquiry were in a "cynical" mood. Bullitt explained that "most of the men with brains on board were being treated like immigrants and felt entirely left out of the game." So Wilson agreed to meet a dozen of the Inquiry men the next morning. Although Wilson asked to be off the record, half a dozen accounts of his talk survive. Bullitt said the president was "overflowing with warmth and good nature."[63] He was also extremely pleased with himself and derogatory about the European statesmen he was traveling to meet. He repeated his favorite contention that the United States was the only nation that was entirely disinterested and that the Allied leaders did not really represent their peoples. (Lloyd George's coalition was in the next few days to win a victory that gave him four out of five seats in the House of Commons, the biggest majority in British parliamentary history up to that date. On December 29 Clemenceau won the support of the French Assembly by more than four to one. President Wilson's party had just lost control of both Houses of Congress.)

Wilson shared a number of his political assumptions with the Inquiry men. He wanted the League of Nations to "evolve," as this was the "Anglo-Saxon" way. He said some of the Allies were "conspiring" to see how much Germany could pay in reparations but that he opposed any indemnities beyond those for the damage inflicted. He thought Germany could not be admitted to the league until it had gone through a probationary period. He boasted about how the American army had saved the French from defeat, that "at Chateau Thierry we saved the world."[64] And he restated his conviction that he could reach over the heads of the European governments because he was more popular with their people than they were. Inevitably much of this reached the ears of the journalists and the diplomats gathered in Paris. None of it was pleasing to the men with whom Wilson would have to deal.

At first, however, President Wilson's reception by the peoples of Europe reinforced his confidence. In Paris, when their boat train arrived from Brest, the Wilsons were greeted by President Raymond Poincaré, Prime Minister Clemenceau, the government ministers, and "practically the entire population of Paris."[65]

State carriages with coachmen and footmen in the red, white, and blue livery of the republic conveyed them to the Murat Palace, where they were staying in splendor. A few days later Wilson was honored by a mass demonstration of Socialists and labor unions. In London, the president and Mrs. Wilson were entertained by the king and queen at Buckingham Palace, and Wilson was invited to a stag dinner by Prime Minister Lloyd George at Number Ten, Downing Street.[66]

Such social glories perhaps meant less to Wilson than his rapturous reception at the Free Trade Hall in Manchester, the high temple of North Country liberal and Protestant radicalism, or a pleasant interview with C. P. Scott, the founding publisher and editor of the liberal *Manchester Guardian.* For a moment, there was support for Wilson's belief that the working masses trusted him more than they trusted their governments: the British Labour Party passed resolutions for a "Wilson peace."[67]

In Rome, which the Wilsons visited next, it was not so much the toiling masses that impressed the president as the fact that the Italian government would not allow a planned mass demonstration in the Piazza Venezia. Edith Wilson recalled that her husband was "fairly blazing with anger."[68] Against the wishes of the Italian government, Wilson made six short speeches in northern industrial areas.

There was something poignant in the outpouring of affection and expectation with which the peoples of Europe greeted Wilson. They saw him as a savior whose country had won a war that many in Britain and France had feared they could never win. They also treasured his hopes for a future of large abstractions: peace, democracy, justice. For a brief historical moment, people in many countries and of many political persuasions, rich and poor, were united in seeing the American president as their symbol of a better life in the future. They did not know much about him, and it did not take long for normal life to be resumed. There was nothing surprising about the fact that politicians in Italy or France or Britain who had hung on grimly for victory continued to battle dourly for what they had promised their people: peace, prosperity, national glory.

At this critical juncture, everything for which House had worked since he had signed on with his friend the president depended on the friendships and the trust he had earned from the statesmen of Europe. Everything hung on his ability to match Wilson's lofty dreams with his own practical idealism. And at this moment, House's health, fragile since boyhood, broke down for two crucial weeks. On January 11, 1919, he went down with a kidney stone. A private telephone wire was run from Wilson's residence, and the president came to consult him almost daily. But House "was really quite miserable after the pain let up."[69] He was still confined to bed after almost a week, "lying in bed unshaven," as Sir William Wiseman found him but "as usual perfectly delightful."[70]

As young Raymond Fosdick wrote: "An American can have anything he wants today—he owns the city. The girls even try to kiss him on the streets. I wonder . . . what will be the greeting of the French when the Peace is finished and Wilson comes to go home. . . . Poor Wilson! The French think that with almost a magic touch he will bring about the day of political and industrial justice. Will he? Can he?"[71]

15 *The Covenant* ❧

"One of the first acts of the Conference of Paris," wrote Colonel House's friend, the lawyer David Hunter Miller, "was the adoption at its opening session January 25 of a resolution declaring that a League of Nations should be created."[1]

Miller played a vital part in the drafting of the league's covenant. He remained one of its most loyal partisans for the rest of his life. But Colonel House had an even more important role in the shaping of Woodrow Wilson's ideas about the league. Indeed, at first overwhelmed by the sheer weight of the wartime presidency, Wilson more or less handed over to House responsibility for defining what the league should be. Just as House's role in the formulation of the Fourteen Points was far more important than many historians have acknowledged, so Edward House could claim to be have been, if not the father, at least the midwife of the league.

The idea of the league did not begin with the draft of its covenant that the colonel and the president had discussed the previous summer at Magnolia, Massachusetts. The conception of some kind of association of nations to enforce or guarantee the peace had been in the air in progressive circles in Europe as well as in America well before the war broke out in August 1914.

The brutal toll of casualties sharpened interest in a league, not only in Left-liberal circles, but also in broad swaths of the ruling elites. After the chaotic muddle of 1914 it was clear that bilateral diplomacy could not be relied on to prevent a crisis turning into war.

By 1915, Sir Edward Grey "dreamed" of a league of nations that would be "a new and much improved substitute for [the] Concert of Europe."[2] In 1915 the Fabian Society, a group of intellectuals committed to a gradual approach to socialism, commissioned Leonard Woolf (husband of Virginia Woolf) to study ways of preventing war.[3] The "peace movement" in Britain had close ties to American groups.[4] The Bryce Group, named for James, Lord Bryce (author of the classic *The American Commonwealth*), kept closely in touch with American colleagues, especially with the League to Enforce Peace, supported by former president William Howard Taft. The Union for Democratic Control in England had close ties to the editors of the *New Republic*, who included Wilson's friends Herbert Croly and Walter Lippmann.

By 1916 both Wilson and House were attracted to some union or association or league of nations to guarantee world peace. In that year Wilson wrote to House: "I agree with you that we have nothing to do with local settlements—territorial questions, indemnities, and the like—but are concerned only in the future peace of the world and the guarantees to be given for that. The only possible guarantees, that is, the only possible guarantees a rational man could accept, are (a) military and naval disarmament and (b) a league of nations to secure each nation against aggression and maintain the absolute freedom of the seas."[5]

That paragraph can be parsed in a number of critical ways. Wilson's lofty indifference to territorial questions was unrealistic. He had a bee in his bonnet about the moral equivalence between German aggression (as evidenced by the invasion of Belgium, France, and Russia) and British sea power used in blockade. But it shows that as early as 1916 Wilson was thinking of a league of nations as a major goal and that House was aware of his thought in that respect.

On both sides of the Atlantic, in fact, schemes for some organization to prevent war were in fashion. Some wanted at least the less dangerous disputes to be resolved by an international court or by arbitration. Many wanted such a council to consist solely of the Great Powers; others wanted some representation for weaker nations. British champions of such schemes were well aware that their chances of success would be greatly enhanced if the United States were on board. Even David Lloyd George—the British prime minister at the end of the war who had started out in life as a radical but was seen by Wilson and House as little better than a reactionary imperialist—said in a January 5, 1918, speech that one essential of a lasting peace settlement must be "the creation of some international organization to limit the burden of armaments and diminish the probability of war."[6] In general the British government (a coalition led by the Liberal Lloyd George) took the idea seriously. At the same time it was uneasy about the implications of a league for the British Empire, an issue that divided the Liberal Party, and reluctant to discuss anything that might inhibit Britain's traditional reliance on naval power.

Three figures apart from Colonel House, all involved in the deliberations of the peace conference, made important contributions to the intellectual pre-history of the league. The French politician and lawyer Léon Bourgeois annoyed the Americans by his passionate defense of what he saw as French interests. Bourgeois, obsessed with the conviction that France must never again be exposed to German aggression, fought hard for a league.

Jan Christiaan Smuts, the Boer general who became a field marshal in the British army, was assigned by Lloyd George to define the sort of league of nations Britain could live with. In December 1918 he proposed much of what ended up in the league's eventual covenant: a general assembly of all member nations, a smaller executive council, a permanent secretariat, steps to settle international disputes, and mandates for people not yet able to rule themselves.[7]

Within the British government, responsibility for thinking about a postwar association to keep the peace fell to Lord Robert Cecil, under-secretary for foreign affairs under first Grey, then Balfour.[8] Tall and thin, with the manner of a highly intellectual monk (he was a committed Anglican layman), Cecil was one of the able sons of the Tory prime minister, Lord Salisbury.[9] On September 3, 1917, Cecil wrote House, "We ought to make some real effort to establish a peace machinery when this war is over."[10] House brought the letter to President Wilson's attention. At the time, Wilson was not interested. He was anxious to prevent public discussion of anything like a league until the Inquiry had finished its work. He spoke disparagingly of American advocates of the league as "woolgatherers."[11]

Wilson's attitude may have been influenced by the fact that the most prominent American organization of the kind Grey and Cecil had in mind was the League to Enforce Peace. Colonel House, however, discussed what form an international organization should take at a luncheon at the House apartment attended by Taft, Elihu Root, President A. Lawrence Lowell of Harvard, House's brother-in-law Sidney Mezes, and the archbishop of York, Cosmo Gordon Lang, later archbishop of Canterbury.

Understandably, because of their grimmer experience of the war, the British were in the lead. The British government had appointed a committee under a senior judge, Sir Walter Phillimore, to look into the various schemes for "a league of nations or other device." In June Cecil reported that the committee had done its work. On June 25, 1918, House wrote Wilson, enclosing a copy of a long letter he had sent Cecil the same day. In it House proposed, as a personal view, that when there was any danger of war, peace delegates would meet and insist that potential belligerents must settle their differences by arbitration. The sanction would be that all other members of the league would break off all diplomatic, financial, and economic relations and, where possible, also use physical force against the belligerent. All members of the league would guarantee each other's territorial integrity. House added that there was a need to act swiftly to wrest the initiative away from Britain and France.

> The trouble that I see ahead is that the English, French, or the groups here may hit upon some scheme that will appeal to people generally and around it public opinion will crystallize to such an extent that it will be difficult to change the form at the Peace conference. It is one of the things with which your name should be linked during the ages. The whole world looks to you as the champion of the idea, but there is a feeling not only in this country but in England and France as well that you are reluctant to take the initiative. . . . Everywhere the most popular slogan is, "This is a war to make future wars impossible."[12]

Wilson was busy—"sweating blood," as he put it—over whether or not to intervene in Russia. So he did not reply to House's letter until July 8. Then he asked House to rewrite the Phillimore Report, which he had been too busy to read, "along the lines of your recent letter to Lord Robert Cecil."[13]

On July 13 House sat down to draft a constitution for the league with the help of David Hunter Miller. Miller had brought voluminous notes and the Phillimore Report, but House deliberately did not use it as the basis of his own draft. By lunchtime the next day they had finished what he called "the first draft for the Covenant of a League of Nations."[14] Comparison of that first draft with later drafts by Wilson and others upholds that claim. Edward House was indeed responsible for the first recognizable version of what became, a little over six months later, the covenant of the league.

For all the league's subsequent failings and failures, it was an unprecedented attempt to bring peace to the world, one that led eventually to the setting up of the United Nations. It was House who suggested to Wilson that the time had come to draft a covenant for the league; House who acted as the channel through which Wilson was informed of the thinking of those in Britain (Grey, Cecil, and Phillimore) who had thought hardest about how a league could be set up; House, finally, who, with Miller, put pen to paper and produced a robust draft. House sent off to the president what he called the "Covenant of a League of Nations." This seems to have been the first time the word "covenant" was used in this context, a favorite word of Wilson's.[15] The brief preamble stated that "International civilization having proved a failure because there has not been constructed a fabric of law to which nations have yielded with the same obedience as individuals submit to intra-national laws . . . it is the purpose of the States signatory to this convention to form a League of Nations having for its purpose the maintenance throughout the world of peace, security, progress and orderly government."[16]

The preamble and the first three articles, House wrote, were the "keystone of the arch." Article I specified that "the same standards of honor and ethics shall prevail internationally and in affairs of nations as in other matters." This same belief underlay, as he admitted, Article IV, banning "secret inquiry," as a means of stamping out what House called "the abominable practice of espionage."[17]

Wilson did not use House's first three articles in his version, though the underlying idea of "open, just, and honorable" dealings among nations and in particular the need for "scrupulous respect for all treaty obligations," incorporated in the preamble, did survive to the final draft accepted by the peace conference. Wilson's biographer, Ray Stannard Baker, was quite accurate in his description of how Wilson used House's and subsequent drafts of the covenant by others: "Practically nothing—not a single idea—in the Covenant of the League was original with the President. His relation to it was mainly that of editor or compiler, selecting or rejecting, recasting or combining the projects that came in to him from other sources. He had two great and central convictions: that a league of nations was necessary; that it might be brought into immediate existence. In voicing these he felt himself only a mouthpiece of the people of the world."[18]

On July 23, 1918, the colonel recorded in his diary that the president and Mrs. Wilson would be coming to visit Magnolia for a few days. House promptly asked Mrs. Thomas Jefferson Coolidge Jr. if the presidential party could stay at her house, to which she agreed. Since the Coolidge home was "the most beautiful on the Shore," with a "beautiful loggia overlooking the sea" and only a stone's throw from what the colonel termed the "little farm cottage" where he and Loulie were staying, the Wilsons were installed there. The house stood "on a point jutting into the water between Manchester beach and Magnolia beach."[19]

The Jefferson Coolidges, fast friends of the Houses since Edward House had used Thomas Jefferson Coolidge Jr. as his stockbroker in the 1890s, had prospered exceedingly thanks to the Old Colony Mutual Trust Company.[20] They claimed descent from Thomas Jefferson, and their house, a replica of Monticello, was decorated with some of the great man's paintings and equipped with his china. They had played a part in introducing the Houses to Brahmin society in Boston.

Even in those simpler days, a presidential visit was no informal affair. House called the State Department to send a Secret Service man to do a reconnaissance. House already had Secret Service protection, but additional Secret Service men arrived for the presidential visit, and a detail of Marines from Boston picketed the grounds. Hydroplanes searched the sea, and two destroyers and a flotilla of submarine chasers protected the Coolidge house, which could be seen plainly from the sea. After all, German U-boats had ventured into American waters before.

At last on August 14 the White House telephoned to say that the president would be there in the morning. When the Wilsons arrived at nine o'clock, House hurried over to greet them. They went from the presidential train to the Coolidge home and went straight to work on the league. Wilson had cut House's draft by ten lines, from 220 to 210.[21] He had taken two of the first three clauses and incorporated them in the preamble. He tried to reduce the number of clauses to thirteen, which he regarded as his lucky number. On only one matter did the two friends differ flatly. House had incorporated a world court. Wilson did not approve. (He did not like lawyers.) He also strengthened the sanctions to be applied to aggressors to include military action, which House had stopped short of recommending.

Much of their discussion concerned questions of presentation. They agreed, for different reasons, that it would be best not to publish the draft covenant. House, who had persuaded the British government not to publish the Phillimore Report so as to prevent the British "anticipating" the American president, feared that the British would be annoyed if Wilson then went public with his version. Wilson was intent on arranging to get all the glory of the League of Nations. To be fair, he was also motivated by the political need to keep control of the idea, which was rapidly becoming the centerpiece of his strategy for peace. Wilson was also more concerned than House was at this stage about domestic opinion. He was already worrying about the reactions of "Senators of the Lodge type," as House put it in his diary.[22]

Vast and perilous as the issues were that they were discussing, the meeting had the atmosphere of a middle-aged summer holiday. The Wilsons arrived on a Thursday. On Friday Edith and Woodrow Wilson played golf with Cary Grayson in the morning. After lunch with the Houses, the two couples and Dr. Grayson drove into Boston along the shore boulevard and went sightseeing, then drove in two cars to the home of the Houses' daughter Mona and her husband, Randolph Tucker, where an embarrassing contretemps took place. House, Wilson, and Grayson went for a walk in the Tuckers' grounds. An alert Boston policeman knew the owners of the house were away. Seeing two cars drive up, one presumably for the loot, and a group of hatless men emerge from the house, obviously burglars, he rushed up to the nearest Secret Service man, who had some difficulty making him believe it was the president of the United States who was under suspicion.

Wilson greatly enjoyed the short break from his labors. The Wilsons left for Washington on Monday evening, and Wilson wrote his daughter, Jessie, how much better he felt as a result.[23] Even so, Wilson and House had found time for serious discussion not only about the League of Nations, but also about the critical situation in Russia. Sir William Wiseman remembered how "one afternoon in particular the President and Colonel House sat on the lawn in front of House's cottage with maps of Europe spread out before them, discussing ways and means of organizing Liberal opinion to bring down the German military machine."[24]

The destinies of Europe were even more obviously affected by events taking place at the same time at the German supreme headquarters at Spa, in Belgium. There, on August 14, 1918 (the day before Wilson's arrival in Magnolia), the kaiser, Field Marshal Hindenburg, and General Ludendorff were joined by the emperor of Austria. Six days earlier the British had launched their decisive offensive, which Ludendorff himself later described as the beginning of the end for imperial Germany. Ludendorff told his imperial masters that the military situation no longer made it possible for Germany to force the enemy to sue for peace.[25]

In the second week of September the Americans and the French jointly pinched out the St. Mihiel salient, and in the third week the French and the British together at last punctured the Hindenburg Line in the north.[26] In the middle of the month dramatic news came from the Balkan front. The joint French and British armies, based in Salonika in northern Greece, routed the German and Bulgarian army in front of them. On September 27 President Wilson, on his way to deliver a major speech at the Waldorf Hotel in New York, learned that the Bulgarian army had surrendered. That made the situation of Germany's major ally, Austria, untenable, and with startling speed the same became true of Germany itself.

By October 1 Ludendorff had to admit that the German army might not last for forty-eight hours.[27] But its leaders' propaganda had predicted victory so loudly and so long that many of the German people believed their army must have been beaten only by a *Dolchstoss,* a stab in the back. The sheer speed of the army's falling apart nourished the paranoid theories that blamed not the Allies' and the Americans' victories in the field, but betrayal by Jews and other "enemies within."

Until the Bulgarian debacle, even Allied military commanders expected the war to last into 1919. Colonel House realized that now Wilson must move fast if he was to reap the fruits of victory. House and Wilson had always seen the war as a strategic opportunity for overthrowing the old regimes of Europe. House had come to see that a league of nations was a key component of that strategy. Although Wilson, preoccupied with winning the war, was slower to see how urgent it was to make the idea of the league his own, now he seized it with the enthusiasm of a convert and made it the centerpiece of his postwar plans.[28]

Wilson's speech in New York was another example of House's influence. The president had been reluctant to go public with his ideas for a league, but on September 3 House wrote to him urging him to make a major speech about it. "Do you not think the time has come," he wrote in his most tactful vein, "for you to consider whether it would not be wise to try to commit the Allies to some of the things for which we are fighting?"[29] Wilson did not reply for three weeks. He had been reluctant to provide the league with a written constitution, arguing that the Anglo-Saxon way was to allow institutions to evolve. Now he seems to have feared that to consult the Allies on the league would make it harder to incorporate the covenant in the peace treaty. House addressed that argument directly, arguing that if the Allies agreed to the covenant in advance, it would make it more, not less, certain that it would become part of the treaty. Once again, as in the setting up of the Inquiry and the framing of the Fourteen Points, it is clear that a prominent motivation for both Wilson and House was their suspicion of the Allies.

House urged Wilson to negotiate directly with the Allies. Wilson was reluctant to do that. He accepted House's argument that the time had come to commit the Allies to his program. But as usual he preferred to rely on his personal eloquence in a public speech. After an interval of three weeks, he summoned House to Washington and showed him the text of a speech he had written. He wanted House's advice on the best venue. Benjamin Strong, the governor of the Federal Reserve Bank of New York, had asked him to speak at a meeting to launch the Liberty Loan fund-raising drive. Wilson did not like that idea, but House persuaded him that the event would be perfect for his purpose.

On September 27 Wilson spoke at the Metropolitan Opera in New York, where the Liberty Loan was launched. It was one of his most brilliant orations. His theme, as always, was the unique moral authority of the United States. Once again, he positioned himself and the United States not as an ally of Britain and France against Germany, but as an arbiter between the two sides. It followed that while the United States would not bargain or compromise with the Germans, by the same token the Allies must accept Wilsonian principles. Once again Wilson seemed motivated by his deep revulsion for the secret treaties. There must be none of that now. The Allies must create the only means by which it could be made certain that the peace agreements would be honored. That indispensable instrumentality was a league of nations.

The speech was hailed as a noble statement of Wilson's lofty principles. But American opinion mainly focused on the fact that the president had now turned his back on the compromise peace he had sought so long. America's blood was up. As House recorded in his diary a few days later, Wilson "did not seem to realize before the nearly unanimous sentiment in this country against anything but unconditional surrender. He did not realize how war-mad our people have become."[30]

At this critical moment Wilson's attention was distracted from the exact shape of his ideas about the League of Nations by further dramatic events in Germany. On October 4 the liberal Prince Max of Baden was formally installed as chancellor of Germany. The very next day he sent a note to Wilson, inviting him to enter peace negotiations on the basis of the Fourteen Points. As everyone knows, the Germans accepted an armistice on November 11, 1918, the eleventh hour of the eleventh day of the eleventh month. That came about as a result of perhaps the most brilliant of all the diplomatic strokes that Woodrow Wilson pulled off, ably seconded by Colonel House.

On New Year's Day 1919, David Hunter Miller went over to Colonel House's office at the Crillon Hotel on the Place de la Concorde, where his law partner, Gordon Auchincloss, in deep confidence handed him two secret papers from the British delegation.[31] (He may have received them from Wiseman.) One was the Smuts proposal for a league of nations. The other was a memorandum by Lord Robert Cecil. Auchincloss asked Miller to return the papers the next day, which he did, after taking notes. As late as January 10, Miller recorded later, only four American drafts of a covenant for a league of nations had been written.[32] Two of them we have already discussed: House's original draft, written with Miller's help at Magnolia the previous July, and the draft in thirteen articles made by President Wilson some time after he received House's draft. The other two were by Miller himself, one written when he arrived in Paris and another drafted by him jointly with another legal expert, Dr. James Brown Scott.

Between the original framing of the covenant by House and its reshaping by the president, dramatic events had happened. House had gone to Europe as Wilson's representative. The war had ended. The president and the colonel had secured an armistice from the Germans on the basis of their own Fourteen Points and so had decisively weakened the leverage of the European Allies over the peace terms. President Wilson had changed his mind and, against House's advice, had decided to attend the peace conference in person. He had been greeted ecstatically by the peoples of Europe. He had installed himself luxuriously but uncomfortably in a Paris palace, while Colonel House, the peace delegates, and a hand-picked team from the Inquiry were accommodated in the Crillon Hotel.

One of Colonel House's problems as he recovered from a nasty bout of the Spanish flu that January, a minor problem in a world in flames, was what to do with Robert Lansing. On January 3 Lansing had sent for the State Department's two legal advisers, Miller and Scott, and ordered them to start drafting the text of a peace treaty. House encouraged Lansing in this "in order to keep him busy."[33]

By January 8, Miller and Scott met in conference with House, Lansing, and Lord Robert Cecil, and their draft was provisionally accepted as final. Their work was far from finished, however. The next morning Miller saw Auchincloss at the Crillon and was handed another paper, entitled "Covenant," which he saw immediately had been drafted by the president himself. Miller read it quickly twice and had no hesitation in telling Auchincloss that it was "very poor." It contained "objectionable" elements lifted from the Smuts draft and features that to a lawyer's eye were clearly unconstitutional.[34] At House's suggestion, Miller spent almost a week (from January 12 to January 18) working on detailed comments on Wilson's paper, and he handed them to Auchincloss to pass to House. On January 21 Auchincloss gave Miller four printed copies of what came to be called "Wilson's second Paris draft."

Now the draft had to be approved by the British, who were especially concerned with what were called "mandatories" but came to be better known as "mandates," arrangements for handing territories not yet deemed ready for self-government to more developed powers in trust for their peoples' future. David Miller had a series of meetings with Lord Robert Cecil. House wanted to get the British to sign off on a text that would not let down Wilson's ideals. He was prepared to make compromises but not to the point where they would threaten

Wilson's vision. He left it to Miller, as the lawyer, to hammer out procedural, textual, and even substantive issues but kept himself ready to step in and deal with political difficulties. One such was the disposition of the German colonies in Africa and the Pacific. These particularly affected the newly independent British dominions. The South Africans had their eyes on German Southwest Africa, the modern Namibia, and the Australians (led by the obstreperous Billy Hughes) and also the New Zealanders had ambitions in the Pacific. ("How I detest him!", muttered A. J. Balfour under his breath in French when Hughes was making some strident demand at the conference.)[35]

While he was patiently working for an agreed text that both the United States and Britain could support, House was also working to get the French on board. On one occasion he took a very considerable risk of offending his principal in the cause of good relations with the French. On January 7, both Wilson and Georges Clemenceau sent word they would come to House's room at five o'clock. Wilson arrived first. House was in the middle of a formal introduction to the other American delegates when Clemenceau arrived. In breach of every rule of protocol—Wilson, after all, as head of state outranked a mere prime minister—House asked his friend if he would mind if he took the Frenchman into another room for "one of our heart to heart talks." House continues: "I convinced him [Clemenceau], I think, for the first time that a league of nations was for the best interests of France. . . . Wilson could force it through because with all the brag and bluster of the Senate they would not dare defeat a treaty made in agreement with the Allies. . . . The old man seemed to see it and became enthusiastic. He placed both hands on my shoulders and said, 'You are right. I am for the League of Nations as you have it in mind and you may count on me to work with you.'"[36]

On January 25 the peace conference met at the French foreign ministry's offices on the Quai d'Orsay. President Wilson made a speech that was generally admired, though some of his hearers may have been irritated by his stressing again that the United States had less selfish interests in creating a league of nations than anyone else. He also made the far-sighted point that it was important to stop war before the scientists created weapons of destruction that would destroy civilization itself.[37] The next day, January 26, House could write in his diary that "this was a red letter day . . . since the Peace Conference adopted the principle of a league of nations."

On Sunday afternoon, February 2, Miller and the British lawyer Francis Hurst finished checking the proofs of the covenant. House told Miller to show it to the president. That evening at a quarter past eight Miller saw Wilson and House alone.

Wilson was unhappy, saying that the British had taken out some things he thought important, but he eventually approved most of the changes. Miller was left to spend all night in the printing office, where the work was finally done at six o'clock in the morning, ready for the first meeting of the League of Nations committee.

This apparently minor but potentially dangerous episode was a good example of the skillful way House handled the president. What Wilson had done, whether he was fully aware of it or not, was to replace an agreed Anglo-American draft with a purely American draft without telling the British. There was reason to expect that the British, whose help would be needed to pass the covenant in any form, would be aggrieved at this high-handed behavior. Wiseman alerted House that Lord Robert Cecil was perturbed. House telephoned the president and persuaded him to meet Lord Robert before the full committee met. For the first seven or eight minutes, House reported, "the meeting bade fair to be stormy," but then things went better and the president finally agreed to take the joint Hurst-Miller draft, rather than his own third draft of the previous evening, as a basis for discussion. After that things went smoothly.[38]

The meeting took place in Colonel House's office on the third flood of the Crillon Hotel. Most of its members were totally unaware how close it had come to breaking down before it even began. President Wilson, as the only head of state, was in the chair. On his right was Orlando, the only head of government on the committee and himself an able lawyer. On Wilson's left sat House, "active, bright-eyed, watchful, silent," and on a chair behind and between the two Americans sat David Hunter Miller, "leaning forward to whisper." The two British delegates, Lord Robert Cecil and General Smuts, sat on the Americans' left, and the two French-men, Bourgeois and Ferdinand Larnaude, were further away. All together there were two representatives on the committee from each of the Great Powers (the United States, Britain, France, Italy, and Japan), and one each from China, Serbia, Brazil, Portugal, and Belgium. Later, members were added for Poland, Czechoslo-vakia, Greece, and Romania. House spoke only at one meeting, when Wilson was away, less than any of the other members of the committee. As David Hunter Miller put it, "A pilot does not have to speak if he steers well."[39]

The league committee met every day in the colonel's room, and in ten days it had finished its work. Afterwards some play was made of the fact that it had taken only ten days to rewrite the rules of the world's game, but in truth the rules had already been rewritten by House, Wilson, Cecil, Smuts, and Miller. All the commit-tee had to do was to scrutinize the draft polished by the lawyers and to resolve a number of detailed but exceedingly knotty points.

One of these was the strong desire of the two Japanese delegates, Baron No-buaki Makino and Viscount Sutemi Chinda, to insert a clause into the covenant banning racial discrimination. It was inoffensive enough: "The equality of nations being a basic principle of the League of Nations, the High Contracting Parties agreed to accord, as soon as possible, to all alien nationals of States members of the League, equal and just treatment in every respect, making no distinction, either in law or in fact, on account of their race or nationality."[40]

The Japanese were thinking primarily of the treatment of their fellow country-men in California, but neither House nor Wilson had any difficulty with that clause. Nor did Lord Robert Cecil personally. The difficulty came from the Austra-lian member of the British delegation, Billy Hughes, prime minister of New South Wales, who saw in the Japanese language a threat to the cherished "white Australia" policy. Lord Robert Cecil, obviously embarrassed, felt obliged to declare formally that he was instructed by his government to vote against the Japanese. "Australia," commented David Hunter Miller acidly, "had more influence with London than Tokyo."[41]

The most difficult day was February 11. Most of the time from 10:30 a.m. to 1:30 p.m. was taken up with Léon Bourgeois's impassioned plea that the league must be backed by an international military force. Wilson told him repeatedly that the U.S. Constitution forbade the United States to join such a league. Cecil agreed. But as House dictated irritably to his diary, Bourgeois could not be silenced. Defeated on an international army, he tried to get agreement on what House called the "insidious" proposal that the league should have its own military staff, but that too was defeated.[42]

At last on February 13 House could rejoice. "This has been a memorable day. We finished the Covenant for the League of Nations. . . . When I telephoned the President at seven o'clock that we had finished, he was astounded and delighted."[43]

It had been a long journey from the car barn in Houston to the Crillon, but House had achieved success in Paris, as in Texas, by applying the same methods: by quietly anticipating opposition, by preparation and consultation, and by allowing others to take much of the credit. Woodrow Wilson took the credit in public, but in private he had the grace that night to tell House that "he preferred the original draft as agreed upon at Magnolia last summer."[44]

The president was due to return temporarily to Washington as the session of Congress was approaching its end. House was already aware that there would be political opposition to the league back home, and he had a plan for meeting it. He wanted the president to invite members of the Foreign Relations Committee of the Senate and its opposite number in the House of Representatives to dine with him on his return. Wilson preferred to address a joint session of Congress. House argued that this would simply confirm the suspicion in Congress that Wilson was a kind of schoolmaster who wanted to lecture them. So House got Gordon Auchincloss to draft a cable to the president's secretary, Tumulty, inviting the senators and congressmen to dinner so that they could go over what he called the "constitution" of the league article by article. Wilson read the cable and changed only one word.

The plenary session of the whole peace conference met at three in the afternoon on February 14 in the gorgeous Salon de l'Horloge at the Quai d'Orsay to hear the president report as chairman of the League of Nations committee. Wilson spoke first, followed by Cecil, Orlando, Eleftherios Venizelos, the prime minister of Greece, and Léon Bourgeois. Wilson sent for a Bible and read the twenty-six articles of the covenant—twice his lucky number—without gestures. Then he launched into a speech that his hearers found noble and uplifting and that many commentators hoped would be the baptism of a new era in international relations. The covenant, Wilson said, was no mere collection of empty words. "If the moral force of the world will not suffice," he threatened, "the physical force of the world shall."

House was impressed, though coolly so. "The president . . . talks entirely too much, but he does it so much better than anyone else. . . . He is in a class unto himself."[45] Wickham Steed, Lord Northcliffe's favorite journalist, agreed that "the affairs of the world were being lifted into new dimensions."[46]

After dinner, Edward and Loulie House went to the Palace Murat to say goodbye to the Wilsons and to go with them to the station. "Practically all official France was at the station," House found.[47] From the roadway to the train, a beautiful red carpet was spread, with palms on either side. Yet all was not well. A row had already broken out that revealed the seething resentment of Wilson that lay behind official enthusiasm.

The French had suffered terribly in the war. Now that it was over, they expected protection against future German aggression, not lectures about their selfishness. Wilson was furious with the French press for suggesting that his obsession with the league had delayed the practical benefits the French people expected from victory. Rightly or wrongly, he suspected the French government was behind the reports. Instead of turning to the colonel, as in the past, to deal quietly with the press, Wilson foolishly asked his doctor, Cary Grayson, to hint to the American correspondents that if the French government continued to campaign against him, the peace conference would move out of Paris, and he issued a press release complaining officially of the French press. "To my mind," House wrote in his diary, "it was a stupid blunder."[48]

From the moment of Wilson's return to France on March 14, 1919, House devoted himself chiefly to the work of revising the covenant so as to meet American objections.

The league committee had reported an agreed text of the covenant, giving Woodrow Wilson a major triumph. But by April, even Wilson was aware that he could not simply ignore the league's opponents in the United States.

One of the most effective political appeals they had was to ask whether this new-fangled league would override the Monroe Doctrine and bring the interfering busybodies and colonial predators of Europe into America's Caribbean and Latin American backyard. Wilson and House saw the Monroe Doctrine as a banner of liberty, protecting the virtuous republics of the New World from the corrupt monarchies of Europe. The Europeans mocked this attitude as Yankee hypocrisy. Wilson's fierce insistence that the covenant of the league make a nod in the direction of the Monroe Doctrine, however, was also motivated by his growing understanding that his opponents would charge him with undermining a cherished principle of American foreign policy.

Both the British and the Japanese saw Wilson's obsession with the Monroe Doctrine as an opportunity to bargain an advantage for themselves. The British wanted an agreement that there would be no costly naval building race, something a straitened postwar British treasury could not afford. But the U.S. Navy refused to have its hands tied by any agreement with Britain.[49]

The Japanese wanted to proclaim East Asia their own sphere of influence, to be covered by a Monroe Doctrine of their own. This troubled the Chinese as well as the Americans. Wilson was able to resist their pressure and even to resist the temptation to buy Japanese acceptance of the Monroe Doctrine by backing the Japanese anti-racism clause. House pointed out the domestic dilemma with his customary clarity: "If a special reservation of the Monroe Doctrine is made, the Japanese may want a reservation regarding a sphere of influence in Asia. . . . If a statement is made that it is not intended to interfere in domestic affairs, this would please our senators from the Pacific Slope, but it would displease all the senators of pro-Irish tendencies, for they would declare it was done at the instance of the English in order to keep the Irish question forever out of the League of Nations."[50]

By April 10 the difficulty with the British had been worked out by House and

Lord Robert Cecil. That night the committee for the League of Nations heard a number of women's representatives plead in five-minute speeches—all the time they were allowed—for the league to take women's interests under its protection. The committee, House felt, was impressed, and the league did in fact theoretically address women's issues.

Then came what House described as "one of the stormiest meetings we have had at all." It began with a "row" with Bourgeois over whether French should be the language for the official text of the league. Then came an hour's hard pounding over the Monroe Doctrine. The French delegates were annoyed that they had failed to get a league "with teeth." House, not to mention Wilson, was annoyed with them. "Of all the stupid performances I have ever witnessed," House wrote crossly, "this was the worst."[51] Why did the United States want a special mention of the Monroe Doctrine? Was it perhaps not in conformity with the covenant? Of course it was, said Wilson; indeed it was the model for the league. Then why was there any need to mention the Monroe Doctrine? Wilson was getting visibly angry. His lower lip quivered. Near midnight he lost his patience. The United States was the guardian of freedom. "Is there to be withheld from her the small gift of a few words which only state the fact that her policy for the past century has been devoted to principles of liberty and independence which are to be consecrated in this document as a perpetual charter for all the world?"[52]

David Miller was impressed. "At the close of the debate President Wilson replied to the French in a speech of witching eloquence, a speech made after midnight, which left the secretaries gasping with admiration, their pencils in their hands, their duties forgotten, and hardly a word taken down; the proposal was then adopted."[53]

Wilson's speech, House commented more cynically, "convinced everybody but the French Delegates at whom it was directed." The Americans and the British went to bed under the impression the clause had been accepted. The French thought otherwise. The whole question of the Monroe Doctrine had to be argued all over again on April 11. The French kept moving amendments, and Cecil and David Miller sought for compromise, but House and Wilson were in no mood to debate language. "It was an exhibition of Anglo-Saxon tenacity," House felt proudly. The president, Cecil, and he were alone, with about fifteen of the other committee members against them. At half past midnight Cecil asked House how long the meeting should go on. "I told him," House wrote, "until daylight or until we had finished."[54]

Once again the Japanese brought up their amendment denouncing racism to the covenant's preamble. Once again it was the Australian, Billy Hughes, who objected. Wilson wanted to accept the Japanese amendment, but House persuaded him to change his mind. House did not want this issue to break the alliance with the British that had forced through the covenant of the league. The French pointed out that a majority—eleven delegates to six—had voted for the Japanese amendment. President Wilson, as chairman, ruled that decisions of the committee were not valid unless unanimous. (Wilson had, however, accepted a majority vote when it was a question of choosing Geneva as the seat of the league.)

Gradually the outstanding questions were answered.

On March 16, only two days after the president's return from Washington, House "consented to be bored with Léon Bourgeois for an hour." What he wants, House wrote impatiently in his diary, "is to make the League an instrument for war instead of an instrument for peace."

House was due to dine with the president on March 18 and spent a long meeting with Lord Robert Cecil and David Miller to prepare for it. He found Wilson "more reasonable that he was the other day as to meeting the wishes of the Senate," but all four men found it nearly impossible to write into the covenant the guarantees that the Senate wanted.[55]

Formally, the covenant was to be amended at three meetings on March 22, 24, and 26. In practice these were meetings for letting the neutral nations in on the decisions that had been taken. Increasingly House's time was taken up not with the league, but with other hard questions we will discuss in a later chapter. In the meantime there was one important decision to be made. Where was the league to have it headquarters? The French wanted Brussels, but the Americans wanted Geneva, and Geneva it was. House had already consulted a friend, Professor William Rappard, and asked him to find a site. "I have in mind a park of about 1,000 acres, within easy distance of Geneva by road and lake, and a beautiful water gate which might well be made a memorial to those who fought and died in the great World War."[56]

At long last, on April 28, a plenary session finally approved the covenant, as amended, without changing a word. House remained committed to the idea of the League of Nations and for the rest of his life did what he could to make it a success. But his wish to be actively involved in making it a reality was only one of his hopes that were now doomed to be disappointed.

16 *The End of a Friendship* ∾

Woodrow Wilson is I believe the only real friend from whom I ever became separated.

—E. M. House, "Memories"

ON FEBRUARY 14, 1919, President Wilson was due to return from Paris to the United States for the end of the congressional session. In his absence, he left no doubt that House was to act in his place and with his full confidence.[1] Within the next four weeks, that confidence had been fatally, but unjustly, shaken.

On March 14, the day of the president's return to France from the United States, Colonel House traveled west on the presidential train, in filthy weather, to the port of Brest. It was not until they were on the way back to Paris that he finally had a chance to speak to the president.

House's diary is laconic. He quotes the president as saying, "Your dinner to the Senate foreign relations committee was a failure as far as getting together was concerned." Wilson "spoke with considerable bitterness," House recorded, about the way he had been treated by some of the senators, particularly Henry Cabot Lodge.[2]

Mrs. Wilson, years later, gave a very different version of what happened. From that talk on the train she dated the wreckage of her husband's plans, his illness, and "tragic years that have demoralized the world."[3] Mrs. Wilson waited in the stateroom while her husband and the colonel talked on next door. It was after midnight when she heard the president's door open and House leave.

She opened the door connecting their two rooms, she remembered. "The change in his appearance shocked me. He seemed to have aged ten years. . . . He was making a superhuman effort to control himself. Silently he held out his hand, which I grasped, crying: 'What is the matter? What has happened?' " Wilson, she remembered, "smiled bitterly." "House has given away everything we had won before we left Paris. He has compromised on every side, and so I have to start all over again and this time it will be harder, as he has given the impression that my delegates are not in sympathy with me."[4]

In Edith Wilson's version, House had explained these compromises by saying that he thought it best to yield some points lest the conference withdraw its approval altogether. "So he has yielded"—that is how Edith Wilson recalled her husband's stark despair—"until there is nothing left."[5]

Mrs. Wilson was writing almost twenty years after the peace conference; her bitterness, and her recollection of her husband's bitterness, had lost nothing with bottle age. So far from lasting until a late hour, the conversation between the president and House was too brief for them to go into all the issues that had arisen in Wilson's absence. House had to wait until Wilson had finished meeting with the French ambassador, Jusserand.[6] Charles Seymour, admittedly a partisan of the colonel, suggested very plausibly what may have happened: "For the first time Wilson realized that it was going to be necessary to compromise with the French and the British; . . . this upset him emotionally; . . . he may have controlled himself in talking to House and then exploded when he got back to Mrs. Wilson."[7]

Edith Wilson's account became the official version of Wilson's friends. His press secretary-turned-disciple, Ray Stannard Baker, interpreted everything that had happened in terms of a cunning plot by smooth, two-faced European diplomats to "wreck the entire American scheme for the peace." "Every militaristic and nationalistic force came instantly to the front when Wilson departed," he wrote. Baker conceded that House had once been "a true friend." But he never saw "the great stark lines of the conflict," never understood what, by "sinuous moves," the "old order" was doing to frustrate the president's dream of peace on earth. He accused House of "giving the greedy ones all they want." From the moment House met Wilson at Brest, Baker pronounced, there began to grow "a coldness between the two men," based not on "trivial personal causes" but on "deep failures in understanding and action."[8]

Both Mrs. Wilson and Ray Stannard Baker, and indeed others—most of them, like Wilson's doctor, Cary Grayson, closely associated with Mrs. Wilson and Baker—laid the foundation for a legend. According to them, the friendship between the president and his confidential adviser was broken because of House's black betrayal of his leader's most cherished ideals. Their version of events is a myth. Like all myths, to be sure, it has some basis in truth. It is true that their friendship never recovered from the events of February and March 1919. It ended in bitterness and mutual incomprehension, with grave consequences for both of them and ultimately—it really is no exaggeration to say—for the peace of the world. But the process was more gradual and more complex than the legend would have it. The cause was as much in Woodrow Wilson's state of mind, not to mention his state of health, as in any betrayal by House, even though the colonel did think he might have conducted affairs in Paris better if the president had not been there.

Wilson did believe that there had been a plot on the part of the European Allies to rush through a preliminary peace treaty that did not include the covenant of the League of Nations, that House had been party to such a plot, and that therefore House had betrayed him. But this was a mistaken belief. There was no such plot. Wilson's belief that there was arose in part from his confusion about the nature of the "preliminary peace treaty" under discussion.

Wilson, however, acted dramatically to undo what he saw as the mischief. And he turned for help to a new instrument of his wishes, Ray Stannard Baker. On Saturday morning, March 15, the day after his arrival in Paris from Brest, Wilson called Baker on a secret line.[9] He asked Baker to deny reports that there would be a preliminary treaty omitting the League of Nations. Baker thereupon drew up a statement, with the president's approval, and made it public. It read as follows: "The President said today that the decision made at the Peace Conference at its plenary session, January 25, 1919, to the effect that the establishment of a League of Nations should be made an integral part of the Treaty of Peace is of final force and that there is no basis whatever for the reports that a change in this decision was contemplated."[10]

Baker described this as a "bold stroke" that destroyed the intrigue that threatened Wilson's greatest achievement. As the British foreign secretary accused of the intrigue later demonstrated, and as overwhelming documentary evidence confirms, there was no intrigue, only a tough diplomatic wrangle.[11] Men sought in good faith to reach the least bad solution. Wilson interpreted his own course as principled resistance to the corrupt bargaining of the "old diplomacy." But in reality it was Wilson, not House, who made the most startling concession—and to the toughest of the bargainers.

On the afternoon of March 14, President Wilson abruptly agreed to a treaty with France guaranteeing that the United States would immediately go to war on France's side if France were ever attacked by Germany. Wilson's behavior was extravagantly praised by Ray Stannard Baker. It was severely judged in an interpretation by Sigmund Freud and William C. Bullitt. Wilson, they wrote, was unconsciously identifying himself with his heavenly Savior: "He was rapidly nearing the psychic land from which few travellers return, the land in which facts are the products of wishes, in which friends betray and in which an asylum chair can be the throne of God."[12]

That may be going too far. But the melodramatic version of events presented by Baker does not hold water. As noted, Balfour stated flatly that the suggestion that there was a plot against the League of Nations was supported by no evidence whatsoever. Wilson's own lawyer, the level-headed David Hunter Miller, wrote that "the effort to prove a plot where none existed could hardly go further."[13]

Charles Seymour's contention is persuasive.[14] Wilson returned to France to find that considerable progress had been made in his absence. If concessions were made, decisions could be quickly reached. Wilson's problem was how much he should concede. But there was another cross-pressure he found so intolerable that in trying to evade it, he blundered into disaster. During his return to the United States, he realized that he was no longer omnipotent. The Republican victory in the midterm elections raised an unbearable dilemma. He might have to choose between a treaty with no league or no treaty at all. For the abrupt decline in his political prospects, unfairly he blamed House.

Before the president left Paris in February 1919, in a businesslike twenty-minute session in the colonel's study at the Crillon, Wilson entrusted House with stewardship over his ideals for the peace. During that time, said House, the two men "settled all the important questions that were on my mind to take up with him before he left for America." The colonel was confident he could "button up everything" while the president was away. At that, Wilson "seemed startled and even alarmed."[15] So House, used to watching Wilson's unpredictable moods carefully, hastened to explain that he did not mean to reach final agreements in Wilson's absence, only to have everything ready for Wilson's imprimatur when he returned.

House laid out his priorities. The conference should fix the program for a preliminary peace with Germany. That meant, first, reducing the German army and navy to a peacetime establishment; second, defining Germany's new boundaries, which included the vexed questions of Alsace-Lorraine, the Rhineland, and the Polish frontier; how much Germany would have to pay by way of reparations for war damage; and how the German economy was to be treated. Since the covenant of the league had been triumphantly passed the previous evening, neither Wilson nor House saw any need to mention that it would be part of the treaty.

Was there anything else? House asked. No, said Wilson; they had covered the essentials. Then House, perhaps with a premonition that his friend was not altogether happy at the brisk self-confidence with which he contemplated standing in for him, asked if the president had anything else to suggest. No, Wilson repeated; those points would be enough. House ended with a warning. "I asked him to bear in mind while he was gone that it was sometimes necessary to compromise in order to get things through; not a compromise of principle but a compromise of detail; he had made many since he had been here." Sometimes it was necessary "to compromise the things of today to obtain the things of tomorrow."[16] Wilson did not demur. And with that the two friends parted, to all appearances the beloved leader and his trusted lieutenant.

Exactly four weeks later, the president was back. In the meantime, the complex machinery of struggle over the peace had rumbled forward. The cheering crowds, the dreams of a new age of innocence, were forgotten. House found himself beset by all the fears of a Europe transformed by the four horsemen of war, revolution, famine, and disease.

The president's head had been more than a little turned by his triumphal reception in Europe. He thought he was more popular than European leaders were with their own people.[17] Only aristocrats and reactionaries—Ray Baker's "greedy ones"—could want to stand in his way as he redrew the map of Europe. These convictions led him into a dangerous mistake. In mid-Atlantic he accepted an invitation to speak in Boston. He checked with House, who saw no harm in it if he spoke in a nonpolitical tone.

He did not take this excellent advice. On February 24, he spoke at the Mechanics Hall in Boston, at length, in passionate praise of the league and in contemptuous denunciation of its opponents. He gave twenty thousand cheering enthusiasts red meat. He pushed for the league. Worse, he insulted those who opposed it. If America did not "make men free"—by which he seems to have meant, more or less, "if the American Senate did not ratify a treaty containing the covenant of the League of Nations"—then the United States would have to "keep her power for those narrow, provincial purposes which seem so dear to some minds that have no sweep beyond the nearest horizon."[18]

Cabot Lodge may have taken this as referring to himself. He certainly took this incursion into his home base as a deliberate insult. "Mr. Wilson has asked me to dinner," he sniffed. "He also asked me to say nothing. He then goes to my own town and makes a speech—very characteristic." He spoke of Wilson's "small cunning."[19] In the bare ten days he was on American soil, Wilson's political position was so shaken that it never recovered, and largely by his own fault.

Tumulty had organized the dinner Colonel House had suggested. Two days after the Boston speech, thirty-four senators and congressmen came the White House. The evening was not a success. It began with a meal that fell below senatorial expectations. More than one guest complained that neither the liquor nor the cigars were up to standard.[20] (There was no wine, only iced water and half a glass of Apollinaris soda water.) The next morning the *New York Sun* reported the Republican senator from Connecticut, Frank Brandegee, as saying he felt as if he had been taking tea with the mad hatter.

Even more deadly was the cold civility of Cabot Lodge. Edith Wilson did not help by gushing about the wonderful reception she and her husband had been given in Boston. Lodge observed that her fingernails were "black with dirt."[21] Asked point blank by the president whether the league covenant would pass the Senate, Lodge replied gnomically (as Edith Wilson recalled twenty years later) that "if the Senate foreign relations committee approves it I feel there is no doubt of ratification."[22] The question, of course, lay very largely within his own power to decide. At another meeting, with the Democratic National Committee, Wilson lost control. He called Lodge and his allies (though not by name) "of all the blind and little provincial people—the littlest and most contemptible" and prophesied that "the gibbets that they are going to be erected on by future historians will scrape the heavens, they will be so high."[23]

Two days after the disastrous White House dinner, Lodge unveiled his batteries with a speech to the Senate. For years, Lodge's feelings about Wilson had amounted to hatred. Lodge the scholar saw Wilson as a pretentious charlatan. Lodge the historian, who had turned down one of Wilson's articles for a journal, despised him intellectually. The Brahmin had no respect for the professor, and the Yankee Republican no time for the Southern Democrat. He dismissed the president as "a man of ability, but he has no intellectual integrity at all."[24]

Nevertheless, Lodge did not intend to prejudge the issue, and he intended to be rational at all costs. A few weeks later he wrote to his friend, the novelist Edith Wharton, that he was in favor of a league of nations "if so constituted that it will . . . not endanger or imperil the United States." But the draft Wilson had brought back, he believed, was "in the highest degree dangerous."[25] He meant to give the league, its covenant, the treaty, and their sponsor, the president, a fair trial. But he would test them to destruction.

Lodge attacked what he called the "really evil suggestion" that any criticism of the covenant was tantamount to opposing peace. Those who supported the treaty, he said, must meet objections with something more than "shrill shrieks" that virtue was better than vice. Was the United States ready to abandon the principles of Washington's Farewell Address and the Monroe Doctrine? Were the American people willing to be forced into war under Article X of the covenant? Would the United States leave it to other nations to decide whether America should admit "a flood of Japanese, Chinese and Hindu labor"?[26] On March 2, 1919, Lodge introduced on the floor of the Senate a declaration signed by thirty-seven senators, later called a "round robin."[27] They were more than enough to vote down ratification of a treaty.[28]

Still Wilson seemed not to realize the mortal danger.[29]

On March 3, having been urged by House to ally himself with William Howard Taft, who supported the treaty, Wilson stepped arm-in-arm with that gigantic person onto the stage of the Metropolitan Opera in New York and delivered a speech that was bound, if indeed it was not calculated, to infuriate his enemies. "So many threads of the Treaty [would be] tied to the Covenant," he boasted, "that you cannot dissect the Covenant from the treaty without destroying the whole vital structure. The structure of peace will not be vital without the League of Nations, and no man is going to bring back a cadaver with him."[31] It did not occur to him that when he came back from Europe, he would bring with him two cadavers—the treaty and his own political reputation.

Wilson's departure from Paris left House busier than ever. His diary records conferences with a dizzy whirl of visitors: British labor leaders, women from the Women's Suffrage Convention, Polish Protestants, Chaim Weizmann. It was an international version, on a vaster scale, of the swarm of office seekers he had received in 1913.

On February 19 House and the British foreign secretary, A. J. Balfour, were due to meet Clemenceau at ten. A little after nine, word came that the Tiger had been shot at seven times by a Communist. (Clemenceau, who had fought duels himself, expressed shock that a Frenchman should miss with six shots out of seven. He refused to allow the would-be assassin, Eugène Cottin, to be executed; he opposed the death penalty.)[32] Two days later House went to see the indomitable old man in his "very humble" apartment. This visit was the beginning of a close friendship. It also prompted sober thoughts. "There are so many disorganized minds and the world is in such a ferment," he dictated to Miss Fanny (who packed a pistol herself in her reticule), "that any of us are likely to be killed at any time."[33]

Even House was overwhelmed by the responsibilities that had fallen on him in Wilson's absence.[34] "No one can ever know," he confided in his diary a week or so later, "how hard pressed I have been during the last months, or how every waking moment has been occupied. . . . It is Archangel and Murmansk at one moment, the Left Bank of the Rhine the next," and he added a global list of his preoccupations.[35] A few days earlier he had confessed to his diary that "when I fell sick in January I lost the thread of affairs and I am not sure that I have ever gotten fully back."[36]

Many parts of the world were indeed in a ferment, none more than Russia, four months after the revolution. House had stormy meetings with Marshal Foch and Winston Churchill, both keen to intervene in Russia. Reports of pogroms in Poland reached Paris. Munich, Vienna, and Budapest were all in chaos. In March, Gustav Noske, the self-styled "bloodhound" of the Social Democratic counter-revolution in Germany, ordered that "anyone found offering armed resistance to Government troops is to be shot at once." "In many German cities," wrote a historian who lived through those days, "horrors were committed . . . of which no history book tells."[37] Everywhere in the East there was hunger, even famine, and on the heels of hunger came epidemic disease in the shape of the Spanish flu.[38] Once again, in Karl Marx's famous phrase from 1848, a specter was haunting Europe, the specter of communism.[39]

The peacemakers themselves were at sixes and sevens, even before their dominant figure, Woodrow Wilson, had left for America, and their presiding officer, Georges Clemenceau, had been shot. There was confusion between a preliminary peace treaty and a definitive one. It might be reasonable to proceed with the former and to reserve for a definitive treaty the covenant of the league. On the other hand, Wilson and other enthusiasts for the league might feel that once even a preliminary treaty was signed, it would be hard to generate the political will for incorporating the league covenant into a final treaty.

The French government was actively lining up allies among the "successor states" of Eastern Europe. The French felt naked before an enemy who had twice in little more than a generation invaded their homeland. This fear was hardly irrational; the Germans would do the same again in another twenty years. Now that Russia had imploded, the French wanted the strongest possible governments in Warsaw, Prague, and Bucharest to take Russia's place.

Even more urgently, the French felt they needed to make territorial gains from Germany while it was still weak. It went without saying that France must recover Alsace-Lorraine. It also wanted to replace the rich coalfields the Germans had devastated in the north with the mines of the Saarland. But the ambitions of some French leaders went further still. They wanted to disarm and occupy the valley of the Rhine. Militarily, that would keep any future war off French territory. Territorially, it would deprive Germany of the Ruhr, perhaps at the time the greatest center of arms manufacture in the world. Symbolically, it would strip Germany of an emotional heartland celebrated from Hermann, the legendary conqueror of the Roman legions of Varus, to Wagner's Ring Cycle. Led by Foch, the generalissimo of victory, the French wanted to occupy undeniably German territory on the west bank of the Rhine, with more than 4 million German inhabitants, and if possible land on the east bank of the river too.

A timetable was at work that linked together two controversial issues. The armistice with Germany was due to be renewed for the third time on February 11, 1919. On February 12—the day of the agreement in committee on the league covenant—the committee duly reported in favor of immediately drawing up naval and military terms of peace and imposing them on the Germans. Balfour, for Britain, agreed, and so did President Wilson. But Clemenceau disagreed. He wanted the Allies to maintain armies big enough to impose, by force if necessary, the hard territorial and economic terms he wanted.

After Wilson's departure on the evening of February 14 House moved swiftly to get on with the drafting of the treaty. On February 16 he saw Balfour, who volunteered to talk the Japanese around.[40] House promised to get the Italians to agree. That left France. On February 22, House met with the wounded but unbowed Clemenceau. The next day he reported to Wilson that Clemenceau was now anxious to make an early peace with Germany. But he was also insistent on creating a "Rhenish republic."[41]

The decision to speed up the drafting of the treaty had made it urgent to decide on the western frontiers of Germany. The French yearning for future security and the American determination not to treat Germany vindictively were incompatible. Compromises were inevitable. But President Wilson, kept in touch by House with the progress in that direction, responded with his usual rigidity.

House met Tardieu in Vance McCormick's rooms at the Ritz to see what could be agreed on the Rhineland. The meeting became one of the chief pieces of evidence for the charge that House had betrayed the president's principles. Unfortunately the record is obscure on exactly what was said. McCormick noted baldly in his diary that "At 5:00, Colonel House and [André] Tardieu came for tea, also Aubert with Tardieu. They agreed on plan for Rhenish Republic and discussed method of getting Lloyd George's approval, also on Saar Coal Basin."[42]

McCormick's evidence need not be taken as conclusive of House's "guilt," however. House went to see Tardieu at the Ritz. (McCormick, of course, had no knowledge of what was said at this later meeting.) After their talk House saw a glimmer of light. In five or ten years, said Tardieu, when the League of Nations was in existence, the French might relent.

This interpretation, House noted in his diary, "relieves that question of one of its most objectionable features since otherwise it would be quite contrary to the policy of self-government."[43] House had already on February 22 reported Marshal Foch's plan to dock Germany of its territory west of the Rhine, to which Wilson responded by telegram on February 23, "I know that I can trust you and our colleagues to withstand such a program immovably." Rightly or wrongly, House interpreted this to mean that he should resist *permanent* but not necessarily *temporary* separation of the Rhineland from Germany.[44]

This distinction too House faithfully attempted to report to the president on February 24. House received no reaction to Tardieu's proposal, however—there were difficulties with a new code—so he felt free to continue to explore it.[45] On February 26, in a message about another subject, he promised to forward a memorandum from Tardieu. This he failed to do, probably because the memorandum made no mention of eventual self-determination for the Rhineland. Perhaps Tardieu realized that he had no authority from Clemenceau to make that concession. Perhaps House was afraid that such an omission would make Wilson dismiss the Tardieu channel out of hand; the colonel well knew how central self-determination was to Wilson's whole project. Perhaps House merely forgot to forward the memorandum, though this seems unlikely. The most serious charge that can be made to stick is that in his anxiety to reach a compromise on the Rhineland, House failed to forward one document that might at least temporarily have ended the negotiation.

On February 27, House discussed the question with Arthur Balfour and felt he was almost home. If only Clemenceau would agree that the Rhineland occupation should be temporary and to be ended after some interval by a plebiscite, then Wilson might accept the compromise. On March 2 House recorded laconically in his diary that he had had a long talk with Tardieu and that they had got nearer together on the question of the Rhenish Republic and Luxembourg. Unfortunately, no detailed account of that conversation survives. McCormick, who was present, recorded in his diary that House and Tardieu "agreed" on the Rhineland, "with proper reservations."[46] House did not go so far. In his diary he said simply "we got nearer." On March 7 House reported to Wilson a conversation that day with Clemenceau and Lloyd George: "The left bank of the Rhine was discussed, but no tentative agreement was reached because of Clemenceau's very unreasonable attitude. He wants the Rhenish Republic to be perpetually restrained from joining the German Federation. Tardieu tells me he will urge him to modify this view."[47]

Wilson, predictably, forbade House to accept any kind of separation of the Rhineland from Germany. Tardieu wrote to House on March 12, recognizing that it would be "very bad to start with German frontiers before the president is here."[48] House bowed to the inevitable: Germany's western frontier would have to be left for decision when Wilson returned.

By chance, on April 4, with Wilson away sick, House was back as America's representative on the Supreme Council. He persuaded Clemenceau and Lloyd George to accept a compromise. There would be no Rhenish Republic. Instead, the left bank of the Rhine, with three bridgeheads on the right bank, would be under temporary Allied occupation. So House saw an opportunity to move the treaty ahead by a compromise that he saw as safeguarding the president's principles. It is possible to criticize him for such a move. Even so, there is no reason to believe that House intended to breach his undertaking to submit any agreements he might make for Wilson's approval. What is hard to understand, except in the light of extraneous factors, which it is now time to confront, is why Wilson's entourage, then and for the rest of their lives, interpreted House's entirely intelligible and honorable diplomatic maneuvers as the blackest treason.

Edith Wilson had always resented House's influence on her husband. By the time she wrote her unreliable memoirs, she blamed House, quite unreasonably, for Wilson's illness and defeat. Nor is Baker a much more credible witness. He had become utterly committed to a view of Woodrow Wilson as a savior betrayed by little men of little faith. The fact remains that the night of March 14, 1919, was a punctuation mark in House's life. Before that, there had been no open change in the relations between the two friends, though seeds of mistrust had been sown. After that point, House's position as the president's most intimate counsellor was in question.

From then on, two camps increasingly bitterly disputed the president's favor, like cabals of courtiers in a baroque court. On one side were Colonel House and his friends, especially his son-in-law Gordon Auchincloss; Sir William Wiseman; Henry Wickham Steed, the editor of *The Times* of London; and the members of the Inquiry, especially the editor of House's *Intimate Papers*, Charles Seymour. Ranged against them was a tight circle of House's detractors: Edith Wilson; Wilson's doctor, Cary T. Grayson; the president's biographer, Ray Stannard Baker; and the enigmatic, though by no means reticent, financier Bernard M. Baruch.

Years later, each side had its say in two articles published in *American Heritage*. They are of interest not only for the light they cast on the quarrel itself, but also for what they reveal of the rancor the two camps felt about it even nearly forty-five years after the event.

The pro-House camp fired its salvo first.[49] It took the form of an article by Charles Seymour that included a memorandum written by Seymour on January 5, 1938, after his last interview with House. About two and a half months before his death, House agreed to see Seymour, who that day drafted his account of House's conversation but agreed not to publish it for twenty-five years. By 1963 those years had passed. The memorandum contains House's last and perhaps most mature reflections on the break with Wilson. Close to death, House said he had reached "absolute conviction." "The main underlying cause," he said, "was, of course, the second Mrs. Wilson." He was "conscious of a certain jealousy among those who wished to be close to Wilson." The beginning of a rift occurred immediately after the armistice. He had received "extravagant praise" for his "diplomatic triumph" in settling the terms of the armistice, and it was then that he "observed a certain unaccustomed lack of warmth in Wilson's cables."[50]

House advised against Wilson's attending the peace conference. "The President," the old gentleman recalled, "was not pleased." "I am told by those who were in Washington that Mrs. Wilson was determined to come to the Peace Conference. I have also been told that she made it plain that she thought I was trying to steal his thunder abroad."[51]

The colonel believed that the president had also been offended by his advice about the membership of the American delegation. "Nevertheless, the rift was slight, was not apparent to my consciousness and probably not to his." There was no coolness, only "less intimacy" until the president sailed for America on February 14, 1919.[52]

When Wilson returned to Paris, House saw at once there had been a change. He was told that "unfriendly persons had carried to Mrs. Wilson the story that during the President's absence I had yielded out unwise suggestions of compromise."[53]

House told Seymour an anecdote about Edith Wilson's resentment of the praise he had received. "I met her one day in her house with a newspaper in her hand, with a eulogistic article by Wickham Steed. I said, 'Is it pleasant?' She replied: 'Pleasant for you but not for Woodrow.'" Still, the old man pointed out, Wilson continue to ask him to stand in for him on the Council of Four. He still passed notes as "intimate and affectionate as ever." But there was no opportunity for long private talks. "I had the sense that [Edith Wilson] did not want me in the intimate family circle."[54]

House dismissed the idea that the Fiume crisis led to a personal break. Even at the end of the conference, "there was no coolness between us: merely a slackening in intimacy." But then, when the two men said goodbye, "I was again aware of an attitude approaching hostility on Mrs. Wilson's part. And for the first time Bernard Baruch . . . spoke to me in a tone that indicated that he felt that he had taken my place as Wilson's confidant."[55]

After the end of the conference, House continued to receive official messages from the president. Then came the crisis over the treaty. House arrived home from Europe a sick man, and Wilson too was sick. House dictated two letters to Wilson but received no direct answer. So when, in December, he was well enough to go to Washington, House simply called and left his card. He expected an answer, but none came. Again, when he went abroad in the spring of 1920, and again in the fall, around election time, House wrote and had a "rather perfunctory" reply. He felt, he told Seymour, "justly or otherwise, that Mrs. Wilson and Grayson did not wish me to see him. Perhaps Baruch did not want me around. They were the three that absolutely controlled Wilson on his sickbed."[56]

That, then, was the version of events House wanted to leave behind him. There had been no absolute breach, only a drifting apart. And any cooling that had taken place was the work of Edith Wilson, Baker, Baruch, and Dr. Grayson, not of Woodrow Wilson himself. "I do not think he could have had hard feelings against me. Why should he? I think he was just too worn out to make the effort to pick up relations again, especially as he was surrounded by people who were hostile to me."[57]

We have no direct evidence as to Wilson's feelings. But about a year after Seymour's memorandum, *American Heritage* published a document that paints an all too vivid picture of the spite felt toward House by the Wilson inner circle.

Two years after Wilson died, the first of four volumes of *The Intimate Papers of Colonel House,* edited by Charles Seymour, appeared. The book provoked Wilson's doctor, Cary T. Grayson, to write the long article that appeared in *American Heritage* thirty-seven years later.[58] Grayson died in 1938, the same year as House. He did not think it right to publish his uncharitable estimate of the colonel in their lifetimes. Only after his death did his sons decide that it was time to publish their father's thoughts.

Grayson affected to have been impressed by most things about the colonel when he first met him, except for his chin, "which was inclined to recede." Having praised the colonel's "tactful, restful, uncontroversial" personality, he suddenly asserted that it was "grotesque" that he should have represented himself "as the originator of the underlying thought of the League of Nations, the Federal Reserve Act and other great constructive measures."[59] He charged House with being a courtier. He accused him of representing himself (in Seymour's book) as a "mastermind."[60]

Grayson directly accused House of "consenting to the separation of the League covenant from the peace treaty."[61] On the contrary, there is no mention in House's diary of any separation of the league covenant from the peace treaty until March 24. On that date, House recorded, he had "advised a showdown." He said he had urged Wilson to tell Clemenceau and Lloyd George that "we would have none of" the peace treaty unless the covenant of the league was written into it.[62] House had acted in that crisis, Grayson said, "as a politician rather than as a statesman." Grayson was also highly critical of House's son-in-law Gordon Auchincloss. He claimed that Auchincloss was in the habit of boasting that it was to Colonel House and not to the president that people went for advice.[63]

Grayson went on to tell a great many ill-natured anecdotes about House. Finally, in more than one sense of the word, Grayson described the last meeting between the two men at the station in Paris when Wilson was leaving to go home. The president, in this account, "turned his head toward him, and, with a stern look, said coldly, "Good-bye, House." Later, Grayson says, after Wilson's stroke on the train, when he was lying on his sickbed, someone mentioned House, and the president said, "Don't mention House to me. The door is closed."[64]

Why? Grayson repeated the charge, made by Mrs. Wilson and Ray Stannard Baker, that House had "agreed to the establishment of a Rhenish republic" and that

Wilson "found to his amazement that Colonel House had consented to a plan for the separation of the peace treaty from the covenant of the League of Nations." The nub of Grayson's angry, even contemptuous critique of House was, however, not political, but deeply personal. It was that "the stage was too big, the pageantry too impressive, the praise too seductive, and, gradually, Colonel House, E. M. House, of Houston and Austin, Texas, of the Texas governor's staff (whence he gained his title of Colonel), got his head turned."[65]

What were the sources of this animosity? Did Wilson himself share it, or was this the president's wife's distress and that of her circle? Was there any substance in policy terms to the harsh judgments of House made by Grayson and also Baker? Did Wilson think that House had become disloyal?

House himself, in his virtually deathbed interview with Charles Seymour, understandably (and characteristically) played down the hurt of the personal quarrel between Wilson and himself, representing it as something worked up by Mrs. Wilson and her circle. No doubt there is truth in this. Still, even if one discounts the emotive language of Edith Wilson and the cavaliers who broke a literary lance for her, it is not possible to miss the authentic distress on Wilson's part that comes through. They may have exaggerated, but they can hardly have invented, Wilson's horror that under the pressures of a world crisis, House's instinct had been that of the politician, an artist of the possible, rather than that of the covenanter.[66]

House himself records Wilson as saying to him, after the crisis in their relationship, "House, I have found one can never get anything in this life that is worthwhile without fighting for it." And House recorded his own revealing response. "I combated this, and reminded him that Anglo-Saxon civilization was built upon compromise."[67]

House had seen a fair bit more fighting, in the literal sense, than Wilson. While Woodrow Wilson was moving through the library and the lecture halls at Johns Hopkins and Bryn Mawr, House had been hanging out with the tough hombres of LaSalle County, Texas, and listening to the war stories of Texas Rangers.

Still, it is true that House's instincts were political, where Wilson's were ideological. Faced with the tangle of incompatible pride and passion that was the peace conference in the spring of 1919, House's instinct was to seek the highest common denominator. Wilson's was to take his stand, even if he had to pull the temple down around his head. He may have threatened the French that he would take to his ship and go home. He certainly did threaten the British that he would build a bigger navy than they could afford. He threatened Henry Cabot Lodge and the

Republicans that he would bring back a treaty so tied together that they must take it or leave it, even threatened a gibbet for them that would "scrape the heavens." Faced with opposition, Wilson's instinct was that anyone wicked enough to disagree with him must endorse his noble vision or face his messianic wrath.

Yet all human personalities are mysterious and contradictory, and Wilson's arrogance grew out of personal insecurity, just as House's accommodating instincts were grounded in very a considerable personal confidence that came from a large and loving family, financial security, and a lifetime of successful political operation. Wilson's experience of practical politics when he entered the White House, after all, could be measured in months; House's, in decades. It is true that House liked to be "all things to all men." That is not a bad quality in a man who seeks common ground between conflicting interests and touchy egos.

If critics such as Baker suspected House of having been corrupted by European society, they were wrong. Where they were on firmer ground was in their suspicion that House thought he was a better diplomat than Wilson. House can be convicted of forgetting, warmed by the flattery that is always lavished on a man who can help powerful people achieve their aims, a basic truth: he was nothing without Wilson's approval. He had no political legitimacy except as the president's friend. His light was always reflected from a greater celestial body.

House earned the trust of some of the shrewdest individuals gathered at the conference, among them Balfour and Clemenceau. His son-in-law, Gordon Auchincloss, was sometimes indiscreetly overloyal to him.[68] The Edith Wilson circle collected examples. Edith herself claimed that the president, at the Crillon, had overheard Auchincloss asking his father-in-law, "What shall we make the president say today?"[69]

The most serious grievance the Wilsons had against House and Gordon Auchincloss had to do with their real or supposed skill at manipulating the press. House briefed the American reporters every evening, and Auchincloss was cheerfully available with his comments, which did sometimes compare the president's performance unfavorably with his father-in-law's. House cultivated relations with Lord Northcliffe, who owned both the largest circulation British newspaper, the *Daily Mail,* and the most influential, *The Times,* and with Henry Wickham Steed, Northcliffe's favorite editor. Gordon Auchincloss had become quite close to a number of the journalists in Paris, including Steed and Charles Grasty of the *New York Times,* and he wrote two sensible and lucid articles for them. It was soon all around Paris that young Auchincloss was putting about the colonel's point of view.

The gravest offense, in Edith Wilson's eyes, came not from Auchincloss, but from one of Wickham Steed's commentaries. An article in the London *Times* on April 7, 1919, contained the following: "During [Wilson's and Lloyd George's] absence Colonel House, who has never found a difficulty in working with his colleagues, because he is a selfless man with no axe to grind, brought matters rapidly forward. The delay that has occurred since the return of President Wilson and Mr. Lloyd George has been due chiefly to the upsetting of the good work done during their absence."[70]

Mrs. Wilson was furious. House himself conceded five years later that the article was one of the "real grievances" of the Wilsons but protested that he "knew nothing of the article until it was published and had as little to do with it as the man in the moon."[71]

Some of the resentment against House that accumulated in Paris can be put down to a certain provincialism in the Wilsons' world.[72] The Wilsons' life at Princeton and even in the White House was scarcely a preparation for the sharp-tongued gossip of conference Paris. Wilson's limited experience of life made him vulnerable to the suspicion that House was hobnobbing with corrupt and cynical European aristocrats—exactly the charge laid against him by Ray Stannard Baker.

Wilson was also more than a little insular. He knew England, but he had not traveled elsewhere in Europe and spoke no foreign language. He was firmly convinced that his American innocence contrasted with the selfish attitudes of European aristocrats.

However House might have behaved, their relationship would have been endangered by the fact that Wilson became increasingly touchy. Two changes affected his behavior, not least toward Colonel House: his second marriage and his physical health.

It is not uncommon for second wives to be suspicious of the influence of their new husbands' old friends. In Edith Wilson's case, she had a specific, though mistaken, reason for resentment of Colonel House—namely, his part in the intriguing matter of Woodrow Wilson's relations with Mary Peck.[73]

In 1906 Wilson became partially blind in his left eye as a result of undiagnosed hypertension. On his doctor's advice, although he had recently returned from a long holiday in England, he went to Bermuda. There he became fascinated by Mrs. Peck, who was there without her husband, whom she was soon to divorce. Next year Wilson returned, again without his wife Ellen. Ellen disliked Mary, and many felt that Mary was—by the standards of a puritanical society—faintly disreputable. She achieved some notoriety in Bermuda for "frank courting of susceptible males," and a photograph survives of her doing just that.[74] It shows her laughing with a group of friends, including Wilson and Mark Twain. She is leaning toward Wilson with an interest that must have been attractive to him; he is smiling broadly and looks almost boyish. Probably, given his repressed personality, Wilson's relations with her were technically innocent. Margaret Hulbert certainly insisted that they were "tender, yes; but hardly erotic."[75] But it is clear he was captivated and guilty that he was captivated.[76] He made matters worse when, just as he was courting Edith, he gave Mary, who was by then financially embarrassed, an enormous present by buying dodgy mortgages from her for $7,500, a substantial sum for a man who was far from rich.[77]

In May 1915, when Wilson was courting Edith Galt with romantic ardor, Edith was already criticizing the man whom she seems to have regarded as her main rival for Woodrow's affections. She lost no opportunity to put House down in her sweet way. House was "a weak vessel and I think he writes like one very often."[78] In fact, as early as 1915 Wilson was conducting a sustained correspondence with his beloved Edith in which she was deliberately undermining, and he was being forced to defend, his friendship with House. Edith was probably not aware of the letter Wilson wrote to House on the last day of August 1915; it began "My dearest friend" and ended "Affectionately yours." In it he said, "Of course you have known how to interpret the silly malicious lies papers have recently been publishing about a disagreement between you and me, but I cannot deny myself the pleasure of sending you just a line of deep affection to tell you how they have distressed me. I am trying to bring to book the men who originated them."[79]

The House-Wilson relationship was further poisoned by the affair of Wilson's letters to Mary Peck. Many of Wilson's closest friends, including his political secretary, the faithful Joseph Tumulty (whom Edith Wilson described as lacking "breeding"), were opposed to the president's remarrying so soon after the death of his first wife.[80] It was Wilson's son-in-law, treasury secretary William Gibbs McAdoo, who blundered into this fraught cat's cradle of human relationships by going public with the story—probably made up by himself and certainly in ignorance of Wilson's vulnerability to gossip on the score of the mortgages—that Mary Peck was blackmailing the president by showing people the letters he had written her.[81]

This "awful earthquake," as Edith Wilson called it, happened at just the moment when she was nudging the fragile craft of her love affair with Wilson into port. As for Wilson, he wrote an "admission" that was found among his papers only after his death. In it he said that "neither in act nor even in thought was the purity or honor of the lady concerned touched or sullied." But he also admitted that his letters did disclose "a passage of folly and gross impertinence," of which he was "deeply ashamed and repentant."[82]

Into this hothouse of refined emotion and "purloined letters" that might have come out of a Victorian novel, Edith Wilson inserted, many years later, a vicious twist of her own. She claimed that Dr. Grayson had visited her and told her that Colonel House had spoken to unspecified newspaper men, who had warned that if rumors about the president's engagement to Mrs. Galt turned out to be true, Mrs. Peck would make her letters from him public. Edith Wilson went on to say that House had admitted, many years later, that he had made the whole story up because he thought Wilson's remarriage might prevent his reelection.[83]

This version of events, published in Mrs. Wilson's memoirs in 1939, is not exactly true. But it seems she blamed House for trying to use Wilson's letters to Mary Peck to prevent her marriage. If she believed that, and it looks certain that at least in later life she did, then no wonder she disliked House. But there is no reason to conclude that her belief was justified.

So much for Edith Wilson's reasons for mistrusting House. But what of the reasons for Wilson's rather abrupt change of heart about his old friend? The explanation may lie in Wilson's health, which was more fragile than had been supposed.

Everyone knows that Wilson broke down with a massive stroke in September 1919. But recent scholarship has been discovering that he was more ill more often than was previously known. As early as 1895, when he was thirty-eight, he complained of indigestion and writer's cramp; modern writers have speculated that this was a minor stroke.[84] As noted above, he suffered blindness in the left eye as a result of arteriosclerosis in May 1906. Two years later his right hand was temporarily paralyzed as a result of "occlusive disease in the internal carotid artery." There were further cerebrovascular "events" in 1900, 1904, 1906, and 1907.[85]

Wilson had a poor vascular system from an early age. It is plain too that there was a close relationship between his physical condition and his moods and behavior. In Paris, it was noticeable that he was tense and bad tempered before he fell ill with what appeared to be the Spanish flu on April 3. (He lost his temper with Jusserand and again with Clemenceau on March 28 and with Wickham Steed on March 30. On April 2 Mrs. Wilson's secretary, Edith Benham, said she had never seen him in such a rage. House commented in his diary on April 1 that his friend was angry and unreasonable.) On April 7, from his sickbed, Wilson summoned the *George Washington*, perhaps an act of temper rather than—as has been supposed—calculated negotiating pressure. The influenza attack changed not only his behavior, but also his opinions. For example, before it, he had been adamant in his opposition to moves to put the German emperor on trial, but on his return to the council he moved a resolution that the kaiser be indicted.[86]

On April 28, 1919, at the height of the crisis over Fiume, which coincided with a critical moment in the conference, Wilson suffered what is now diagnosed as a minor stroke. For a long time Dr. Grayson, who was in the best position to know, refused to admit that Wilson had a stroke in Paris, though later he admitted that Wilson had several minor strokes there. Dr. Malford Wilcox Thewlis, who examined him in Paris on April 29, said the stroke Wilson had experienced the previous day was "so destructive that it had made of him a changeling with a different personality and a markedly lessened ability."[87] Dr. Bert E. Park, who studied the whole question in the 1990s, concluded that the series of strokes brought on by Wilson's high blood pressure and stress affected "virtually all . . . his later behavioral and cognitive changes." Park spoke of the President's "dementia."[88]

The consensus of expert opinion now is, in other words, that although Wilson's condition was elaborately hidden from the world by Edith Wilson and Grayson, Wilson underwent serious physical illness with behavioral and mental consequences at roughly the time of his falling out with House. That was also the time when he realized that his cherished dreams for the postwar world might well be shattered by the Senate.

The causal relationship between physical illness and behavior is complex. Wilson's erratic behavior in Paris may have been in part the consequence as well as the cause of his loss of trust in Colonel House. But that the president was, as the telling old phrase goes, "not himself" in April, and perhaps as early as March, cannot easily be denied.

17　The End of the Treaty　∾

While our friendship was not of long duration, it was as close as human friendships grow to be.

　　　　　　　　　　　　　　—Edward House to Charles Seymour, March 1920

HOUSE WAS RELUCTANT, almost to the end, to admit that there had been any break between him and Wilson. As late as August 28, 1919, when the Associated Press called to ask him about a story that had broken in New York headlined "Mr. Wilson breaks with Colonel House," House brushed it off as something invented by the press.[1] Only years later, with close friends like Stephen Bonsal, did House come to admit that "the President was peeved with him even while they were together in Paris."[2]

　　The end of the friendship was not as sudden as it was made to seem in the recollections of Edith Wilson and Cary Grayson; nor was it a mere invention of malicious journalists. For the fourteen weeks between the president's return to Paris and his final departure, House continued to be a busy member of the American delegation. But the political and personal intimacy between the two men faded away.

　　From time to time—and at an accelerating rhythm as 1919 went on—House allowed himself, in the nightly dictation of his diary, to admit the president's foibles and mistakes. He had good reason, of course, to deny that he had forfeited his friendship with the president. His whole political position depended on others' perception that he possessed influence. There are less cynical explanations, however. House and Wilson had after all been brothers in arms for seven years, fellow true believers in high purposes.

Some observers have picked out as the decisive break the moment, as early as April 1917, when Wilson changed the form of his address to House from "Dearest friend" and even "My dear, dear friend" to a more Presbyterian "Dear House."[3] The end of the friendship may have been plain to see in mid-March. But the acutest crisis for the conference came in April. Until then, House could still hope to be readmitted to Wilson's favor.

The immediate occasion of the crisis was the Italian claim for territorial gains on the Dalmatian coast, across the Adriatic. But that was only the most immediate of a whole series of problems—Danzig, Teschen, Palestine, and Shantung; many more in Europe, the former Ottoman Empire, and the Far East; not to mention reparations, France's insistence on guarantees against a future attack by Germany, and Britain's determination to cling to supremacy at sea.[4]

The Fiume crisis came to a head on April 23, 1919, when Orlando, the Italian premier, stormed out of the conference. The Italian parliament backed Orlando, and the Italian people demanded all, and more than all, the British and the French had offered in the secret treaty of London: the Trentino, Trieste, Istria, Fiume, the Dalmatian islands, and concessions in Asian Turkey. The fate of Fiume (now known by its Slavic name of Rijeka) and its twenty-four thousand Italian inhabitants, isolated in a predominantly Slav population, brought out into the open the conflict between Wilsonian ideals of self-determination and the secret treaties. But Wilson himself did not always behave in a Wilsonian way. He handed over the South Tyrol in the Alps, with three hundred thousand German-speaking Austrian citizens, to Italy, where their descendants have remained an angry enclave ever since.

The differences between Wilson and House were not disagreements over policy so much as differences of temperament, revealed by the relentless pressure to decide questions of insistent urgency. Wilson's sense of personal mission led him to attack the hosts of Midian with the sword of righteousness. House's experience and temperament led him instead to look for solutions across the green baize cloth of diplomacy.

Britain and France, bled white by the war, wanted peace. The signing of a treaty to end the war was their first priority, even though they also wanted to get something out of the peace for which they had made such sacrifices. They wanted as much money as they could get by way of reparations, if only to pay their war debts to the United States. They also had territorial and colonial ambitions—for France, Alsace-Lorraine and Syria; for Britain, in Africa and the Arab Middle East. But most of all they wanted security. That was why the French were so desperate to protect themselves on the Rhine and why the British clung so stubbornly to naval superiority.

Wilson too, after all, wanted something out of the peace, and no small thing: he wanted a league of nations in which the United States would be the dominant power. House shared Wilson's dreams. But he had understood the European thirst for peace in the literal sense of an end to war.

There was, especially after Wilson's fateful return from Washington, another difference between the two men, as wide as the Atlantic: the difference between the concerns of Paris and those of Washington. House's mind had been fixed on the conference in Paris and on the rumors that reached Paris from a Europe and a Middle East in convulsion. He had to focus on the myriad incidents, some—revolution and the collapse of great empires—of truly historic import, others—like the political difficulties of Lloyd George or Orlando—less cosmic but still bulking large in the minds of the men with whom he was dealing. Wilson, on the other hand, was belatedly concerned and eventually obsessed with the political situation in Washington. He realized with growing trepidation that his whole political future, including the hopes he privately cherished of a third term in the White House, depended on his ability to persuade the Senate to ratify the treaty.[5]

Wilson, like others at the time and since, seems to have been confused by the distinction between a preliminary treaty, scarcely more than a definitive armistice with Germany, and a final treaty that would inaugurate a new era in international relations.

It is hard to believe that an expert on constitutional government could have made such a mistake, but the president initially supposed that a preliminary treaty, including the covenant of the league, would not need ratification by the Senate. Robert Lansing recorded after the Council of Ten's meeting on March 17 that "[the President] astounded me by practically saying that he had not thought the preliminaries of peace ought to go to Senate. I told him it was a treaty of peace and he could not avoid it."[6] Lansing's legal advisers, James Brown Scott and David Hunter Miller, agreed. Attorney General Gregory confirmed to Miller that "it was true that the President had had an idea that he could make a treaty with Germany and put through the League of Nations, military terms etc., without having it ratified by the Senate."[7]

The Council of Ten's record reveals Wilson's hesitation on this point. The same day on which Lansing, Scott, and Miller put him right about the constitutional position, Wilson admitted that "he had assumed that this preliminary convention would only be temporary until the complete treaty was prepared. . . . If this preliminary convention would have to be submitted to the Senate for a general discussion there . . . it would be several months before it could be ratified."[8] Kurt Wimer suggested that Wilson deliberately planned to conclude a preliminary treaty without sending it to the Senate.[9]

House was increasingly critical of Wilson's performance. On April 1 he wrote in his diary, "The President is becoming stubborn and angry, and he never was a good negotiator. . . . It is maddening to see the days go by and nothing decided."[10]

At his meeting with Lloyd George and Clemenceau on March 14, his first day back in Paris, Wilson agreed to a joint guarantee of French security by the United States and Britain in the event of a future German attack (as noted above). But House did not learn of this agreement until March 17, when he saw a French summary of the guarantee.

House was whistling in the dark to convince himself that he had not lost all influence. He comforted himself that Wilson had entrusted him with choosing an emissary to Montenegro—scarcely a major task. After Wilson's return House was in fact largely cut off from top-level negotiations and even, with the exception of one brief meeting, from contact with the president until March 24.

On that day, House tried to clear the air. He told Wilson that he must force a "showdown."[11] But after that House found himself once again excluded until April 2. Then the real showdown took place. Like all such explosions, long repressed by politeness and the parties' fear of a breakdown, it was a complex crisis. Discordant ambitions and hidden motives converged on the conference. The atmosphere was ominous, as on the eve of a thunderstorm.

Wilson had lost his former unclouded faith in House but was not sure who else he could trust. Exhausted and sick, he now understood that his own future, as well as his vision, was at stake.

House, anxious to get the best treaty through that he could, was trying to work with Clemenceau. Lloyd George, unhappy in Wilson's world of noble sentiments, was facing a rebellion from some of the Tories in his multiparty coalition in Parliament and a hostile press campaign. House, through Gordon Auchincloss, was more or less knowingly drawn into an intrigue against Lloyd George by Wickham Steed, Northcliffe's right-hand man. Wilson, with one eye on the political situation in the United States, was tense and touchy. He was also sickening for a bout of influenza so severe that in the opinion of his doctor it almost killed him.[12]

At last, on April 2 came the approach House had been hoping for. At 8 o'clock in the evening Wilson telephoned. They spoke for forty-five minutes. "We went over the whole matter from start to finish. The Saar Basin, the Rhenish Republic, the protection of France, Danzig, Fiume, reparations and whatnot." Wilson said he felt that no one liked him and complained about Clemenceau. "What he really means," House commented somewhat cynically in his diary, "is that he cannot get Clemenceau to come round to his way of thinking."[13] It was not as if House had any illusions about the French premier. He is "of the old regime," House wrote in his diary. "He told Steed yesterday that the President thought himself another Jesus Christ come upon the earth to reform men. He is the ablest reactionary in the Conference, but it is almost impossible to deal with him except in ways . . . which we hope to make forever obsolete."[14]

The next day, House promised Wilson, he would go to see his friend André Tardieu and tell him that if the French did not go along, the president would have to go back to Washington. The colonel did just that, but when he telephoned to report to the president, Wilson had collapsed with influenza. He had raged at the British at a meeting and had been taken seriously ill at the Supreme Council, which was discussing Fiume.

The next morning, House received a message from Wilson asking him to take the president's place at the Council of Four meeting, due to take place that morning.[15] Now House took over. There was no one else with his knowledge of the tangle of affairs who could have done the job. This was his chance to prove what he had long suspected: that his talents as a diplomat were superior to Wilson's, that he had the reins of the conference in his hands, and that he could drive the quarreling powers like a four-in-hand.

To this extent, Mrs. Wilson and her friends were correct. House did believe he could get a peace treaty, and get one fast. He had come to see Wilson's weaknesses, and he was annoyed by what he saw as Wilson's indifference to the realities of a world in anguish. However, they were wrong in suspecting House of wanting to sell out the League of Nations in order to get a peace treaty. If anything, he wanted to buy support for the league from the leaders of Britain, France, and Italy by offering each of them some of what they wanted. If he was willing to sell out anything, it was not Wilson's grand vision, which he shared, but Wilson's "principles"; he had lost patience with Wilson's proud reluctance to play the necessary political game of compromise.

Or rather House was irritated by Wilson's *selective* unwillingness to play the political game. When it suited him—for example, in giving France Alsace-Lorraine or a favorable position on the Saar or in conceding more than Orlando even asked for in the Alps—Wilson could play it with the best.

That same day, Friday, April 4, the Steed editorial, which so disgusted Edith Wilson when she saw it in the *Washington Post* two weeks later, appeared in the Paris edition of the *Daily Mail*, which was read by all the delegates with their morning coffee. It contrasted the colonel's modesty and efficiency with Wilson's pompous bungling. The colonel disclaimed any responsibility for the article. It had been suggested to Steed by Gordon Auchincloss with the loyal intention of strengthening his father-in-law's hand, but Steed ruined the effect by going too far. Lloyd George, who had eyes in the back of his head where political intrigue was afoot, suspected as much. He met Auchincloss with the colonel after the Council of Four meeting on the following Monday morning and said, as Auchincloss recorded in his diary, "Steed had been using matter that we (looking at me) had no doubt given him in confidence and that he, George, thought that was the worst thing a newspaperman could do. I did not comment but just stared George back. He is playing a slick game. . . . He sees Steed almost daily. Of course I realize that I am playing with fire but I may be able to escape getting burned."[16]

Steed had also concerted with House, on March 31, an approach to Wilson on giving France some control of the Saar coal mines. Wilson himself seized on this concession as a compromise that might break the deadlock. House and Steed wanted to get Wilson to do a deal with Clemenceau on the Saar. But when a letter from Steed proposing as much was handed to the president by the American diplomat Arthur Hugh Frazier, Wilson lost his temper. "He . . . flew into a terrible rage," Frazier reported to Auchincloss. " 'I will not have it. I will not have it. . . . What do you mean by bringing me things which are in flagrant contradiction with my principles?' And literally turned me out of his room."[17]

House had no illusions about the self-interested side of his colleagues' deliberations. On April 4, the Council of Four discussed reparations, which House said might just as well be called "loot." The statesmen reminded House of "a lot of children." The conference, he congratulated himself, "so far has been run by the President, Lloyd George, Clemenceau, Balfour, Tardieu and myself."[18]

On Sunday, April 6, Wilson was sufficiently recovered to meet the American delegates in his room. It was agreed that the president would say to the prime ministers that unless peace was made on the basis of the Fourteen Points, the president would either have to go home or give up the Council of Four and conduct business through plenary sessions, which would slow the negotiations down to a snail's pace.

The next day there occurred an incident that has been much misunderstood. Early in the morning the president asked Admiral Benson to find out, "carefully concealing the fact that any communication on this subject has been received," what the earliest date was on which the *George Washington* could reach Brest to take the president home.[19] There was no sign that sending for the *George Washington* had any effect on the conference. It is not even certain that Wilson intended it as a means of putting pressure on the other parties. The fact is that, perhaps as a result of his illness, the president's behavior was increasingly erratic. The next day he gave in and backed Clemenceau's position, and the day after that, he himself suggested that German sovereignty over the Saar should be suspended for fifteen years. Clemenceau quickly assented, and Wilson's proposal, hardly an example of the principle of self-determination, was adopted.

The president's illness was serious but not prolonged. House was never again the chief American delegate. However, he continued to see a bewildering variety of visitors, sometimes as many as a couple of dozen a day. He still carried a substantial share of the burden of negotiating on specific matters, some of them important, with the members of the Council of Four and their deputies. Historians who claim that he lost Wilson's confidence after the middle of March 1919 have to confront the continuing, if diminished, responsibility House was given until the treaty was signed. For example, on April 10 he had an important conference with Lord Robert Cecil about British and American naval building. House took a tough line. He insisted that the United States must be allowed to continue its planned program of battleship building.[20]

Even more important in the context of getting agreement on a peace treaty was House's meeting with Clemenceau on April 14, 1919. The French premier asked for the appointment himself, and they spoke for an hour. They started by discussing Syria. Clemenceau said that although France had been promised control of the province of Cilicia, where Turkey joins Syria, he would give it up if the United States would accept a mandate from the league to run Armenia. After briefly discussing Orlando's threat to walk out of the conference, Clemenceau got down to what was for him the most important business of all. He accepted the American terms for France's protection on the Rhine. With a guarantee from the United States of

France's future security he was prepared to take on Foch and the other marshals if President Wilson would agree to let France occupy three strips of German territory, the first for five years, the second for ten, and the third for fifteen.

House commented in his diary that night that he felt that the reason he got along better than Wilson with Clemenceau was that he would never think of using the same arguments with Clemenceau as he would use with the president. "One is an idealist," he said, "the other a practical old-line statesman." It was, in any case, House felt, an afternoon of great accomplishment. He got Wilson to agree to everything Clemenceau had said, though he made a wry face over the French stipulation of three five-year periods of occupation of parts of the Rhineland.[21]

House believed that political differences could and should be overcome by political means, by bargaining. Wilson believed it was his duty to make his vision prevail, by agreement if possible and by the threat of force if not. The irony is that House, the political realist, never fully grasped the most elementary political reality: his own position depended wholly on the president's trust and favor.

Even before the Fiume crisis had been finally resolved, the Germans were formally invited on April 14 to send delegates to sign a peace treaty at Versailles. On May 7 the peace conference proper met at last to present the Germans with the terms of the treaty. It was a painful occasion. House drove out to Versailles and found Clemenceau, Balfour, Orlando, and the other leading delegates waiting. Only House's friend the Polish president, Ignazy Paderewski, was late.[22] "He evidently cannot get it out of his head," House commented with amusement, "that he is not giving one of his great concerts in which the audience is always supposed to be seated before he enters."[23]

Clemenceau made a short speech. The leader of the German delegation, the foreign minister, Count Ulrich von Brockdorff-Rantzau, received the terms of the treaty standing, his face chalk white with humiliation. But when he spoke, at great length, he gave great offense to many of the Allied statesmen by remaining seated. Most of the Allies took Brockdorff-Rantzau's defiant, even truculent speech for a studied insult. He acknowledged Germany's violations of the laws of war. But he also complained of the starvation of hundreds of thousands by the Allied blockade. He denounced as a lie the charge that Germany was guilty for starting the war. Clemenceau was furious. Wilson exclaimed, "What abominable manners!" House, as ever, was more realistic. "If I had been in his position," he commented, "I should have said: 'Mr President and members of the Congress: War is a great gamble; we have lost and are willing to submit to any reasonable terms.'"[24]

For the next two weeks the German delegation tried in vain to change the terms of the treaty. There was no realistic chance of that. Brockdorff-Rantzau was not the man to succeed in opening rifts among Germany's enemies, though the rifts were there. As soon as the terms were known, there was an explosion of anger in Germany. "It is incomprehensible," said the president of the new national assembly in Weimar, that Wilson, "who promised the world a peace of justice . . . has been able to assist in framing this project dictated by hate."[25]

The American delegates were all in one way or another unhappy about the treaty. Its legal expert, James Brown Scott, passed a severe judgment: "The statesmen have . . . made a peace that renders another war inevitable."[26]

There was indeed nothing ineluctable about World War II, still less was it "the fault" of the peacemakers of 1919. Yet both Wilson and House knew all too well that the treaty they had helped to write was very different from the one they had hoped to write. Three weeks later House confided his private judgment to his diary: "The Treaty is not a good one, it is too severe, and notwithstanding the President believes it is well within the Fourteen Points, it is far afield from them. . . . It is also a question as to the effect upon the Germans. I desired from the beginning a fair peace, and one well within the Fourteen Points, and one that could withstand the scrutiny of the neutral world and of all time. It is not such a peace."[27]

The closing weeks of the peace conference were frustrating and seemed barren of achievement. Yet this time of dangerous failure was perhaps more determinant for the future of Europe and the Middle East, and indeed for the world, than the early weeks of optimism, when it seemed that the world's peace could be guaranteed by the Fourteen Points and the League of Nations. The world's political arrangements were fluid. Boundaries were being changed, states founded, and political hostages given to fortune at a dizzy pace. President Wilson, who once seemed to tower over a stricken world that had turned to him for salvation, had lost interest in everything but his own dreams. Now House judged his friend, in the privacy of his diary, without sentiment. On May 30, for example, he said of Wilson, "I believe that it is as an orator that he excels rather than as a statesman. The feeling has become fairly general that the President's actions do not square with his speeches. There is a *bon mot* going the round in Paris and London: 'Wilson talks like Jesus Christ and acts like Lloyd George.'"[28]

On June 10 House went to see Sir William Orpen's portrait of Wilson and contrasted it with an earlier painting by John Singer Sargent.[29] "I think I never knew a man whose general appearance changed so much from hour to hour,"

House commented. "He is so contradictory that it is hard to pass judgment on him. He has but few friends. . . . He seems to do his best to offend rather than to please, and yet when one gets access to him, there is no more charming man in the world than Woodrow Wilson."[30]

House was still in the thick of the political grappling and intrigue. His diary is studded with casual notes, such as that on May 24: "Alexander Kerensky came by appointment in the afternoon to tell again of Russia. Felix Frankfurter called to talk of the Jews of Palestine." First, House got caught in crossfire on the Irish question.

On April 15, 1919, House was visited by Frank P. Walsh, a well-known labor attorney from Kansas City and later a close political ally of President Franklin D. Roosevelt.[31] In January, a revolutionary Irish Republic had been declared in defiance of the British government. Walsh and two colleagues had been dispatched by an Irish American convention to exert American pressure on the British government to allow an Irish delegation to put the case for Irish independence before the peace conference. On Good Friday, House saw Walsh and his two colleagues, ex-governor Edward F. Dunne of Illinois and the former city solicitor of Philadelphia, Michael J. Ryan, and volunteered to do what he could to get the British government to agree. House had lunch with Lloyd George, who agreed to see the three Irish Americans the following week. Nothing happened. Walsh, Dunne, and Ryan said Lloyd George was giving them the run around, and Sir William Wiseman confirmed that the prime minister had no intention of seeing them. House was furious. So when Walsh and his colleagues said they would go to Ireland, House arranged for the British to give them passports.

While in Ireland, however, Walsh, Dunne, and Ryan made outspoken statements on behalf of Irish independence. Now it was Lloyd George's turn to be annoyed. He was being roasted in the British press for allowing American agitators to muddy the waters in Ireland, and he fired off a letter accusing House of misleading him. After ten days of ill-tempered exchanges, House took the matter up with President Wilson. He and Secretary of State Lansing were for giving the Irishmen a "brusque refusal." House, always the politician, favored telling them that it was the British government that had turned them down. The row rumbled on. Wilson always assured Tumulty that he had Ireland's interests at heart, but he was not prepared to have a row with the British over Irish home rule.[32]

By August the foreign affairs committee of the new and unofficial Dáil, the embryo Irish parliament, had to report that "M. Clemenceau has declined to take action upon the resolution of the American Senate requesting that the case of

Ireland should be heard before the Conference."[33] Walsh, Dunne, and Ryan returned to America to join the president of the still illegal Irish Republic, Eamon de Valera, in his campaign to seek support for Irish independence in America.

The episode shows neither Wilson nor House at their best. The president, self-proclaimed champion of self-determination, seemed largely indifferent to Irish independence. House, Wilson's political adviser, saw his Irish visitors primarily as a potential irritant in his relations with the British.

The closing weeks of the conference were the time when decisions of lasting import were taken over the Ottoman provinces that would become Syria, Lebanon, Palestine, and Iraq. Colonel House never played a leading role in the great debates over the Middle East and Zionism. Others influenced the confused political struggle left behind by the collapse of the Ottoman Empire far more than President Wilson.

Still, for anyone who sought to influence the peace conference, Colonel House was still a man to see. British and American Zionists in particular kept in contact with him. They regarded him, rightly, as broadly sympathetic to their aspirations, even though House's knowledge of the Middle East was limited. He probably devoted as much energy to the prospects of American Christian missionary colleges as to the future of Palestine. Wilson and House did take a lively interest in the fate of the Armenian Christians, massacred by the Ottoman government from 1915 on.

House's role in the great dramas being played out in the Near East came down to keeping various parties, including Weizmann, Brandeis, and Frankfurter, informed about the intentions of the Great Powers.[34] Zionism came low on the list of Wilson's priorities. In October 1917 he sent a memo to House saying, "I find in my pocket the memorandum you gave me about the Zionist Movement. I am afraid I did not say to you that I concurred in the formula suggested by the other side [Britain]. I do, and would be obliged if you would let them know it."[35]

Over the winter of 1918–1919 there were fierce differences among three groups: Chaim Weizmann, who stressed the importance of keeping on good terms with his allies in British politics; the Russian Jews, led by Nahum Sokolow; and the American delegation, sent by Brandeis.[36] On February 27, 1919, Weizmann won a great victory when resolutions drafted by his Zionist organization were accepted by the Council of Ten. However, Wilson had matters on his mind to which he gave far higher priority than the future of some sixty thousand Jews in Palestine.

In June 1919 House found himself in the middle of a first-rate row between the State Department and leading Zionists. He was on very friendly terms with

Paderewski, who early in 1919 had become the first president of an independent Poland. He was also friendly with the American diplomat Hugh Gibson, whose confirmation as ambassador to Warsaw was before the Senate. (Gibson was a leading advocate of opening the foreign service up to a more democratic entry.)

In the chaos resulting from the liberation of Poland after two centuries of Russian rule, there were pogroms against Jews. There were also reports of pogroms that House and many Americans sympathetic to the new Poland thought were exaggerated. Gibson reported to this effect, for which he was roundly denounced by the great Jewish civil rights lawyer Louis Marshall, a Zionist representative in Paris.

On June 23 House reported in his diary, "Justice Brandeis was another caller. . . . I called in Hugh Gibson, our minister to Poland. I suggested to Gibson that he explain to the Jews that they were hurting their cause by giving out exaggerated statements of conditions in Poland and elsewhere."[37] Two days later House introduced Gibson to Frankfurter, who, in House's words, "had the temerity to tell Gibson that the Jews had almost determined to keep him, Gibson, from being confirmed by the Senate because of what he called his anti-Jewish feeling."[38]

Brandeis and Frankfurter did not mince their words. In Gibson's later recollection, they started by telling him that he had "done more mischief to the Jewish race than anyone who had lived in the last century."[39] Frankfurter then hinted that if Gibson continued his reports, Zionists would block his confirmation as ambassador to Poland by the Senate. Secretary Lansing confirmed this by telegram the following day.

House must have been taken aback by the ferocity of the reaction to Gibson's reporting. He was motivated chiefly by his sympathy for the newly independent Polish republic. It is clear that Gibson thought the Zionists were deliberately painting an exaggerated picture of anti-Semitic violence in Poland in order to encourage Jews to emigrate to Palestine. House misunderstood the seriousness of the issues at stake, and certainly he miscalculated the likely Zionist response.

At last on June 28 House could write in his diary, "This is the great day." He took as many of his personal staff as he could get tickets for—Gordon Auchincloss, Fanny Denton, his chief interpreter Arthur Hugh Frazier (a member of the Paris embassy staff who was an aide to Colonel House), Whitney Shepardson (later one of the founders of the Council on Foreign Relations), and a couple of the military aides—through the dense crowds to Versailles to see the ceremony. At the palace, there were cavalry with pennants flying and on the grand stairway "chasseurs in gorgeous uniforms" right up to the entrance of the Hall of Mirrors. House's feelings were for the defeated Germans. They were being dragged at the conquerors' chariot wheels, he thought, without any hint of chivalry. He felt this was "out of keeping with the new era which we profess an ardent desire to promote."[40]

If the French were not in a chivalrous mood, nor was Woodrow Wilson. He bitterly insulted the French by trying to refuse to attend a state dinner offered to him by the French president, Poincaré, who had annoyed him by taking the Italian side over Fiume. Wilson told House he would "choke if he sat at the table with him." House had the temerity to remind the president that, like him or not, Poincaré represented the French people, whose guest he had been for nearly six months. Wilson tried to pretend he had not been properly invited, but House, Jusserand, and the veteran diplomat Henry White all explained that the normal procedure for invitations from one head of state to another had been followed. The next day Wilson "completely capitulated," and the dinner went forward. House commented that the episode was "a revelation to everyone excepting myself of something in his character [that] accounted for his many enemies."[41]

The very day the Germans signed the peace treaty Wilson left for Washington. House went to see him off. Neither man knew it at the time, but this was the very last conversation they were ever to have. Brief as it was, it epitomized the difference between their approaches to politics. House ventured to urge Wilson to "meet the Senate in a conciliatory spirit." Wilson said, "House, I have found one can never get anything in this life that is worthwhile without fighting for it." House replied—one can imagine with a small shrug—that a fight was the last thing that was wanted and then only if it could not be avoided. His own plan in negotiations, he said, was to get all he wanted by friendly methods, but if driven to it, to fight so effectively that no one would wish to drive him to it again.[42]

That day House set down some of his thoughts about the conference and about his colleagues. It was easy to say what should have been done, he said, but harder to have found a way to do it. An attempt had been made to make peace on conventional lines. But that ignored the bitterness left by the war, the hopes raised by victory, and the fact that civilization had been shattered. Once again, he returned to his old conviction that it would have been better if Wilson had stayed away. "When he stepped from his lofty pedestal," he said, "and wrangled with representatives of other states upon equal terms, he became as common clay."[43]

The treaty was bad, he acknowledged. But the same forces that made it bad, he believed, would have hindered the enforcement of peace of any kind. A better settlement could have been made only by "an unselfish and idealistic spirit which was . . . too much to expect of men come together at such a time and for such a purpose."[44]

That night House was driven from Paris to Boulogne, and the next day he crossed the English Channel. After a week of total rest, spent largely playing with his daughter Janet's baby Louise, the Houses launched on a summer of furious social activity. Every aristocratic door was open to them now. The colonel jested that the poorest people he had met in England were Mrs. Astor and the Duchess of Marlborough (the former Consuelo Vanderbilt).[45] The Astors did not know how they were going to keep warm next winter, and the duchess said she had to sell jewels to meet her expenses. It might soon be necessary, House commented drily, to take up a collection to help the rich.[46]

House also met old friends with whom he discussed the darkening world scene, among them the diplomat Sir William Tyrrell; the secretary-general-elect of the League of Nations, Sir Eric Drummond; and especially Viscount Grey. A pleasant interlude was a weekend with Grey at the latter's sanctum, a fishing lodge on a famous trout stream a couple of miles outside Winchester.[47]

House had several meetings with Grey, who said it was House who had convinced him that it was his duty to go to Washington as a special ambassador.[48] (Grey was now aging and growing blind.) Grey even asked about what clothes to buy for the Washington summer. House also had long conversations with his friend about the relationship between the United States and Britain. Immediately after the end of the war, there was tension between the two countries, focusing on naval rivalry and Ireland but also reflecting American suspicion of Lloyd George's policy on reparations and the Middle East.

Grey dismissed dire predictions of trouble between the two Anglo-Saxon powers. The United States, he recognized, could always build a fleet bigger than the Royal Navy, but there was no reason to fear war. Grey would not go to Washington unless the British government had an Irish policy he could defend. The Lloyd George government was moving slowly toward granting Ireland home rule, with the proviso that the majority Protestant North could opt out if it chose.

House spent the summer of 1919 with the friends he had made in Britain during the war, friends who accepted him as a man of power, with whom he discussed what was to be done with Ireland, Russia, or the Middle East. They did not understand that the sun of the president's favor no longer shone on him so that he would have little influence on these matters. Understandably, House continued to sit in on the intimate discussions of the Anglo-American elite as if he too had not understood that he had been eclipsed. He was particularly keen on selling his idea for a financial settlement that would relieve Great Britain of some of its burden of debt and believed he had interested Benjamin Strong, the chairman of the Federal Reserve, in his plan.[49]

In mid-September House was back in Paris, where he saw Clemenceau and tried to persuade him to visit the United States. (Clemenceau had lived in the United States for some years after the Civil War and had married an American.) Clemenceau spoke with his usual freedom about his various bêtes noires, including Lloyd George and Poincaré, and said he planned to retire. This prompted the colonel to muse about whether the president would run for a third term. House was watching Wilson's speaking tour of the West with great interest. "What a gamble it all is," he reflected, "and how easily he might have made it a certainty."[49]

On July 10 Wilson had commended the treaty to the Senate in a speech of characteristically biblical rhetoric. "It was of this that we dreamed at our birth. America shall in truth show the way."[51] But if he were to prevail over a Senate where the treaty's opponents probably held a majority, there was only one way: the classic technique of presidential leadership. He must appeal over the heads of the senators to the people who had elected them. To do that, in those days when radio was in its infancy, he could reach the people in only one way. He must meet them himself. So on September 3 he set forth on the long journey. He started his tour in Columbus, Ohio. Then Indianapolis, St. Louis, Kansas City, Des Moines, Omaha, Sioux Falls, Minneapolis, and into the Far West.

Over and over Wilson hammered at the same themes.[52] His wish, he said, was not to punish Germany but to right "the age-old wrongs which characterized the history of Europe." He denounced his opponents, extravagantly comparing Senator Lodge and his friends, though not by name, to the Bolsheviks. He expounded his view of the league and in particular of Article X. Above all he appealed to patriotism and to America's new-found pride in its soldiers. Again and again he invoked the soldiers dead as if they had died for the league. Sometimes, seeing small children in the crowds, he said it was to them that he must report because "the task—that great and gallant task which our soldiers performed—is only half finished." In one speech, he proclaimed that "if, by any chance, we should not win this great fight for the League of Nations," it would be those children's death warrant.

As Wilson's journey went on, the price it was exacting on his health became painfully clear. He suffered from sore throats, "asthma," coughing, and constant headache.[53] Dr. Grayson did what he could, but especially at the high altitudes of the mountain states Wilson was in great discomfort. Later doctors diagnosed congestive heart failure caused by arteriosclerosis. The president's courage was beyond praise. He spoke in damp heat to fifteen thousand in Salt Lake City, and to thirty thousand in San Diego he excelled. On September 25 he gave two speeches in Colorado, the first in Denver and the second in Pueblo.

That day he climbed the emotional zenith of his whole amazing tour. In Denver again he recalled the mothers and the small children who came to hear him and said, "These are the little people I am arguing for. These are my clients." He warned that if the league were defeated and war were to come again, it would be infinitely worse even than the horrors of the Western Front, with "great projectiles which guided themselves, capable of travelling one hundred miles or more, and bursting tons of explosives on helpless cities." In the evening in Pueblo, he gave the supreme speech of his life, in both senses of the word: the greatest and the last. Senator Daniel Patrick Moynihan called it "a speech from the Cross."[54]

Wilson recalled the military cemetery where he had spoken in Paris on Memorial Day and evoked "the serried ranks of those boys in khaki, not only these boys, who came home, but those dear ghosts that still deploy upon the fields of France." In his peroration he proclaimed that the American people had seen "the truth of justice and of liberty and peace" and said it would "lead us, and through us, the world, out into the pastures of quietness and peace such as the world has never dreamed of before."

After he finished, Wilson was almost mortally exhausted. Twenty miles out of town, Grayson ordered the engineer to stop the train so that Wilson could have an hour's walk. He shook hands with a farmer and climbed over a fence to talk to a young soldier. He had dinner and went to bed. At two in the morning, Wilson called Grayson. The doctor wanted to call off the rest of the trip. He had probably detected premonitory symptoms of a stroke. He contacted the neurologist who had treated Wilson for the attack that left him partially blind in 1906 and arranged for him to examine the president on October 3. In the morning, Grayson finally prevailed on the president to cancel his tour.

The presidential train headed 1,700 miles straight back to Washington. On October 2, the day before he was due to see the neurologist, the president woke up in the night and tried to go to the bathroom. He collapsed. Mrs. Wilson summoned Grayson, who realized he had suffered a massive stroke. Dr. Francis X. Dercum, the neurologist, was summoned from Philadelphia. He diagnosed hemiplegia, probably caused by occlusion of the carotid arteries. This is a less violent form of stroke than the apoplectic kind and not necessarily life-threatening. It still meant that the president was gravely ill and incapable of carrying out the functions of his office.

For the next several months, the president of the United States, to all intents and purposes, was Edith Wilson. She succeeded in carrying off a sort of charade in which the president was propped up in bed if visitors simply could not be kept away. In one of the most bizarre episodes in the entire history of the presidency, Edith Wilson ruled the United States through little notes saying "The President wishes. . . ." She could now exclude her enemy, Colonel House, entirely from her husband's life. And that is what she did.

House, in Paris, had no idea of what had happened. On October 5, while the president was in seclusion in the White House, he and Loulie House left Paris by special train. House too was seriously sick. The kidney stone that had troubled him in January had flared up again. The doctors could not operate until his general condition had improved.[55] With a high fever, the colonel had to be half carried on board the *Northern Pacific* at Brest. On arrival in New York, he was helped off the ship and put to bed for almost a week.[56] It was October 20 before he was well enough to see Edward Grey. At this point Loulie House received a letter from Edith Wilson, telling her that the president did not know of House's return from France or of his illness. House commented in his diary, "This indicates how seriously ill he is."[57]

On November 6 House went up to Boston to spend a week with his daughter Mona Tucker. Before leaving, he recorded in his diary that "last week I sent Colonel Bonsal to Washington to see Senators Hitchcock and Lodge to tell them I was ready to go before the Committee." That was the Senate Foreign Relations Committee, then holding hearings into the treaty.

That laconic diary entry covers one of the most intriguing episodes in House's political life. Critical historians brush it aside as unimportant, if not fantasy or even fraud on the colonel's part. It was a last, opportunistic bid by House to save the treaty. The president had played to his own long suit: political persuasion on the high road of gorgeous rhetoric. Colonel House sought to save the treaty and the league by the means he knew best: the search for political consensus.

Sick and exhausted as he was, House recognized the potential of the merest chance. Colonel Stephen Bonsal was no more a military man than Colonel House. Born in 1865 and brought up in Baltimore, he had had an extraordinary career as a journalist, diplomat, and special agent. His parents sent him to study at the university in Vienna. He learned good German and later a dozen other languages. In 1919, with the rank of lieutenant-colonel, he was on the staff of the peace conference and worked as an interpreter for Colonel House. House liked him and entrusted him with missions—for example, with General Smuts to Budapest. There was another biographical fact about Bonsal that counted for more in late 1919 than the rest:

Bonsal had been at boarding school at St. Paul's in New Hampshire with Augustus Peabody Gardner, later a member of Congress, who had died while serving as a major in the U.S. Army in Georgia.[58] And Gardner had been married to the daughter of Senator Henry Cabot Lodge, with whom Bonsal had remained on friendly terms.

Bonsal arrived back in the United States a few days after House and went to see him. "I regard you," Bonsal remembered the colonel saying, "as a messenger from heaven."[59] At the time Bonsal had been told by his friends in Paris that Senator Lodge and his ally Senator Brandegee were sharpening their knives. "They mean to learn from the Colonel what really happened in Paris—or else." House asked Bonsal to go to Washington and find out how the land lay. Bonsal saw Lodge, who received him as an old friend, on October 28, and the senator authorized him to send House "a reassuring letter."[65]

Bonsal's story, recorded in his diary, published in 1944 as *Unfinished Business,* is as follows. He met Lodge twice, the first time at a "hideaway" office in the capitol in October, the second in the library of Lodge's home on Massachusetts Avenue.[61] After assuring Bonsal that there was no urgency about House giving evidence to the committee, the senator talked about the treaty. Bonsal came to the conclusion that the chairman was in a mood to compromise. He telephoned House, who asked him to get from the senator, if he could, a statement of his minimum demands.

At a second meeting Lodge and Bonsal, so the latter claimed, went over the covenant of the league, article by article. On a printed copy of the covenant that Bonsal had brought with him, the senator made certain changes and also certain "interlineations," which, he thought, would "smooth the way to ratification."[62] The changes ran to about forty words, the "inserts" to fifty. Lodge made them in pencil and signed them. Lodge said, more than once, that his worries centered on Article X, the clause that bound the United States to go to war in response to a breach in the league covenant.[63] Bonsal ventured to say that the article itself disposed of Lodge's objections.[64] Lodge went on to criticize the language of the covenant. Then, as a joke, he added, "it might get by at Princeton, but certainly not at Harvard."

The conversation ended with some chat about the English writer George Borrow, of whom Lodge was a great admirer. These courtesies decently completed, Bonsal dashed to the post office at Union Station and mailed to Colonel House the copy of the covenant on which Lodge had penciled his notations. The colonel was in bed, "but when he heard the news he whooped for joy." Bonsal's memo states that "when our conferences" [that is, Bonsal's with Lodge] "were completed I hurried to New York more than delighted with the result. We spent a day drafting a covering letter to President Wilson which concluded with a most eloquent appeal to the President to accept." The assumption is that House sent Lodge's annotated copy of the covenant, or a summary of it, to President Wilson in the hope of persuading him to approach Lodge and find out whether a deal could be done and the treaty saved. Lodge's biographer accepts this as true, though he acknowledges that a careful search of the Lodge papers turned up no evidence of a willingness to compromise.[65]

There are many and great difficulties with this story, however. For one thing, as Charles Seymour, the guardian of the House archives at Yale, wrote Bonsal in a letter after publication of Bonsal's diary/memoir, "There is not, and since 1922 there never has been, any reference" to the annotated copy of the covenant. He could understand, Seymour wrote politely, that the document might have been sent to the White House without Fanny Denton taking any record of Lodge's vital annotations, but he was surprised that the colonel never mentioned the incident and mystified by Bonsal's lame reply that House kept all reference to Lodge's annotations out of the Yale library.

There are, it seems to me, three possible explanations of this conundrum. The first is that Bonsal did send House the document and House did send it on, in one form or another, to the White House but that Mrs. Wilson or Admiral Grayson kept it, no doubt with the best of wifely or medical motives, from the husband and patient. That is all too likely, given their distaste and paranoia with regard to House, evidenced in Mrs. Wilson's memoir and in Grayson's posthumous article. But that still leaves an unusual lack of supporting evidence, given the voluminous size of the House archives and the scrupulous way in which they were maintained by both House himself and Fanny Denton and by Seymour and his successors at Yale.

The second alternative is the one preferred by John Milton Cooper in his impressive history of the treaty fight after a rigorous review of the documents. "There is a more likely explanation," he writes bluntly, "namely that House never sent the papers to the White House and was lying when he claimed to have done so."[66] This is bold, because House had an international reputation for trustworthiness. It does have a certain plausibility, if it is assumed that House was desperate to show that he could succeed where the president had failed. Certainly House passionately wanted the League of Nations to survive with American membership. Cooper's skepticism, though not his accusation of lying, is supported by a comment in a letter from the historian Arthur Walworth, who, as Cooper noted, was sympathetic to House.

In a letter written in 1953, Walworth wrote that there was evidence that Bonsal had one conversation with Lodge, but not that the senator proposed a compromise.

"While we think Mr. Bonsal a thoroughly reliable authority," Walworth concluded tactfully, "we cannot understand the absence of documentary evidence or the void in the memory of Miss Denton and we hesitate to accept the story as historical without evidence."[67] It is notoriously hard, however, to prove a negative. Until the records of the White House mail room, if they exist, yield up their secrets, there can be no definite proof.

The third explanation is that it is Stephen Bonsal's account, or rather accounts, of the incident that are unreliable. He was writing a quarter of a century after the event. There are contradictions in his account, not least on the subject of how many times he met Senator Lodge. He may have wanted to spice up his diary; the style suggests that he was quite capable of that. That he met Senator Lodge is clear. That they discussed the treaty is likely. That the senator whipped out a pencil and committed himself, to a social acquaintance known to be associated with Colonel House, who, for all Lodge knew, was still the man of confidence of his hated antagonist and who in any case was an astute and inveterate Democrat, strikes me as implausible to the brink of the ridiculous. Bonsal's case, presumably, is that Lodge, fearing defeat, was looking for a way to run up a flag of truce and saw his late son-in-law's school friend as an intermediary he could trust. Perhaps. But there were surely many safer alternatives. It strikes me as more likely that Bonsal exaggerated and dramatized the longest of long shots at saving the treaty. To be as blunt as Professor Cooper, it is more likely that Bonsal was fantasizing than that House was lying.[68]

Where Cooper is no doubt correct is in questioning how important the Bonsal affair was. Even if Senator Lodge, in a short-lived moment of doubt about the outcome of the league fight, did take this odd and—it must be said—uncharacteristic way of putting out feelers for a compromise, certainly nothing came of it. And whether or not Colonel House sent the parcel with the senator's penciled annotations to the White House, he certainly did send two messages to the president about the treaty. He had no answer to either.

Even after President Wilson's return to the United States at the end of June, Colonel House continued to write letters to him. On July 30, he wrote at great length, warning of dangers in Anglo-American relations. What worried the colonel was the possibility of naval rivalry of the kind that had poisoned Anglo-German relations before 1914, and in this context he reported to Wilson the assurance he had been given by his friend Lord Grey. But he also pointed out that it was the freedom of the seas that had brought the United States into the war, and that problem was no nearer to solution than in 1914.

On September 30 House wrote another long missive, this time expounding his favorite ideas for a financial settlement. He wanted to shift the burden of debt from Britain and France. (He pointed out that Britain had lent $3 billion to Russia and nearly $4 billion to France and Italy.) Once the inter-Allied debt had been adjusted, it would be possible to scale down Germany's reparations payments. Unless some such settlement were made, House wrote, "we will not be able to collect our debts in full, and it is also certain that we will incur the everlasting ill will of those to whom we have advanced loans."[69]

House's two most important letters, however, dealt with the vital issue of the league, the treaty, and the Senate. The first letter was dated November 24, 1919, by which time the presidency had been in the hands of Mrs. Wilson for more than seven weeks.[70] The president was bedridden. His left hand was paralyzed. He was not at first strong enough to walk or even to use a commode. Undaunted, Edith Wilson decided she could stage-manage visits in such a way that the president would appear less stricken than he was. Her choice of the first two visits was revealing. Ahead of all the people—senators, diplomats, congressmen, officials of many kinds—who needed to see the president, Mrs. Wilson chose to wheel in first the king and queen of the Belgians, then the debonair but inconsequential Prince of Wales.

For months, Edith Wilson conducted herself as acting president, in a bold interpretation of the Constitution and in a manner that reflected her personal prejudices and those of her clique. She was helped in the various undignified dodges her imposture required by her accomplices—notably Dr. Grayson and Bernard Baruch—and also by the loyalty of White House staff like Joseph P. Tumulty and Irwin "Ike" Hoover. In early December, she decided she had no alternative but to allow in two senators, ungraciously described by Wilson as a "smelling committee," sent to try to assess how fit he was to govern. Edith staged an elaborate charade, arranging the bedclothes, the lighting, and other props to hide how ill the president still was.

House felt he must try to save something from the wreckage of their joint achievement. With the crucial vote looming in the Senate, he tried to save his former friend from disaster. He dispatched a letter to the president, with a tactful covering letter to Mrs. Wilson: "You can never know how long I have hesitated to write to the President about anything while he is ill, but it seems to me vital that the Treaty should pass in some form. His place in history is in balance. If the Treaty goes through with objectionable reservations it can later be rectified. The essential thing is to have the President's great work in Paris live."[71]

The letter to Wilson himself began by saying that House felt the defeat of the treaty "would be a disaster not less to civilization than to you."[72] His advice was that Wilson should send for Senator Gilbert Hitchcock, the Democratic minority leader, and say that he had done his duty by refusing to change the treaty but would now turn the document over to the Senate. Hitchcock should ask the Democrats to vote for the treaty with its reservations. If the Allies accepted the treaty with those reservations, the president would have done his duty. If they did not, he would at least be vindicated. The implication, though House did not spell it out, was that a league of nations, even with some American reservations, would be better than no league and no treaty at all.

House himself may have realized the psychological flaw in this reasonable argument. At their last meeting, after all, Wilson the prophet had brandished the sword of righteousness and promised to go down fighting. So three days later, House tried again. In a second letter, again enclosed in a covering note to Mrs. Wilson, he emphasized that he was not counseling surrender. If Wilson did as House advised, it would guarantee the passage of the treaty. He ended, as he had so often done when he wanted to persuade his friend in the past, with flattery: "Your willingness to accept reservations rather than have the treaty killed will be regarded as the act of a great man."[73]

It was all in vain. On November 7 Senator Hitchcock was allowed into the presence. The president lay on his back, saying he found it tiring to read or discuss important matters.[74] Later that day Hitchcock drafted a letter for Wilson to send to the Senate, asking its members to vote against the Lodge reservations. Edith Wilson, after some discussion with her husband, took a pen and slashed away at the letter, changing, for example, a sentence that said that if this course were followed, "the door will probably be open for a possible compromise" and allowing only "for a genuine resolution of ratification."[75]

Two days after Hitchcock's visit, the catastrophe took place. The senators, presented with the treaty with the Lodge reservations attached, voted it down by fifty-five votes to thirty-three. Passionate supporters of the treaty voted with the treaty's "irreconcilable" opponents. The treaty came before the Senate again on March 19, 1920, and fell seven votes short of the necessary two-thirds majority. By then, few even seemed to care.

House's letters were never answered. Indeed, they were never even opened. No one saw them until they were deposited in the Library of Congress in 1952. House had done his duty, but Edith Wilson's resentment was implacable.

18   *Watching the World Go By*   ∾

Edward House, a supercivilized person escaped from the wilds of Texas, who sees everything, who understands everything, and, while never doing anything but what he thinks fit, knows how to gain the ear and the respect of everybody. A good American, very nearly as good a Frenchman, a sifting, pondering mind—above all, the traditional gentleman.

—Georges Clemenceau

FROM JUNE 29, 1919, when Woodrow Wilson left France to return to Washington, we can now see that Colonel House's career as a public man was essentially over. That was not, however, plain to House himself at the time, still less to others. The remaining twenty years of his life were not spent watching the world go by in resignation. He still sought, and from to time he still wielded, some influence on the world's great affairs.

House lobbied for the League of Nations; for generous solutions to Europe's problems of debt and reparations; and for policies he thought would reduce the risk of war. And in the last decade of his life he had a surprisingly close personal and political friendship with Franklin Roosevelt as governor, presidential candidate, and president.

House's expectations of making a greater contribution to relations between the United States and Britain were derailed by the bizarre tragicomedy of his friend Edward Grey's special diplomatic mission to Washington.

Grey trusted House to such an extent that he even discussed with him his personal financial affairs.[1] (House learned that the British landowner and railway director had almost exactly the same income as House, between $15,000 and $20,000 a year.)[2] In August 1922 and again in July 1925, the Houses overcame their reluctance to visit cold English country houses and stayed with Grey at his home in Northumberland, Fallodon.[3]

As early as 1919 House and his British friends were alarmed at the deterioration of relations between Britain and the United States, made worse by the absence of a high-level British diplomat in Washington.[4] In August 1919, House lunched with Lloyd George, Grey, and Lord Haldane to discuss sending Grey to Washington on a special mission to improve relations. (It is remarkable that once again House was so trusted that he was included in the intimate discussions of a foreign government.) House planned to travel with Grey on the *Mauretania* on September 20, but Wilson ordered him to stay in Europe. In October, House fell ill, and it was not until late in that month that he was able to get together with Grey in New York. By that time Edith Wilson was in charge of the White House, and the Grey mission was poisoned by a farcical episode. Grey had been told by the president that he would be very welcome. But when he reached Washington, he was not received at the White House.

The chief reason lay in the Craufurd-Stuart affair. Major Charles Craufurd-Stuart was an officer from the British Indian army assigned to work for British intelligence in America. He was a great social success in Washington, whether because of his talent for writing popular songs or his smart Indian army regimentals with their purple satin pants. He dined out on jokes such as his contention that Edith Galt was so surprised when Woodrow Wilson proposed to her that she fell out of bed. This joke came to Edith Wilson's ears, and she was not amused.

For this and other indiscretions, Craufurd-Stuart was sent back to London. But Edward Grey needed an aide. Craufurd-Stuart knew his way around Washington. Grey took him on. The first contact he had from the State Department was when he was curtly told to fire his new aide. Grey refused to ruin a man's career without evidence. So he was not received at the White House. It is possible that the climate in Washington, with Edith Wilson now to all intents and purposes acting president, had already changed so much that Grey would not have been received in any case. The Craufurd-Stuart affair made failure a certainty.

In the course of his duties as an intelligence officer, the gallant major suspected Bernard Baruch of having a relationship with Mrs. Archibald White, the former actress Olive Moore, who had previously been the mistress of no less a personage than Count von Bernstorff.[5] Later Craufurd-Stuart's professional suspicion fell on the young and beautiful May Ladenburg, who had inherited $6 million from her father, a German banker. Versions of the story differ. The more highly colored, supplied by President Theodore Roosevelt's daughter, Alice Longworth, relates that she, Longworth, wife of the Speaker of the House of Representatives, was persuaded by General Marlborough Churchill, head of American military intelligence, to snoop on Ladenburg.[6] Major Craufurd-Stuart obtained entrance to Ladenburg's home at 18th and M Streets in Washington to install a listening device by sweet-talking the maid. Between noises that sounded like kissing, Ladenburg was overheard asking Bernard Baruch how many locomotives were being sent to Romania. Sir William Wiseman's more prosaic version pointed out that May Ladenburg was Bernard Baruch's niece and that he would not have had any secrets worth telling in any case.

In any event, Major Craufurd-Stuart had made implacable enemies of Edith Wilson and Baruch. The major could hardly have been in more trouble. Edward Grey refused to fire him. And Mrs. Wilson refused to let Grey see the president. "It all shows the power of the Baruch-Grayson influence," wrote Colonel House, "at this time when no one other than Grayson has access to the President."[7]

On January 3, 1920, Edward Grey sailed for home. He had written to a friend about his three months in Washington: "I love the Americans. They seem to me more easy to get on with than English people, but they are very civilized and wear white waistcoats, and have not as a rule got any passion for country life; and I, being at bottom primitive and uncivilized, would have to go and live in the backwoods if I stayed in the country."[8]

Back in London, Grey fired his shot. It was a letter to *The Times* of London, reprinted immediately by the *New York Times* and the *Philadelphia Public Ledger*. Grey was a passionate advocate of a league of nations. Now he argued that it would be better to have the United States in the league willingly but with reservations than to have it as a reluctant and resentful partner. The effect was to demolish Wilson's insistence on passing the treaty without the Lodge reservations. Lodge himself could not have put it better.

"The ground is cut from under the President's feet," House saw. He supposed "the White House entourage will make the President believe I am in some way responsible."[9] In fact, he knew nothing of it. The failure of Grey's mission, House concluded, was a great misfortune, and it was all the fault of the White House.

In the same breath in his diary House recorded that he was besieged by one publisher after another pressing him to write his memoirs and by authors offering to write his life. It was as if Edith Wilson's foolish spite, Grey's humiliation, and the collapse of their hopes for the league freed him to put the record straight. That was to be one of his main preoccupations for the rest of his life.

House found his principal instrument in this project among the bright young academics from the Inquiry. Charles Seymour was the son of a Yale professor of Greek who had two former presidents of Yale in his family tree. Born in 1885, he studied at Cambridge from 1901 to 1904. He returned to Yale, where he was tapped for the secret society, Skull and Bones, in whose Egyptian tomb so many of the makers of American foreign policy were once initiated.[10] He graduated from Yale in 1908 and studied in Paris and Freiburg. He was teaching at Yale when in 1917 Colonel House recruited him to the Inquiry.

It was to this pluperfect Connecticut Yankee, a confident young man, a future president of Yale, that House first turned for help.[11] In March 1920 Seymour presented himself a little nervously at 115 East 53rd Street for the first of a series of interviews that went on until near the end of House's life. Seymour helped House and his friend Edward W. Bok, publisher of the *Ladies' Home Journal,* set up a series of lectures under the general title "What Really Happened at Paris." The lectures were held in the splendidly refurbished Academy of Music building in Philadelphia. There were fifteen lectures, one every week from December 10, 1920. House himself gave the final lecture, on "The Versailles Peace in Retrospect," and the lectures were subsequently published as a book.

By late 1921 House was thinking of entrusting to Seymour the book that would vindicate his own career. (It came out under the title *The Intimate Papers of Colonel House,* published in four volumes between 1926 and 1928.) Those looking to the intimate papers for intimate revelations would be disappointed. But they are an invaluable guide to House's life. Seymour was handicapped by Edith Wilson's refusal to allow him to quote Wilson's letters and cables to House textually. The volumes must be seen as what they were: House's defense of his life and work against the effort being made to minimize his contribution to Woodrow Wilson's achievement. In time, a superb edition of the Wilson papers was to be produced at Princeton under the direction of Arthur S. Link.[12] But in the 1920s House felt he had to contend with the aggressively partisan account being written by Ray Stannard Baker on the basis of the papers deposited at Princeton by Mrs. Wilson, papers which Seymour was not allowed to cite, though Baker demanded access to the House papers.[13]

House was aware that a battle of the books was being fought. His solution was a clever one. He deposited his papers at Yale in 1923. He encouraged others—his son-in-law Gordon Auchincloss, Sir William Wiseman, and David Hunter Miller among them—to do the same. He entrusted his reputation to Charles Seymour. Seymour did not betray his trust.

Every year during the war Colonel House, accompanied by Mrs. House, spent some time in Europe. With the coming of peace, their visits to Europe were longer and more leisurely. They were vacations. But House was also keeping in touch with his contacts in Europe. These were spectacular by any standards. Everyone wanted to meet the colonel. Whenever they were in London, the Houses were invited to lunch or dinner at Buckingham Palace. As we have seen, they saw a dazzling array of duchesses, marchionesses, and society hostesses, many of them American heiresses. In 1920, after a garden party at Buckingham Palace, House could write that "there were several thousand people there and I was surprised at the number I knew."[14]

House routinely saw the top political leaders in London: successive British prime ministers Herbert Asquith, David Lloyd George, Ramsay MacDonald, Bonar Law, and Stanley Baldwin, as well as other major figures like Grey, Balfour, and Winston Churchill. Once, in August 1923, as they were leaving the Ritz Hotel in Paris, the Houses ran into Lord and Lady Curzon, who were checking out at the same time. It seemed the most natural thing in the world for the four of them to go off and stay in a French country hotel, where they had a long, relaxed chat about world politics.[15]

It is plain from occasional affectionate grumbles in the diary that Colonel House did not share his wife's enthusiasm for going out every night.[16] He would turn up after dinner for the political talk without the turbot and the foie gras. He enjoyed the way he was fully accepted in the most elevated social and political circles.[17] But his head was not turned. Invited to Blickling Hall in Norfolk, the exquisite Elizabethan mansion belonging to Philip Kerr, House complained that the guests were "not very exhilarating. A country squire and a gouty earl have little to talk about other than hunting, dogs, horses and the growing of their fruit and flowers."[18]

The Houses could afford to travel in style. In May 1920 House contracted an agreement with Cyrus Curtis, publisher of the *Philadelphia Public Ledger* and the *Saturday Evening Post,* on his own terms, to serve the *Public Ledger* in an advisory capacity. He was to be paid $2,500 a month, with passage to Europe paid for himself, his wife, and Fanny Denton and a letter of credit for $10,000.[19] They put up at the most fashionable hotels of the day, the Connaught in London and the Ritz in Paris, and gave handsome little dinners for a dozen or so to repay hospitality. "We have never travelled in Europe with less inconvenience than on this trip," House recorded in his diary, "thanks to the courtesies shown by our embassies, legations and the governments whose countries we have visited."[20]

From 1920 to 1926, the Houses spent a serious proportion of their life on these leisurely European progresses. In 1920, they sailed on June 12 and returned to New York on September 8. In 1921, commissioned again by the *Public Ledger* to write a weekly article, House sailed on the *Aquitania* on May 3. House had long talks on deck with the new American ambassador to the Court of St. James, none other than George Harvey, the victim of a famous Wilson snub. In Paris, House had lunch *à trois* with Prime Minister Aristide Briand and the philosopher Henri Bergson.[21] Then the Houses traveled on to Berlin, Vienna, and Prague before spending July and August in England. They were away for just under four months.

In 1922, the Houses sailed from New York to Boulogne on May 30 and sailed for home on September 6. They were met by Prime Minister Clemenceau in a Rolls Royce he had been given by his admirers.[22] They drove over to see Claude Monet's water lilies in his garden at Giverny and then fought the war all over again, with pungent judgments from the aging Clemenceau.

The vacation was from June 4 to August 19 in 1923. One of the highlights was a dinner with Rudyard Kipling, the American-born but Anglicized painter John Singer Sargent, and Lytton Strachey.[23] In 1924 they reached London on May 25, spent the next weekend with Ramsay MacDonald, the Labour prime minister, at Chequers, his official weekend retreat, and stayed three and a half months. In 1925 they sailed on an American ship, the SS *Minnewaska,* on May 23 and returned on the *Duilio* from Genoa at the beginning of October, more than four months later.

In 1926 came the most ambitious European holiday of all. It began with a Mediterranean cruise on the *Mauretania.* The Houses visited Madeira, Gibraltar, Algiers, and the French Riviera, then sailed by way of Naples and Athens to Haifa in Palestine and Alexandria in Egypt, before returning by Cannes and Paris to London. The Houses spent most of their time on these extended jaunts in London and Paris, but they also visited Germany, Austria, Czechoslovakia, Holland, Belgium, and Switzerland.

House had political interests as well as pleasure in mind, foremost among them the league. Like many of his contemporaries in Britain and the United States, House believed the peace of the world could be guaranteed only by a close alliance between these two countries. In practice, it was hard to distinguish this belief from a distinctly elitist Atlanticism, in which those who could afford to cross the Atlantic in first-class cabins featured more prominently than the general public. In this patrician world, Colonel House figured prominently.

House remained to the end of his life a liberal and a Democrat. But there is no getting away from the fact that after the Paris peace conference he was a grandee on a world scale. He rubbed shoulders with other grandees, and some of their less democratic attitudes rubbed off. When he visited Germany in 1921, he observed that "Berlin is full of profiteers spending their money recklessly. The Jews predominate in this class of undesirable citizenship."[24]

House was not, however, obsessed with Europe to the exclusion of all interest in American politics. In public, House was careful to avoid criticism of Wilson.[25] In private, he did permit himself criticism, almost always balanced with expressions of loyalty. There is no mistaking a degree of satisfaction, for example, in House's account of a reported conversation between Wilson and Raymond Fosdick in 1923 in which the president made some odd remarks, among them that Cabot Lodge "died years ago, I mean morally."[26]

House was nevertheless moved by Wilson's death when it came in February 1924: "It was not alone my interest in the success of his undertaking, but I had a deep and abiding affection for the man which all that has happened since June 28, 1919, has not shaken."[27]

House had intended to go to the funeral but was told by Bernard Baruch that he would not be admitted. So he gave up and went to Madison Square Garden, where the service was broadcast, but he arrived too late and had to stand outside in the rain.[28]

House had intended to support William G. McAdoo, a "dry" and endorsed by the Ku Klux Klan as he was, in the 1924 presidential election, but he was put off by McAdoo's involvement in the Teapot Dome scandal.[29] He flirted with support of several candidates, but by April 1924 he was pushing two of them: John W. Davis and his former acquaintance from the days of the Federal Reserve Act, Carter Glass of Virginia. In the spring of 1925, he had lunch with John W. Davis to talk about plans for a conference to discuss the future of the Democratic party: "We did not disagree in the opinion that the time might come when there would be a serious clash between capital and labor in this country. . . . I thought it merely needed a proper setting—hard times, and an arrogant administration in Washington determined to hold labor in check. We both thought that if anything akin to a revolution started here it would be of a serious and violent nature because our people are lawless."[30]

A few days later House gave a luncheon to which he invited prominent Democrats—including Ohio governor James M. Cox, the 1920 nominee—to exchange ideas about the "rehabilitation" of the Democrats. A few days later he was reaching out to the man who in due course would rehabilitate the party in earnest. He tried to rescue Franklin Roosevelt from an awkward position. Roosevelt had called a Democratic conference, but no one wanted to come. Franklin D. Roosevelt was to be the last political cause of House's life. But before that happened, House had become involved with a less salubrious character.

Understandably, House continued to be fascinated by his relationship with Wilson until the end of his life. His cooperation with Charles Seymour on the *Intimate Papers* was his first attempt to define it. His second drew him into a sad episode, a friendship with an unhappy and sinister figure: George Sylvester Viereck.

House may have contacted Viereck before the United States entered the war as a source of German American opinion. In 1919 Viereck sent House a postcard from Doorn, across the German border in Holland, where he had been to interview his grandfather on the wrong side of the blanket, the German kaiser.[31] His father, Louis Viereck, edited a socialist newspapers and served as a Social Democratic member of the Reichstag and even spent nine months in prison under Germany's anti-socialist laws. In 1896 he emigrated to the United States. His wife and twelve-year-old son Sylvester joined him there a year later. In his teens, Sylvester Viereck established a reputation as an aesthetic poet.

When war came, Viereck set up a bureau to offset British propaganda, subsidized by the German government. He was careful to avoid violating the Espionage or Sedition Acts, but he was interrogated by the Justice Department.

After the war, he became a vehement opponent of President Wilson. A disciple of Richard von Kraft-Ebbing, Havelock Ellis, Freud, and other students of the psychosexual, Viereck collaborated with a Jewish writer, Paul Eldridge, on the amorous adventures of the Wandering Jew. He was also an early admirer of Adolf Hitler.[32]

In 1929, House sent Viereck a note congratulating him on his recently published study of propaganda, *Spreading Germs of Hate*. Viereck responded by asking for a "chat," and House agreed. By October Viereck was asking for House's help; he was unblushing and devious in his requests for introductions and in various more or less subtle ways for money. Viereck was in contact with the German espionage and sabotage network in the United States. He asked for House's help in recovering papers handed over to the U.S. attorney.[33] House passed on the request to his old friend, T. W. Gregory, U.S. attorney general at the time.

Over the next few months Viereck spread his net. He said he was writing about House for the Hearst papers but needed to know whether House's eyes were gray or blue. He almost groveled. When he wrote to House asking him to do an interview for Fox-Hearst-Movietone, he said, "Your graciousness would be the final and indisputable proclamation that I have achieved respectability."[34]

By October 1930, Viereck had asked House to collaborate with him in writing "the story of your friendship with Woodrow Wilson." This was the genesis of *The Strangest Friendship in the World,* published in 1933. It was neither a publishing nor a critical success. The even stranger friendship between House and Viereck survived, though the strain of collaboration with someone as pushy and thick-skinned as Viereck was not to be underestimated. By the fall of 1932, House had had enough. "I do not think we can make a go of cooperating in these articles."[35]

Before long Viereck was angling for House to help pay for his son Peter to go to Harvard, and House actually wrote to Princeton asking for a scholarship for him.[36] A few days after Hitler took over as chancellor in Germany, Viereck wrote, "What do you think of the new developments in Germany? I am glad Papen is there to act as a brake. It seems to me that he really controls the situation."[37] In the pages of folder after folder of House's correspondence with Viereck, it is painfully obvious why Viereck is keeping up the friendship: he hopes to persuade the old gentleman to share his increasingly brutal anti-Semitic views.[38] But House mattered to Viereck primarily as a source of influence and money. He is constantly proposing ideas for articles and broadcasts for House to do.[39] What he does not say is that he will take a cut of the proceeds. In the end, Viereck went too far. He drew House's attention to the fact that because his middle name was Mandell, it was being put about that he was a Jew. (As we have seen, he was called Mandell after a friend of his father's.) House replied: "Everything has been said of me except that I was a Jew, and now that point is covered the circle is complete. My people on both sides are English. For many generations they lived in Somerset, and the church at Stoke St. Gregory is surrounded with the graves of my ancestors."[40]

Viereck promised to pass on the correction to his friend, Dr. Josef Goebbels.[41] The very next day he wrote to Reichsminister Dr. Josef Goebbels: "Colonel House assures me that he has not a drop of Jewish blood in his veins. . . . The Mandell family is of pure Aryan descent and belonged then, as it still does today, to the 'Blue Blood' of New England."[42]

In early 1937 House, no longer in good health, repurchased rights to his own memoirs for $10,000, the amount originally advanced to him by the publisher of *The Strangest Friendship*. House and Viereck last met in October 1937. To the end Viereck wrote letters suggesting that House owed him money. He also continued to write propaganda on behalf of Nazi Germany, loudly advocating the thing most objectionable to his friend and patron, Edward Mandell House.[43]

The episode would be almost amusing if it were not so disgusting on Viereck's side and so sad on that of an old man who tried to help someone he thought of as a friend.

House knew and liked Franklin Delano Roosevelt when the latter was assistant secretary of the navy under Josephus Daniels. Throughout the 1920s, the two men kept in touch, and Eleanor Roosevelt occasionally attempted to engage both the colonel and Loulie House in her charitable projects. After he decided to run for governor of New York, FDR frequently asked House's advice. On election day 1930, FDR sent a telegram saying, "Mrs. Roosevelt and I hope you will come in to headquarters at the Biltmore on Tuesday evening to see us and hear the returns," to which House scribbled acceptance in pencil, adding, "Your overwhelming victory makes me very happy, for it foreshadows your election to the Presidency two years from now. Edward House."[44]

As early as 1928 Franklin Roosevelt had written to House, "I would rather have your approval than that of any other man I know."[45] It was, of course, political flattery with a purpose. Roosevelt saw House as a connection with the Progressive Democrats of the Wilson tradition. After Roosevelt's resounding victory by three-quarters of a million votes in the 1930 gubernatorial election, "Colonel House had joined the small inner group which was promoting the presidential aspirations of F.D.R."[46]

House's friendship with FDR was political on both sides. House saw FDR as his way back into the higher councils of the Democratic Party. Perhaps he even dreamed of being once again a Democratic president's intimate friend and counselor. Roosevelt was keen to avail himself of House's political judgment, experience, and vast acquaintanceship in the Democratic Party. House saw Roosevelt as the best hope for the party if it was to end its twelve-year crossing of the desert. House wanted nothing better than to help Roosevelt replace Wilson as the leader

of a progressive yet pragmatic Democratic Party. At the end of his life he recalled that he had been "close to the movement that nominated Roosevelt," and
it was true.[47]

A strange chance enabled House to do Roosevelt a good turn. House wanted to
wean the Massachusetts democracy from its Irish loyalty to Al Smith. (House had
nothing against Smith except that he could not be elected.) With this in mind, he
arranged one of his little lunches for some of the leading Democrats in the state to
meet Governor Roosevelt and be overcome by his charm and political horsepower.
Governor James B. Ely, a Yankee Democrat from western Massachusetts, and the
state's two senators, David Ignatius Walsh and Marcus A. Coolidge, were the chief
guests. House also invited carefully chosen reporters, including his friend Robert
Washburn, a liberal Republican columnist, and Ellery Sedgwick of the *Atlantic
Monthly*.

On the train from New York, FDR ran into no less a Massachusetts Democrat
than James Michael Curley, the mayor of Boston, who was on his way home from a
colorful tour of Europe, where he had presented Mussolini with the flag of Boston,
dedicated to "the savior of Christian civilization," and declared that his natural gifts
made it unnecessary for him to kiss the Blarney stone.[48] Curley heard that Roosevelt was on the *Yankee Clipper*, sent his card to the governor's suite, and was asked
to stop by for a chat. By the time the train reached Boston, the news was out
that Curley had endorsed Roosevelt for president. And when that reached Colonel House, Mayor Curley was asked to lunch at Manchester too. The lunch was a
huge success.

Roosevelt's strategic difficulty was that to be elected, in the big eastern cities he
badly needed the Irish vote, which was still in the main fanatically loyal to Al Smith.
Roosevelt desperately needed Democrats, and if possible Irish Democrats, to admit
that Smith's chance has passed. Of course Curley had political motives of his own:
he wanted to discomfit Governor Ely, whose job he wanted.

House had prepared the lunch with care. He had even checked with Roosevelt's
man, Louis Howe, whether or not to serve alcohol. Prohibition or no prohibition,
Boston was hardly dry. In 1928 there were said to have been four thousand speak-
easies in town.[49] Yet House asked Howe: "Would you advise serving a light wine
at the lunch? I do not do so as a rule but my son-in-law offers a few bottles of
home made wine and there are one or two newspaper men coming who might
appreciate it."[50]

Caution prevailed. Nothing stronger than sweet cider was served. Yet after lunch, on the sun-soaked lawn of Colonel House's cottage, Curley linked arms with Roosevelt and said, "Within the next two years we hope that you will come back to us in an even more exalted capacity. We expect to welcome you as President of the United States."[51] Colonel House, naturally, concurred. Thanks to Jim Curley, the cat was out of the bag. Ten days later Franklin Roosevelt wrote Colonel House that "the reverberations of that delightful luncheon are still rising from the hills, not only of Massachusetts but of a dozen other states."[52]

More than a year before Roosevelt was nominated, his right-hand man, Louis Howe, was consulting House regularly on tactical matters. (By August 1931 House was writing to Howe, "May I presume on our intimacy to call you by your first name?")[53] Throughout 1931 and 1932 both the House Papers at Yale and the Roosevelt Papers at Hyde Park are full of examples of FDR asking House's advice and House offering suggestions, encouragement, and criticism. For example, on February 10, 1932, House wrote Roosevelt warning that many of his friends—those very old Wilsonians FDR was counting on House to deliver to his camp—were unhappy about FDR's position on the League of Nations and would be unable to support him if he took the same (negative) position on the World Court. House also, as ever, expressed his suspicions of Tammany.[54]

As the election approached, in August 1932 Governor Roosevelt asked House to join a small advisory group led by Raymond Moley. This was the famous Brain Trust. Roosevelt's letter crossed one from House saying that his "many contacts throughout the country" were telling him that Roosevelt's campaign was slipping.[55] One of House's major contributions to the 1932 victory was to persuade his friend Judge Robert Bingham, wealthy publisher of the *Louisville Courier-Journal,* to make large donations to the Roosevelt campaign chest. Bingham was rewarded by being made Roosevelt's ambassador to London.

House soon fell into the habit he had kept up with Wilson of sending warm little congratulatory notes after FDR's more important speeches. Twice, in October and November 1932, Roosevelt thanked him for these, saying it was a boost to his morale. On the day of Roosevelt's inauguration, March 4, 1933, House congratulated the new president, and Roosevelt responded by sending a signed photograph. House said he would hang it alongside that of Woodrow Wilson.

In May 1933 House invited the president to come and stay on the North Shore, saying that he was sure one of his friends would be glad to lend their home, as Clara Coolidge had done for the Wilsons. Roosevelt replied almost a month later, saying he hoped to be able to land at somebody's private wharf in his chartered schooner,

Amberjack II, and on June 20 a Western Union telegram arrived. "Hope reach Gloucester tonight," it read. "Can you come aboard about ten thirty Wednesday morning. Franklin D Roosevelt."[56]

This was no idle vacation trip. For Roosevelt, who loved sailing, it was a rest after the rigors of the hundred days.[57] It was also a personal quest. *Amberjack's* voyage took him from Marion, on Buzzard's Bay, around Cape Cod to the North Shore, and then up the coast of Maine to Campobello on the Bay of Fundy. He had not been back there since he was carried on a stretcher to the dock in agony from polio twelve years before. The voyage of the *Amberjack* was an exorcism of the darkest memories of his life. It was also a moment of high international drama. As the president sailed north, accompanied by a small flotilla (the cruiser *Indianapolis,* a Coast Guard cutter for White House staff, the press boat *Mary Alice,* and a patrol boat carrying the Secret Service detail), representatives of sixty-six nations were meeting in London to address the world financial crisis.

While the president rested at anchor in his schooner off the Pollock Light, Raymond Moley arrived post-haste from Washington by navy plane and destroyer from Nantucket to put steel into the secretary of state, Cordell Hull. Hull, the elegant Tennessean, was not pleased. "That piss-ant Moley," the secretary cried out in mortification. "Here he curled up at mah feet and let me stroke his head like a hunting dog and then he goes and bites me in the ass!"[58] Moley had interrupted his journey to London to get authorization from Roosevelt.

On his way north, steering *Amberjack* himself, FDR duly arrived at Gloucester. Colonel House came on board with Lewis Douglas, the president's budget director, and had a long discussion of monetary policy in the cockpit of the schooner.[59] House had brought with him a memorandum arguing against stabilization and a copy of *Planned Money,* by Sir Basil Blackett, newly published in Britain. In the event Roosevelt "wrecked" the London conference by insisting on America's freedom to allow the currency to reach its own level in the market. He changed his mind and denounced the efforts of the European powers to stabilize the dollar-pound exchange rate, ruthlessly undercutting Moley. It is impossible to know how much Roosevelt was influenced by a paper and a book that both took the anti-stabilization side of the argument. Certainly, faced with a difficult decision about the currency crisis, Roosevelt listened to House's advice.

House was becoming almost a family friend. A handwritten letter from the president to House, undated but probably from the spring of 1934, was passed on with a scrawled note from FDR's mother, Mrs. James Roosevelt.

Dear Colonel,

Mama will give you this and it carries with it my affection and the
wish that I could stop in N.Y. and run in to see you—I have had some
days here with absolutely no interruptions except the news from Germany and England—I so wish you could go over and get a true picture
for me! I hear from London that Chamberlain really believes there is a
chance to buy Italy away from Germany and that his moves are based on
that assumption[.] Meanwhile we can and should do nothing at this moment[.] Public opinion begins urgently to understand the potential dangers of the spread of fascism throughout the world, including this
hemisphere.

I do hope to get to N.Y. early in May and see you then.

As ever yours,
Franklin D Roosevelt.[60]

House did not "go over" to Europe for Roosevelt as he had done for Wilson,
but the president did value his opinion, both about domestic politics and about the
situation in Europe. Early in 1935 Colonel House, already looking forward to the
1936 elections, warned FDR of a movement among "Republicans and liberals" to
put forward "some such man as Glenn Frank" as their candidate.[61] FDR replied
two days later with a sharp analysis of the situation as he saw it.[62] About a month
later, Roosevelt wrote again in a more cheerful mood, saying that the "diversion
by the trinity of [Huey] Long, [Father Charles E.] Coughlin and [General Hugh S.]
Johnson was long over due and it is vastly better to have this free side-show
presented to the public at this time than later on when the main performance
starts."[63]

In the spring of 1935 FDR was already beginning to wrestle with the dilemma
that was to dominate his political thinking for the next six years: how to respond to
what he already saw as the mortal challenge of fascism in Europe and Japan at a
time when American public opinion was dead set against military involvement. On
April 10 that year the president wrote House that he was "of course, greatly disturbed by events on the other side—perhaps more than I should be." He had
thought over two or three different courses of action to stop the armaments race
and the drift to war before rejecting each of them. Any American suggestion, he
feared, would meet with "the same kind of chilly, half-contemptuous reception on
the other side as an appeal would have met in July or August 1914."[64] So he asked

House to give some thought to the idea of collective naval action against Germany by France, Italy, Britain, and the "Little Entente" countries of Central Europe.

Roosevelt continued to ask House his opinion of the European situation, and House continued to offer it. In 1934 House thought the British were overpessimistic. "The British are obsessed with the idea that Germany is almost as much of a menace now as she was in '14."[65] But by the next year he was gloomy himself. "War is much more probable at present than it has been for several years," he wrote. "Great Britain does not want war, and I doubt if they would send a single soldier to the Continent."[66] His opinions were colored by those of his contacts. House had always moved in two broad circles in England. One was that of what might be loosely called establishment liberals, such as Grey, Bryce, C. P. Scott and the like.[67] These were the friends who had favored the negotiated peace that President Wilson and Colonel House tried so hard to arrange before the United States entered World War I. House may have underestimated the strength of the other group, led by Winston Churchill, who favored a robust confrontation of Hitler.

By the mid-1930s, House was in his late seventies. He no longer had the grasp of European and world politics that had been his in Paris. He was growing old. In the summer of 1937 his friend the president wrote tactfully, "Your signature is strong and characteristic as ever and confirms the report that you are well as interested as always in the affairs of humanity." By the fall the president found time to write, "I am sorry to know that you are not quite strong enough to come up to Hyde Park."[68]

Since his painful kidney stone attack in 1919, House had in fact enjoyed relatively good health for a man who had seen himself as something of an invalid all his life. But there were bouts of ill health. He suffered a recurrence of the kidney infection in 1928 and 1930, and on April 2, 1929, he entered Harbor Hospital in New York City for two major surgical operations, one on a tumor on the bladder and the other for prostate cancer. He was not fully recovered until July.[69] He told Stephen Bonsal that he was lucky to have survived "for the operations were much more serious than the statements given to the newspapers indicated."[70] He was surprised by how calm he could be and put it down to his age. As you grow old, he discovered, "you naturally look upon death as becoming soon inevitable, and you are guided by a philosophy that aids you in such hours."[71]

By the late 1930s, as he approached his eightieth year and all that he had hoped and worked for seemed to be threatened by the twin perils of communism and fascism, Edward House at last withdrew into a private world that was intimate and happy. He spent his summers on the North Shore rather than in Europe. In 1934, when Fanny Denton was ill, he wrote her like a man for whom the rise of the dictators in Europe and the world economic crisis were now far away: "The dogs are having a *grand time*. I am devoting myself to them, and am enjoying the woods, the rabbits & throwing the sticks as much as they are."[72]

In the fall of 1937 House was seriously ill with pleurisy. He recovered to some degree over the winter. Charles Seymour saw him in early January 1938. He found the colonel dressed and lying on the sofa in the little front sitting room of his apartment on East 68th Street. "He looked like a wax effigy, motionless except for the hand he raised to greet me, the face of an eastern philosopher who has discovered the answer to the riddle of life."[73] House had written to Seymour, saying that if he had any more questions about his relations either with Wilson or with Franklin Roosevelt, he should not wait too long. He answered Seymour's questions fully, insisting once again that "my love and admiration for Woodrow Wilson have never faltered or lessened."[74]

House made it plain that he was tired of life: "The doctors tell me there is nothing wrong with me organically," he said. His voice was husky, but every now and then his ironic amusement expressed itself in his characteristic high-pitched chuckle. "I can live for ten years, they say, if I adjust my manner of life to a certain level. . . . I know that just the little extra exertion will carry me across the river." He had decided to live over Christmas and the New Year, he said. He wanted to see the grandchildren and he had work to finish. But he thought he would "go out sometime in the late spring." He could not read. He was too weak. He got tired of the radio and of "having the women fuss over me." He wanted Miss Fanny to travel. (He had made a generous provision for her as early as 1905.) As for himself, he had fulfilled his aspirations. He had lived close to the center of things. "My hand has been on things. But now I am too weak to go on with this. And it's not worth living as a vegetable. So I think I will cross the river shortly."[75]

In mid-March Fanny Denton reported to Stephen Bonsal that the colonel was "much better, but he looks woefully weak and is in bed most of the day."[76] On March 16 he was able to write to Bonsal himself, saying he had had a "pretty severe" setback two weeks before but was now gaining strength daily.[77] Twelve days later the newspapers reported his death.

As he grew older, House occasionally took to philosophical reflection. He was of the stoic school. "As life's shadows lengthen," he wrote on Thanksgiving Day in 1926, aged sixty-eight, "I sometimes wonder whether my activities in behalf of the things lying near my heart were worth while. Who knows? Who really cares? I am sure that working for the general welfare has made my life fuller and happier than if I had devoted myself to the furthering of my personal fortunes."[78]

House saw himself as "an inconsequential atom" in the cosmos. The "living or dying of the entire human race would make as little difference to the universe as the stamping out of an individual anthill would to this globe. Now that the end cannot be far distant I have learned to live serenely and happily. Each day brings with it certain joys, and I find myself eager to live, but contented to die when my hour has come."[79]

As a much younger man, House had apparently played with some idea of a life after death. He asked Edward Grey what he believed about the survival of the soul. In a letter written to Fanny Denton in 1908—incongruously on the bright red letterhead of a hotel in Brittany—he commended to her an article by the well-known British physicist and psychic researcher Sir Oliver Lodge in the *Atlantic Monthly:* "It is a great promise that is held out to us, and death is robbed of its sting. How fine it will be for us to have another trial in another field of endeavor. You and I will work it out together and what a joy it will be in the working. His assertion that those who have depended on material things and possessions for happiness will likely be miserable there, is satisfactory. In another sphere it should be the soul and intellect that count."[80]

House did not claim any profound spiritual faith. His way was the stoic path of the nineteenth-century American gentleman, a pattern of belief influenced equally by Christian ideals and the scientific skepticism of the late nineteenth century. House had absorbed the values of that culture, its reticence, discipline, and sense of duty. He was blessed in a happy family life with his wife and his daughters, their husbands and children, and a dwindling but staunch circle of friends. But his life was his work.

Ideas had a place in that work. But what made him notable was neither the authoritarian progressivism of *Philip Dru* nor any special talent for political philosophy. House's gift was for political action, political management, political advice, and political persuasion. In those fields, he had few equals among his contemporaries in any country.

House first entered the political lists as an adviser to Jim Hogg, a character who excited his interest and his loyalty. House's position in the politics of Texas during the Populist insurrection was centrist. He sympathized with the Populist emotions, but he did not share the Populist faith in the monetary panacea. Each of his three successive governor-protégé leaders in Texas—Culberson, Sayers, and Lanham—earned less of his respect than Hogg had done, and House visibly chafed for a wider field for his abilities. He liked and admired Bryan but could not respect his judgment. When, at fifty-three, he recognized the opportunity afforded by Woodrow Wilson, he had the good sense to give Wilson the political knowledge and experience he so lacked and to ask nothing for himself—except, of course, what he really wanted: the satisfaction of using his great gifts in a great cause.

House was able to help Woodrow Wilson through the unfamiliar thickets of domestic politics and to relieve him of the dangerous burden of patronage. But it was abroad that he could help Wilson most.

The second decade of the twentieth century was a time of promise and disaster. For some years before the outbreak of war in Europe, artists and poets had sensed the imminence of a great upheaval. The great Austrian novelist Robert Musil, looking back on the second decade of the century from the fourth, remembered how "out of the oil-smooth spirit of the last two decades of the nineteenth century, suddenly throughout Europe there arose a kindling fever. Nobody was able to say whether it was to be a new art, a New Man, a new morality or perhaps a reshuffling of society."[81]

It was all of those things. Something similar was happening in the United States. Technical change—electric power and light, the internal combustion engine, radio, film, new tools, and new weapons—swept away the cast-iron rigidities of the Victorian age. A first round of globalization, brutally imposed by imperialism on the peoples of Asia, Africa, and South America, enriched the metropolitan countries but taxed their strength as well as their political wisdom. Years of economic crisis, from 1873 until the 1890s, created the "social question" and evoked new solutions, especially various schools of socialism, all hoping to harness the power of the state to deliver prosperity and social justice. At the same time, new, disturbing ideas about art, religion, social and industrial relations, nations, families, and the most intimate aspects of life and love threatened to shake the established pillars of society.

It is hard to think our way back into what seems at first a strangely sheltered world, of long summers on the North Shore and in the palace hotels of Europe, slow journeys by train and ocean liner, luncheons and dinners with urbane statesmen who behaved, most of the time, like gentlemen—even when doing their best to blow each other's armies to smithereens and drown enough ships to drive each other's peoples into starvation. But the scope of Colonel House's work was not mere clever manipulation of gentlemen in stiff collars. It was an idealistic and often desperate attempt to control vast, murderous forces that were marching the civilized world toward Armageddon.

In Colonel House's brief prominence on the international stage, we can see the United States moving, half consciously, half in blind unknowing, to fulfill the destiny Theodore Roosevelt and his friends had foreseen it must occupy. House and Wilson both meant the United States to be the greatest power of the twentieth century, through the weight not only of economic and military power, but also of moral and ideological influence.

Edward House sensed this change, though he did not claim to understand it. He saw that the Old World was hurtling toward the disaster of war. He sensed that America could offer a political vision, and the political skills, to prevent that catastrophe and, once it had started, to end it. For his five most creative years, from 1914 to 1919, he devoted himself to trying to prevent the war, then to stop it, to win it, and at last to turn its hideous sacrifice to lasting gain by creating a new international system.

That was his broad strategy. He shared Woodrow Wilson's vision of a New Freedom at home and a new international order abroad. He agreed with Wilson that this system must reflect the American conviction that sovereignty came not from God or by descent from kings but from the people. House shared Wilson's beliefs enough to have played a large part in formulating Wilson's two most characteristic achievements, the Fourteen Points and the covenant of the League of Nations, though others contributed greatly. Where House differed from Wilson was not in fundamental ideas about political philosophy but in his instinctive talent for political action. Unlike Wilson, House saw how things could be done—by patient persuasion, using other people's hopes, fears, and ambitions to forward his own and Wilson's ideas.

These skills, concealed and enhanced by modesty and great charm, made House the ablest diplomat the United States had produced up to his time and one of the ablest it has ever bred. A. J. Balfour, one of the wisest and most experienced of the Paris peacemakers, was not alone in considering that the breach between Wilson and House was a tragedy because of what House could have done to make Wilson's dream a reality. "Balfour, after mature deliberation, said he had come to the conclusion that the break between the President and me was one of the disasters of history. He said that it sounded like a foolish remark to say that a difference between two individuals should be of such consequence as to affect the welfare of the entire world, but that the conjunction of circumstances made it so."[82]

House's greatest claim to our attention, however, is not his ability, impressive though it was to his ablest contemporaries. It was the absolutely crucial part he played in getting the United States involved in the affairs of the world. No one should underestimate his commitment to defending American interests or his determination that American values should prevail. No individual, however gifted, or however fortunate in his historical opportunities, can have more than a small part in shaping the history of the great world where nations struggle. But few men have had more influence on the style as well as on the purposes of American diplomacy.

House's failures were large and obvious. But they were not all his own. His successes were less visible, but they were no mere reflections of Woodrow Wilson's glory. He understood, earlier and more clearly than Wilson, that the United States was too strong, and that at the same its strength was too bound up with the fate of other countries, to remain aloof from the world's urgent moral conflicts. He saw too that its entry onto the world scene could be best achieved not by boasting about the exceptional virtue of American society, but by finding partners in other societies who would work toward the same goals.

Notes ❧

1 A Coming Together and a Falling Apart

1. Specifically, Wilson wanted to endow Princeton with a graduate school to rival those at Harvard and Johns Hopkins. He also wanted "quadrangles," modeled on those of Oxford and Cambridge colleges
2. *The Nation*, February 15, 1917, p. 195. The phrase is attributed to an anonymous European journalist.
3. Seymour, *Intimate Papers*, vol. 1, pp. 96–97.
4. House to Seymour, April 20, 1928, E. M. House Papers.
5. Wilson did not in fact move into the governor's mansion but continued to live in Princeton and drive the eleven miles to Trenton, the state capital, every day. J. A. Thompson, *Woodrow Wilson*, p. 57.
6. See W. F. Johnson, *George Harvey*, pp. 186–192.
7. "And like that mighty river [the Platte]," continued the joke about Bryan, he is "a mile wide at the mouth and only six inches deep." The "Great Commoner" was a name given to William Pitt, the eighteenth-century British prime minister, before he was created Earl of Chatham. Bryan's newspaper, in which he promoted the silver credo, was called *The Commoner*.
8. "An overwhelming majority of all farmers, landowners and landless alike, were locked into the crop lien, the discriminatory freight rate and the chattel mortgage." Goodwyn, *The Populist Moment*, p. 304n.
9. Brogan, *History of the United States of America*, p. 437.
10. Goodwyn, *The Populist Moment*, pp. 20–25.
11. Hofstadter, *The Age of Reform*, p. 5.

12. Ibid., p. 5.

13. P. L. Levin, *Edith and Woodrow,* p. 92.

14. McComb's co-manager, William Gibbs McAdoo, complained that at one important meeting, McCombs consumed six drinks. On another occasion House thought he was on "some kind of dope." On October 24, 1912, just before the presidential election, House wrote in his diary that "I found him 'half seas over,' as he usually is at this hour (5 p.m.)."

15. In 1924, after no fewer than 103 ballots, the Democrats chose John W. Davis after their convention had been deadlocked about a plank in the platform condemning the Ku Klux Klan. McAdoo was one of the leading candidates.

16. McAdoo, *Crowded Years,* p. 127.

17. Ibid.

18. *Papers of Woodrow Wilson,* vol. 23, p. 458. Cited hereafter as *PWW.*

19. Ibid.

20. For example, Link, "The Wilson Movement in Texas," pp. 166–185.

21. See Daniels, *The Wilson Era,* p. 48.

22. House, "Reminiscences," p. 51.

23. House, "Diary," January 27, 1915.

24. Seymour, *Intimate Papers,* vol. 1, pp. 118 and 121. I have used the British edition of the *Intimate Papers* (published by Ernest Benn, 1926), whose pagination is not identical to that of the American edition.

25. P. L. Levin, *Edith and Woodrow,* p. 93.

26. The correspondence between the two men in *PWW* reveals House claiming more influence over the fact that "we now have everything in good shape in Texas" on March 6. But it also shows Wilson expressing, on the same date, "his warm and deep appreciation of the intelligent work done." On June 7 House was advising against some suggestions made by Love.

27. House, "Reminiscences," p. 28.

28. *PWW,* vol. 24, July 31, 1912.

29. House, "Memories," p. 40.

30. For the kaiser's comments on Colonel House, see Viereck, *The Strangest Friendship in History,* p. 55, and chapter 8 below.

31. Grey and House became close friends for the rest of their lives.

32. The only public office he ever occupied was as the president's special representative in Paris and later as a member of the American delegation to the peace conference. His expenses were reimbursed, but he drew no salary.

33. Seymour, *Intimate Papers,* vol. 1, p. 118.

34. Auchincloss, *Woodrow Wilson,* p. 35.

35. House, "Diary," June 24, 1915.

36. Ibid., March 31, 1913.

37. Ibid.

38. House, "Memories."

39. Cited in P. L. Levin, *Edith and Woodrow,* pp. 107–108.

40. J. Enoch Powell, classics professor, reactionary Conservative and later Ulster Unionist member of Parliament, and cabinet minister, was infamous for his "rivers of blood" speech, in which he predicted that nonwhite immigration into Britain would lead to a

bloodbath. He quoted the Roman poet Juvenal—"I see the Tiber foaming with much blood"—and more in the same vein. His career certainly ended in failure.

41. The phrase "short twentieth century" was coined by the British historian Eric Hobsbawm to describe the seventy-five years from the collapse of the European system in 1914 to the end of Communist government in Europe in 1989.

2 Origins of a Texas Gentleman

1. House, "Reminiscences," p. 4.
2. Ibid., p. 1.
3. Ibid., p. 2.
4. Garner, "Galveston during the Civil War," p. 106.
5. House said he was the seventh son of a seventh son, traditionally marked out for distinction in life. House, "Reminiscences," p. 6.
6. Alfred, Lord Tennyson, *Idylls of the King.*
7. For the history and ecology of the Somerset Levels, see Colebourne and Gibbons, *Britain's Natural Heritage,* and Sutherland and Nicolson, *Wetland.*
8. *A Guide to Stoke St. Gregory Parish Church.* In 1967 a Miss Ethel House presented the church with a valuable silver chalice and paten for use in the communion service.
9. House, "Reminiscences," p. 6.
10. See *A True Report of Certain Wonderful Overflowings of Waters.*
11. *Handbook of Texas Online.*
12. In 1924, Edward and Loulie House visited a Shearn descendant living near Bristol. The same trip took them to Stoke St. Gregory. There was no longer the Shearn name "since the male line is extinct." House, "Diary," July 14, 1924.
13. *Handbook of Texas Online.*
14. House "Memories," p. 1.
15. House, "Reminiscences," p. 6.
16. House, "Memories," p. 9.
17. Ibid., p. 8.
18. House, "Reminiscences," p. 6.
19. House, "Memories," p. 10.
20. Garner, "Galveston during the Civil War," p. 133.
21. The original Ebbitt House was founded in 1856 by innkeeper William E. Ebbitt. The Ebbitt was a favorite of politicians. President McKinley lived there when he was in Congress, and the modern restaurant claims, very plausibly, that Presidents Grant, Andrew Johnson, Cleveland, Theodore Roosevelt and Harding all drank at the Ebbitt bar.
22. For more on *Philip Dru,* see chapter 4.
23. House, "Reminiscences," p. 11.
24. After William Marsh Rice, the founder of Rice University, and Edward Hutcheson. See Richardson, *Colonel Edward M. House,* p. 30, quoting Harris County probate records, vols. U and V; and Grover, "The Dissolution of T. W. House and Company.
25. John Hunter (1728–1793), born near Glasgow, was a co-founder of the Royal College of Surgeons.
26. House, "Reminiscences," p. 12.
27. Richardson, *Colonel Edward M. House,* pp. 31–32.

28. Ibid., pp. 32–33. Richardson consulted the deed records of House properties in at least six of the sixty counties were House properties were found.

29. House, "Memories," p. 6.

30. House, "Reminiscences," p. 35.

31. House, "Memories," p. 32.

32. House, "Reminiscences," p. 38.

33. Richardson, *Colonel Edward M. House*, p. 39.

34. Ibid., citing 1958 interview with T. B. Poole (Richardson cites him also as "Pool"), a former employee of the House ranch at Cotulla.

35. Ibid., p. 211.

36. Ibid., citing interviews with C. W. Malone, son of the Monadale manager, and the Monadale foreman, Sam A. Sharp.

37. House-Barkley letters, passim; quoted in ibid., p. 216.

38. The $17,500 was clear profit, after the salary of the manager had been paid and after expenses and investments in improvements had been deducted. Bushnell, *All the World and the Fullness Thereof*, p. 27. At the conservative multiple of 30:1, it would have been the equivalent of $525,000. It would have been free from income tax until 1913. There was an income tax during the Civil War, eliminated in 1872. It had a short-lived revival in 1894 and 1895. In 1913, the Sixteenth Amendment to the Constitution made the income tax a permanent fixture.

39. The extraordinarily negative account of House's business career by Romney Clark Bushnell, written largely on the basis of House's letters to E. J. Barkley, announces itself forthrightly enough as "an attempt to probe the progressive image attributed to Colonel House and his deceitful, contradictory, problematic nature antithetical to this image." Bushnell presents House, largely on the basis of his letters to Barkley, as "a frugal, miserly man; a modern day 'Scrooge.'" Bushnell, *All the World and the Fullness Thereof*.

40. Cited in ibid., p. 13.

41. Richardson, *Colonel Edward M. House*, p. 34.

42. Ibid., p. 219.

43. E. M. House Papers, Yale Collection 466, Series I, Box 30, Folder 937.

44. Ibid., Coolidge to House, October 10, 1910.

45. Tinsley, *Letters from the Colonel*.

46. Baker was the Texas representative of the Equitable Life Company of London.

47. Clark and Halbouty, *Spindletop*; DeGolyer, "Anthony F. Lucas and Spindletop."

48. E. H. Harriman was the father of the governor of New York and diplomat Averell Harriman. On the Boll Weevil Line, see Allhands, *Boll Weevil*.

49. Coolidge to House, November 5, 1904, E. M. House Papers.

50. E. M. House Papers, Box 30. Mrs. Catherine Coolidge Lastavica believes that she can account for the occupants of the houses on the Coolidge Point property for most of the period when the Houses spent the summers there (personal communication).

51. House, "Reminiscences," p. 26.

52. This account of the House home, at 1704 West Avenue, Austin, is based on Bond, "The Residence of E. M. House"; "Austin Home May Be Razed," *Texas Public Employee*, May 1965; and Gilliland, "The E. M. House House."

53. Among the visiting dignitaries were Charles W. Eliot of Harvard and Baron D'Estournelles de Constant, a French diplomat and senator, pioneer of motoring and aviation,

and Nobel peace laureate in 1909 (in recognition of his work at the Hague peace conferences.)

54. House, "Reminiscences," p. 43.

3 The Texas Kingmaker

1. "While Hogg came of a good family he presented a rough exterior which I think he cultivated because of the popularity it gave him with the masses. . . . It is a pity that some of his unique expressions are entirely too coarse to be recorded here." House, "Reminiscences," p. 18. House was dictating to his unmarried secretary, Miss Frances (Fanny) Denton, when he made this comment.
2. Cotner, *Hogg*, p. 301.
3. Ibid. Another distinguished Texas historian, Lewis L. Gould, came to a strikingly similar conclusion: "Through the shrewd and intelligent leadership of Governor James S. Hogg, the party found a middle ground between its conservative, pro-railroad wing and the more radical demands of the Populists. . . . After 1896 the Populists disappeared as a viable state party leaving the Democrats undisputed arbiters of Texas politics." Gould, *Progressives and Prohibitionists*, p. 6.
4. The following brief account of Texas politics at the time Edward House first got involved is based on the following: E. M. House Papers, especially House's correspondence with James S. Hogg, Charles A. Culberson, Thomas W. Gregory, Joseph D. Sayers, and S. W. T. Lanham; Tinsley, *Letters from the Colonel*; Cotner, *Hogg*; Goodwyn, *The Populist Moment*; Gould, *Progressives and Prohibitionists*; Richardson: *Colonel Edward M. House*, and "Edward M. House and the Governors"; Martin, "The People's Party in Texas"; Smith, "The Farmers' Alliance in Texas, 1875–1900"; Crane, "Recollections of the Establishment of the Texas Railroad Commission"; Wagner, "Culberson."
5. Substantial numbers of African Americans still voted in Texas in the early 1890s. The black vote, however, was notoriously manipulated by corrupt bosses, some white, some black. Indeed, according to Roscoe Martin ("The People's Party in Texas," p. 93), in some counties in 1890 120 percent of registered African American voters voted!
6. Eighty-four percent of the population in Texas was rural in 1890, according to the Bureau of the Census. Seventy percent of all those employed were farmers in 1870, and the proportion was still 65 percent in 1900, on the eve of the first oil boom.
7. House himself was not sure this was a good idea. "He chose to enter the scramble for wealth," House wrote, "a field in which he was easily outstripped by those of less ability. He did not seem to know that the money making instinct cannot be acquired in a day." House, "Reminiscences," p. 18.
8. Kolko, *The Triumph of Conservatism*, p. 2.
9. The same could be said of other southern states in the 1890s: "Southern politics . . . did not lack for competition and their monolithic quality was deceptive." Gould, *Progressives and Prohibitionists*, p. 4.
10. Cited in ibid.
11. House to Andrews, February 10, 1903; in Tinsley, *Letters from the Colonel*.
12. E. M. F. Smith, *Memoirs of Mollie McDowall* (Mary Ann Nicholson), p. 38. Actually, Mrs. Nicholson was some years older than House. She could remember being taken upstairs to see him, as a baby, sleeping in "a very handsome canopied crib." Ibid., p. 35.

13. Goodwyn, *The Populist Moment,* pp. 16–17.

14. Tinsley, "The Progressive Movement in Texas," p. 26.

15. House, "Memories," p. 36.

16. Richardson, *Colonel Edward M. House,* pp. 48–49, quoting the *Fort Worth Gazette* and the *Dallas News.*

17. House, "Memories," p. 37.

18. Richardson, *Colonel Edward M. House,* p. 50.

19. House, "Memories," p. 38.

20. John Henninger Reagan (1818–1905) was born in Sevier County, Tennessee. A surveyor, lawyer, judge, U.S. representative (1857–1861, 1875–1887), and U.S. senator (1887–1891), he was the author of the Interstate Commerce Bill of 1887. He was a member of the Texas Railroad Commission (1891–1903).

21. Richardson, *Colonel Edward M. House,* p. 59.

22. Ibid., p. 61.

23. Cotner, *Hogg,* p. 393. The Supreme Court's decision, in the case *Reagan v. Farmers' Loan and Trust Co.,* 152 U.S. 362, was not made in favor of the commission's constitutionality until May 26, 1894. Ibid., p. 402; *Austin Daily Statesman,* May 27, 1894.

24. Cotner, *Hogg,* p. 399.

25. Ibid., p. 401.

26. Cited in Wagner, "Culberson," p. 53.

27. Richardson, *Colonel Edward M. House,* p. 92.

28. Cited in Wagner, "Culberson," pp. 55 and 56.

29. Ibid., p. 129, quoting *Dallas Morning News,* August 17, 1896.

30. Cited in ibid., p. 56.

31. Ibid., p. 150.

32. Sayers is said to have been wounded, then returned to the Confederate ranks and fought on crutches. Richardson, *Colonel Edward M. House,* p. 139.

33. See Crane, "Recollections of the Establishment of the Texas Railroad Commission."

34. House, "Reminiscences," p. 21.

35. Ibid.

36. Tinsley, *Letters from the Colonel,* p. 2.

37. Ibid., p. 3.

38. House, "Reminiscences," p. 26.

39. House's admiring biographer, Rupert Richardson, says he was a "loyal friend" of Prairie View Normal School for Negroes, and he guesses that House may have been the author of the plank in the Democratic platform of 1896 calling for an appropriation of fifty thousand acres of land to endow the school and make it a university for black students, but he admits that there is no evidence of any great change due to House's direct influence. Richardson, "Edward M. House and the Governors," p. 65.

40. House, "Reminiscences," p. 23.

41. "Colonel House's effective organization . . . dominated state politics for almost a decade." Tinsley, "The Progressive Movement in Texas," p. 32.

42. Burleson was postmaster general of the United States, 1913–1921. Gregory was attorney general of the United States, 1914–1919. Jameson (1871–1904) worked as an aide for Governors Sayers and Lanham. More completely than the other members of "our crowd," he was a creature of House; in a letter to Culberson after Jameson's death, House wrote,

"He was my political right hand. I had him trained for so many years that he knew exactly what I wanted without telling him and he had the political instinct which made him absolutely invaluable." House to Culberson, May 14, 1904, E. M. House Papers, Box 33; Richardson, *Colonel Edward M. House,* p. 197.

43. House, "Reminiscences," p. 27; Gould, *Progressives and Prohibitionists,* p. 14.

44. Cotner, *Hogg,* p. 483.

45. House, "Reminiscences," p. 28.

46. Jones had been an Arkansas legislator and U.S. congressman from Arkansas (1879–1885) and was a U.S. senator from 1885 to 1903.

47. House's correspondence briefly records several visits by the Bryans—for example, in 1902, 1903, and 1907. E. M. House Papers, Box. 19.

48. House, "Reminiscences," pp. 29–30.

49. Ibid., p. 31.

50. Ibid., p. 25.

51. Ibid., p. 26.

52. Gould, *Progressives and Prohibitionists,* p. 11.

53. Ibid., p. 49.

54. House, "Memories," p. 48.

55. As told by Colonel Edward M. House to "Tyler Mason" (Miss Mason-Mannheim), *Riding for Texas: The True Adventures of Captain Bill McDonald* (New York: Reyhnal and Hitchcock, 1936).

56. In August 1906 the stationing of African American soldiers from the all-black Twenty-Sixth Infantry Regiment gave rise to a riot, and the Texas Rangers were called out. The black soldiers were blamed, though no reliable evidence was found against them. President Theodore Roosevelt blamed and collectively punished the black regiment. Captain McDonald of the Rangers favored arresting twelve black soldiers. See Tinsley, "Roosevelt, Foraker and the Brownsville Affray," p. 56.

57. House, "Reminiscences," p. 27.

4 Going National

1. Swanberg, *Citizen Hearst,* pp. 137ff.

2. Lipset and Marks, *It Didn't Happen Here,* pp. 138–143. Lipset and Marks make the point that though many Germans were socialists, states with a high German immigrant population often had a low socialist vote because German socialists came from industrialized, Protestant Prussia, while immigrants from rural, Catholic south Germany were often hostile to socialism.

3. There is of course a voluminous literature on the Progressive era. For a short but comprehensive introduction with documents and notes, see Gould, *America in the Progressive Era 1890–1914.*

4. House, "Reminiscences," p. 31.

5. Neu, "In Search of Colonel Edward M. House."

6. McCombs, *Making Woodrow Wilson President,* p. 75.

7. Seymour, *Intimate Papers,* vol. 1, p. 42.

8. Thornton, "William Jay Gaynor."

9. House, "Reminiscences," p. 48.

10. Ibid., p. 52.

11. Ibid., p. 58.

12. House, *Philip Dru*, p. 67.

13. Theodore Roosevelt, speech at Provincetown, Massachusetts, August 20, 1907.

14. House, *Philip Dru*, p. 68.

15. Ibid., p. 103.

16. Ibid., p. 106.

17. Ibid., p. 120.

18. Ibid.

19. Ibid., p. 137.

20. Ibid., p. 156.

21. Ibid., p. 168.

22. House, "Memories," p. 49.

23. House, *Philip Dru*, p. 185.

24. Ibid., pp. 214–215.

25. Ibid., p. 268.

26. Seymour, *Intimate Papers*, vol. 1, p. 157.

27. House, *Philip Dru*, p. 222.

28. Ibid., p. 272.

29. Ibid., p. 280.

30. Caro, *Master of the Senate*, p. 34.

31. Seymour, *Intimate Papers*, vol. 1, p. 161.

5 Making Woodrow Wilson President

1. Seymour, *Intimate Papers*, vol. 1, p. 85.

2. On an occasion when McCombs saw McAdoo's name favorably mentioned in print, his "face instantly took on the expression of an infuriated animal. He locked the door, seized his cane and beat it into splinters over the desk, cursing and shrieking like a maniac." Broesamle, *William Gibbs McAdoo*, p. 51.

3. Link, "The Wilson Movement in Texas."

4. Ibid., p. 171. The papers of Congressman (and later Postmaster General) Albert S. Burleson are at the Library of Congress. Link undoubtedly has a point when he shows that House and his admirer Seymour exaggerated House's contribution to the Wilson campaign in Texas.

5. Ibid., p. 179, n. 37; Link cites a letter from Love to R. S. Baker, June 7, 1928, in Baker Papers.

6. Love to House, November 8, 1912, E. M. House Papers, Box 72.

7. Ibid.

8. House to Culberson, July 26, 1911, E. M. House Papers.

9. House, "Reminiscences," p. 49.

10. This guarantee, at least, is corroborated by contemporary evidence. "Sells started to close the headquarters at one time and I had to guarantee the contingent expenses such as rent and stenographer. He does not know this so please do not repeat it. I had it done through others." House to Culberson, April 19, 1912, E. M. House Papers.

11. House, "Diary," October 6, 1921.

12. T. W. Gregory to Woodrow Wilson, September 4, 1911, E. M. House Papers, Box 51. See also Gregory's letter to Culberson on October 10, 1911, cited below.

13. House to Culberson, September 30, 1911, E. M. House Papers, Box 33.

14. House to Culberson, October 10, 1911, E. M. House Papers, Box 33.

15. Culberson to House, October 13, 1911, E. M. House Papers, Box 33.

16. House to Wilson, October 16, 1911, *PWW*, vol. 23, p. 458. This is the first reference to House in *PWW*.

17. Ibid., October 18, 1911.

18. Ibid., October 20, 1911.

19. Wilson to House, October 24, 1911, *PWW*, vol. 23.

20. House to Wilson, November 18, 1911, E. M. House Papers.

21. House to Culberson, November 27, 1911, E. M. House Papers.

22. House, "Reminiscences," p. 52.

23. Houston, *Eight Years with Wilson's Cabinet,* vol. 1, pp. 18–20. Henry Watterson (1840–1921), congressman from Kentucky and editor and publisher of the *Louisville Courier-Journal,* had played a key part in the backstairs negotiations leading to the Compromise of 1877 which made possible the election of Rutherford B. Hayes.

24. House to Bryan, December 6, 1911, E. M. House Papers.

25. Ibid.

26. Seymour, *Intimate Papers,* vol. 1, p. 54.

27. In his "Reminiscences," House says he traveled on December 6, but this date must be a mistake as his dinner for Wilson and Houston was on December 7, 1911.

28. Denton to Wilson, December 30, 1911; E. M. House Papers; *PWW*, vol. 23.

29. Wilson to House, January 27, 1912, E. M. House Papers.

30. House to Wilson, February 2, 1912, *PWW*, vol. 24.

31. House to McCombs, February 10, 1912; cited in Seymour, *Intimate Papers,* vol. 1, p. 58.

32. House to Wilson, March 6, 1912, *PWW*, vol. 24.

33. Broesamle, *William Gibbs McAdoo,* p. 52.

34. House to Love, April 30, 1912, E. M. House Papers, Box 72.

35. Love to House, May 5, 1912, E. M. House Papers, Box 72.

36. House to Love, May 7, 1912, E. M. House Papers.

37. Love to House, August 16, 1912, E. M. House Papers.

38. It is interesting that T. W. Gregory made much of this in his letter to Wilson of September 4, 1911, E. M. House Papers, Box 51.

39. Seymour, *Intimate Papers,* vol. 1, p. 62.

40. Ibid., p. 64.

41. House to Wilson, June 20, 1912, E. M. House Papers. The friends to whom House referred were T. W. Gregory and T. A. Thomson (a Texas delegate to the 1912 convention), who visited him at Beverly in June. McCombs also visited him there at the beginning of June. House, "Reminiscences," p. 56.

42. Broesamle, *William Gibbs McAdoo,* p. 56.

43. McCombs, *Making Woodrow Wilson President,* p. 230.

44. House, "Diary," October 6, 1921.

45. Culberson to House, June 18, 1912, E. M. House Papers.

46. Ibid., June 21, 1912.

47. "Under no circumstances would it have been possible for me to have been in Baltimore because of the heat." House, "Reminiscences," p. 56.
48. Ibid., p. 58.
49. Ibid., pp. 58–59.
50. Ibid., p. 59.
51. Broesamle, *William Gibbs McAdoo*, p. 74.
52. House, "Diary," October 28, 1912.
53. McAdoo, *Crowded Years*, p. 174.
54. House, "Memories," p. 53.
55. E. M. House Papers, consulted on microfilm.
56. House, "Diary," September 25, 1912.
57. Ibid., October 26, 1912.
58. Chace, *1912*, pp. 238–239.

6 *The Hungry Horde*

1. House to Culberson, November 5, 1912, E. M. House Papers, Box 32.
2. Speech in the Senate, January 1832.
3. House: "Reminiscences," p. 23; "Diary," January 8, 1913. Newton Diehl Baker was born and raised in Martinsburg, West Virginia; attended high school in Alexandria, Virginia; and did his undergraduate work at Johns Hopkins, where he met Woodrow Wilson; he had a law degree from Washington and Lee.
4. House was interested, for example, in two Democratic politicians from Minnesota— former governor John Lind and Fred Lynch.
5. House, "Diary," January 8, 1912.
6. McAdoo, *Crowded Years*, p. 177.
7. When House got to London in 1914, he found that may British politicians and diplomats thought Bryan must be a wild man.
8. Bryan's daughter Ruth was married to a British officer, Lt. Reginald Owen.
9. Wilson was afraid that Bryan would not approve of the currency reform project he intended to propose.
10. House, "Diary," January 18, 1913. House underlined the words "not to ask his advice" for emphasis.
11. House, "Diary," January 31, 1913.
12. Ibid., January 15, 1913.
13. McCombs, *Making Woodrow Wilson President*. McCombs ran for the Senate from New York in 1916 and was defeated. He died the same year.
14. For Brandeis's biography, see Strum, *Louis D. Brandeis*, and Gal, *Brandeis of Boston*.
15. It is possible that House had been influenced by whispering campaigns against Brandeis. In his diary he suggested as much—"He was not thought to be above suspicion"—then scratched the sentence out. House, "Diary," November 16, 1912.
16. Strum, *Louis D. Brandeis*, p. 198.
17. Gal, *Brandeis of Boston*, p. 196.
18. Brandeis to Hapgood, undated; quoted in ibid. As an editor at *Collier's*, Norman Hapgood was in the forefront of the muckraking movement and campaigned for clean food and for votes for women.

19. Ibid., p. 189.

20. Ibid., p. 188.

21. Ibid., p. 196.

22. Wilson to Bryan, February 27, 1913, *PWW,* vol. 27.

23. House, "Diary," February 13, 1913.

24. Ibid., January 14, 1913.

25. Ibid., February 22, 1913.

26. Ibid., March 31, 1913.

27. O'Gorman (1860–1943) was a former New York judge and Tammany Hall member who sat in the U.S. Senate for New York from 1911 to 1917.

28. House, "Diary," March 7, 1913.

29. O'Gorman to Wilson, April 1, 1913, *PWW.*

30. House, "Diary," March 9, 1913.

31. Davis, Polk and Wardwell traces its history back to the 1840s, but Polk (who was John W. Davis's campaign manager) and Davis became senior partners in the 1920s.

32. House, "Diary," May 1, 1913.

33. Ibid., May 2, 1913.

34. Ibid., January 19, 1913. For the Panama tolls controversy, see chapter 7.

35. *PWW,* vol. 27, pp. 396–397.

36. Wilson to O'Gorman, May 5, 1913, *PWW,* vol. 27, pp. 399–401. Lawson Purdy was head of the Department of Taxes and Assessment in New York City. He was a follower of Henry George, a Progressive but a Tammany appointee.

37. Mitchel (1879–1918), the youngest mayor of New York ever, served as mayor from 1914 to 1917, made a good record, but was not reelected, possibly as a result of resentment due to the collectorship affair.

38. Kerney to Wilson, May 8, 1913, *PWW,* vol. 27, pp. 409–410, from Tumulty Papers.

39. House, "Diary," April 16, 1913.

40. Ibid., April 18, 1913.

41. For the recruitment, morale, and salaries of American diplomats before the Foreign Service Reorganization Act of 1924, see Byrnes, *Awakening American Education to the World,* pp. 152–156.

42. Henry Morgenthau (1856–1946) was a lawyer and successful real estate developer. His account of the Armenian genocide was *Ambassador Morgenthau's Journal,* published in 1918. For Wilson's remark about Turkey, see House, "Diary," December 18, 1912.

43. See chapter 7. Samuel Untermyer (1858–1922), a successful Wall Street lawyer and vice president of the American Jewish Congress, acted for a client who sued Henry Ford for anti-Semitic remarks and made a famous speech denouncing Hitler on ABC radio in 1933.

44. Gerard, *My First Eighty-three Years in America,* p. 168.

45. Ibid., pp. 193–196.

46. House, "Diary," October 30, 1912.

47. Ibid., March 23, 1913.

48. Cited in Hendrick, *Life and Letters of Walter H. Page,* vol. 1, p. 131.

49. House to Culberson, November 5, 1912, E. M. House Papers, Box 33.

50. Lane was a lifelong friend of House's brother-in-law, Sidney Mezes. In 1902 he ran unsuccessfully for governor of California as a Democrat. He attributed his defeat to

William Randolph Hearst's stirring up the wine growers and saloon keepers against him, as he was a "dry." He and House once thought of going into the railroad business in California but backed out when it became clear that their plans would be blocked by Southern Pacific.

51. House, "Diary," August 27, 1913.
52. Wilson to House, September 5, 1913; in full in House, "Diary," September 6, 1913.

7 Wall Street and Mexico

1. Aside from the Wilson and House papers, the account in this chapter of the creation of the Federal Reserve system is based on the following sources: Dean, "The Federal Reserve Act of 1913"; Houston, *Eight Years with Wilson's Cabinet;* R. T. Johnson, *Historical Beginnings;* Metzger, *A History of the Federal Reserve;* and Willis, *The Federal Reserve System.*
2. "If we have done anything wrong," said Morgan to President Roosevelt, "send your man" [meaning the attorney general] to my man and they can fix it up." Roosevelt replied, "That can't be done." Cited in Burns and Dunn, *Three Roosevelts,* p. 70.
3. The split was executed by Congressman Robert W. Bulkley of Ohio. Willis, *The Federal Reserve System,* pp. 107–108.
4. House, "Diary," December 16, 1912.
5. Willis, *The Federal Reserve System,* pp. 170–176.
6. House, "Diary," February 25, 1913.
7. Henry Clay Frick started as a coke producer in western Pennsylvania. A millionaire by the age of thirty, he became a partner of Andrew Carnegie, though later the two men fell out. In 1892 he ruthlessly suppressed the Homestead strike, and an anarchist, Alexander Berkmann, tried to assassinate him. In 1901 he was involved in the formation of United States Steel, the "Steel Trust." In 1905 he moved to New York, and in 1913 he purchased the former Vanderbilt mansion at 70th Street and Fifth Avenue to house his art collection. Henry P. Davison (1867–1922), educated at Yale, became a partner in J. P. Morgan and head of the Morgan Guaranty Trust Company. In 1915 he became the head of the American Red Cross. Otto H. Kahn, (1867–1934), a partner in Kuhn, Loeb since 1897, is said to have been America's most influential patron of the arts. He gave lavishly to the New York Metropolitan Opera and the Provincetown Playhouse and helped such diverse artists as Ezra Pound, Serge Eisenstein, Luigi Pirandello, and Vaslav Nijinsky.
8. House, "Diary," February 26, 1913.
9. Ibid., March 22, 1913 (on Morgan), and March 31, 1913 (on Warburg).
10. Ibid., March 29, 1913.
11. Link, *The New Freedom,* p. 212.
12. Willis, *The Federal Reserve System,* p. 251, quoting Glass's letter to him.
13. Ibid., p. 169.
14. Ibid., p. 177.
15. Dean, "The Federal Reserve Act of 1913," p. 2.
16. R. T. Johnson, *Historical Beginnings,* p. 21.
17. Ibid., p. 19.
18. Ibid., p. 27.
19. Ibid., p. 21.

20. Ibid., p. 22.
21. Wolf, "Mexico," p. 14. Wolf goes so far as to say that the *científicos* wanted to "obliterate" Mexicans of Native American descent.
22. Calvert, *The Mexican Revolution,* p. 19.
23. Gardner, "Woodrow Wilson and the Mexican Revolution," p. 5.
24. Swanberg, *Citizen Hearst,* p. 246.
25. Gardner, "Woodrow Wilson and the Mexican Revolution," p. 9.
26. Ibid.
27. Calvert, *The Mexican Revolution,* p. 38.
28. Cited in ibid., p. 163.
29. See, for example, Cronon, *The Cabinet Diaries of Josephus Daniels,* p. 43: "The general opinion in the cabinet was that the chief cause of this whole situation in Mexico was a contest between English and American oil companies to see which would control; . . . and it was largely due to the English company that England was willing to recognize Mexico before we did."
30. House, "Diary," May 14, 1913.
31. Seymour, *Intimate Papers,* vol. 1, p. 215.
32. Gardner, "Woodrow Wilson and the Mexican Revolution," p. 16.
33. See Bryan and Bryan, *The Memoirs of William Jennings Bryan,* p. 361: "I was gratified to find the President resolutely opposed to intervention except as a last resort."
34. House, "Diary," July 7, 1913.
35. House, "Diary," November 11 1913.
36. Ibid., September 6, 1913.
37. Ibid., November 13, 1913.
38. Ibid., November 14, 1913, and House to Wilson, November 29, 1913, *PWW.*

8 *The Schrippenfest Affair*

1. Viereck, *The Strangest Friendship in History,* p. 55.
2. House, "Diary," January 22, 1913.
3. See, for example, Herring, *A History of Latin America,* p. 293.
4. House, like many Americans of his generation, habitually used the term "England" to mean "Britain," although England was only one of the four "home nations," together with Scotland, Ireland, and Wales.
5. House, "Diary," May 9, 1913.
6. Trevelyan, *Grey of Fallodon,* p. 161.
7. See, for example, Lloyd George, *War Memoirs,* vol. 2, p. 859.
8. House, "Diary," December 2, 1913.
9. Ibid.
10. Ibid., January 1, 1914.
11. Ibid., April 9, 1914.
12. Ibid.
13. Ibid., April 10, 1914.
14. Ibid., April 28, 1914.
15. Ibid., May 27, 1914.
16. The following account of House's interview with the kaiser is taken from House,

"Diary," June 1, 1914; from the letter House sent to Wilson once he had reached Paris, June 3, 1914, *PWW,* vol. 30, p. 139; and from Gerard's memoirs, *My First Eighty-three Years in America,* pp. 193–194.

17. House to Bryan, June 13, 1914, E. M. House Papers, Box 19, Folder 651.
18. Wilson to House, June 16, 1914, *PWW,* vol. 30, p. 187.
19. House, "Diary," June 17, 1914.
20. House to Wilson, June 17, 1914, *PWW,* vol. 30, pp. 189–190.
21. House to Wilson, June 26, 1914, *PWW,* vol. 30, p. 256.
22. House to Wilhelm II, July 8, 1914, *PWW,* vol. 30, pp. 266–267.
23. Gerard, *My First Eighty-three Years in America,* p. 193.
24. Personal information from Professor Fiebig von Hase.
25. Fischer, *Germany's Aims in the First World War,* p. 477. See also, in a vast literature, Joll, *The Origins of the First World War,* p. 5.
26. Lloyd George, *War Memoirs,* vol. 2, p. 657.
27. House to Wilson, August 22, 1915, *PWW,* vol. 34, p. 297.
28. Hobsbawm *The Age of Extremes.*
29. Musil, *Der Mann ohne Eigenschaften.*

9 Trying to End the War in Europe

1. Seymour, *Intimate Papers,* vol. 1, p. 328.
2. Strachan, *The First World War,* p. 58.
3. Bulgaria joined the Central Powers later.
4. Cited in unpublished manuscript of Charles Swem, Wilson's personal stenographer, Firestone Library, Princeton University.
5. Reinertson, "Colonel House, Woodrow Wilson and European Socialism," p. 75, citing M. P. Howard Whitehouse's recollection.
6. Ibid., p. 78.
7. Ibid., p. 140, citing *FRUS 1917,* supp. 2, Russia.
8. Wilson to House, July 11, 1917, E. M. House Papers.
9. Walworth, *Wilson and His Peacemakers,* p. 341.
10. Link, *Wilson: Campaigns for Progressivism and Peace,* pp. 201–203.
11. House to Wilson, May 17, 1916, *PWW,* vol. 36.
12. Walworth, *America's Moment,* pp. 132–135. See also diary of Edith Benham Helm, Helm Papers, Library of Congress, and the transcript of Wilson's talk to members of the Inquiry on the voyage, in Papers of Charles L. Swem, Princeton University.
13. At the time Wilson spoke, he had just lost control of Congress. Lloyd George had a majority of more than 250 in the House of Commons, while Clemenceau had just received the support of more than four-fifths of the French national assembly.
14. Wilson said as much to Raymond B. Fosdick, diary letter; cited in Walworth, *America's Moment,* p. 133. Fosdick, later president of the Rockefeller Foundation, traveled to Europe on the *George Washington* with Wilson.
15. Some French friends, like Clemenceau, who had lived in the United States as a young man, or the former journalist André Tardieu, spoke fluent English.
16. House, "Diary," January 25, 1915.
17. Ibid., February 5, 1915.

18. Ibid., February 7, 1915.

19. There was a cruel little rhyme going the rounds that began, "My name is George Nathaniel Curzon, I am a most superior person."

20. House, "Diary," March 1, 1915.

21. Ibid., February 27, 1915.

22. Ibid., March 13, 1915.

23. Among them were this writer's step-grandfather, Sergeant Saxelby of the Lincolnshire regiment, killed at Suvla Bay.

24. House, "Diary," May 7, 1915.

25. Seymour, *Intimate Papers*, vol. 1, p. 435.

26. Ibid., p. 437.

27. Ibid., p. 442.

28. Ibid., p. 445.

29. House, "Diary," May 30, 1915.

30. Wilson to Nancy Saunders Toy, November 9, 1914, *PWW*, vol. 31.

31. P. L. Levin, *Edith and Woodrow*, p. 59. Though Mrs. Galt liked to reminisce about how the family silver was saved by a loyal old slave retainer, her grandfather's will listed only two pieces of silver, one a ladle and the other a watch. There were, however, nine slaves in her grandfather's estate.

32. Irving Hood Hoover Papers; cited in P. L. Levin, *Edith and Woodrow*, p. 52.

33. Ibid., p. 83.

34. House, "Diary," June 13, 1915.

35. Ibid., June 20, 1915.

36. Note to German government, June 9, 1915, *PWW*.

37. House, "Diary," June 13, 1915.

38. Seymour, *Intimate Papers*, vol. 1, p. 471.

39. House, "Diary," July 10, 1915.

40. Ibid., August 21, 1915.

41. Ibid., August 26, 1915.

42. Seymour, *Intimate Papers*, vol. 2, p. 30.

43. Ibid., p. 35.

44. Ibid., p. 33–34. See also Witcover, *Sabotage at Black Tom;* Warner, "Protecting the Homeland the First Time Around."

45. House, "Diary," September 22, 1915.

46. Seymour, *Intimate Papers*, vol. 2, pp. 84, 88–90.

47. House, "Diary," October 8, 1915.

48. House to Grey, October 17, 1915, E. M. House Papers.

49. Grey to House, November 1, 1915, *PWW*, vol. 35.

50. Ibid.

51. House, "Diary," November 25, 1915.

52. Ibid., January 11, 1916.

53. Ibid., January 14, 1916.

54. Ibid., January 27, 1916, quoting the kaiser.

55. Ibid., January 28, 1916.

56. Ibid., February 2, 1916; House to Wilson, February 3, 1916 (letter 11 on this trip).

57. Cambon's account is printed in translation in *PWW*, vol. 36, p. 126. The original, "Con-

versation du Colonel House avec M. Jules Cambon, le 2 février, 1916," is to be found in the French Ministry of Foreign Affairs Archives, Guerre 1914–1918, Etats-Unis, vol. 498, pp. 174–177. Cited hereafter as FFM-Ar.

58. House to Wilson, February 9, 1916, *PWW*, vol. 36, p. 147.

59. In *PWW*, vol. 36, pp. 148–150; original: "Deuxième Entrevue du Colonel House, 7 février 1916" (Guerre 1914–1918, Etats-Unis, vol. 498, pp. 206–208, FFM-Ar).

60. Ibid.

61. House, "Diary," February 7, 1916.

62. Ibid.

63. Ibid., February 8, 1916; House to Wilson, February 9, 1916, *PWW*, vol. 36, p. 150.

64. House, "Diary," February 9, 1916.

65. House to Wilson, February 10, 1916, *PWW*, vol. 36, p. 167.

66. *London Globe*, February 11, 1916; cited in Seymour, *Intimate Papers*, vol. 2, p. 187.

67. Seymour, *Intimate Papers*, vol. 2, p. 171; *PWW*, vol. 36, p. 180, editor's note.

68. Seymour, *Intimate Papers*, vol. 2, p. 170.

69. House, "Diary," February 11, 1916.

70. House to Wilson, February 11, 1916, *PWW*, vol. 36, p. 170.

71. House, "Diary," February 14, 1916.

72. Ibid., February 17, 1916.

73. Ibid., February 15, 1916.

74. Ibid., February 23, 1916.

75. Text in E. M. House Papers; also in Seymour, *Intimate Papers*, vol. 2, pp. 200–202.

76. House to Grey, March 10, 1916.

77. Lloyd George, *War Memoirs*, vol. 2, p. 688.

78. Taylor, *The Struggle for Mastery in Europe*, p. 554, note 1.

79. N. G. Levin, *Woodrow Wilson and World Politics*, p. 40.

80. House, "Diary," March 6, 1916.

81. House to Wilson, April 3, 1916, *PWW*, vol. 36, p. 405; House, "Diary," April 6, 1916.

82. Grey to House, May 12, 1916, *PWW*, vol. 37, p. 43.

83. Wilson to House, May 16, 1916, *PWW*, vol. 37, pp. 57–58.

84. House to Grey, May 23, 1916, *PWW*, vol. 37, p. 100.

85. Footnotes to speech, May 27, 1916, *PWW*, vol. 37.

86. House, "Diary," May 20, 1916.

87. Seymour prints parallel texts of House's memo and Wilson's speech as an appendix in *Intimate Papers*, vol. 2, pp. 337–339.

88. House to Wilson, June 1, 1916, *PWW*, vol. 37, p. 135. Link, the editor of *PWW*, prints Jusserand's own report of his meeting, including the judgment that "the status of Mr. House remains truly extraordinary." He also says that "if we may believe Jusserand's account of this conversation . . . House began to fabricate at this point." Cited in Seymour, *Intimate Papers*, vol. 2, p. 338.

89. House to Wilson, July 25, 1916, *PWW*, vol. 37, p. 475; Seymour *Intimate Papers*, vol. 2, p. 316.

90. House, "Diary," June 23, 1916.

91. Ibid., September 24, 1916.

92. Ibid.

93. Robert Browning, "Epistle Containing the Strange Medical Experience of Karshish, an Arab Physician."
94. House, "Diary," September 24, 1916.
95. House, "Diary," November 15, 1916.
96. Ibid., November 17, 1916.

10 America Drifts into the War

1. Seymour, *Intimate Papers*, vol. 1, p. 457.
2. House, "Diary," June 17, 1916.
3. Ibid., October 18, 1916.
4. The Tennessee-born McAdoo tied with Al Smith for ballot after ballot in large part because he refused to repudiate the Ku Klux Klan.
5. House, "Diary," September 23, 1916.
6. Ibid., September 30, 1916.
7. Cited in ibid., October 17, 1916.
8. Ibid., October 19, 1916.
9. Ibid., November 19, 1916.
10. Ibid., November 2, 1916.
11. Ibid.
12. Ibid., November 9, 1916.
13. Ibid., November 15, 1916.
14. Cited in ibid., November 2, 1916.
15. Tuchman, *The Zimmermann Telegram*, p. 125.
16. Gradually, as a result of further adventures in the North Sea, in Belgium, and in Iran, of all places, the British cryptographers were able to read most of the German codes. Ibid., pp. 17–22.
17. Ibid., pp. 10–12, 104, 128–130.
18. House, "Diary," November 26, 1916.
19. The sketch of Wiseman presented here owes much to Fowler, *British-American Relations*. The Wiseman Papers are at Yale.
20. House, "Diary," December 20, 1916.
21. Plunkett to House, December 27, 1916, *PWW*, vol. 40, pp. 331–342.
22. House, "Diary," January 3, 1917.
23. House to Wilson, January 17, 1917, *PWW*, vol. 40, p. 508.
24. House to Wilson, January 18, 1917, E. M. House Papers.
25. Tuchman, *The Zimmermann Telegram*, p. 108.
26. Wilson speech to Senate, January 22, 1917, *PWW*, vol. 40, p. 536.
27. House to Wilson, January 20, 1917, *PWW*, vol. 40, p. 526.
28. Wilson to House, January 24, 1917, *PWW*, vol. 41, p. 3.
29. Bernstorff to House, January 20, 1917, *PWW*, vol. 40, pp. 528–529.
30. Editor's note at January 20, 1917, *PWW*, vol. 40, p. 529.
31. Wiseman to Balfour (foreign secretary), January 26, 1917, Wiseman Papers.
32. House, "Diary," January 31, 1917.
33. Bernstorff to Bethmann-Hollweg, January 27, 1917, telegram no. 23, *PWW*, vol. 41, translation pp. 51–52.

34. Bernstorff to House, January 31, 1917, *PWW*, vol. 41, pp. 80–82.

35. House, "Diary," February 1, 1917.

36. Lansing memorandum on the severance of diplomatic relations with Germany, February 4, 1917, *PWW*.

37. Wilson address to joint session of Congress, February 3, 1917, *PWW*, vol. 41, pp. 108–112.

38. House, "Diary," March 3, 1917.

39. Ibid., March 5, 1917.

40. Ibid., March 18, 1917.

41. Ibid.

42. Ibid., March 27, 1917.

43. Ibid., April 2, 1917.

44. Wilson to Congress, April 2, 1917, *PWW*, vol. 41, pp. 519–527.

11 1917

1. Haffner, *Die Verratene Revolution*. The German title translates as "the betrayed revolution."

2. See Fromkin, *A Peace to End All Peace*, pp. 405–411.

3. See Crankshaw, *The Fall of the House of Habsburg*.

4. See D. M. Smith, *Italy and Its Monarchy*, pp. 219–233.

5. Strachan, *The First World War*, p. 310.

6. The following details are taken from a memo Charles Seymour made of a conversation with Colonel House on January 27, 1922.

7. John Reinertson, "Colonel House, Woodrow Wilson and European Socialism."

8. Lincoln Steffens, in particular, kept House informed about Mexico. See letters, E. M. House Papers.

9. Fowler, *British-American Relations*, passim.

10. Seymour memo, January 27, 1922, p. 1.

11. Balfour, *Chapters of Autobiography*, p. 236.

12. Robinet et al., *Correspondances/Bergson*, passim.

13. House, "Diary," April 28, 1917.

14. Ibid.

15. House to Wilson, May 13, 1917.

16. House to Wilson, May 20, 1917.

17. Baker cited in Seymour, *Intimate Papers*, vol. 3, p. 64.

18. Cited in ibid.

19. Cited in ibid., p. 52.

20. Cited in Dugdale, *Arthur James Balfour*, p. 201.

21. The agreements are enumerated in a footnote at May 18, 1917, *PWW*. The editor of *PWW* points out that Balfour did not include any of the Allied treaties with Japan dealing with the postwar settlement in the Far East.

22. House to Wilson, May 30, 1917, *PWW*.

23. Wilson to House, June 1, 1917, *PWW*.

24. House to Wilson, May 30, 1917, *PWW*.

25. Balfour cable to House, in Seymour, *Intimate Papers*, vol. 3, p. 106.

26. Wiseman to Drummond for Balfour, June 29, 1917, in ibid.

27. House to Wilson, June 29, 1917, in ibid., p. 107.

28. House, "Diary," June 30, 1917.

29. Cited in Steed, *Through Thirty Years*, vol. 2, p. 143.

30. Seymour, *Intimate Papers*, vol. 3, p. 108.

31. Ibid.

32. Ibid., p. 125.

33. Ibid., p. 154. See also Ryder, *The German Revolution of 1918*. Text of resolution is in Scheidemann, *Der Zusammenbruch*. The key passage read as follows: "The Reichstag strives for a peace of understanding and the permanent reconciliation of peoples. Forced territorial acquisitions and political, economic and financial oppressions are incompatible with such a peace."

34. Taylor, *The Struggle for Mastery in Europe*, p. 560, n. 1.

35. House to Wilson, August 15, 1917, Seymour, *Intimate Papers*, vol. 3, p. 157.

36. House to Balfour, August 18, 1917; Seymour, *Intimate Papers*, vol. 3, p. 159. This was a letter passing on to Balfour the president's position and also adding House's comments.

37. House to Wilson, August 17, 1917; Seymour, *Intimate Papers*, vol. 3, p. 160.

38. Ibid., pp. 162–163.

39. House, "Diary," September 4, 1917.

40. Wilson to House, August 22, 1917; Seymour, *Intimate Papers*, vol. 3, p. 167.

41. House to Wilson, August 24, 1917; ibid., p. 168.

42. House to Wilson, August 25, 1917; ibid., pp. 168–169.

43. House, "Diary," September 2, 1917.

44. Ibid., September 9, 1917.

45. Ibid.

46. "In my opinion it would be disastrous for W. W. to supplant L. this time. He is an awfully sweet man and he is thoroughly loyal to W. W." Diary for September 10, 1917, Gordon Auchincloss Papers.

47. House to Wilson, September 4, 1917, *PWW*.

48. Fromkin, *A Peace to End All Peace*, pp. 176–178.

49. House to Wilson, September 18, 1917, *PWW*.

50. House, "Diary," September 22, 1917.

12 *The Inquiry and the Fourteen Points*

1. Wilson to House, September 2, 1917, *PWW*; House, "Diary," September 4, 1917.

2. Buckler to House, April 27, 1917, William Hepburn Buckler Papers. Buckler, the son of well-to-do Americans who lived in Paris, had been educated at Trinity College, Cambridge, where he had made a number of friends, particularly among the liberal elite, on whose pacifist sentiments he kept House well informed. He had worked as a secretary in the U.S. embassy in Madrid before the war. He was later to go on to a distinguished career as an archaeologist at Oxford and made important discoveries of Hittite antiquities in Turkey.

3. Seymour, *Intimate Papers*, vol. 3, p. 173.

4. Walworth, *America's Moment*, p. 75; Gelfand, *The Inquiry*, p. 24. See also House to Buckler, August 21, 1917, E. M. House Papers.

5. Mayer, *Political Origins of the New Diplomacy,* p. 18. See also Cocks, *The Secret Treaties and Understandings;* Baker, *Woodrow Wilson and World Settlement,* vol. 1, chs. 3 and 4.

6. See Reinertson, "Colonel House, Woodrow Wilson and European Socialism," esp. pp. 38–79.

7. "At the core of Wilson's poitical creed was a conception of American exceptionalism and of the nation's chosen mission to enlighten mankind with the principles of its unique liberal heritage." N. G. Levin, *Woodrow Wilson and World Politics,* p. 13.

8. Wilson to House, September 19, 1917, *PWW,* vol. 44, p. 216.

9. House, "Diary," September 5, 12, and 21, 1917; Byrnes, *Awakening American Education to the World,* p. 163.

10. Wilson to House, September 24, 1917, *PWW.*

11. House, "Diary," October 17, 1917.

12. Bowman, a Latin American specialist, was later accused of being both a racist and anti-Semite. There is no reason to believe that House was aware of his views.

13. See two documents by Bowman in the James T. Shotwell Papers: Notes on the Inquiry, November 30, 1918, and Statement Made by Dr. Bowman Concerning the Reorganization of the Inquiry, March 14, 1932. Cf. Gelfand, *The Inquiry,* pp. 94–99.

14. Steel, *Walter Lippmann,* p. 130.

15. Byrnes, *Awakening American Education to the World,* p. 154.

16. Charles Homer Haskins was the author of *The Renaissance of the Twelfth Century;* Samuel Eliot Morison (1887–1976) was a biographer of Columbus, a historian of the European discovery of America, and admiral in World War II; Charles Seymour (1885–1963) was the editor of House's *Intimate Papers;* Wallace Notestein was the author of *The English People on the Eve of Colonization;* E. S. Corwin was a constitutional authority.

17. Gelfand, *The Inquiry,* p. 57.

18. Cited in ibid.

19. Ibid., p. 205.

20. Ibid., pp. 218–219.

21. House, "Diary," November 18, 1917. See also Reinertson, "Colonel House, Woodrow Wilson and European Socialism," p. 312.

22. The *Guardian*'s correspondent in Russia was the famous children's book author Arthur Ransome, who later married Trotsky's secretary Evgenia Petrovna Shelepina.

23. House to Wilson, November 30, 1917, *PWW.*

24. Wilson to House, December 1, 1917, *PWW.*

25. Seymour, *Intimate Papers,* vol. 3, p. 325.

26. Cited in Baker, *Woodrow Wilson: Life and Letters,* vol. 7, p. 270.

27. House, "Diary," November 20, 1917.

28. Lippmann memorandum, December 7, 1917; text in *PWW,* January 4, 1918; see Steel, *Walter Lippmann,* pp. 133–134.

29. Steel, *Walter Lippmann,* p. 609n, quoting "The Reminiscences of Walter Lippmann," Yale Lippmann Collection, oral history collection.

30. Steel, *Walter Lippmann,* writes "three weeks," but this must be a mistake as House did not brief the team until December 18.

31. Text in *FRUS, PPC,* vol. 1, pp. 41–53.

32. "A Suggested Statement of Peace Terms Revised and Enlarged from the Memorandum of December 22," Wilson Papers, Series II, Library of Congress.

33. The phrase is that of the Inquiry. See Mayer, *Political Origins of the New Diplomacy,* p. 323.
34. House, "Diary," January 3, 1918.
35. Ibid., January 9, 1918.
36. Ibid.
37. Ibid.
38. Ibid.
39. Milenko Vesnić (1862–1921) had been the Serbian minister in Paris and had played a part in the negotiations to end the first Balkan war. He was the Yugoslav representative at the peace conference and afterwards was the minister of the Kingdom of Serbs, Croats, and Slovenes in Paris.
40. Ibid. *"Actuel"* in French means "contemporary."
41. Link, *PWW,* vol. 46, p. 459.
42. Gelfand, *The Inquiry,* p. 134.
43. The language of Point 5, stating that the interests of the people concerned should have only equal weight with the claims of the colonial powers, was modest, reflecting American rule in the Philippines as well as the colonial empires and ambitions of America's associates, Britain, France, and Italy.
44. Gelfand, *The Inquiry,* p. 153.
45. "A Suggested Statement of Peace Terms," Wilson MSS, Series II, *PWW,* p. 470.
46. President Wilson's January 8, 1918, speech to Congress, as delivered.
47. The word is that of Charles Seymour, who was the Inquiry's specialist on the Balkans before editing House's *Intimate Papers.*
48. E. M. House Papers, Box 5, Folders 18–33.

13 Russia

1. Wilson cited in Kennan, *Russia and the West,* p. 123; House, "Diary," March 5, 1917.
2. Kennan, *Russia and the West,* pp. 122–123.
3. Quoted in Betty Miller Unterberger, "Woodrow Wilson and the Russian Revolution," in Link, *Woodrow Wilson and a Revolutionary World,* p. 51.
4. What was known in Russia as the October Revolution took place in November according to the Western calendar.
5. J. M. Thompson, *Russia,* p. 240.
6. House, "Diary," September 19, 1918.
7. House to Wilson, quoted in Unterberger, *America's Siberian Expedition,* p. 7.
8. Strachan, *The First World War,* p. 269.
9. Cited in ibid., p. 309.
10. Ibid., p. 269.
11. J. M. Thompson, *Russia,* p. 47.
12. Seymour, *Intimate Papers,* vol. 3, p. 392.
13. House, "Diary," February 25, 1918.
14. House to Wilson, March 3, 1918, E. M. House Papers.
15. *PWW,* vol. 47, pp. 79–80, n. 1. See also Kennan, *Russia Leaves the War,* pp. 512–513.
16. Reinertson, "Colonel House, Woodrow Wilson and European Socialism," pp. 575–580.
17. House to Wilson, September 3, 1918, Wilson Papers, Library of Congress.

18. Kennan, *Russia and the West*, p. 125.
19. Churchill, *The World Crisis*, vol. 5, p. 263.
20. Procès-verbal of Council of Ten, E. M. House Papers, Box 191.
21. Ibid.
22. Ibid.
23. House, "Diary," March 25, 1919.
24. Ibid., March 27, 1919.

14 *Armistice*

1. Ludendorff was nominally quartermaster general. In practice he and Field Marshal Paul von Hindenburg operated as the team that had been victorious on the Eastern Front; given Germany's draconian wartime military control, Ludendorff has been described as a "virtual dictator." Ryder, *The German Revolution of 1918*, p. 67.
2. This is the thesis of Haffner, *Die Verratene Revolution*. Haffner points out that very few knew and few would have believed that it was Ludendorff who was behind the peace overtures, for which the chancellor, Prince Max of Baden, took responsibility. I find his interpretation persuasive.
3. Keynes, *The Economic Consequences of the Peace*, pp. 34–49.
4. House, "Diary," October 15, 1918.
5. Renouvin, *L'Armistice de Rethondes*, p. 377.
6. Philipp Scheidemann (1865–1939), was a typesetter, Socialist member of parliament, and minister in the Weimar government. Friedrich Ebert (1871–1925), was a saddler, journalist, Socialist politician, and president of the Weimar Republic. Gustav Noske (1868–1946), a basket maker, journalist, and Socialist politician, suppressed the revolution in 1919.
7. House, "Diary," October 9, 1918; House to Wilson, October 6, 1918, *PWW*, vol. 51, p. 254.
8. Seymour, *Intimate Papers*, vol. 4, p. 81.
9. Wilhelm Solf (1862–1936) was an interesting figure. A cultivated cosmopolitan and linguist who had traveled in the United States, he was a strong supporter of Germany's colonial ambitions in the Pacific but also made a great reputation as a liberal governor of German Samoa before being appointed as minister for the colonies. He was imperial Germany's last foreign minister and resigned two days after the armistice, on November 13, 1918. He was sent as the Weimar Republic's first ambassador to Japan and belonged to the liberal bourgeois elite in Wilhelmine Germany. See Hempenstall and Mochida, "The 'Yin' and the 'Yang' of Wilhelm Solf."
10. The texts of Wilson's three notes are to be found in *PWW*, vol. 51, as follows: October 8, 1918, note—pp. 263–264; October 14, 1918, note—pp. 333–334; October 23, 1918, note—pp. 417–419.
11. House, "Diary," October 15, 1918. "There can be no question of agreement to an armistice on the part of the nations allied against Germany so long as inhuman acts, pillage, and devastation continue, which justly fill them with horror and indignation." Renouvin, *L'Armistice de Rethondes*, p. 378, my translation. The German note of October 20 said, "The German government protests the reproach of illegal and inhuman acts, directed against German land and sea forces and consequently against the entire nation." Some "destruction had always been necessary to cover a retreat and to that extent was permitted by the law of nations."

12. House, "Diary," October 22, 1918. The diary has "Tonkinsville," but it was Tompkinsville, on the northern shore of Staten Island.

13. Afterwards, much was to be made by House's enemies of the fact that his son-in-law, Gordon Auchincloss, and his brother-in-law, Sidney Mezes, were in Paris as part of the American peace delegation. But Auchincloss had been a responsible State Department official for some time, and Mezes was one of the heads of the Inquiry; both had valid qualifications for the work. Joseph Grew (1880–1965) was an under-secretary of state in 1924 and again in the Franklin Roosevelt administration and ambassador to Turkey and Japan. Admiral Benson (1855–1932) of Georgia oversaw the huge wartime expansion of the navy, the extension of its operations to European waters, and the transportation of the U.S. Army to France.

14. Telegram from House to Wilson, October 6, 1918, *PWW*, vol. 51, p. 254.

15. Wilson note to Germany, October 23, 1918, *PWW*, vol. 51, pp. 417–419.

16. Ibid.

17. House, "Diary," October 24, 1918.

18. Wilhelm Groener (1870–1939) was a "social general," as opposed to an aristocratic one, a noncommissioned officer. He wanted reform of the three-class German franchise and wrote during the war that the war was "the greatest democratic wave. . . . The point is how to ride it." He was trusted by labor, and it was Groener who telephoned Friedrich Ebert late at night on November 9, 1918, when the Social Democrats took power, and privately assured him of the army's support. Ryder, *The German Revolution of 1918*, pp. 125, 135. See also Watt, *The Kings Depart*, pp. 223–224.

19. Watt, *The Kings Depart*, p. 279; Haffner, *Failure of a Revolution*, pp. 133, 186–187.

20. General Tasker Bliss, the American military representative with the Supreme War Council, severely criticized the French critic Gabriel Terrail, who wrote under the pseudonym "Mermeix" (*Les Negotiations Secrètes et les Quatre Armistices avec pièces justificatives*). Bliss pointed out that by October 8, when the military representatives met to discuss an armistice, it was already "commonly believed in every Allied capital in Europe that a German Note on this subject was then pending before the Government at Washington." Bliss, "The Armistices," p. 521.

21. Tasker Bliss, an astute, well-informed, and militarily qualified observer, makes the point that the armistice was defective not because it prevented the Allies from marching on Berlin, but because it should simply have asked for the surrender of the German army. As it was, at first the Allies were so confident of their military strength that they could rely on it to control the Germans.

22. The historian John Milton Cooper Jr. writes that "this presidential appeal has been almost universally judged to be probably the greatest political blunder of Wilson's career." But Cooper argues that these judgments are "overdrawn." He thinks Wilson might have done even worse if he had not "gone out on a limb" for his partisans. *Breaking the Heart of the World*, p. 31n. See also Livermore, *Politics Is Adjourned*, pp. 224–227.

23. Livermore, *Politics Is Adjourned*, p. 210.

24. *PWW*, vol. 49. But see also Cooper, *Breaking the Heart of the World*, p. 155, where Lodge appears to favor a treaty with France, which would be endangered by the "curse of the League."

25. Cited in Livermore, *Politics Is Adjourned*, p. 220.

26. Gregory to House, E. M. House Papers.

27. Livermore, *Politics Is Adjourned,* argues, oddly, that the vote was not so much a protest against the Wilson administration as a rejection of the previous Congress. The two were surely at least closely linked in many voters' minds.

28. House, "Diary," October 26, 1918.

29. Ibid.

30. Steel, *Walter Lippmann,* pp. 149–150, citing Lippmann's oral history in the Yale Lippmann Collection. (Steel, in error, gives House's address as 74 rue de l'Université.)

31. Text in telegram number 5 from House to Wilson, October 29, 1918, *PWW,* vol. 51, pp. 495–504.

32. Telegram from House to Wilson, October 30, 1918, *PWW,* vol. 51, p. 511.

33. Telegram from House to Wilson, October 30, 1918, "Urgent. Number 8. Secret," *PWW,* vol. 51, p. 511. The decoded copy in *PWW* is slightly garbled, so the version used here is from the E. M. House Papers, cited in the footnote to *PWW.* It is not absolutely clear when this optimistic telegram was sent. It appears plausible that House and Lloyd George first had a private talk, at which Lloyd George was reassuring. Then at lunch with the British officials he expressed doubts. Third, at a meeting with the French and Italians House was unequivocal that Britain could not accept point 2.

34. Seymour, *Intimate Papers,* vol. 4, pp. 170–171.

35. Telegram from Wilson to House, October 30, 1918, *PWW,* vol. 51, p. 513.

36. Telegram from House to Wilson, October 30, 1918, *PWW,* vol. 51, p. 515.

37. Telegram from Wilson to House, October 31, 1918, *PWW,* vol. 52, p. 533.

38. House, "Diary," November 3, 1918.

39. Telegram from Wilson to House, October 31, 1918.

40. Nicolson, *Peacemaking,* pp. 15–16. Nicolson was a Foreign Office official and a young but responsible member of the British team at the peace conference. He makes abundantly plain his admiration for the concept of the Fourteen Points, his respect for Colonel House, and his closeness to younger members of the American delegation, especially Charles Seymour and Clive Day. He was critical of Wilson, but his attitude was far from that of Keynes or of the traditionalists conjured up by Wilson's biographer, Ray Stannard Baker.

41. Seymour, *Intimate Papers,* vol. 4, p. 109.

42. Chief cable censor's reports telephoned, November 6, 1918. See also Watt, *The Kings Depart,* pp. 180–190.

43. House to Wilson, November 3, 1918, number 41, *PWW.*

44. House, "Diary," November 3, 1918.

45. Telegram from House to Wilson, number 6, Paris, November 5, 1918, *PWW.*

46. Telegram from House to Wilson and Wilson statement, November 11, 1918, *PWW,* vol. 53, p. 34.

47. November 5, 1918, *PWW.*

48. House said as much to Lloyd George, though he blamed the British, not the president. "I told George that his course was placing the United States in the same position toward Great Britain as Germany occupied during the war [but] in a contest, Great Britain would lose." House, "Diary," November 4, 1918.

49. General Pershing estimated that the Allies (including the Americans) mustered 1,564,000 "rifles" (i.e., soldiers) on the Western Front, as against the German strength of 1,134,000—an advantage of 37 percent—and an advantage of 35 percent in guns (i.e.,

artillery pieces). In addition, Germany was utterly exposed by the collapse of its allies (Austria, Turkey, and Bulgaria) in the south. Telegram from House to Wilson, number 14, October 31, 1918.

50. See Bliss, "The Armistices," p. 521: "The American representative [Bliss himself] expressed the following opinion: that the Allies had every reason for supporting the then existing government in Germany . . . as nearly a democratic one as could be expected . . . that the continual pin-thrusts being made by the Allies were playing into the hands of the opponents in Germany of this government," and that this made either a Bolshevik or a new imperial government more likely.

51. Wilson to House, November 7, 1918, *PWW*, vol. 51, p. 617.

52. Henry White (1850–1927), a former ambassador to Italy and France, was sometimes called the first U.S. career diplomat.

53. Seymour, *Intimate Papers*, vol. 4, p. 235.

54. For a memo to House from his friend T. W. Gregory, Wilson's second attorney general, who pressed Wilson to take distinguished Republicans, see ibid., p. 233. Cooper's recent study of the failure of the treaty suggests that Wilson could not offer a place on the delegation to any senator without offering one to Henry Cabot Lodge, who, as noted, was both majority leader and chairman of the Foreign Relations Committee, and given the "two men's cordial hatred for each other, it is hard to fault Wilson for not wanting to have Lodge at his side." But it is not perhaps unreasonable to ask a president to rise above personal feelings in such a vital matter, and in Root, Taft, and the Republican candidate he had beaten in 1916, Charles Evans Hughes, there were distinguished, nonsenatorial Republican alternatives. Cooper, *Breaking the Heart of the World*, pp. 34–36.

55. House to Wilson, Paris, November 14, 1918, *PWW*, vol. 53, p. 71.

56. Lansing, *The Peace Negotiations*, p. 22.

57. Telegram from Wilson to House, number 15, November 16, 1918, *PWW*, vol. 53, pp. 96–97.

58. Willard Straight diary, November 16, 1918, quoted in Walworth, *America's Moment*, p. 118.

59. Ibid., p. 120.

60. House, "Diary," July 24, 1919.

61. Lansing, *The Peace Negotiations*, p. 16.

62. Fosdick, "Diary of Trip on the *George Washington* with W. W."; photocopy in E. M. House Papers.

63. Walworth, *America's Moment*, p. 131, citing Bullitt to the writer, April 2, 1951.

64. Not all Americans agreed. General Billy Mitchell (1879–1936), air commander of the American Expeditionary Force in France and the first pilot to fly behind enemy lines, told Colonel House's friend Stephen Bonsal that "our . . . actual performance except in depressing enemies [*sic*] morale was, in his judgment, close to nil. . . . Wherever we fought we were buttressed on the French." Bonsal note on stationery of Office of the Chief of Staff, War Department, Stephen Bonsal Papers.

65. Diary of Dr. Cary T. Grayson, December 14, 1918, *PWW*, vol. 53, p. 383.

66. At Buckingham Palace, the Virginian Dr. Grayson reported (humorously?) that Mrs. Wilson was aghast that her maid, Miss Susie Booth, "who is of great width and blackness," might be entertained with the royal servants. Grayson diary, December 6, 1918, *PWW*, vol. 53, p. 328.

67. Brand, "The Attitude of British Labour toward President Wilson during the Peace Conference," pp. 244–245.
68. Edith Wilson, *My Memoir*, p. 217.
69. Dr. Albert Lamb notes, cited in Walworth, *Wilson and His Peacemakers*, p. 29.
70. Wiseman diary, January 17, 1919, cited in ibid., p. 29, n. 31.
71. Fosdick, "Diary of Trip on the *George Washington* with W. W."; p. 20, photocopy in E. M. House Papers.

15 The Covenant

1. David Hunter Miller, "The Making of the League of Nations," twenty-six-page typescript in E. M. House Papers, Box 210; one copy has a cover note reading, "Dear Colonel House, This is my final draft for your consideration. You may want to change p. 17, DHM. 29 Jan. 1921."
2. Trevelyan, *Grey of Fallodon*, pp. 107–108.
3. Winkler, *The League of Nations Movement in Great Britain*, pp. 7–34.
4. Phillimore, *Schemes for Maintaining General Peace*, is an official survey (the Phillimore Report) of proposals for a league or association of nations to keep the peace. It goes back to Dante, Leibniz, and Kant but is exhaustive on proposals made since 1914.
5. Wilson to House, December 24, 1915, *PWW*, vol. 35, pp. 387–388.
6. Cited in Walworth, *America's Moment*, p. 3.
7. Macmillan, *Peacemakers*, p. 98.
8. "Lord Robert Cecil" in the strict usage of the day denoted the younger son of a duke or marquess, which Lord Robert was; other peers would be addressed as Robert, Lord Cecil.
9. Prime minister from 1895 to 1905, the Marquess of Salisbury was a keen amateur chemist, as well as a statesman of great ability and the champion of "splendid isolation" for Britain.
10. Cecil to House, E. M. House Papers; published in Seymour, *Intimate Papers*, vol. 4, p. 6.
11. Ibid., p. 8, citing Wilson to House, March 20, 1918.
12. Seymour, *Intimate Papers*, vol. 4, p. 20.
13. Wilson to House, July 8, 1918, *PWW*.
14. House, "Diary," July 14, 1918.
15. Charles Seymour acknowledges that Ray Stannard Baker called the document a "covenant—the word was his own." Indeed Seymour lists four previous uses of the word "covenant" by Wilson in similar contexts. But Seymour also points out that Baker, who at the time he wrote Wilson's biography was a member of the group who was determined to minimize House's role in Wilson's achievement, ignored the fact that in his letter to House "Wilson specifically uses the word 'constitution,' " not "covenant." *Intimate Papers*, vol. 4, p. 27.
16. E. M. House Papers, Box 210.
17. Ibid.
18. Baker, *Woodrow Wilson: Life and Letters*, vol. 1, p. 214.
19. House, "Diary," July 23, 1918; Baker, *Woodrow Wilson: Life and Letters*, vol. 8, pp. 339–345E. The Coolidge house is there no longer.
20. E. M. House Papers, Box 30.

21. Seymour, *Intimate Papers*, vol. 4, p. 48.

22. House, "Diary," August 15, 1918.

23. Wilson to Mrs. Francis B. Sayre, August 22, 1918, *PWW*, vol. 49, p. 319.

24. Seymour, *Intimate Papers*, vol. 4, p. 50.

25. Seymour, *Intimate Papers*, vol. 4, p. 55, quoting *Ludendorff's Own Story*, vol. 2, pp. 334–335.

26. The Germans had in fact decided to abandon the St. Mihiel salient. Strachan, *The First World War*, p. 319.

27. Ludendorff, *Concise Ludendorff Memoirs*, p. 317.

28. Robert Lansing was largely cut out of the inner circle who had access to the president's thinking. But it is interesting that he reported that "some believed [House] to be the real author of Mr. Wilson's conception of a world union." As early as May 25, 1916, Lansing wrote Wilson, arguing (in the context of the League to Enforce Peace) that the United States should not put itself, by joining in a league, in the position of being compelled to choose between sending American armed forces to Europe or Asia and repudiating a treaty obligation. As a result Wilson kept Lansing entirely in the dark as to his thinking about the league, but Lansing suspected that House was behind it. See Lansing, *The Peace Negotiations*, p. 36.

29. Seymour, *Intimate Papers*, vol. 4, p. 65.

30. House, "Diary," October 9, 1918.

31. D. H. Miller, *My Diary at the Conference of Paris*.

32. "A Memorandum Regarding the Covenant," in ibid., pp. 331–369.

33. House, "Diary," January 3, 1919.

34. D. H. Miller, "A Memorandum Regarding the Covenant," p. 334, citing his own diary for January 11, 1919.

35. Cited in ibid., p. 369.

36. House, "Diary," January 7, 1919.

37. Miller, *My Diary at the Conference of Paris*, January 25, 1919.

38. House, "Diary," February 3, 1919.

39. D. H. Miller, "The Making of the League of Nations," p. 11. Cf. Seymour, *Intimate Papers*, vol. 4, p. 316, citing Baker, *Woodrow Wilson and World Settlement*, vol. 1, pp. 278–279. Miller's paper is dated January 1921; Baker's book was published in 1922.

40. Seymour, *Intimate Papers*, vol. 4, p. 324.

41. Quoted in Walworth, *Wilson and His Peacemakers*, p. 310.

42. House, "Diary," February 13, 1919.

43. Ibid.

44. Ibid.

45. House, "Diary," February 14, 1919.

46. Steed, *Daily Mail*, February 15, 1919; cited in Seymour, *Intimate Papers*, vol. 4, p. 329.

47. House, "Diary," February 14, 1919.

48. Ibid., February 11, 1919.

49. Seymour, *Intimate Papers*, vol. 4, pp. 432–439.

50. House, "Diary," March 18, 1919.

51. Ibid., April 11, 1919.

52. Cited in Macmillan, *Peacemakers*, p. 105.

53. D. H. Miller, "The Making of the League of Nations," E. M. House papers. p. 18.

54. House, "Diary," April 12, 1919.
55. Ibid., March 16, 1919.
56. Ibid., March 29, 1919.

16 The End of a Friendship

1. Seymour, *Intimate Papers,* vol. 4, p. 340.
2. House, "Diary," March 14, 1919.
3. Edith Wilson, *My Memoir,* p. 293.
4. Ibid.
5. Ibid.
6. Floto, *Colonel House in Paris,* p. 168.
7. Seymour to Bonsal, February 7, 1939; letter in Stephen Bonsal Papers.
8. Baker cited in Seymour, *Intimate Papers,* vol. 4, p. 399. Neither Clemenceau nor Lloyd George was a diplomat, and no one could possibly call either of them smooth. Clemenceau fought several duels, and Lloyd George was the fieriest orator of his generation.
9. The Wilsons' new lodgings, which Mrs. Wilson found more "homey" than the Murat Palace, were in a home built by a banker under the Second Empire. It sported a grand marble staircase; a ballroom imported from a palazzo in Naples; and canvases by Rembrandt, Rubens, and Hals, among others.
10. Baker, *Woodrow Wilson and World Settlement,* vol. 1, p. 311.
11. See Balfour's lengthy demolition of Baker's charges in Seymour, *Intimate Papers,* vol. 4, pp. 373–391.
12. Freud and Bullitt, *Thomas Woodrow Wilson,* p. 208.
13. Seymour, *Intimate Papers,* vol. 4, p. 391, citing David Hunter Miller, *The Drafting of the Covenant,* vol. 1, p. 98.
14. Seymour, *Intimate Papers,* vol. 4, p. 373.
15. House, "Diary," February 14, 1919.
16. Ibid.
17. "The President talked at some length on the general spirit in which he was approaching the conference, saying that the United States was the only nation which was absolutely disinterested, that he felt that the leaders of the allies did not really represent their peoples." Diary of William C. Bullitt, *PWW,* vol. 53, p. 351.
18. Wilson speech at Mechanics Hall, Boston, February 24, 1919, *PWW,* vol. 55, p. 243.
19. Cited in Auchincloss, *Woodrow Wilson,* p. 111.
20. P. L. Levin, *Edith and Woodrow,* p. 257, quoting Senator Brandegee's recollection, recorded in Chandler Anderson diary, March 10, 1919, Chandler P. Anderson Papers.
21. P. L. Levin, *Edith and Woodrow,* p. 257.
22. Cited in Edith Wilson, *My Memoir,* pp. 241–242.
23. *PWW,* vol. 55, p. 323.
24. Cited in Auchincloss, *Woodrow Wilson,* p. 104.
25. Cabot Lodge to Wharton, April 8, 1919, cited in Levin, *Edith and Woodrow,* p. 276.
26. Cabot Lodge to Albert Beveridge, February 18, 1919, cited in Cooper, *Breaking the Heart of the World,* p. 5.
27. A round robin was originally a protest by sailors in the British Royal Navy in the eigh-

teenth century in which signatures were written around the periphery of a document so that no signers could be picked out for punishment as ringleaders.

28. Macmillan, *Peacemakers*, p. 163; Walworth, *Wilson and His Peacemakers*, pp. 184–185.

29. "Cabinet: President discussed League of Nations and Peace Conference. Told him no money for Peace Mission after July 1. Told me to apply to Congress for $5 million dollars, as Secretary Lansing had indicated. I did so, but Senators Martin and Sherley both said it was hopeless to try." Frank Lyon Polk diary, February 25, 1919, cited in Walworth, *Wilson and His Peacemakers*, p. 184.

30. President Taft weighed 300 pounds. When told the President was out riding, Elihu Root is said to have replied, "How is the horse?"

31. Wilson address at Metropolitan Opera House, New York, March 4, 1919, *PWW*, vol. 55, p. 418.

32. Macmillan, *Peacemakers*, p. 161.

33. House, "Diary," February 19, 1919.

34. Ibid., February 16, 1919.

35. Ibid., March 3, 1919.

36. Ibid., February 26, 1919.

37. Haffner, *Failure of a Revolution*, p. 161.

38. The epidemic killed an estimated 20–40 million people worldwide, or more people in one year than the Black Death killed in Europe in more than four years. It appeared to infect young, healthy people more than the old or the very young, and it was at first associated with the trench warfare on the Western Front. Some even suspected, without evidence, that it was deliberately introduced by the Germans.

39. Karl Marx, *The Eighteenth Brumaire of Louis Napoleon* (London: Lawrence and Wishart, 1954), p. 1.

40. Lloyd George was in Britain, winning a massive majority in the so-called "khaki election." Khaki, from the Hindi word for dust, is the British equivalent of the American "olive drab."

41. House to Wilson, *PWW*, vol. 55, p. 233.

42. McCormick diary, March 2, 1919, Vance McCormick Papers, Yale University.

43. House in his diary has "self-government." Seymour (*Intimate Papers*, vol. 4, p. 357) has "self-determination," which may well be what House meant and even what he dictated.

44. "House then remained steadfastly opposed to the permanent separation of the Rhineland from Germany, but nevertheless he continued, as a responsible diplomat, to work for a possible compromise." Walworth, "Considerations on Woodrow Wilson and Edward M. House," p. 85.

45. Walworth, *Wilson and His Peacemakers*, p. 153, n. 44, citing House to Wilson, February 19, 1919, and Auchincloss diary, February 28, 1919, Gordon Auchincloss Papers.

46. McCormick diary, March 2, 1919, Vance McCormick Papers, Yale University.

47. House to Wilson, February 23, 1919, *PWW*, vol. 55, pp. 229–230.

48. Tardieu to House, March 12, 1919, E. M. House Papers. See also Tardieu, *The Truth about the Treaty*, pp. 172–176; Walworth, *Wilson and His Peacemakers*, p. 155.

49. Seymour, "End of a Friendship."

50. Ibid., p. 7.

51. Ibid., p. 8.

52. Ibid., p. 9.

53. Ibid.

54. Ibid. The anecdote is confirmed, with a more hostile spin, in Grayson's article in *American Heritage,* "The Colonel's Folly and the President's Distress."

55. Seymour, "End of a Friendship," p. 78.

56. Ibid.

57. Ibid.

58. Grayson was a navy doctor, Virginia-born, assigned to be the personal physician to Theodore Roosevelt when he became president and retained by William Howard Taft and Wilson, who promoted him to admiral in 1916.

59. Grayson, "The Colonel's Folly and the President's Distress."

60. Grayson consistently described *The Intimate Papers of Colonel House* as House's book, as if Seymour's editorial role were simply a mere fiction or the work of a mere amanuensis.

61. Grayson, "The Colonel's Folly and the President's Distress."

62. Walworth, "Considerations on Woodrow Wilson and Edward M. House."

63. Grayson, "The Colonel's Folly and the President's Distress." Vance McCormick told Ray Stannard Baker that he thought Colonel House and Gordon Auchincloss had broken up the Council of Ten "because it left him out and the Colonel could not bear it as he and Gordon have become obsessed to be the whole show." McCormick memo for Baker. McCormick resented what he saw as House's efforts to get him out of the way by having him sent on a mission to Syria. Henry Morgethau commented as follows in his diary on May 6, 1919: "Got impression that V. [Vance McCormick] does not admire House as much as formerly—and resents A[uchincloss] and H[ouse] not being quite loyal to W. W." McCormick and Morgenthau references cited in Floto, *Colonel House in Paris,* p. 322.

64. Grayson, "The Colonel's Folly and the President's Distress."

65. Ibid.

66. Wilson liked to think of himself as descended from the Covenanters, seventeenth-century Scots Presbyterian militants.

67. House, "Diary," June 29, 1919.

68. There are several references in Henry Morgenthau's diary (quoted by Floto, *Colonel House in Paris,* p. 322) to Gordon Auchincloss's tendency to compare Wilson unfavorably to the colonel.

69. Cited in Hatch, *Edith Bolling Wilson,* p. 161.

70. Cited in P. L. Levin, *Edith and Woodrow,* p. 293.

71. House, "Diary," April 23, 1924.

72. J. A. Thompson, *Woodrow Wilson,* p. 29.

73. P. L. Levin, *Edith and Woodrow,* pp. 124–138.

74. Morgan, "The President and Mrs. Peck."

75. Hulbert, "The Woodrow Wilson I Knew."

76. See the "admission" cited below and P. L. Levin, *Edith and Woodrow,* p. 114.

77. Ibid., p. 136, citing Woodrow Wilson Papers on microfilm at the Library of Congress, reel 14.

78. Cited in ibid., p. 105.

79. Cited in ibid., p. 108.

80. Ibid., p. 106. Ellen Wilson died on August 6, 1914.

81. Ibid., p. 110.

82. Ibid., p. 114.

83. Edith Wilson, *My Memoir*, pp. 90, 93.

84. P. L. Levin, *Edith and Woodrow*, pp. 30–31.

85. Weinstein, "Woodrow Wilson's Neuropsychological Impairment," p. 633.

86. Park, "The Impact of Wilson's Neurologic Disease during the Paris Peace Conference", p. 614. For changed attitude to Germans, see Weinstein, "Woodrow Wilson's Neuropsychological Impairment."

87. Cited in P. L. Levin, *Edith and Woodrow*, p. 295.

88. Park, "The Impact of Wilson's Neurologic Disease during the Paris Peace Conference," p. 614.

17 The End of the Treaty

1. House "Diary," August 28, 1919.

2. Memo, April 24, 1920, Stephen Bonsal Papers.

3. For example, Freud and Bullitt, *Thomas Woodrow Wilson*, p. 188.

4. Teschen was a disputed parcel of territory on the borders of the new Poland and the new Czechoslovakia.

5. At this time and after, there was a widespread expectation that Wilson would be nominated for a third term. At the time of the Democratic convention in 1920, after Wilson had been seriously incapacitated for months, Postmaster General Albert S. Burleson said that if it had not been for reports of physical incapacity deliberately circulated by Grayson, Tumulty, and others, with Mrs. Wilson's approval, "nothing could have kept the Convention, notwithstanding the third term bogey, from giving the President the nomination." Cooper, *Breaking the Heart of the World*, pp. 386–387, citing *PWW*, vol. 65, p. 511, n. 3.

6. Lansing desk book, March 19, 1919, Robert Lansing Papers, Box 63, Library of Congress.

7. Floto, *Colonel House in Paris*, pp. 172–173, citing D. H. Miller, *My Diary at the Conference of Paris*, vol. 1, March 19, 1919.

8. Floto, *Colonel House in Paris*, p. 32.

9. Wimer, "Woodrow Wilson's Plan to Enter the League of Nations through an Executive Agreement," pp. 800–812. See also Floto, *Colonel House in Paris*, p. 320.

10. House, "Diary," April 1, 1919.

11. House, "Diary," March 24, 1919.

12. Wilson was seriously ill twice in April 1919. On April 3 he fell "violently ill," coughing so that he could hardly breathe, with diarrhea and a fever of 103 degrees. By April 8 he was sufficiently recovered to chair a meeting. On April 28, at the height of the bitter negotiations over Fiume and Shantung, Wilson had a "vascular" incident, probably a small stroke. Dr. Grayson denied that it was a stroke, but there is evidence that Wilson was examined by two neurologists, Dr. John Chalmers Da Costa, a lieutenant commander in the Navy Medical Corps, and Dr. Malford Wilcox Thewlis, who thought otherwise. P. L. Levin concludes that Wilson's personality was changed by this incident and perhaps by other minor cerebrovascular incidents and that "Wilson's illness might also explain certain of his political and diplomatic blunders." *Edith and Woodrow*, pp. 290–297.

13. House, "Diary," April 2, 1919.

14. Ibid., April 1, 1919.

15. Ibid., April 4, 1919.

16. Walworth, *Wilson and His Peacemakers*, p. 296, n. 91, quoting Auchincloss diary, April 4, 1919.

17. Cited in Floto, *Colonel House in Paris*, p. 201.

18. Cited in ibid.

19. Wilson to William S. Benson, April 6, 1919, *PWW*, vol. 57, p. 61.

20. House, "Diary," April 9, 1919.

21. Ibid., April 15, 1919.

22. On January 12, 1917, Ignazy Jan Paderewski (1860–1941), the supreme nineteenth-century virtuoso of the piano and Poland's first president, handed Colonel House the memorandum calling for Polish independence that was to be passed on to President Wilson.

23. House, "Diary," May 7, 1919.

24. Ibid.

25. Cited in Seymour, *Intimate Papers*, vol. 4, p. 475.

26. Cited in Walworth, *Wilson and His Peacemakers*, p. 395.

27. House, "Diary," May 30, 1919.

28. Ibid.

29. House was also sitting to Orpen for his collective portrait of the peacemakers in these weeks.

30. House, "Diary," June 10, 1919.

31. Ibid., April 15, 1919.

32. Tumulty, *Woodrow Wilson as I Knew Him*, p. 402.

33. Dáil Eireann report on foreign affairs, Dublin, August 19, 1919.

34. House's diary records meetings with Brandeis, Frankfurter, Rabbi Wise, and other Zionist leaders on January 3 and 6, February 4 and 18, March 26 and May 24, 1919.

35. Wilson to House, October 13, 1917, *PWW*; cited in Neff, *Fallen Pillars*, p. 19.

36. Reinharz, *Chaim Weizmann*, pp. 284–299.

37. House, "Diary," June 23, 1919.

38. Ibid., June 25, 1919.

39. Neff, *Fallen Pillars*, pp. 19–20.

40. House, "Diary," June 28, 1919.

41. Ibid., June 25, 1919.

42. Ibid., June 29, 1919.

43. Ibid.

44. Ibid.

45. This was the famous Nancy Astor (1879–1964), the first woman to sit in the British House of Commons.

46. House, "Diary," July 14, 1919.

47. Ibid. and Trevelyan, *Grey of Fallodon*, p. 161.

48. Walworth, *Wilson and His Peacemakers*, p. 538n, quoting a memorandum from Grey to Lord Curzon, August 5, 1918.

49. House, "Diary," September 12, 1919.

50. Ibid., September 21, 1919.

51. Wilson, speech to Senate, July 10, 1919, *PWW*, vol. 61, p. 436.

52. The following paragraphs owe much to Cooper, *Breaking the Heart of the World,* pp. 158–197.

53. "Asthma" is in quotes because medical authorities think Wilson's shortness of breath was not classical asthma but a consequence of his cerebrovascular problems.

54. Moynihan, *On the Law of Nations,* p. 53.

55. Bonsal, *Unfinished Business,* p. 245.

56. House told Seymour that he "had to be carried off the ship on a stretcher." Seymour pointed out that according to the *New York Times,* "Colonel House said he could walk down with assistance, and descended slowly supported by Dr. Lamb and an army officer." Footnote to Seymour, "End of a Friendship."

57. House, "Diary," October 21, 1919.

58. Gardner was born in 1865 in Boston and was a member of Congress from Massachusetts.

59. Bonsal, *Unfinished Business,* p. 245. There are small discrepancies in Bonsal's account.

60. Ibid., p. 246.

61. Perhaps they met more than twice. In an undated typewritten memo Bonsal wrote, "I now had extending over a month some three or four conferences with the chairman of the Foreign Relations Committee generally in his committee room but once late in the evening at his request in the library of his Mass Ave residence. The openly avowed purpose of this or rather these meetings was to draw up changes and reservations in the Covenant, if possible, so that the votes Lodge controlled could be cast for it." Stephen Bonsal Papers. The phrase "this or rather these" suggests a certain vagueness in the writer's mind, to say the least.

62. Bonsal, *Unfinished Business,* p. 248.

63. The text of Article 10 reads as follows: "The Members of the League undertake to respect and preserve as against external aggression the territorial integrity and existing political independence of all Members of the League. In case of any such aggression or in case of any threat of danger of such aggression the Council shall advise upon the means by which this obligation shall be fulfilled."

64. The following version of Bonsal's story has been derived from the typewritten memo in the Stephen Bonsal Papers and Bonsal, *Unfinished Business.* It is my assumption that the typewritten memo was written in the course of Bonsal's preparing the published diary. No contemporary manuscript or typescript Bonsal diary has survived.

65. Garraty, *Henry Cabot Lodge,* p. 375n.: "While it must be admitted that a careful search of the Lodge papers fails to reveal other evidence of this willingness to compromise, the fact remains that he did make, in his own hand, this important effort. (Both the House papers and Bonsal's diary contain irrefutable evidence on this point.)" That overstates the case.

66. Cooper, *Breaking the Heart of the World,* p. 257.

67. Cited in ibid., p. 256n. Walworth's letter is preserved in the Robert W. Woolley Papers, Library of Congress. Arthur Walworth died in early 2005 at the age of 101.

68. It is interesting that House, in commenting in his diary on Josephus Daniels's suggestion that he had written to Wilson approving the Lodge reservations, House said, "This of course is wholly wrong," but he does not mention having sent any comment on the Lodge reservations to the White House. It is possible that this was part of a deliberate plan to avoid mentioning the Bonsal-Lodge affair and Lodge's comments, but it is hard

to see what interest House would have had in misleading future readers of his diary after Wilson's death.

69. House to Wilson, September 30, 1919, Seymour, *Intimate Papers*, vol. 4, pp. 517–518.

70. I am indebted for much in the following paragraphs to Phyllis Lee Levin, *Edith and Woodrow*, for her successful penetration of the smokescreen erected by Edith Wilson.

71. House to Wilson, November 24, 1919, *PWW*, vol. 64, p. 89.

72. Ibid.

73. House to Wilson, November 27, 1919, *PWW*, vol. 64, p. 96.

74. P. L. Levin, *Edith and Woodrow*, p. 377.

75. The letter, with Edith Wilson's emendations, is reproduced in facsimile in ibid., opposite p. 379.

18 Watching the World Go By

1. On May 22, 1917, Grey wrote to an American friend, W. K. Richardson, "I like both House and Page immensely. [They have] that sympathy of temperament and intimacy of spirit that beget friendship and confidence." Cited in Trevelyan, *Grey of Fallodon*, p. 333.

2. House, "Diary," August 29, 1922.

3. Ibid., July 31, 1925.

4. Sir Cecil Spring-Rice had died in 1918, and Lord Reading (Rufus Isaacs) had returned to London in May 1919.

5. P. L. Levin, *Edith and Woodrow*, p. 405.

6. Ibid., p. 406, quoting Michael Teague, *Mrs L.: Conversations with Alice Roosevelt Long-worth* (Garden City, NY: Doubleday, 1981).

7. House, "Diary," December 7, 1919.

8. Cited in Trevelyan, *Grey of Fallodon*, p. 352.

9. House, "Diary," February 3, 1920.

10. Averell Harriman, four Bundys, nine Tafts, and half a dozen Bushes among them.

11. Harold Nicolson, who came to admire Seymour and to be friendly with him, described him on first meeting as "young, dark, might be a major in the Sappers" (i.e., the Royal Engineers; an obscure reference). "They—meaning Seymour and other members of the Inquiry—evidently know their subject backwards. Nice people." Nicolson, *Peacemaking*, diary entry at January 6, 1919, p. 223.

12. Even Link's work shows signs of unfairness toward House—as, for instance, in the mini-mizing of House's part in Wilson's 1912 electoral victory, the low estimate of House's contribution to the Fourteen Points and the league covenant, and the adoption of Edith Wilson's view of House's behavior in February–March 1919. Link took the view privately that House was an unreliable witness.

13. House, "Diary," passim, especially November 22, 1925: "At the last moment, Mrs. Wilson through Ray Stannard Baker and by letter direct to Dr. Seymour declined to give per-mission to publish the President's letters to me. Baker came to me prior to that to tell me of the decision. I asked him how they had the face to refuse when they had used let-ters of mine to the President in *Woodrow Wilson and World Settlement* without referring to them or asking my permission. Baker admitted that they should not have done this, nevertheless Mrs. Wilson was adamant."

14. Ibid., July 23, 1920.

15. House, "Diary," August 10, 1923.

16. Ibid., March 8, 1924: "Loulie likes to go and I hate to deprive her of the pleasure although it is a constant strain upon me."

17. House met the playwrights J. M. Barrie and John Drinkwater; Herbert Baker, Sir Edwin Lutyens's partner in the design of the government buildings in New Delhi and Capetown; and the Socialist intellectuals Sidney and Beatrice Webb, among a host of others.

18. House, "Diary," July 8, 1923. Philip Kerr was Lloyd George's secretary at the peace conference and later, as Lord Lothian, British ambassador to Washington at the beginning of World War II.

19. Ibid., May 27, 1920.

20. Ibid., September 4, 1920.

21. House and Bergson exchanged correspondence for years. Robinet et al., *Correspondances/Bergson.*

22. The previous year, Clemenceau had told House he had turned down the Rolls-Royce! House, "Diary," May 20, 1921.

23. Ibid., June 11, 1923.

24. Ibid., June 3, 1921.

25. Ibid., February 22, 1921.

26. Ibid., November 23, 1923.

27. Ibid., February 9, 1924.

28. Private communication from House's grandson, Edward H. Auchincloss.

29. McAdoo was the attorney of Edward L. Doheny Sr., the California oil man who bribed Albert B. Fall, President Harding's secretary of the interior, for secret access to oil-drilling rights on thirty-two thousand acres of federal land at Elk Hills, California. LaBotz, *Edward L. Doheny.*

30. House, "Diary," May 10, 1925. John W. Davis (1873–1955) was solicitor general; ambassador to the Court of St. James (1916–1921); and co-founder of the great New York law firm Davis, Polk. He argued many cases before the Supreme Court. At the end of his life Davis defended separate but equal education before the court in *Brown v. Board of Education.*

31. It was widely believed that Viereck's father, Louis, was the son of a leading German actress, Edwina Viereck, and that Wilhelm II was the father. Louis von Prillwitz, son of a royal prince, acknowledged the child, but such shielding of royal personages was common practice.

32. Keller, *States of Belonging,* p. 176.

33. Epstein, "German and English Propaganda in World War I."

34. Viereck to House, January 2, 1930, E. M. House Papers, Box 113.

35. House to Viereck, September 10, 1932, E. M. House Papers.

36. E. M. House Papers, April 10, 1933. Peter Viereck eventually went to Harvard. He became a far more distinguished poet than his father, winning a Pulitzer Prize. He also published *Metapolitics* in 1941, a brilliant study of the intellectual roots of nazism in German romanticism and Wagner (republished in 1961 as *Metapolitics: The Roots of the Nazi Mind*).

37. Viereck to House, February 2, 1933, E. M. House Papers, Box 113. Franz von Papen (1879–1969) was responsible for German sabotage in the United States during World

War I. He was the last German chancellor before Hitler and helped Hitler to come to power. Convicted as a major war criminal, he served only a short term in prison.

38. E. M. House Papers, Box 113, Folder 3947.
39. Ibid., Folder 3946.
40. House to Viereck, January 26, 1936, E. M. House Papers.
41. Viereck to House, January 27, 1936, E. M. House Papers, Box 113, Folder 3948.
42. Viereck to Goebbels, January 28, 1936, ibid.
43. In 1942 George Sylvester Viereck was convicted of violating the Foreign Agents Registration Act. In spite of a number of mistrials and numerous appeals, he was fined, sentenced to imprisonment, and served five years before he received a parole. His son, Peter, broke with his father over the latter's pro-Nazi views but took him into his home when he emerged from prison.
44. E. M. House Papers, Box 95, Folder 3281. Both FDR's invitation and House's acceptance are in same folder.
45. Cited in Beatty, *The Rascal King*, p. 296.
46. E. Roosevelt, *F.D.R.*, p. 201.
47. Memorandum by Charles Seymour, January 5, 1938, Seymour Papers, Yale University.
48. I am indebted to Jack Beatty's magnificent biography of Curley for these and other details and for a helpful account of the background to Colonel House's lunch.
49. Beatty, *The Rascal King*, p. 272.
50. House to Howe, E. M. House Papers, Box 95.
51. Beatty, *The Rascal King*, p. 298.
52. FDR to House, June 23, 1931, E. M. House Papers, Box 95.
53. House to Howe, August 14, 1931, E. M. House Papers, Box 95.
54. House to FDR, February 10, 1932, E. M. House Papers, Box 95, Folder 3287.
55. FDR to House and House to FDR, August 30, 1932, E. M. House Papers, Box 95, Folder 3288.
56. Telegram from FDR to House, June 1933, E. M. House Papers, Box 95.
57. The following account of Roosevelt's cruise is based on Davis, *FDR*, pp. 158–198, and Schlesinger, *The Age of Roosevelt*, pp. 205–224.
58. Cited in Davis, *FDR*, p. 197.
59. On April 5, 1933, FDR wrote to House that Lewis Douglas was "in many ways the greatest 'find' of the administration"; cited in E. Roosevelt, *F.D.R.*, p. 342.
60. E. M. House Papers, Box 63.
61. House to FDR, February 14, 1935, E. M. House Papers, Box 95. Glenn Frank (1887–1940) was an editor and educator. In 1925 he was appointed president of the University of Wisconsin, where he won a record as an innovator, starting the Experimental College and promoting "the Wisconsin idea." Frank was killed in an automobile accident when running for the U.S. Senate.
62. FDR to House, February 16, 1935, E. M. House Papers, Box 95, Folder 3291.
63. FDR to House, March 20, 1935, ibid. Huey Long (1893–1935) was governor of Louisiana (1928–1932) and senator (1930–1935). Father Charles E. Coughlin (1891–1979), who won a national following as a radio priest, developed increasingly fascist and anti-Semitic ideas. He was first a supporter then a bitter enemy of Roosevelt. General Hugh S. Johnson (1882–1942), who had served under General Pershing in Mexico and in France, was not an ally but a noisy opponent of Long and Coughlin.

64. FDR to House, April 10, 1935, E. M. House Papers, Box 95, Folder 3291.

65. House to FDR, October 9, 1934, E. M. House Papers.

66. House to FDR, April 30, 1935, ibid.

67. James, Viscount Bryce (1838–1922) was a Liberal cabinet minister, author of *The American Commonwealth,* and British ambassador to Washington (1907–1913).

68. FDR to House, October 19, 1937.

69. House, "Memories," p. 34.

70. House to Bonsal, May 13, 1929, Stephen Bonsal Papers.

71. House, "Memories," p. 34.

72. House to Denton, June 6, 1937, E. M. House Papers.

73. Seymour memorandum, January 5, 1938, Seymour Papers, Yale.

74. Ibid.

75. Ibid. In August 1905 House told Miss Denton that he had left her the interest on $20,000 at 6 percent "as some recompense for your labors." E. M. House Papers.

76. Denton to Bonsal, March 11, 1938, E. M. House Papers.

77. House to Bonsal, March 16, 1938, E. M. House Papers.

78. House, "Diary," November 25, 1926. This is the last entry in the diary.

79. Ibid.

80. House to Denton, August 17, 1908, E. M. House Papers.

81. Musil, *Der Mann ohne Eigenschaften,* English translation: *The Man Without Qualities* (London, 1955), vol. 1, p. 59.

82. House, "Diary," March 28, 1926.

Bibliography ∾

Documents

U.S. National Archives. *Foreign Relations of the United States.* Cited as *FRUS.*
——. *Foreign Relations of the United States, 1900–1919, Paris Peace Conference,* 10699. 13 vols. Cited as *FRUS, PPC.*
House, E. M. "Diary." In E. M. House Papers.
——. "Memories." In E. M. House Papers.
——. "Reminiscences." In E. M. House Papers.
E. M. House Papers. Department of Manuscripts and Archives, Yale University Library.
The Papers of Woodrow Wilson. 69 vols. Ed. Arthur S. Link. Princeton, NJ: Princeton University Press, 1966–1994. Cited as *PWW.*
Gordon Auchincloss Papers. Department of Manuscripts and Archives, Yale University Library.
Chandler P. Anderson Papers. Library of Congress.
Stephen Bonsal Papers. Library of Congress.
William Hepburn Buckler Papers. Department of Manuscripts and Archives, Yale University Library.
Irving Hood Hoover Papers. Library of Congress.
E. M. House correspondence with E. J. Barkley, 1904–1914. Five volumes of typescript letters in Austin Public Library.
Report of a committee chaired by Senator John Sherman of Ohio to President Grant. Sen Exec. Doc., 44th Congress, 2nd Session, vol. 1718.
Seymour, Charles, ed. *The Intimate Papers of Colonel House.* London: Benn, 1926.
Charles Seymour Papers. Department of Manuscripts and Archives, Yale University Library.
James T. Shotwell Papers. Nicholas Murray Butler Library, Columbia University.

Smith, Ethel Mary Franklin, ed. *Memoirs of Mollie McDowall* (Mary Ann Nicholson). National Society of the Colonial Dames of America in the State of Texas, Bastrop Historical Society.

Tinsley, James A., ed. *Letters from the Colonel: Edward M. House to Frank Andrews 1899–1902. Texas Gulf Historical Association* 4, no. 1 (December 1960).

George Sylvester Viereck Papers. Department of Manuscripts and Archives, Yale University Library.

Wilson Papers, Library of Congress. "A Suggested Statement of Peace Terms Revised and Enlarged from the Memorandum of December 22."

Sir William Wiseman Papers. Department of Manuscripts and Archives, Yale University Library.

Books, Articles, and Web Sites

Acheson, Sam Hanna, *Joe Bailey: The Last Democrat.* New York: Macmillan, 1932.

Allhands, J. L. *Boll Weevil: Recollections of the Trinity and Brazos Valley Railway.* Houston: Anson Jones Press, 1946.

Anders, Evan. "Thomas Watt Gregory and the Survival of His Progressive Faith." *Southwestern Historical Quarterly* 93 (July 1989): 1–24.

Auchincloss, Louis *Woodrow Wilson.* New York: Penguin Putnam, 2000.

"Austin Home May Be Razed." *Texas Public Employee,* May 1965.

Baker, Ray Stannard. *Woodrow Wilson: Life and Letters.* 8 vols. Garden City, NY: Doubleday, Page, 1927–1939.

——. *Woodrow Wilson and World Settlement.* 3 vols. New York: Doubleday, Page, 1922.

Balfour, A. J. *Chapters of Autobiography.* London: Cassell, 1930.

Beatty, Jack. *The Rascal King: The Life and Times of James Michael Curley (1874–1958).* Reading, MA: Addison-Wesley, 1992.

Bliss, Tasker H. "The Armistices." *American Journal of International Law* 16 (1922).

Bond, Richard W. "The Residence of E. M. House." *Texas Architect,* June 1968.

Bonsal, Stephen. *Unfinished Business.* London: Michael Joseph, 1944.

Brand, Carl F. "The Attitude of British Labour toward President Wilson during the Peace Conference." *American Historical Review* 42 (1937).

Brands, H. W. *Woodrow Wilson.* New York: Henry Holt, 2003.

Broesamle, John J. *William Gibbs McAdoo: A Passion for Change.* Port Washington, NY: Kennikat Press, 1973.

Brogan, Hugh. *History of the United States of America.* London: Longman, 1985.

Bryan, W. J., and Mary B. Bryan. *The Memoirs of William Jennings Bryan.* Chicago: John C. Winston, n.d.

Burns, James McGregor, and Susan Dunn. *Three Roosevelts.* New York: Atlantic Books, 2001.

Bushnell, Romney Clark. "All the World and the Fullness Thereof: The Business Career of E. M. House 1885–1920." Submitted for Master's thesis, University of Texas, 1982.

Byrnes, Robert F. *Awakening American Education to the World.* Notre Dame, IN: Notre Dame Press, 1982.

Calvert, Peter. *The Mexican Revolution 1910–1914: The Diplomacy of Anglo-American Conflict.* Cambridge: Cambridge University Press, 1968.

Caro, Robert. *Master of the Senate.* New York: Knopf, 2002.

Chace, James. *1912: Wilson, Roosevelt, Taft and Debs: The Election That Changed the Country.* New York: Simon and Schuster, 2004.

Churchill, Winston S. *The World Crisis.* London: Thornton, Butterworth, 1923.

Clark, James Anthony, and Michel T. Halbouty. *Spindletop.* New York: Random House, 1952.

Clemenceau, Georges. *Grandeur and Misery of Victory.* London: Harrap, 1930.

Cocks, F. Seymour. *The Secret Treaties and Understandings: Text of the Available Documents.* London: League for Democratic Control, 1918.

Colebourne, Phil, and Bob Gibbons. *Britain's Natural Heritage: Reading Our Countryside's Past.* Poole, Dorset, England: Blandford Press, 1987.

Cooper, John Milton, Jr. *Breaking the Heart of the World: Woodrow Wilson and the Fight for the League of Nations.* Cambridge: Cambridge University Press, 2001.

Cotner, Robert C. *James Stephen Hogg.* Austin: University of Texas Press, 1959.

Crane, M. M. "Recollections of the Establishment of the Texas Railroad Commission." *Southwestern Historical Quarterly* 50 (April 1947).

Crankshaw, Edward. *The Fall of the House of Habsburg.* London: Longmans, 1963.

Cronon, E. David, ed. *The Cabinet Diaries of Josephus Daniels 1913–1921.* Lincoln: University of Nebraska Press, 1963.

Daniels, Josephus. *The Wilson Era: Years of Peace.* Chapel Hill: University of North Carolina Press, 1944.

Davis, Kenneth S. *FDR: The New Deal Years, 1933–1937.* New York: Random House, 1986.

Dean, Paul. "The Federal Reserve Act of 1913." www.geocities.com/Athens/2391/federal.

DeGolyer, Everett. "Anthony F. Lucas and Spindletop." *Southwest Review* 30 (Fall 1945).

Dugdale, Blanche E. C. *Arthur James Balfour.* London: Hutchinson, 1939.

Epstein, Jonathan A. "German and English Propaganda in World War I." Paper given to NYMAS, December 1, 2000, by CUNY Graduate Center/NYMAS.

Ferren, John M. "Edward Mandell House: The Preparation." Harvard University senior essay, 1959.

Fischer, Fritz. *Germany's Aims in the First World War.* With introduction by Hajo Holborn and James Joll. Translated from *Griff nach der Weltmacht* by Marion Jackson. London: Chatto and Windus, 1967.

Fitzhardinge, L. F. "W. M. Hughes and the Treaty of Versailles, 1919." *Journal of Commonwealth Political Studies* 5, no. 22 (July 1967).

Floto, Inga. *Colonel House in Paris.* Princeton, NJ: Princeton University Press, 1980.

Fowler, Wilton B. *British-American Relations, 1917–1919: The Role of Sir William Wiseman.* Princeton, NJ: Princeton University Press, 1969.

Freud, Sigmund, and William C. Bullitt. *Thomas Woodrow Wilson: Twenty-eighth President of the United States—A Psychological Study.* Boston: Houghton Mifflin. 1967.

Fromkin, David. *A Peace to End All Peace: The Fall of the Ottoman Empire and the Creation of the Modern Middle East.* New York: Henry Holt, 1989.

Gal, Allon. *Brandeis of Boston.* Cambridge, MA: Harvard University Press, 1980.

Gardner, Lloyd C. "Woodrow Wilson and the Mexican Revolution." In Link, *Woodrow Wilson and a Revolutionary World.*

Garland, Joseph E. *The North Shore.* Beverly, MA: Commonwealth Editions, 1998.

Garner, Ruby. "Galveston during the Civil War." Master's thesis, University of Texas, 1927.

Garraty, John A. *Henry Cabot Lodge: A Biography.* New York: Knopf, 1953.

Gelfand, Lawrence E. *The Inquiry: American Preparations for Peace 1917–1919.* New Haven and London: Yale University Press, 1963.

Gerard, James W. *My First Eighty-three Years in America.* Garden City, NY: Doubleday, 1951.

——. *My Four Years in Germany.* New York: George H. Doran, 1917.

Gilliland, M. "The E. M. House House in Austin, Texas: Frank Freeman, New York, NY, as Architect." Essay for Architecture Department, University of Texas, April 15, 1974. Austin History Center, Austin Public Library.

Goodwyn, Lawrence. *The Populist Moment: A Short History of the Agrarian Revolt in America.* Oxford: Oxford University Press, 1978.

Gould, Lewis L. *America in the Progressive Era, 1890–1914.* London: Pearson, 2001.

——. *The Presidency of William McKinley.* Lawrence, KS: Regnets Press of Kansas, 1980.

——. *Progressives and Prohibitionists: Texas Democrats in the Wilson Era.* Austin: University of Texas Press, 1992.

Grayson, Cary T. "The Colonel's Folly and the President's Distress." *American Heritage,* 1964.

Grey, Viscount of Fallodon. *Twenty-five Years 1892–1916.* London: Hodder and Stoughton, 1925.

Grover, Henry Cushing. "The Dissolution of T. W. House and Company." Master's thesis, University of Houston, 1960.

A Guide to Stoke St. Gregory Parish Church.

Haffner, Sebastian. *Die Verratene Revolution.* Berne: Scherz Verlag, 1969. Published in English as *Failure of a Revolution: Germany 1918–1919.* London: André Deutsch, 1973.

Handbook of Texas Online, www.tsha.utexas.edu/handbook/online. Esp. House, Thomas William.

Hatch, Alden, *Edith Bolling Wilson.* New York: Dodd, Mead, 1961.

Haworth, Paul L. *The Hayes-Tilden Disputed Presidential Election of 1876.* New York: AMS Press, 1979.

Hempenstall, Peter, and Paul Mochida. "The 'Yin' and the 'Yang' of Wilhelm Solf." *Journal of Pacific History,* September 1998.

Hendrick, Burton J. *Life and Letters of Walter H. Page.* 2 vols. New York: Doubleday, 1922.

Herring, Hubert. *A History of Latin America.* New York: Knopf, 1964.

Hewitt, Abram S. "Secret History of the Election 1876–7." In *Selected Writings of Abram S. Hewitt.* Ed. Allan Nevins, pp. 156–194. New York: Columbia University Press, 1937.

Hobsbawm, Eric. *Age of Extremes: The Short Twentieth Century.* London: Michael Joseph, 1994.

Hodgson, Godfrey. *Carpetbaggers et Ku-Klux-Klan: Les Etats-Unis après la Guerre de Succession.* Paris: Julliard, 1966.

Hofstadter, Richard. *The Age of Reform: From Bryan to F.D.R.* New York: Knopf, 1985.

House, Edward M. *Philip Dru, Administrator: A Story of Tomorrow.* New York: B. W. Huebsch, 1912. Authored by Edward House.

House, Edward M., and Charles Seymour, eds. *What Really Happened at Paris.* New York: Scribner's, 1921.

Houston, David F. *Eight Years with Wilson's Cabinet, 1913 to 1920.* 2 vols. Garden City, NY: Doubleday, 1926.

Hulbert, Margaret Allen. "The Woodrow Wilson I Knew." *Liberty Magazine,* January 3, 1925.

Johnson, Roger T. *Historical Beginnings: The Federal Reserve.* Boston: Federal Reserve Bank of Boston, 1999.

Johnson, William Fletcher. *George Harvey: A Passionate Patriot.* London: George Allen and Unwin, 1930.

Joll, James. *The Origins of the First World War.* London and New York: Longman, 1984.

Keller, Phyllis, *States of Belonging: German-American Intellectuals and the First World War,* Cambridge, MA: Harvard University Press, 1979.

Kennan, George F. *Russia and the West under Lenin and Stalin.* London: Hutchinson, 1961.

——. *Russia Leaves the War.* Princeton, NJ: Princeton University Press, 1956.

Keynes, J. M. *The Economic Consequences of Peace.* London: Macmillan, 1919.

Kolko, Gabriel. *The Triumph of Conservatism: A Reinterpretation of American History 1900–1916.* Glencoe, IL: Free Press, 1963.

LaBotz, Don. *Edward L. Doheny: Petroleum, Power, and Politics in the United States and Mexico.* New York: Praeger, 1991.

Lansing, Robert. *The Peace Negotiations: A Personal Narrative.* Boston: Houghton Mifflin, 1921.

Levin, N. Gordon. *Woodrow Wilson and World Politics: America's Response to War and Revolution.* New York: Oxford University Press, 1968.

Levin, Phyllis Lee. *Edith and Woodrow.* New York: Scribner, 2001.

Link, Arthur S. *The New Freedom.* Princeton, NJ: Princeton University Press, 1956.

——. *Wilson: Campaigns for Progressivism and Peace, 1916–1917.* Princeton, NJ: Princeton University Press, 1965.

——. "The Wilson Movement in Texas, 1910–1912." *Southwestern Historical Quarterly* 48 (1944–1945): 169–185.

——. ed. *Woodrow Wilson and a Revolutionary World, 1913–1921.* Chapel Hill: University of North Carolina Press, 1982.

—— *Woodrow Wilson: Revolution, War, and Peace.* Wheeling IL: Harlan Davidson, 1979.

Lipset, Seymour Martin, and Gary Marks. *It Didn't Happen Here: Why Socialism Failed in the United States.* New York: Norton, 2000.

Livermore, Seward W. *Politics Is Adjourned: Woodrow Wilson and the War Congress, 1916–1918.* Middletown, CT: Wesleyan University Press, 1966.

Lloyd George, David. *War Memoirs.* London: Nicholson and Watson, 1933.

Ludendorff, Eric von. *Concise Ludendorff Memoirs.* London, Hutchinson, 1933.

McAdoo, William G. *Crowded Years.* Boston: Houghton Mifflin, 1931.

McCombs, William F. *Making Woodrow Wilson President.* Ed. Louis Jay Lang. New York: Fairview, 1921.

McGerr, Michael. *A Fierce Discontent: The Rise and Fall of the Progressive Movement in the United States.* New York: Free Press, 2003.

McKitrick, Eric L. *Andrew Johnson and Reconstruction.* New York: Oxford University Press, 1960.

Macmillan, Margaret *Peacemakers: The Paris Peace Conference of 1919 and Its Attempt to End War.* London: John Murray, 2001. Published in the United States as *1919.*

Manchester Historical Society, www.manchesterhistorical.org/coolidge.htm.

Martin, Roscoe C. "The People's Party in Texas: A Study in Third Party Politics." *University of Texas Bulletin,* no. 3308. Austin: University of Texas, 1933.

Mayer, Arno J. *Political Origins of the New Diplomacy.* New Haven: Yale University Press, 1959.

——. *Politics and Diplomacy of Peacemaking: Containment and Counterrevolution at Versailles 1918–1919.* New York: Knopf, 1967.

"Mermeix" [Gabriel Terrail]. *Les Negociations secrètes et les quatre armistices avec pièces justificatives.* Paris: Ollendorf, 1921.

Metzger, Allan H. *A History of the Federal Reserve.* Chicago: University of Chicago Press, 2003.

Miller, David Hunter. *My Diary at the Conference of Paris, with Documents.* 8 vols. New York, 1924, privately printed.

Miller, Worth Robert. "Building a Progressive Coalition in Texas: The Populist-Reform Democrat Rapprochement 1900–1907." *Journal of Southern History* 52 (May 1986): 163–182.

Moneyhon, Carl H. *Texas after the Civil War: The Struggle of Reconstruction.* College Station: Texas A and M Press, 2004.

Morgan, John S. "The President and Mrs. Peck. *The Bermudian,* January 3, 1984, pp. 19–32.

Moynihan, Daniel Patrick. *On the Law of Nations.* Cambridge, MA: Harvard University Press, 1990.

Musil, Robert. *Der Mann ohne Eigenschaften* [The man without qualities]. Berlin: Rowohlt, 1930, 1933.

Nasaw, David. *Chief: The Life of William Randolph Hearst.* Boston: Houghton Mifflin, 2000.

Neff, Donald. *Fallen Pillars: U.S. Policy towards Palestine and Israel since 1945.* Washington, D.C.: Institute for Palestine Studies, 1995.

Neu, Charles. "In Search of Colonel Edward M. House: The Texas Years, 1858–1912." *Southwestern Historical Quarterly* 93 (July 1989): 25–44.

Nicolson, Harold. *Peacemaking 1919.* London: Constable, 1933.

Ninkovich, Frank. *The Wilsonian Century: U.S. Foreign Policy since 1900.* Chicago: University of Chicago Press, 1999.

Offner, John L. *An Unwanted War: The Diplomacy of the United States and Spain over Cuba 1895–1898.* Chapel Hill: University of North Carolina Press, 1992.

Park, Bert E. "The Impact of Wilson's Neurologic Disease during the Paris Peace Conference." In *Papers of Woodrow Wilson,* vol. 58. Ed. Arthur S. Link.

Phillimore, Walter. *Schemes for Maintaining General Peace.* London: His Majesty's Stationery Office, 1920.

Political Graveyard, http://www.potifos.com/tpg/.

Reinertson, John. "Colonel House, Woodrow Wilson and European Socialism 1917–1919." PhD dissertation, University of Wisconsin, 1971.

Reinharz, Jehuda. *Chaim Weizmann: The Making of a Zionist Leader.* New York: Oxford University Press, 1985.

Renouvin, Pierre. *L'Armistice de Rethondes.* Paris: Gallimard, 1968.

Richardson, Rupert Norval. *Colonel Edward M. House: The Texas Years.* Abilene, TX: Abilene Printing and Stationery, 1964.

——. "Edward M. House and the Governors". *Southwestern Historical Quarterly* 61 (July 1957): 51–65.

Robinet, André, et al., eds. *Correspondances/Bergson* [Bergson letters]. Paris: Presses Universitaires de France, 2002.

Roosevelt, Elliott, ed. *F.D.R.: His Personal Letters 1928–1945.* New York: Duell, Sloan and Pearce, 1947, 1950.

Ryder, A. J. *The German Revolution of 1918.* Cambridge: Cambridge University Press, 1967.

Sarasohn, David. *The Party of Reform: Democrats in the Progressive Era.* Jackson: University of Mississippi Press, 1989.

Scheidemann, Philipp. Der Zusammenbruch. Berlin: Verlag fur Sozialwissenschaft, 1921.

Schlesinger, Arthur M., Jr. *The Age of Roosevelt: The Coming of the New Deal.* Boston: Houghton Mifflin, 1957.

Seymour, Charles. "End of a Friendship." *American Heritage* 14, no. 5 (August 1963).

Smith, Denis Mack. *Italy and Its Monarchy.* New Haven: Yale University Press, 1989.

Smith, Ralph. "The Farmers' Alliance in Texas, 1875–1900: A Revolt against Bourbon and Bourgeois Democracy." *Southwestern Historical Quarterly* 48 (January 1945).

Stampp, Kenneth. *The Era of Reconstruction.* New York: Knopf, 1965.

Steed, H. Wickham. *Through Thirty Years.* 2 vols. London: Heinemann, 1924.

Steel, Ronald. *Walter Lippmann and the American Century.* London: Bodley Head, 1980.

Stone, Norman. *The Eastern Front 1914–1917.* London: Penguin, 1998.

Strachan, Hew. *The First World War.* New York: Viking Penguin, 2004.

Strum, Philippa. *Louis D. Brandeis: Justice for the People.* Cambridge, MA: Harvard University Press, 1984.

Sutherland, Patrick, and Adam Nicolson. *Wetland: Life in the Somerset Levels.* London: Michael Joseph, 1986.

Swanberg, W. A. *Citizen Hearst.* New York: Macmillan, 1961.

Tardieu, André. *The Truth about the Treaty.* London: Hodder and Stoughton, 1921.

Taylor, A. J. P. *The Struggle for Mastery in Europe 1848–1918.* Oxford: Oxford University Press, 1954.

Thompson, John A. *Woodrow Wilson.* London: Longman, 2002.

Thompson, John M. *Russia, Bolshevism and the Versailles Peace.* Princeton, NJ: Princeton University Press, 1966.

Thornton, Robert M. "William Jay Gaynor: Libertarian Mayor of New York," www.libertyhaven.com.

Tinsley, James A. "The Progressive Movement in Texas." PhD dissertation, University of Wisconsin, 1973.

——. "Roosevelt, Foraker and the Brownsville Affray." *Journal of Negro History* 41 (1956).

Trevelyan, G. M. *Grey of Fallodon.* London: Longman, 1937.

A True Report of Certain Wonderful Overflowings of Waters, Now Lately in Summersetshire Etc. 1607.

Tuchman, Barbara W. *The Zimmermann Telegram.* New York: Ballantine, 1958.

Tumulty, Joseph. *Woodrow Wilson as I Knew Him.* Garden City, NY: Doubleday, 1921.

Unterberger, Betty Miller. *America's Siberian Expedition.* Durham, NC: Duke University Press, 1956.

Viereck, George Sylvester. *The Strangest Friendship in History: Woodrow Wilson and Colonel House.* London: Duckworth, 1933.

Wagner, Robert L. "The Gubernatorial Career of Charles Allen Culberson." Master's thesis, University of Texas, 1954.

Walworth, Arthur. *America's Moment: 1918—American Diplomacy at the End of World War I.* New York: Norton, 1977.

——. "Considerations on Woodrow Wilson and Edward M. House: An Essay Letter to the Editor." *Presidential Studies Quarterly* 24, no. 1 (Winter 1994).

——. *Wilson and His Peacemakers: American Diplomacy at the Paris Peace Conference.* New York: Norton, 1986.

Warner, Michael. "Protecting the Homeland the First Time Around: The Kaiser Sows Destruction." www.cia.gov/csi/studies/vol4no1/article02.

Watt, Richard M. *The Kings Depart.* London: Pelican, 1973.

Watterson, Henry M. *Marse Henry.* New York: Doran, 1919.

Weinstein, Edwin A. "Woodrow Wilson's Neuropsychological Impairment at the Paris Peace Conference." In *Papers of Woodrow Wilson,* vol. 58. Ed. Arthur S. Link.

Willis, Henry Parker. *The Federal Reserve System: Legislation, Organization and Operation.* New York: Ronald Press, 1923.

Wilson, Edith Bolling Galt. *My Memoir.* Indianapolis and New York: Bobbs-Merrill, 1939.

Wimer, Kurt. "Woodrow Wilson's Plan to Enter the League of Nations through an Executive Agreement." *Western Political Quarterly* 11 (1958).

Winkler, H. R. *The League of Nations Movement in Great Britain 1914–1919.* New Brunswick, NJ: Rutgers University Press, 1952.

Witcover, Jules. *Sabotage at Black Tom: Imperial Germany's Secret War in America, 1914–1917.* Chapel Hill, NC: Algonquin, 1989.

Wolf, Eric. "Mexico." In *Peasant Wars of the Twentieth Century.* Ed. Eric Wolf. London: Faber, 1971.

Woodward, C. Vann. *Reunion and Reaction: The Compromise of 1877 and the End of Reconstruction.* Boston: Little, Brown, 1951.

Index ∾